For

t one

THE W.. .. .. OOD:
SINGLE WOMEN IN FICTION

(AND HOW THEY CAN HELP US NOW)

By

Anthea Ingham

Published by New Generation Publishing in 2024

First Edition

ISBN: 978-1-83563-360-1

www.newgeneration-publishing.com

New Generation Publishing

O, fellow, come , the song we had last night,
Mark it, Cesario, it is old and plain;
The spinsters and the knitters in the sun,
And the free maids that weave their thread with bones
Do use to chant it; it is silly sooth,
And dallies with the innocence of love,
Like the old age.

William Shakespeare, 'Twelfth Night'

CONTENTS

The letter 'S' defining the description of each chapter is not used only because it describes particular strands of spinsterhood, nor simply for its alliterative effect, but because of all the letters of the alphabet, it most resembles the trailing of one particular thread, each of which will be interwoven with the others, to form skeins that will weave the web of spinsterhood explored in Part Two.

PROLOGUE

She was only a spinster. I must put flowers on her grave.
Muriel Spark, 'The Prime of Miss Jean Brodie'.

They don't exist anymore, do they? There are single women: career girls independent women, unmarried women in relationships, but there are no 'spinsters'. I think any single woman would laughingly, or perhaps angrily, dismiss such an antiquated soubriquet. They have, like the dodo, disappeared – but only recently. In my own lifetime, admittedly spanning numerous decades, they were alive and well – or, at least alive. Who were they and what were they?

When I was about four years old in 1950 my mother, always one for social climbing, made me write a Christmas card to the two sisters of the Archdeacon (we lived in the Cathedral Close at Canterbury).Their name was 'Waugh' – I don't know if they were related to Evelyn and Auberon because my mother always pronounced the name as 'Woff'. I did not know what 'Misses' meant so I wrote 'To the Mrs Woff'. It was told that I was a very stupid little girl: not only did I not know how to spell Waugh, but I couldn't even write Misses properly. I was puzzled on two accounts, not so much by the peculiar spelling of Waugh because I had learned to expect spellings to be inexplicable: why was what I heard as 'key' spelt quay, for example? But 'Misses? What *were* these misses? All the mothers of my friends were Mrs with an 'r' in the middle and only one 's', so who or what were they? Apparently they were 'maiden ladies', but what were *they*? What did 'maiden' mean? It was explained to me that they were 'ladies not lucky enough to find a husband'. This didn't seem an entirely satisfactory explanation, particularly when I heard some cricket commentary from the radio: 'A maiden over', it said, and later when I came across the word in my school poetry book, 'maiden' seemed to mean girl, so how could these husbandless Misses be girls and ladies all at the same time? And then there were maids who did housework; were *they* doomed to spend the rest of their life as lonely drudges? It was all very confusing, but there had been something in the tone of my mother's voice as it pronounced the words 'maiden ladies', a kind of nuance, a hint of embarrassment just as when I had once said, "Oh, look Mummy, there are two birds outside and one is standing on top of the other!" There was a pause and then she replied angrily, "Don't be so silly, they are getting married." More puzzlement: how could a bird be a bride and wear a white dress and how could her groom wear a smart suit? And anyway, they weren't dressed like that, they were in their own feathers. But I didn't ask; I sensed this was another of those strange areas into which little girls (maidens?) were not to be allowed to stray.

But when I started my education at the small and smelly St Christophers, I thought I had finally understood what Misses or maiden ladies were. Of course, they were all school mistresses! It was self-evident because all the teachers were called 'Miss'. There was Miss Armstrong, large and frowning, who had wet patches under her arms which showed when she wrote on the blackboard. There was Miss Williams, small with coarse black hair on her head and more black hair under her nose; then there was Miss Tudor-Jones, generally referred to as Miss Tudor-Bones, not because of any ossuary reference, but because of her strange triangular pointed frontage: a breastplate consisting of two aggressive pyramids that could only be held together by an intricate structure of bones like the body of some sharp-beaked bird. Then there was the headmistress, a Miss Prior, very distant and important with a flushed face and a strange flapping black suit. There was not a Mrs among them. The accuracy of my new understanding and opportunity to examine and define them was enhanced by my mother, who having – beyond her wildest dreams – managed to number herself among the cohort of Mrses, liked to patronise these ladies by asking them to tea. If there were any Mrses among my teachers, and indeed, I never encountered any, they remained unasked. They seemed, I thought, to possess a common attribute: a sort of oddness, something that my friends' mothers somehow avoided.

But when I moved on to the grammar school, matters became less clear. Yes, they were still all Misses, and they ran true to form in exhibiting oddity: terrifying Miss Bristow who strode through the corridors wearing a transparent blouse beneath which a multiplicity of straps wriggled and entwined like the snakes of Laocoon; Miss White with orange plaits bound about her head and an orange moustache to match, Miss Russell (History) who aptly looked like a tonsorless monk, and poor deaf, fluttering Miss Donnelly who lived with an aged mother and whom we all cheerfully tormented. There was another similarity about them too, a sort of purse-lippedness, a lack of any sort of jollity.

Of course, there were still so many unmarried women in the fifties because of the devastation wrought by two World Wars, but there was, I think, another factor: a lack of opportunity. There were very limited places outside the family circle where these middle-class women could go and meet the opposite sex. The tennis club might be a useful place if the woman was sporty, and there was the church where a lucky one might catch the eye of a vicar or curate, but neither venue offered huge supplies of men. And even if she made it to university, the young woman would live in a strictly female hall of residence with no male visitors allowed. And if she were to meet a suitable partner, the relationship would have to be a chaste one; extra marital sex without the pill was too fraught with danger, and besides, where would you go? And these women had been reared on Victorian novels where sex was only viewed, if viewed at all, in the context of marriage, where it formed a necessary but, it seemed, unpleasant part of the bargain. So women's time was spent mainly with other women in similar circumstances, and as their maiden years increased, so, by way of compensation, did their oddness.

But things were altering among the schoolmistresses. Beautiful Miss Higginbottom, looking like a Greek goddess and suitably employed in teaching the classics, was not doomed to spinsterhood; she upped and became Mrs Reynolds and returned with Thucydides in her hand and a smile on her face. There was sprightly Miss Jones who was surprisingly friendly and told us she liked to have 'interesting holidays'. Then there were the schoolmistresses who lived together in pairs. Strange difficult-to-understand rumours floated about them, but they too, like the erstwhile Miss Higginbotham and other newly-married colleagues seemed somehow unlike those dyed-in-the wool spinsters. Why should that be? Then, all of a sudden, there was an influx of cheerful married women which seemed somehow to alter the dynamic of the whole school.

Life was widening out; we were about to enter the swinging sixties – not that much was swinging either at home or at school, as far as I was concerned; we were all (or nearly all) not *innocent,* certainly not that, but ignorant. Girls had boyfriends, there was snogging and 'petting','heavy petting' and even 'going all the way', but that three letter word s-e-x was not used; sex itself was not discussed, but we sensed it all around us in that All Girls' School, and we felt that it was something the old archytypal school-misses had 'Missed' out on.

And gradually they began to melt away; they married, they retired, they died, the terms 'maiden ladies', 'spinsters' and 'old maids' disappeared, leaving behind them only a faint memory like the sharp odour of an old scent bottle. But before that scent goes cold, as surely it soon must, I felt it was important to sniff out the perfume of these ladies, and try to discover what it meant to be a spinster.

I have a further aim. I want to appease my guilt. How uncaring I was towards all those schoolmistress spinsters. How brave they were forging a way through life at a time when people in the world outside, and I one of them, showed them no compassion, but regarded them as mere oddities.

Now that the whole position of women is further understood (although not yet understood enough), and the abuse of women is under scrutiny, I hope my spinsters – although they will all be fictional – can provide a reference point for vulnerable women who are still subject to abuse, and I hope too, that these fictional spinsters can offer some support and hope, because in spite of male abuse, they have managed to leave behind them their own remarkable unique identities.

INTRODUCTION

Spinster; ORIGIN MIDDLE ENGLISH (in the sense 'woman who spins') from SPIN+STER
Online Etymology Dictionary

When I started thinking about how to tackle this, I saw so many ghostly figures fluttering before me that I felt dazed. If I were to write about actual spinsters the remit would be impossibly wide, and besides, reams have already been written about the famous ones, and even lesser-known ones have their biographers.

Real life-stories are so far reaching, dependent on time and place and chance, and there is so much ground already covered, with doubtless more angles from which to approach them, that there seems no end to what could be said about them and I did not want to re-trace old stale biographies.

Instead, I thought I would look at spinsters and spinsterhood through the spectrum of fiction. More information may be uncovered about Jane Austen, but no more will ever be found about Miss Bates in her 'Emma'. Furthermore, while we will never have the opportunity to actually hear Austen speaking, we can learn all we need to know about Miss Bates, because we can eavesdrop on her as she rambles on, and 'hear' what other people thought of her. In reading fiction we can credit as gospel what the authors are telling us; there are parameters around the characters, and we can be satisfied that we have a complete picture. Like medieval portrayals of the Virgin Mary, these fictional spinsters occupy their own enclosed spaces, their own *horti inclusi*, and there we can view them in their entirety. *These* were the spinsters I would use to guide me through the web of spinsterhood.

I began by reading and re-reading novels in which spinsters played a predominant part; everywhere I went I asked, "Have you come across any spinsters in your reading?" And suggestions poured in, but so often these women seemed to have played no major role, but hovered in the background, almost obliterated by a charismatic, nubile heroine: kind, good Sonya in 'War and Peace' would always be overshadowed by her fascinating cousin, Natasha; and who remembers poor Miss Briggs in 'Vanity Fair' when Becky Sharpe is so much more enticing?

So I decided to dig these shadowy figures out, and show how they too, had their own, important roles to play and their own stories to tell. But there were an awful lot of them. Where to begin and where to stop? I was never going to write the definitive work on spinsters and spinsterhood, and I had no overarching ambition like Mr Casaubon's in 'Middlemarch' in writing his 'Key to All Mythologies', no wish to ape Maurice Zapp in David Lodge's 'Changing Places', who would write about Austen from every conceivable angle, thus making redundant further attempts by others. I knew I would have to be selective, that I might well be castigated by readers for glaring omissions, or for including relatively unknown examples, but the spinsters I have chosen have become my close acquaintances, sometimes they have even felt like friends, and most importantly, they seemed to me, to represent a credible cross-section of these women. But how to set about it and what would be my aim in this investigation?

My first thought was to simply select spinsters with or within an interesting story, to look at each for herself and see what new aspects I could show about them as individuals. However, as I got to 'know' more and more spinsters and tried to understand them, I became aware that there were constant strands in spinsterhood, some difficult to define like suffering, subservience or saintliness, even scheming and silliness, while other strands were more definable by virtue of belonging to

2

distinct activities such as sleuthing, scholarship or teaching. I could see that one thread might interweave with another: a sleuthing spinster might be a saintly spinster, and a suffering spinster a scholarly spinster. So while I wanted to re-tell enticing individual stories, I could see that in order to understand the nature of spinsterhood, these women needed to be looked at as a *material* group, because they had not acted in isolation, but they had spun yarns of interweaving threads together. They had made a web, and it was this web that would reveal the fabric of spinsterhood.

And while thinking of spinners, it struck me how pertinent the etymological root of spinster is, that spinning in its various forms lay at the heart of the lives of these single women, and that spinsterhood was, in fact, all about spinning ever metamorphosing strands. Indeed, threads that were first spun in the Ancient World twirl and twist their ways into the lives of spinsters living millennia later. These were strong and durable threads providing a framework like the warp on the loom. But in contrast, there were also threads that were very different and colourful, such as those that might appear on the weft. Then, over the centuries, all these threads began to intermesh and become woven together into a complex web, a vibrant tapestry of spinsterhood, one I wanted to put on display.

However, before this tapestry can be unrolled I must first disentangle these threads, sort and gather them into separate skeins, even if at first glance they appear quite disparate. Miss Marple, for instance, will be gathered into the same skein as the Erinyes of Ancient Greece. The academic spinsters of Dorothy L. Sayers' 'Gaudy Night' will occupy their skein along with the harpies.

The skeins will be as colourful and various as the spinsters they contain. Some will have a clear pure colour like the skein of saintliness; others will remain somewhat tangled such as the one containing the scheming spinsters; some will be rather grubby like that of the soiled and scarred spinsters, others will wind themselves into tight balls like the superior spinsters and the schoolmistress spinsters; while another skein will be partially hidden beneath the rest, such as that containing the subordinate spinsters. A skein of dark hue will contain the sinister spinsters.

Once I have separated them into the various skeins and shown their various hues, it will be time to bring them together and start weaving them back together into a complex web. And in course of the weaving – it won't be easy – I will be forced to consider what sort of fabric this spinsterhood is made of, I will try to unravel secrets that still lie hidden in the skeins. And out of their many threads I hope to spin their *yarn* and write my own *text*, a word that originates from the Latin: 'textum' meaning something woven. In doing this I want to *feel* the texture of the material, and make it tactile for my readers too.

What had caused this spinsterhood in the first place; was there some common root factor? Were these spinsters always the subject of male abuse or were there, in fact, women who were 'born spinsters'? Was spinsterhood the result of early family influence? Could a married woman ever be classed as a spinster? Was there a difference between the willing and unwilling spinster? If so, what did this constitute? Could a spinsterly woman escape spinsterhood? How had they managed to sustain the privations so often imposed on them, and what strategies had they employed to survive them, if indeed they had? Was there still a connection between 'spinner' and 'spinster'?

Finally, I want to consider how these brave women – for they were brave, even if their motives were not always of the highest order – can help us in understanding the difficulties faced by women today.

PART 1: SKEINS OF SPINSTERHOOD

The one drew the thread and trod the wheel, the other whetted the thread with her finger, and the third twisted it, and as often as she struck it, a skein of thread fell to the ground that was spun in the finest manner possible.

Brothers Grimm, 'Fairy Tales'.

CHAPTER ONE

SPINNING SPINSTERS

I will begin in the Ancient World with the three Fates or Moirai who are responsible for life and death, because they are the first true 'spinsters', accomplishing their allotted tasks through the act of spinning: Laches assigns the length of the human's lot, Clotho spins the thread of life and Atropos, she who cannot be turned away – from snipping off that fragile cord – deals out death. Their parentage is unclear: Hesiod makes them the daughters of Zeus and Themis, i.e. of God and Law, but in Pindar they serve Themis as bridal assistants. But most interestingly, Plato makes Anangke, best translated as 'Necessity', their mother, and places in her lap the adamantine spindle on which the world turns, while her daughters occupy three thrones about it. It seems that life and death and indeed, the world itself is intimately bound up with spinning and spinsters.

We see a similar trio of fateful spinsters in Norse mythology where there are the Norns who are descended from giants. These are the three Fates: Urdhr, Verdandi and Skuld who represent Past, Present and Future, exactly like the Moirai. They attend the birth of a child and measure its life, observe its fate, both good and bad, and weave it into the thread of life; they decide on its length and the proper time to bring it to an abrupt end with the scissors.

The Hopi Indians regard Spiderwoman of primordial importance; they believe that at the beginning of time she was one of only two deities: Tawa was the god of the sun and Spider Woman the goddess of the earth. She is regarded as 'both old as time and young as eternity' (Mullett). So although she differs from the Fates and the Norns in not actually deciding the destiny of individuals, her web spans the nourishing earth.

We can see that the original Spinsters have a job to do and must remain spinsters; marriage would seriously disrupt the life of (wo)mankind. These are spinsters are who are responsible for humanity.

The Erinyes:

We will return to the all-important original spinners, the Fates or Moirai, to see how they perform their roles. Acting as their agents are the Furies, the Erinyes, euphemistically renamed 'Eumenides' meaning 'the kindly ones', so called to propitiate them since their nature is far from kindly; they act as avenging spirits, particularly on behalf of wronged women. We see them in action in Aeschylus' play: 'The Eumenides', the last in the 'Oresteia Trilogy'. In the first, 'The Agamemnon', the eponymous hero returns home, only to be murdered along with his mistress Cassandra, (another spinster to whom we shall return later), by his wife Clytemnestra and her lover, Aegisthus; in the second play her son returns home and murders his mother and her lover in revenge for his father's death, as the god Apollo has ordered him, and who has cleansed him of the 'blood guilt'.

In 'The Eumenides' Orestes seeks sanctuary at Delphi, the home of Apollo, presided over by yet another spinster to whom again we shall return, the Pythia, priestess of Apollo, but the titular deities demand revenge for the murder of Orestes' mother, (they are unconcerned about Aegisthus' murder as they are interested only in revenge for the woman). And they certainly are vengeful; indeed, they have a strong claim on justice: matricide cannot go unpunished. They describe their actions with sadistic glee: these are not one-offs, but their usual modus operandi.

'For with a long leap from high
Above, and dead drop of weight,
I bring foot's force crashing down
To cut the legs from under even
The runner, and spill him to ruin.'

In these Furies we see the origin of the vengeful spinster that we will meet later in a variety of different forms as diverse as Miss Havisham, Cousin Bette and Mrs Danvers, but unlike them, the Furies act on behalf of Justice itself rather than for themselves, as they claim:

' For we are strong and skilled;
We have authority; we hold
Memory of evil; we are stern
nor can men's pleading bend us. We
drive through our duties, spurned, outcast
from gods, driven apart to stand in light
not of the sun.'

But in the end, like later spinsters, they have to accept the judgement of society rather than their own; the Athenian jury brought in to decide the fate of Orestes is equally divided; six for his punishment, six for his pardon, but the goddess Athene has the casting vote, and she votes for forgiveness. The Eumenides themselves, like spinsters everywhere, must settle for the paltry compensation offered by Athene:

'Do good, receive good, and be honoured as the good
Are honoured. Share our country, the beloved of god.'

The offer of religious rites by way of compensation and a reputation for virtuous behaviour is, as we shall see, exactly what so many spinsters will have to accept. We shall also see what an integral part religion, in its various forms, plays in the life of spinsters.

The Harpies:

There is so much bitter and vengeful work to be done by the Erinyes that they are often in need of help, and the Harpies are enthusiastic instruments in carrying out their orders. Originally they do not seem to have been malignant but merely vague ghostly wind spirits, but as time goes on they begin to be portrayed as birds with women's faces, and etymologically their name is connected with the Greek verb 'harpo' to snatch, and greedy snatchers they become, particularly revolting ones.

In Virgil's 'Aeneid' we meet them on the shores of the Strophades in the Ionian sea where Aeneas and his men on their way to discover a site for their new colony, have disembarked and are setting about making a meal:

'No sooner had they started when… suddenly with a terrifying swoop down from the hills and loudly flapping wings the Harpies were upon us. They pillaged our meal, making everything filthy with their unclean touch; their stench was foul and their screams horrible' (Jackson Knight).
Again and again Aeneas and his men drive them off 'but they did not feel our blows on their feathers, and no wound ever reached the skin on their backs.'

The harpies, it seems, do not act out of a sense of justice or injustice like the Eumenides, but just for the hell of it – maybe they are simply in need of a meal, or perhaps they are just unhappy, unattractive, unmarried 'ladies' who want to make life as unpleasant for men as they can. However, their revenge is particularly horrible: they not only snatch the food, they excrete over it because they do not seek simply to spoil, but to create a miasma of filth, leaving pollution in their wake. We shall meet such spinsters later. Cousin Bette will be one.

The Moirai, assisted by the Harpies and the Erinyes are the primordial spinners, but there are other spinning spinsters in Antiquity, albeit of rather a different sort. Let's look at a selection because they too provide strands that we will meet again in their 'descendants'.

Arachne:

Arachne was a young Lydian woman, very skilled in weaving; she was so proud of her work that she challenged the goddess Athene to a weaving contest. This was not a good idea because Athene was the goddess who presided over women's handicrafts and furthermore, gods and goddesses do not like being challenged. Arachne should have known better.

Athene wove four tapestries, pointedly depicting the fates of mortals who dared challenge the gods; you might have thought this would have put Arachne off. Not a bit of it; equally pointedly, but rather less than tactfully, she wove four perfect tapestries depicting the disguises taken by gods in their discreditable affairs with mortals. Rather a foolish choice of subject matter. The enraged Athene tore the tapestries to pieces and attacked her with a handy weapon – a shuttle. Arachne, understandably upset by this, and obviously not altogether a balanced person, set about hanging herself – plenty of thread lying about – but finally Athene took pity on her, pity of a sort, and changed her into a spider so she could continue spinning forever, or at least, other arachnids could.
Arachne spun a legacy of weavers, not simply spiders, but unmarried females who must occupy themselves with thread. And we shall see later how important threadwork in its various forms, will be to the spinster.

Ariadne:

Although not a spinner in her own right – although of course, she may have been – Ariadne has an important role to play as a thread-bearer.

She was the daughter of Minos, King of Crete. His wife, Passiphae had fallen in love with his pet bull, and the result of their union was the minotaur who was confined in the labyrinth beneath the palace. Every year King Minos required a tribute from Athens of seven youths and seven maidens to feed the hungry beast. One year, Theseus was among the chosen youths, and naturally Ariadne fell in love with him. Understandably, not wanting him stuck in the labyrinth and eaten by its inhabitant, she gave him a ball of thread so he could find his way out again once he had killed the minotaur. This was very successful and Theseus took her to the Island of Naxos, promising to marry her, but instead he seduced her and promptly sailed away. This will have a familiar ring about it. So often the woman makes sacrifices for the male, only to be abused and deserted.

Fortunately she was spotted by the god Dionysus who may or may not have married her, but anyway, he gave her a golden crown that was later set among the stars to become the Corona Borealis. I suppose things could have been worse.

There is another link to Ariadne which reinforces her importance in threadwork. The Roman poet, Catullus' poem 'The Marriage of Thetis and Peleus' depicts the whole of her story woven into a sumptuous quilt for the marriage bed. Stories can be woven in many different ways.

Philomela:

Procne was married to Tereus, king of Athens, but missing her sister Philomela, she asked her husband to bring her to Athens. However, when Tereus saw her he was struck by her beauty and raped her, subsequently incarcerating her, and to make doubly sure of her silence, ripped out her tongue. On his return, he told his wife that Philomela was no longer alive. However, Philomela wove the whole story into a tapestry and sent it to her sister via a servant. Procne had her secretly conveyed to the palace and together they plotted revenge. They killed her son, Itylus, and served him up for supper to his father; only after he had eaten did they tell him what they had done. In his poem 'Itylus' Swinburne points to the role played by weaving in the tragic story.

> 'The woven web that was plain to follow.
> The small slain body, the flowerlike face.'

To pre-empt Tereus' revenge the gods turned Philomela into a swallow (because a swallow cannot sing melodiously), and Procne into a nightingale because her mournful song would reveal her enduring sadness at having killed her own son. Tereus himself was turned into a hoopoe, a bird distinguished by a showy crest, as if to parody the crown he had once held, or perhaps to suggest a misplaced penis. Rape, weaving and metamorphosis become inextricably entangled.

Bacchantes or Maenads:

In Euripides'play 'The Bacchae' we meet women who 'spin' in yet another, more dangerous way. They will substitute spinning thread for spinning themselves – into a state of ecstasy. The chorus tells us of ' The Theban women leaving / Their spinning and their weaving / Stung with the maddening trance / Of Dionysus.' Now they must prepare themselves to take to the mountains where spun thread will be used for a new purpose; the chorus instructs them:

'Fringe and bedeck your dappled fawnskin cloaks
With woolly tufts and locks of purest white…
Soon the whole land will dance
When the god with ecstatic shout
Leads his companies out.'

The women have gathered on the mountainside where they have been holding an all-night vigil. They begin in a comparatively low key:

'… brandishing their wands and preparing to dance, calling in unison on the son of Zeus, Iacchus Bromius. And the whole mountain, and the wild beasts too, became part of their joyful dance – there was nothing that was not roused to leap and run.'

Dancing has become the new spinning, but then things begin to get nasty; seeing they were being spied on by men, the women become violent:

'Cattle were feeding on the fresh grass and the Bacchae attacked them with their bare hands… tearing our cows limb from limb, and you could see some ribs or a cleft hoof being tossed high and low; and pieces of bloody flesh hung dripping on the pine branches… they bore down on the villages of Hysiae and Erythrae… and ransacked them. They snatched children out of the houses… then they went back to the place they had started from… And they washed off the blood and snakes licked the stains clean from their cheeks.'

These are women who have spun out of control. Removed from their habitually tightly controlled domestic role, these women reveal their inner violence – as we shall see later in the case of Hilda Cherrington. However, if they had not been spied on by prurient men, none of this would have happened; all they wanted was a girls' night out.

I see all these ancient spinners as providing the original threads of what will become a complex web of spinsterhood.

CHAPTER TWO

SUNDRY SIGNIFICANT SPINSTERS

They could hear Circe within, singing in her beautiful voice as she went to and fro at her great and everlasting loom, on which she was weaving one of those delicate, graceful, and dazzling fabrics that goddesses love to make.

Homer, 'The Odyssey'.

The Ancient World brims with spinsters of all sorts and one is spoilt for choice, but out of the hundreds – possibly thousands – I have chosen just a few who will have direct bearing on our later spinsters. Although these are not spinners and weavers like those we have met above, they too will spin colourful strands that contribute to the web of spinsterhood. I have made my selection from five categories: goddesses, nymphs, prophetesses, Amazons and monsters.

Goddesses

It has been difficult to decide whether I can class unmarried goddesses as spinsters, but I think I can because although they will always be viewed like Miss Jean Brodie (whom we shall meet later), in their prime, their immortality means that their unmarried presence has lingered on indefinitely, so like the sculpted figures on Keats' Grecian Urn, they remain in a permanent unchanged state, in their case, one of spinsterhood. I have chosen to cite those who will resonate in different ways with our more modern spinsters.

Diana:

She was associated by the Romans with the Greek Artemis, goddess of wild nature, hunting and the moon. She did not appreciate being seen naked, and she wreaked a horrible revenge on the viewer, although in this case, he was just a man in the wrong place at the wrong time. Purely by chance this hunter, Acteon, came across the goddess and her nymphs bathing in a forest pool, and inadvertently caught sight of them naked; goddesses brook no excuses: so offended was Diana that she turned Actaeon into a deer, and as he fled, he was hunted down and torn to pieces by his own hounds. An extreme act of revenge on outraged spinsterhood, something we shall meet again later.

Eris:

Eris, daughter of Night is the goddess of Strife, but she is more often seen as a personification of discord rather than as a 'flesh and blood' goddess – if one can be so designated. However, it was she in person who was the instigator of the Trojan War by throwing the apple of discord among three of the most important goddesses: Athene, Hera and Aphrodite. The Trojan prince Paris was chosen as arbiter. Predictably, each goddess resorted to bribery: Athene would give Paris wisdom, Hera worldly success and Aphrodite would give him the most beautiful woman in the world for his wife. For Paris it was a no-brainer: he chose the woman, although Helen was already married to the Greek, King Menelaus, but undaunted, Paris abducted her, and to cut a long story short, that was the start of the Trojan War. A pretty successful outcome to Eris' machinations. We shall meet other such cruel spinsterly agents of discord later. But… but… but wasn't it all really Paris' fault?

Hecate:

Hecate is an Underworld goddess associated with the darkness of night, sorcery and black magic. I mention her here only briefly as I shall be returning to her in more detail later.

Hestia:

A goddess of the hearth and home, she was sought in marriage by Poseidon, and Apollo, but she renounced sexual love and swore eternal chastity.

Athene:

We have already briefly met the vengeful Athene in her role of mistress of handicraft, but she had a very different side. At birth she had sprung fully armed from the forehead of Zeus. Unsurprisingly, she was also a formidable warlike figure. She has her favourite men, being instrumental in getting Odysseus safely back home to Ithaca from Troy. On the other hand, she does her best to thwart the Trojan Aeneas getting to Italy and founding Rome, not just because she favours the Greeks rather than the Trojans, but because he is the son of Aphrodite against whom she bears resentment because of the apple incident. We shall meet such spinsters later, similarly motivated by vindictiveness and resentment.

Nemesis:

Daughter of Night, she regards it as her moral duty to punish anyone who has shown excess, whether in possessing riches, showing pride or simply having too much happiness. She is the goddess of retribution. We shall meet a number of spinsters who see themselves in just that role.

Nymphs

Do nymphs count as spinsters? I think I can include them as they are unmarried and often undergo metamorphosis into a different form of unmarriedness, and like the goddesses mentioned above, their presence is still with us in the form of painting and sculpture.

Nymphs are numerous: there are mountain nymphs (oreads), nymphs associated with groves (alseids), water nymphs (naiads), nymphs who inhabited trees (dryads), hamadryads who lived symbiotically with trees, nymphs of ash trees (meliads). Out of their vast numbers I will select only a very few who will have resonance with our later spinsters.

Victimised Nymphs:

Daphne:

In order to escape the advances of Apollo, Daphne, who had vowed herself to chastity, prayed for help to her father, the River God, Peneius. He saved her by turning her into a laurel tree. (One wonders if that was the best he could do!). I think of Bernini's wonderful sculpture of Daphne, showing the nymph in the process of change from nymph to laurel.

Callisto:

She was the object of sexual abuse, having been raped by Zeus. Subsequently she gave birth to a son, Arcturus, who became a famous hunter, but that was not the end of her troubles; she was then pursued by Zeus' wrathful wife Hera and turned into a boar; unfortunately her hunter son, failing to recognise his mother, killed her. So she was a double victim of male sexual abuse and female spite.

Syrinx:

Pursued by the god Pan, she escaped by being turned into a reed. Then she was utilised by the god to become part of a musical instrument: the pan pipes. In her poem, 'A Musical Instrument', Elizabeth Barrett Browning describes him as 'half beast', and concludes with the lines:

'The true gods sigh for the cost and the pain –
For the reed which grows nevermore again
As a reed with the reeds in the river.'

The gods might sigh, but she was literally simply made into something to be played with, objectified. We shall see that eons later, happening to the geisha, Chiyo and the AF, Klara. All these nymphs have been sexually violated by different gods; later spinsters are also violated by beings who have overwhelming influence.

Slighted Nymphs

There is a second category of nymphs: those who suffer, not by being sexually assaulted, but by being spurned by males.

Echo:

Spurned by Narcissus, she was reduced by sadness to a gabbling voice, then eventually to a faint… well, echo.

Calypso:

Having detained Odysseus on her private island of Ogygia for seven years, she was finally told by Zeus to let him return to his wife. She even had to help him make his boat.

All these nymphs met with unhappy fates, but not all nymphs were victims; there is a third category of successful nymphs:

Successful Nymphs:

Circe:

A powerful sorceress who turns men into animals, she turned Odysseus' men into pigs – just, it seems, for the hell of it. There are more recent spinsters too, who will turn men into beasts.

The Water Nymph:

The youth Hylas gets his comeuppance by being pulled underwater by the nymph whose advances he has rejected; there is a wonderful painting by Waterhouse: 'Hylas and the Water Nymphs'. I used to have the painting hanging in the hall which attracted the interest of a visiting plumber. "What's that?" he asked. I explained the best I could. He regarded it further for a moment and then remarked, "I wouldn't mind being pulled under water by that lot." Nymphs obviously still exercise their power.

Sinope:

This is a cunning nymph who attracted the attentions of Zeus to such an extent that he promised to give her whatever she asked for. She asked for enduring virginity. Not often someone got the better of Zeus. Not often do later spinsters get the better of their suitors

Prophetesses

Cassandra:

In Aeschylus' 'Agamemnon' the chorus question Cassandra about her relationship with the god Apollo and her gift of prophecy:

Chorus: Struck with some passion for you, and himself a god?
Cassandra: There was a time when I blushed to speak about these things.
Chorus: True; they who prosper take on airs of vanity.
Cassandra: Yes then; he wrestled with me and breathed delight.
Chorus: Did you come to the begetting of children as people do?
Cassandra: I promised that to Loxias [Apollo], but I broke my word.
Chorus: Were you already ecstatic in the skills of god?
Cassandra: Yes, even then I read my cities destinies.
Chorus: So Loxias' wrath did you no harm? How could that be?
Cassandra: For this my trespass none believed me again:

Cassandra is a victim of rape. It would appear that she was initially happy to be seduced by Apollo, but later changed her mind and refused him sex. This has always been an unforgivable sin in male eyes, one which for some justifies rape: 'She wanted it, really', is a horribly familiar excuse. But rape wasn't enough for Apollo, he wanted revenge for the insult to his male pride. He wasn't just a man, he was a god. How could she refuse him? And so he doomed her to have her true prophecies disbelieved; and she was further tormented by foreseeing her own future: murder at the side of her lover, Agamemnon. Later we will meet other women who can see a disastrous future that nobody else believes.

The Sibyl:

Perhaps Cassandra once existed outside myth, but now she has been reduced simply to a definition: one who utters prophesies of doom. There will be a repeated problem with holy women because they hover between actuality and representation. Are they fictional or not? However, the Apollo-inspired Sibyl described by Virgil in the 'Aeneid' is entirely his creation, so she can certainly count as a fictional spinster.

We last met Aeneas and his men on the Stromphiades, having their food spoilt by the Harpies. Now they have landed on the shores of Italy at Cumae (which can still be visited), and Aeneas is in need of some guidance, wanting to discover what lies in store for him in his mission to found the colony that will become Rome. I quote from Jackson Knight's translation:

'Aeneas made his way to the fastness where Apollo rules enthroned on high, and to the vast cavern beyond which is the aweful Sibyl's own secluded place; here the prophetic Delian God breathes into her the spirit's visionary might, revealing things to come.'

But this business is not a happy one for the Sibyl:

'There is a cleft in the flank of the Eubean rock forming a vast cavern. A hundred mouthways and a hundred broad tunnels lead from it, and through it the Sibyl's answer comes forth in a hundred rushing streams of sound. They had reached the threshold when the maiden cried: "… the time to ask your fate has come. Look the God! The god is here" …as she spoke the words, there, beyond the double doors, suddenly her countenance and her colour changed, and her hair fell in disarray. Her breast heaved and her bursting heart was wild and mad.'

Eventually she speaks and gives him some useful advice, and she even agrees to conduct him down into the Underworld to look into the future and to have a word with his old dad. But what is this strange relationship she has with Apollo? It reads suspiciously like rape. She does everything she can to avoid being 'shaped to his will', and this is a violation that will be repeated every time a prophecy is required. Centuries later, in 'Cena Trimalchionis' by Petronius, we are told of the Sibyl who has become an ageing old woman, hanging from a bottle in her cave and saying, "I want to die." But unfortunately, unlike other spinsters she does not have this option, because along with her prophetic powers comes the unwelcome gift of immortality. When we reflect on the lot of this wretched spinster, constantly subject to rape, denied marriage and forced to live forever in this situation, even Miss Havisham (whom we will meet later) will seem fortunate.

The Pythia:

With the figure of the Sibyl we again touch on territory that waivers between the real and the mythical because there were *actual* oracles, and priestesses to go with them. Alexander the Great visited one at Memnon. But the most famous was the one at Delphi where Apollo's mouthpiece was the Pythia, (regularly replaced, no fear of the bottle). It was consulted by the Greeks and Asiatics when faced with making any important decision; and so numerous were the consultations by potentates and even by ordinary people, that it became known as 'the omphalos', the belly button of the world. It was an important centre of information, a bit like the Vatican, in fact, although with one important difference, it was not staffed by bachelors, but by spinsters.

Amazons

These were mythical women who lived apart from men somewhere near the Black Sea and delighted in hunting and war. Occasionally they would mate with men for the purpose of raising female offspring (they got rid of the male babies).

Hippolyte:

She was the queen whose girdle was taken by Heracles as one of his twelve labours. When her female army rose against him, he killed her.

Penthesilea:

Another Amazon queen who headed an army to aid King Priam in the Trojan war, but was slain by Achilles – who fell in love with her as he delivered the fatal blow.

However strong women are, it seems it is near impossible to get the better of men who have treated them unfairly. Sadly, we shall see that repeated all too often.

Monsters

Scylla and Charybdis:

There are numerous unsavoury mythical spinster monsters; there are Scylla and Charybdis, for instance; the latter being a whirlpool is a spinner in her own way, but it is difficult to plumb the depths of her. Scylla is much more easily defined with her six rows of heads and three rows of teeth, and long arms reaching out to catch and devour unlucky sailors.

Gorgons:

These are Euryale and Medusa, having heads entwined with writhing snakes, great tusks like a boar, hands of bronze and wings of gold; the sight of any one of them would turn a mortal into stone. Even this ability does not save Medusa who is beheaded by Perseus. Sometimes, it seems, nothing can protect single women from male violence – although in Medusa's case, perhaps, one's sympathy is less forthcoming.

The Graiae:

They are three hideous old immortal sisters who pass their single eye and tooth between them. Seeking directions from them to discover the whereabouts of the gorgons, and having obtained them, Perseus ungallantly throws the all-important organs into the sea. An early example of male contempt for the ugly spinster.

For the moment I have finished with the Ancient World, but we shall recall these personae later when we come to more familiar spinsters, as they constitute the same colourful threads that will be twisted into different but recognisable forms. Now it is time to move on some millennia and take a good look at some of them.

CHAPTER THREE

STEREOTYPICAL SPINSTERS

Spinster: n. chiefly derogatory, an unmarried woman, typically beyond the usual age for marriage.'

OED

Perhaps nobody does spinsters as well as Barbara Pym; and this in itself poses questions: can spinsters only be depicted by a – I was going to say 'fellow' spinster – but I can see that is an inappropriate term, so I'll settle for 'sister' spinster, or is their status wrongly, even illegally appropriated by women who are not spinsters, or worse still, by a man, whether a bachelor or not? Anyway, Pym herself never married, although she had numerous affairs, so she, at least, was well-placed to write about them. And while we're on the subject, why does the adjective 'derogatory', given in the definition above, not apply to the bachelor? And indeed, the very word bachelor has faded away too. Who speaks of 'bachelors' now? Yet this term was never regarded as derogatory, even amongst the Victorians who must have known that in many cases such men were people deemed by society to be that unspeakable thing, 'an invert'! Perhaps another example of injustice perpetrated by a patriarchal society.

'Some Tame Gazelle' by Barbara Pym

"You need not make fun of doting spinsters," said Belinda, "after all it isn't always our fault..." She stopped in confusion.

I start with Pym because she provides a very gentle introduction to different types of spinsters. I say, 'gentle', because they mostly belong to that now dead category of 'gentlewomen'. They are not the more deeply etched spinsters we shall meet later, marked by suffering and bent on revenge, true descendants of their Greek sisters, but like them, they do have their crosses to bear – albeit not very heavy ones – and they provide a wonderful selection of the different types, many of which we shall meet again later.

Pym's novels all concern spinsters and one is very spoilt as to selecting one rather than another, but I have chosen 'Some Tame Gazelle' published in 1950, (although she had written an earlier version in the thirties). Its title, taken from Thomas Haynes Bayly's poem shows the leitmotif of the book:

'Some tame gazelle or some gentle dove;
Something to love, oh, something to love.'

The story revolves around the uneventful lives of the Misses Bede, Harriet and Belinda. The story is delightfully simple, and it is the skill of Barbara Pym that makes a story out of so little, but that is the point really. It is not meant to be a story with an exciting plot, but a study of women whose lives have so little in them.

As we saw with some of our the Classical spinsters, Harriet and Belinda's lives are closely connected with religion, not that their connection has a particularly spiritual dimension, but the link lies in their close association with the church, the church being, of course, The Church of England.

Harriet's life is spent in cossetting whatever new curate has appeared in the parish; she invites each new one to special meals, takes him baskets of fruit, inquires into every aspect of his life and regards him as her own special property. Apart from this curatophilia, Harriet is what I would term a robust spinster, sadly, one of few we shall meet. She likes fashionable clothes, enjoys long scented baths and the company of men; she has regular proposals of marriage from an ageing Italian count; and although she is a spinster she is not 'spinsterish' at all.

Her sister, Belinda is quite different, a much more spinsterish spinster: she is a well-meaning and sensitive woman with a university education; her connection with the church is more practical than her sister's, and she is always ready to offer sensible help in church events; she also thinks deeply about theological matters:

"'If only we could get back to some of the fervour and eloquence of the seventeenth century in the pulpit today,'" she sighs to her sister, but her real religious crutch is the Archdeacon, Canon Hocleve; for twenty years she has been hopelessly and romantically in love with this lazy, self-indulgent and petulant man whom she knew at university. He is married to a very spinsterish sort of wife, Agatha; one suspects a distinct lack of sexual relations there; at any rate, they have no children. Belinda has no thought of any sexual relationship with Henry – being a strict Anglican she would have regarded any such thing as wicked, and I do not think she has any thought about sex at all. So in their different ways both Harriet and Belinda support their spinsterhood through their own form of religious fervour; they are in their different ways, gentle, unaroused Bacchantes.

Excitement is generated when the Archdeacon, very unwillingly has visitors to stay: Mr Mould, in spite of being assistant librarian at an Oxford college, is a rather vulgar man who likes a drink. Harriet, however, quite admires him and is very pleased when he proposes to her, but she refuses him, preferring comfortable spinsterhood with her curates and kindly sister. Belinda too, has an unexpected proposal from another of the archdeacon's visitors, the desiccated unpleasant bishop of Mbawawa who is looking for a wife – any wife – to look after him on his return to Africa. His proposal is not flattering:

"'Miss Bede, I am sure you must have realised – have noticed, that is, my preference for you above all the other ladies of the village," he said.

"No, I don't think I have," she said anxiously. "In any case, you can hardly know me very well or you would realise there is nothing very special about me."

"Ah, well, one hardly looks for beauty at our time of life," he said with a return of his usual complacency. "*She is not fair to outward view*, how does Wordsworth put it?"

"Not Wordsworth," said Belinda automatically. "Coleridge, Hartley Coleridge, I think." She felt rather annoyed. Not even a middle-aged spinster likes to be told in so many words that she is not fair to outward view.'

The bishop is not a pleasant person and Belinda naturally refuses him. Like her sister she is comfortable with her spinsterhood, spiced as it is, with her melancholic adoration of the archdeacon. Each sister has adopted an unexacting spinsterhood in preference to marriage. But they are in a fortunate situation: not only have they actually opted for spinsterhood in preference to marriage, they have enough money to make a pleasant life for themselves. I think the following sums it up:

'Although the Misses Bede had a maid, they were both quite domesticated, and helped her in various small ways, clearing away the breakfast things, dusting their own bedrooms and doing a little cooking when they felt like it.'

The telling words are the adjectives 'quite' and 'small' and the phrase 'when they felt like it'. Theirs is an easy life and unlike other spinsters they do not suffer – or, not much. Harriet has her moments of unease when it is rumoured that her pet curate is to become engaged "'I don't like the way Mr Donne keeps mentioning that Olivia Berridge,'" Harriet complains to Belinda. But the archdeacon's wife is loud in her praise, though not necessarily of her nubility:

"'She's a very clever girl… and she's doing some excellent work on certain doubtful readings in *The Owl and the Nightingale*…" . "Olivia is a very forceful young woman," said the archdeacon, "and rather a bluestocking appearance.'" He addresses the curate: "'What do you think, Donne?'" The curate, who is a rather pallid and sexless young man (a sort of male spinster, perhaps?), replies, "'Oh, I can't say I've really noticed, I mean it's what a person is that matters most.'"

And when the wedding finally takes place, Harriet is mollified by the bride's appearance: "'She is taller than he is… and she looks much older. What a pity. She's rather plain too, isn't she? Why doesn't she use lipstick?'" Harriet can reflect that this Oliva Berridge with her academic research and plain appearance is really only another spinster. In spite of their marriage one imagines the life of bride and groom will be pretty celibate. And solace comes to Harriet as a pale and interesting-looking new curate is appointed; she will waste no time in planning ways of feeding him up.

Spinsters proliferate in this very middle class society. There are the two spinsters living together: Edith Liversidge and Connie Aspinall. Belinda reflects: 'Sometimes one almost forgot that she [Edith] was a gentlewoman, with her cropped grey hair, her shabby clothes which weren't even the legendary 'good tweeds' of her kind, and her blunt, almost rough way of speaking.'

Although there is talk of a long-ago romance with a colleague when she did work 'of a sanitary nature' in the Balkans, one suspects that it was no more than a working relationship, and that she is by nature a lesbian, and not discontented with her lot; again, she has (just) enough money. Her companion Connie Aspinall is a poor dependant, a feeble fluttering creature given to wearing floating draperies:

'"Now, she's a decayed gentlewoman, if you like," said Harriet, "she can talk of nothing but the days when she used to be companion to a lady in Belgravia Square who was a kind of waiting-woman to Queen Alexandra."

"She plays the harp beautifully," murmured Belinda weakly, for poor Connie was really rather uninteresting, and it was hard to think of anything nice to say about her.'

She has no money and must depend on the tender mercies of Edith. However, her luck turns when the bishop, refused by Belinda, meets her unexpectedly, and decides she will do instead as a wife to look after him on his return to Africa. However, one does wonder how this will ever come to be, as it seems likely that poor Connie will be equally appalled by any amorous advances on the part of the bishop as dealing with the primitive tribes with whom the bishop works; one cannot imagine her having much success, as she puts it, ' in teaching them the gentler arts'. Can such a spinster ever metamorphose into a wife? One doubts it. Like Olivia Berridge, one suspects that marriage for her, will be a continued spinsterhood.

There are other spinsters whose lot is not so comfortable because they have neither 'class' nor money. Poor Connie at least had the former which 'bought' her the unlikely and probably unfortunate marriage. But for those who have neither, spinsterhood is not such a comfortable state.

Miss Prior, the woman – the sisters certainly wouldn't call her a 'lady' – who does their sewing, is the prime example.

Belinda, looking back at her own classical education, regards Miss Prior with the Aristotelean concepts of 'pity and fear'. Miss Prior is to be pitied because she has to work for her living, and she is acutely sensitive about her ambiguous social situation. She cannot be asked to join the sisters for lunch because of her 'inferior' position, but equally, she can't be asked to have lunch in the kitchen with their maid in the kitchen, because her position is superior to Emily's.

Belinda's Aristotelian fear (Harriet doesn't care) is of offending Miss Prior. There is a wonderful episode when she is due to come and do some sewing for the sisters – obviously they cannot do such mundane work themselves. Belinda, motivated by her fear, is anxious to give her a nice lunch in the room where she does the sewing, thereby effecting a compromise between her eating with them in the dining room, or in the kitchen with the maid. She suggests to her sister that they give her some chicken, a suggestion which Harriet dismisses: the chicken is for the curate who will be visiting that evening. Belinda reluctantly gets the maid to prepare cauliflower cheese, and all her fears are realised when she sees the lunch left uneaten. The maid has not washed the cauliflower properly.

'"Oh dear, I'm afraid you haven't enjoyed your lunch. Miss Prior," said Belinda who now felt close to tears, "don't you like cauliflower cheese?"
"Oh yes, I do sometimes," said Miss Prior in an off-hand tone, not looking up from her work... And then in a flash she realised what it was... the long greyish caterpillar... Belinda bust into a torrent of apologies...
"I'm afraid I didn't feel like going on with it after that," said Miss Prior almost smugly.'
Belinda tries to make amends:
'"Perhaps you would like a poached egg – or even two, Emily could easily make them."

"Well no, Miss Bede, thank you all the same. It would seem funny to have a meal the wrong way round, wouldn't it. You wouldn't fancy that yourself now, would you, Miss Belinda?"'

And here is the nub of the difference in the two spinsters. Belinda is horrified at the grey intruder, but nevertheless, reflects that *she* would have eaten the caterpillar, or at least got rid of it. The spinster who is a 'lady' knows how to behave, but the spinster who is not, must wreak her meagre revenge by showing up the 'lady', and take solace in a masochistic delight in exhibiting her inferior position. Like an enfeebled harpy, all Miss Prior can do is to leave behind a spoiled meal. Spinsterhood is not so pleasant for the less well-heeled.

Another difference between the spinster who has status and the one who has not, is shown by Miss Jenner, the woman who runs the wool shop:

"'I was only saying to the traveller the other day that I knew this would be a popular line. He even suggested that I might knit *him* a pullover" – she laughed shrilly – "the idea of it." Belinda smiled; she could well imagine the scene. Miss Jenner was so silly with the travellers that it was quite embarrassing to be in the shop when one of them arrived.'

But Belinda reflects kindly: 'poor thing… it was probably the only bit of excitement in her drab life… she was getting on now, and with her sharp foxy face and prominent teeth had probably never been very pretty. Living over the shop with her old mother must be very dull. And perhaps we are all silly over something or somebody without knowing it; perhaps her own behaviour with the archdeacon was no less silly.'

And here is the crucial difference: the middle class spinster with plenty of money and no dependents can afford to be 'a bit silly' because she knows how to channel her silliness into acceptable and respectable behaviour.

Other 'inferior' spinsters are represented as a sad entity. We are invited to view the Sunday School teachers, 'Miss Beard, Miss Smiley and Miss Jenner, standing in a corner by themselves.' Like the Greek chorus in Euripides' 'Ion' they might as well have claimed: 'We only want to do what is allowed. We like looking round outside.'

Earlier we see them grouped together at the bishop's lantern slide talk, collectively getting out notebooks and pencils to take notes in order that they can contribute towards his charities. Like the Eumenides at the end of Aeschylus' play, they must be content 'to do good, receive good, and be honoured as the good / are honoured.' It is not much to write home about.

Interestingly, almost everyone in the book is a spinster of one sort of another: the only married women mentioned are the sexless Agatha, wife of the Archdeacon, Miss Jenner's old mother and Mrs Rampage, a woman who comes to buy the Misses' Bede's cast-off clothes; even the three male visitors to the archdeaconry are a kind of species of male spinster, the desiccated Bishop Grote, the rubicund Mr Mould, and Nicholas Parnell, who is married to the university library. Even Count Bianco who proposes regularly to Harriet is, one suspects, really a lonely gay, obsessed with his the memory of his dear, dead friend, John Akenside.

This spinsterhood shown by Pym in muted tones, presents a variety of different types: the robust spinster Harriet, the rejected spinster Belinda, the lesbian spinster, Edith; the scholarly spinster, Olivia Berridge; the silly spinster, Miss Jenner; the poor companion spinster, Connie Aspinall; and the overlooked spinsters, the Sunday school teachers. Later we shall see such figures intensified, their sufferings greater, their intentions more deadly. The Ancient World provided us with a warp of spinsters; Barbara Pym has presented us with some more colourful threads; we shall see them all woven into the lives of the spinsters we are about to encounter.

CHAPTER FOUR

SACRED AND SAINTLY SPINSTERS

Some find me a sword; some
The flange and the rail;' flame.
Fang or flood' goes death on drum,
And storms bugle his fame.

Hopkins, 'Wreck of the Deutschland'

Of course, there was a lot of religious fervour amongst the spinsters of 'Some Tame Gazelle': there is Harriet's mania for curates, Belinda's adoration of the Archdeacon; there is the enthusiasm of the Sunday school teachers for Bishop Grote, there is the faithful flock of spinsters who follow the archdeacon's rival, Father Plowman, and there is assiduous Sunday churchgoing by all and sundry; but of course, all this enthusiasm has little or nothing to do with spiritual values; but nevertheless, religion in whatever form is an important thread of spinsterhood, and it will be seen over and over again to intertwine with figures from the Ancient World, some of whom we have already met. Now I would like to introduce the Pythia, Arieka.

'The Double Tongue' by William Golding

Arieka:

Earlier on we met the Pythia at Delphi. We cannot now know anything about these ancient priestesses, but in his novel, 'The Double Tongue', published posthumously, William Golding presents us with a fictional one. He imagines the life of a plain young girl named Arieka who is forced to become a Pythia because of the difficulty of marrying her off:

'In addition to being scrawny with a lopsided face, I am on the sallow side… my nurse told me that my father would have to pay an extra large dowry to get me off his hands, which was why he was so stern with me'.

She is also aware that they would have liked to have disposed of her at birth. When a wretched marriage is finally arranged for her, she runs away and is brought back in disgrace.

Now that she will be unmarriageable, an arrangement is made with the Foundation at Delphi. The High Priest, Ionides explains:

'"…you have heard of the Pythia, of course. Or should I say the Pythias? At the moment there are two of them. Those distinguished ladies are sacred and divine and utter the oracles of the god…"

"You must think yourself lucky, my girl," said my father. "Don't imagine you are not costing us anything."'

He is, in fact, disposing of her, as many medieval fathers would when they dispatched daughters unlikely to make a good marriage, to the nunnery.

Once she is there, Arieka realises that Delphi is in fact, nothing more than a huge business concern; visitors consulting the oracle must bring expensive gifts, and the prophecies are based on information gained from agents sent abroad and composed with cunning ambiguity. (Herodotus tells us of King Cyrus who consults the oracle on the outcome of a military enterprise, and who is told that 'a great kingdom will fall.' Foolishly he assumes the oracle refers to that of the enemy; it doesn't; it refers to his own). Sometimes, when stuck for an answer, the priestess would resort to mumbo jumbo.

When two presiding Pythias die in succession, Arieka is promoted to the position. Sitting on the sacred tripod in a subterranean chamber she must utter words which will then be re-issued by the High Priest in a form he considers suitable to the client. But when she is first left alone in the dark and frightening cave, something strange happens:

'Suddenly the whole tomb place was filled with rolling, rollicking laughter that went on louder and louder, and I knew as my body worked like some automaton, it had come from my own mouth.' She crawls to the tripod. 'The god would have me there in the holy seat whether I would or no; oh yes, it was rape, this was Apollo who fitted me into the seat, twisted me anyway he would, then left me.'

But was it rape? Here we see a frightened young girl in a state of aroused sexuality that becomes entwined with a sense of religious awe. Surely 'Apollo' is nothing other than naked sexual desire on the part of a frustrated young woman? We saw something similar in the case of Cassandra and the sibyl in their interactions with Apollo. Millennia later, Bernini would sculpt such an ambiguous emotional experience in his 'The Ecstasy of Saint Teresa'.

(It is worth mentioning that Arieka's 'rape' does not occur again. Her subsequent life settles into a routine of uttering of words and receiving gifts, and she survives to a ripe old age, a much respected spinster, like an abbess of a famous convent.)

It is perhaps, worth bearing in mind that 'The Double Tongue' and 'The Ecstasy of Saint Teresa' were both produced by men, so both are only male projections of female sexuality. However there is a modern novel which also considers the lot of the incarcerated spinster and this is written by a woman.

The Anchoress by Robyn Cadwallader

Upon entering, the reclusendus [anchoress] would climb inside a grave dug inside their cell. Once inside their grave they were sprinkled with earth… the door of the cell was bolted. Once inside they were enclosed for the rest of their lives.

Wellesley, 'Hidden Hands'

In the Middle Ages there were numerous anchoresses, Julian of Norwich being the most famous. These women elected to have themselves walled up alone in a cell no bigger than a large cupboard, with three windows or hatches to the outside world. Although they were not prophetesses as such, one of the cell's three small windows was designed to allow for consultations from visitors who came for advice, thus enabling a kind of prophetic utterance. Like the Pythia she would spend the rest of her life walled up, unlike the Sibyl she was allowed to die, and eventually she would be buried in her small dark cell.

Cadwallader's novel aims to recreate the first years of the seventeen-year-old Sarah's incarceration. She has three reasons (not necessarily in this order) for becoming an anchoress: a means of assuaging her grief for the loss of her beloved sister, Emma; an escape from the advances of an important man whom she dislikes; and a long-felt yearning for a life devoted to Christ.

She describes her first moments: 'The dark mouth of the cell stood open, I took a breath and stepped inside. Blackness yawned around me, damp on my face… they laid me down on the floor, scatterings of dirt and words falling on me, into my mouth and eyes. Death desired me and I accepted. Here I will stay forever, this is the home I have chosen.'

It is clear her life is not going to be a bundle of laughs. However, she does her best; within her dark cell she endeavours to follow the Rule for Anchoresses (penned by a male writer); she follows the religious round of set services; she prays to a former occupant of the cell, the revered anchoress Agnes (now buried under the floor) to make her equally holy.

In her efforts she has the staunch support of her old confessor, Father Peter, she has two servants to bring her food and there are women from the village who visit her and who speak to her through the window. But temptation and the outside world are inescapable: she refuses a meagre portion of food to a leper who begs at her window because she must have no contact with men, (even a hand placed inside the cell is regarded as a penetration of virginity), but her conscience pricks her, she does not know if she has done right. Then her old confessor who has given her so much support, is replaced by a young awkward monk who cannot understand her problems; her old suitor, a man of importance manages to force her to speak to him, and she feels the stirrings of sexual desire; then one of her servants falls pregnant, and Sarah is further torn: by the rules of her calling she should dismiss the girl for her immorality, but is this right? She does not know how to talk to the married village women who seek her advice as a holy woman because what does she know about marriage? The pressures begin to tell on her, she suffers from anorexia, loneliness, the cold, the dark, and the hardness of her daily round; she tries to subsume herself in her subjection to Christ and His Passion as she gazes at the crucifix above the altar:

"'Jesus, my honeydrop, my lover, your beauty marred for love of me; your wounds, the blood running down your arms, down your white chest, onto your legs, streams of life in which I bathe... take me in your arms, embrace me on your cross, pierce me with nails and let me bleed.'" But it becomes obvious that this devotion – after all Sarah is only seventeen – will turn into something else:

'We embraced, his warmth flowed into my flesh, his lips on my cheek, my neck, my mouth. I have never known such warmth in every part… His love was a pain, deep in my belly that I had desired so long, a pain that I could hardly bear, so sweet was it… "My beloved," I whispered and I swooned.'

Chaste devotion, this isn't, orgasm it is. It is exactly like the sensation suffered by the Pythia, Arieka and by the Sibyl in their encounters with 'Apollo'. Starved of sex, enclosed in narrow dark places, they seek the same relief.

The next day, Sarah realises that she has confused piety and sex: 'I'd heard of holy women becoming one with Christ, but surely it wasn't one like that, so much like the act of a man with a woman… the words I read of Christ as lover and spouse; surely they told of his care, pure and chaste, not of the pleasures of the body?'

She soldiers on; her pregnant maid dies in childbirth, she repulses the advances of her lover, and comes to an understanding with her confessor, she learns how to deal with village women, but she cannot stand the confines of her cell. Eventually she requests a small garden which she is finally allowed (I'm not sure that actually she would have been), and she revels in the feel of sun on her flesh:

'I walked to a patch of garden where the sun was shining… I lifted my robe and pulled it over my head. My shift was thin and the air was cool on my arms and legs, but the sun warmed my skin, licked at me, played around my face, ran its fingers along my arms, across my breasts and down my legs.' Here she is, in effect, enjoying sensory pleasure while justifying it with piety – something she had realised earlier was not what she should be indulging in. She continues:

'It seemed to me that Christ called to me and touched me. My Rule tells me I must come to know God by controlling my senses, by keeping the flesh in need and not allowing my eyes or nose or ears to lead me back towards the world. I had read and reread the words, wearied myself, tried so hard to be a holy woman, beaten my heart and body against stone. But that morning it was as if I turned, and love was there, simple without rules… I remembered then the story near the end of my Rule; it says that Christ is my lover-knight who longs passionately for me, who went into battle to rescue me and died for the sake of his deep love. It advises me to touch him, my lover, with as much love as I might feel for another person; when I read that I see Emma [her sister] kissing Godric [her husband], and other things I can barely say, of skin and mouths and faces caught somewhere in pain or ecstasy…'

Again, she is conflating piety and sex, but one could argue that Arieka, the sibyl and Sarah are all victims of controlling relationships – not with another man, but with a deity.

The book ends on a somewhat ambiguous note; she recalls a Tumbler called Swallow whom she had seen in her childhood:

'I thought of Swallow, how I had gasped to see him tumble, his red and grey stripes spinning against the sky. I stretched out my arms and looked up as he had during that first leap, looking for flight, but knowing he could fall. That moment of risk – now it was mine.'

I am not sure what we are meant to make of this. Will the future of this holy anchoress lie in repression of sexual urges, masturbatory relief, or in abandoning her calling, and becoming a married woman? We will never know.

Saints

In looking at these religious spinsters we have seen there is a constant ambivalence between the legendary and the actual, a blurring between truth and fiction. We meet the same lability with that formidable body of holy spinsters, the female saints. What, then, is the actual status of these women? Can I include them amongst my fictional spinsters? Indeed, do they count as spinsters at all, being, it seems relatively young? But, like the classical figures we met earlier, goddesses, harpies, nymphs etc., they didn't achieve the married state and, as an extra bonus, not given to all spinsters, they were certainly virgins. Furthermore, as they have hung about for centuries, even millennia, they can no longer be looked at as spring chickens. So, yes, I think they qualify, and like the Sibyl and the Pythia, they are religious spinsters. But *are* they fictional?

Undoubtedly many female saints were real women who once actually existed, but as a result of later veneration of their relics, their shrines, or even their names, and endless hagiographies – each one adding further embellishments – fiction accrues around them to the point where truth becomes so overshadowed that the original is hopelessly blurred; then a representation or multiple representations occur, with the result that the original metamorphoses into whatever shape or form the worshiper wishes to receive her.

Much of the blame for this blurring can be laid at the pages of 'The Golden Legend', a book written in Latin in the mid-fourteenth century, purporting to recount the lives of various saints; it gained enormous popularity and came to be regarded as an authentic account. Stories of saints' lives proliferated, and it was the lives of female saints that predominated in the later Middle Ages. Countless 'biographies' were written whose purpose was often purely didactic, exemplars of how spinsters should live – and naturally, they were written by men! Osbert Bokeham, for example, composed in different verse forms, accounts of the lives of thirteen female saints which he then dedicated to patronesses, or presented to nunneries. I wonder how they were received.

Saint Catherine:

So are these saintly iconic figures in fact, fictional? Even the Catholic Church, the arbiter of such matters cannot make up its mind. Take the case of St. Catherine, she of the wheel, venerated for centuries, who was removed from the Church Calendar in 1969 through lack of historic evidence, and then in 2002 reinstated, although no further historic information was forthcoming. She was supposedly martyred in the fourth century at the hands of the Roman Maxentius by being broken on a wheel, and undergoing 'a mystic marriage with Christ' (does that stop her being a spinster?) Anyway, assuming she is a spinster, we can see how images of her multiply: Perugio in 1489 has her enthroned at the side of the Virgin along with saints Cal and Rose of Alexandria, Raphael has her stylishly dressed, nonchalantly leaning on her wheel as though it were a theatre prop; Caravaggio has his Catherine fashionably dressed in contemporary clothes, sitting comfortably by... yes, her wheel. But perhaps the strangest and most macabre metamorphosis is in the saint's identification with a firework. Now the actual fate of Catherine herself is forgotten, and it is the wheel that becomes the centre of attention, a two minute wonder, but sadly, perhaps that was what Catherine actually was.

None of these images can actually *be* the saint, they can only be representations of what may once have been a real woman. So I think I am justified in including Catherine among my fictional spinsters.

Saint Ursula:

Saint Ursula also emerges from 'The Golden Legend'. She too, like Saint Catherine was ignominiously removed from The Church Calendar in 1969, but less fortunately, was not restored, so I suppose we can unambiguously state that she is fictional.

Ursula, the pious and of course, beautiful daughter of a Breton king is sought in marriage by an English king whom she promises to marry as long as he converts to Christianity. This seems to be no problem, and off she goes to Rome to seek the Pope's blessing along with eleven accompanying maidens. All goes well, but on their return journey, travelling along the Rhine, they are, most unfortunately, attacked by some Huns outside Cologne; Ursula and her entourage are captured and martyred. A fairly straightforward story, but then all sorts of embellishments occur: Ursula, it seems, had already seen visions of martyrdom, the women appear to be able to cross great seas in a single day, (prior to their death), and angels perform sherpa duties for them in the Alps. Unsurprisingly there is no historic record of any of this.

Then another twist occurs. In 922 the pious Bishop of Cologne, intentionally or unintentionally, mistranslated the Latin abbreviation XI. M. V. into 'undecim millia virginum', thereby turning the eleven maidens into 11,000, a number which stuck, making, I suppose, for a better story, and certainly a greater number of martyrs. Apparently, there are over thirty tonnes of human remains scattered all over Europe, purporting to be the very bones of the 11,001. In the Cologne Basilica alone there is 'The Golden Room of Saint Ursula' where bones line every wall, and skulls are kept in golden reliquaries. The fact that many of the bones are male, some are of children and there are even those of dogs, seems irrelevant. These bones were discovered in the nineteenth century by workers on a building site, and the somewhat less than miraculous explanation seems to be that the bones belonged to an old Roman burial site outside Cologne.

However, in 1492 a series of nineteen paintings were commissioned by a church in Cologne and executed by the Master of The Saint Ursula Legend, who gave free rein to his imaginings with plenty of gory details.

The story inspired Renaissance painters all over Italy, Germany and Spain, perhaps the most famous being 'The Matryrdom of Saint Ursula' by Caravaggio in 1610, who has her – a new twist this – dying in the arms of her fiancé, now given the name of Etherius, no explanation being given as to how this person managed to get to the spot so opportunely – or perhaps, not opportunely enough.

Perhaps the liveliest and most imaginative series of the representations of the story of her life is told in a series of pictures by Carpaccio, originally commissioned for the Scola Di Sant' Orsola, now in the Galleria Dell' Accademia. In the first two we see the arrival and subsequent departure of the English ambassadors who have succeeded in obtaining the marriage agreement; then we see the arrival of these same ambassadors, very pleased with themselves, reporting back with the good news in the English court; the next shows the betrothal and departure of Ursula for Rome along with (some of) the eleven thousand spinsters who are to accompany her; the next picture entitled: 'The Dream of Saint Ursula' shows her cosily tucked up in her bed, with her pet dog looking on; then we see the majestic arrival in Rome; finally, alas, the fateful events in Cologne, followed by 'The Martyrdom of the Pilgrims and Funeral of Saint Ursula'; and lastly, we have the 'Apotheosis of Saint Ursula', as she coyly stands on a pedestal surrounded by cherubs, while God looks down with his arms outstretched, ready to receive her into Heaven. At her feet kneel countless female figures with their hands clasped in prayer, perhaps the less blessed survivors of the eleven thousand. After all, eleven thousand is quite a lot to execute; I daresay some got away.

What sort of spinsters are they? Of course, owing to their untimely and unpleasant deaths they are certainly suffering spinsters, victims of male cruelty, resembling some of the nymphs we met earlier, and like them becoming translated into a different state. On the other hand, perhaps like other spinsters we have met, they rather pointlessly and stupidly brought disaster on themselves – and on others too. Think of all those eleven thousand – or at least, eleven other spinsters. Couldn't Ursula just have got hitched up to the British guy and sent a letter to the pope, thereby saving everyone a lot of trouble?

Couldn't Catherine not have been a bit diplomatic with Maxentius? But perhaps he didn't get it all his own way: there is a fine piece of stained glass in the *Victoria and Albert Museum* showing a very fierce looking Catherine trampling a diminutive Maxentius underfoot.

Whether or not they are religiously inclined, the trouble so often with spinsters, as we shall see later in Harriet Herriton, Hilda Cherrington, Jean Brodie, and even the worthy Miss Clare, is tunnel vision, an obstinacy, a monstrous belief that their way of doing things is the right and only way. Any compromise on the part of Catherine or Ursula would have been as unthinkable. There are many who, no doubt, would not agree.

Nuns

Surely these are among the first spinsters that come to mind when we think of holy women, and there are plenty of nuns in fiction, creations with no claim on historic figures. There is Chaucer's Madame Eglantine, that dainty dog-loving nun with her affected French; there is an indispensable Sister Leander, in Thomas Mann's 'Buddenbrooks' (a book we shall meet later), always ready to attend to those in extremis – and much better, says Tom Buddenbrook to have her to attend his dying mother because she is a White Sister, whereas the Black Protestant sisters are flighty, too interested in the outside world, and even on the look out for husbands. Novels abound with them: Rumer Godden's 'In this House of Brede' looks at relationships within convent life; there is Victoria Glendenning's 'The Butcher's Daughter', exploring what happened to nuns after the dissolution of the monasteries. Antonia Fraser's 'Frost in May' is a polemic against Catholicism, dealing with the unsavoury nature of a convent school. There is a recent novel by Lauren Groff: 'Matrix', fictionalising the life of a medieval French nun and abbess.

Novelists are not alone. Television producers and film makers have been keen to get into the 'habit'. There are plenty of nuns in Rumer Godden's 'Black Narcissus', and two films have been made of the books, one only recently. Some decades ago there was the much fêted 'Nun's Story'. In 1963 Sidney Poitier starred in 'Lilies of the Field', as a travelling handyman helping nuns make repairs to their home in Arizona, and 'The Sound of Music' is always on our screens. More recently we have 'Sister Act', and we are now familiar with the sisters of Nonnatus House in 'Call the Midwife'. Last year Romola Garai presented us with a very sinister nun in 'Amulet'. There are countless others. The public, it seems, is always a ready audience for these women – perhaps with salacious interest. What do they really get up to, these nubile and not so nubile women? Unlike the saints hovering between legend and a dubious actuality, these are actual figures of fiction, but there is a problem – one of a different kind than that appertaining to the saints: nuns are, in fact, married women; I don't mean they are widows who have joined a Covent, although there are such women, the protagonist in Godden's 'In This House of Brede' is one, but they are – by their own admission – married; they may be bound to chastity, poverty and obedience, but they are also 'Brides of Christ'. So this is a bit of a puzzler: clearly as brides, nuns cannot be regarded as spinsters, or does their state of chastity keep them in a state of spinsterhood since a spiritual marriage cannot actually be consummated?

Nuns are not the only 'brides of Christ'; in the medieval poem 'Pearl' translated by Simon Armitage there are quite a lot more, albeit dead ones: the grieving father who has lost his daughter, 'the priceless pearl' has a vision of Heaven and asks his daughter now elevated above, how she has been chosen by Christ to be 'His bride', but she explains that she's not the only one: 'the brides who live with our Lord in bliss / Are a hundred and forty thousand strong'. A rather bigamous arrangement, one might think. But to return to nuns: theirs is a specific form of spinsterhood we have not met before, an elected spinsterhood that masquerades as marriage, a sort of having your cake and eating it. An ambiguous lot, nuns.

Some, but not all, of these 'holy' women have been have been the objects of male abuse, but they have all been enclosed in some way or other, whether actually in cells or caves, or within a consciousness of their own rectitude.

'Babette's Feast' by Karen Blixen

There are lay figures who, although not belonging to any particular conventional religious order, can nevertheless, lay claim to a form of saintliness.

Martine and Philippa:

In 'Babette's Feast' we meet the elderly spinster sisters christened Martine and Philippa, after Martin Luther and his friend Philip Melanchron.

'Their father had been a Dean and a prophet, the founder of a pious ecclesiastical party or sect, which was known and looked up to in all the country of Norway... The dean's daughters spent their time and their small income in works of charity.'

However, these women had not always been old spinsters; 'in their youth they had been extraordinarily pretty and various proposals had been made to them through their father.' But the Dean 'had declared that to him in his calling, his daughters were his right and left hand. Who could want to bereave him of them? And the girls who 'had been brought up to an ideal of heavenly love did not let themselves be touched by the flames of this world.'

Nevertheless, Martine attracts the attention of the handsome young officer Lorens Loewenhielm. When the Dean 'proclaims righteousness and bliss have kissed one another', 'the young man's thoughts were with the moment when Lorens and Martine should be kissing each other.'

However, so sacrosanct does the Dean's house seem to the young man that he dare say nothing and departs in despair. He subsequently makes an advantageous marriage and enjoys a successful career. Philippa, we are told, would sometimes try to speak to her sister about him, but 'She would answer gently, with a still clear face, and find other things to discuss.'

Then it is the turn of her sister Philippa who attracts the attention of the 'great singer, Achille Papin of Paris who is visiting the area. He was 'a handsome man of forty with curly black hair and a red mouth.' Not only is Philippa beautiful but she has an outstandingly beautiful voice which she uses for the singing of hymns at church. He immediately sees her potential as an opera diva and wants to train her for stardom. He gives her music lessons, and swept away by the duet they were singing together, 'he seized Philippa's hands, drew her towards him and kissed her as solemnly as a bridegroom might kiss his bride before the altar.' Philippa goes home and tells her father that she does not want any more singing lessons. So Papin departs. The sanctity of the Dean's house has forbidden her to 'be touched by the flames of this world.' So the sisters grow into their spinsterhood, doing good and supporting the local community of 'brothers and sisters' who are growing somewhat grumpy with old age.

One day a refugee named Babette arrives from revolutionary France with a letter from Monsieur Papin begging the sisters to take her in. In fact, she is a famous chef and is soon cooking delicious meals for the sisters, but claiming it is only plain food because she realises that is all they will eat.

When the anniversary of their father's death comes round, the sisters envisage a modest celebration: '... a very plain supper with a cup of coffee was the most sumptuous meal to which they had ever asked any guest to sit down'. However, Babette, who has unexpectedly won the lottery, has other ideas. She will cook the meal of her lifetime, although she merely tells the sisters that it will be ordinary French food; even this alarms the sisters, and Martine goes round the community apologising to her neighbours for the forthcoming feast and begging them to eat it without making any comments.

The great day arrives and Babette cooks the most superb meal, the apogee of her skill. The pious brothers and sisters arrive and the good smells from the kitchen inspire them to start singing hymns. Then Lorens Loewenhielm, now an elderly general, visiting his aunt, arrives unexpectedly. 'Tall, broad and ruddy, in his bright uniform, his breast covered with decorations', he makes a marked contrast with 'the sedate party' of brothers and sisters.

The meal is the last word in *haute cuisine,* but the brothers and sisters who have been told not to comment on this strange French food, remain silent. However, but they feel a tremendous sense of happiness as they eat the wonderful food and drink (what they do not know is) wine. Then General

Loewenhielm who cannot believe what he is eating, is moved by the effects of 'the noblest wine in the world' to make a speech about grace. 'None of the guests later had any clear remembrance of it. They only knew that the rooms had been filled with heavenly light.'

As he is leaving Loewenhielm says to Marianne, '"I have been with you every day of my life; you know, do you not, that it has been so?"' But the fact is he has had a successful worldly life and has been carried away by the superb food and wine. He has not been with her at all, but she believes in some chaste and spiritual sense that his words are true.

'"Yes," said Martine. I know that it has been so."'

Afterwards the sisters go into the kitchen to thank Babette. Martine says with superb unconscious meiosis: '"It was quite a nice dinner, Babette."' When the sisters realise that she has spent all her ten thousand francs on it, they are astounded:

'Philippa's heart was melting in her bosom. It seemed that an unforgettable evening was to be finished off by an unforgettable proof of human loyalty and self sacrifice.'

'"Dear Babette," she said softly, "you ought not to have given away all you had for our sake."'

But here we realise the total lack of understanding of the saintly sisters:

'Babette gave her mistress a deep glance, a strange glance. Was there not pity, even scorn in it?

"For your sake?" she replied. "No. For my own… I am a great artist."'

Babette knows that her final masterpiece is a purely sensual one, while the sisters see the whole evening as an act of piety.

And Philippa can only say: "In Paradise you will be the great artist God meant you to be." "Ah," she added with tears streaming down her cheeks, "Ah, how you will enchant the angels."'

Both sisters have lost their opportunities in life: Philippa could have joined Monsieur Papin and been a great opera singer, Martine could have been the wife of a great general. But they have been prevented by being confined in a prison of sanctity. In a way they have been as incarcerated as the ancient prophetesses or indeed as nuns and anchoresses. Yet they have not been unhappy; they have busied themselves like all good spinsters in works of kindness. They have earned great respect within the community and have love for each other. Like Athene's gift to the Eumenides they have been allowed to 'do good, receive good, and be honoured as the good /Are honoured. Share our country, the beloved of god.'

Was their spinsterhood such a bad thing? I can't decide. However diverse the reasons for our interest in religious women, be it salacious or mere curiosity, we cannot help but admire something in their elected spinsterhoods. Whatever their shortcomings they can lay claim to a sort of mysterious sanctity, call it grace, that we can only envy, even if we regard them as misguided. They have left us their own unique representations of holiness, a strand twisted down from the Ancient World. Perhaps we can learn something from them.

CHAPTER FIVE

SUFFERING SPINSTERS

Echo fell in love with the beautiful, but cold youth Narcissus. Her love unrequited, she wasted away until only her plaintive voice was left.
Jenny March, 'Dictionary of Classical Mythology'

In 'Some Tame Gazelle' we saw spinsters who suffered in small ways: Belinda yearned after the archdeacon, Miss Prior was upset by the caterpillar in her salad, Harriet was put out by the loss of her curate, Miss Prior was resentful of her 'inferior position'; Connie hankered after her days with Lady Grudge; but their sufferings are not great – or Pym does not present them as so. Anyway, like the saintly and sacred women discussed above, they all have a religious crutch in the form of the local church. By and large these spinsters lived unexciting, but not unhappy lives. Now I move on to spinsters who in different ways really do suffer. I will start with two who, although they resemble the Misses Bede in possessing status and money, are not willing spinsters; they have had spinsterhood thrust on them through rejection by the men they loved, rather like some of the nymphs we met earlier.

The two spinsters whom I have chosen are placed in remarkably similar positions: Catherine Sloper in Henry James' 'Washington Square' and Mary Jocelyn in F.M. Mayor's 'The Rector's Daughter'. Each is the victim of a callous father who blights his daughter's chance of marriage.

Washington Square, by Henry James

Catherine… became an admirable old maid. She formed habits, regulated her days upon a system of her own, interested herself in charitable institutions, asylums, hospitals, and aid societies; and went, generally, with an even and noiseless step, about the rigid business of her life.

Catherine Sloper:

Catherine, daughter of the wealthy and successful Dr Sloper of New York is an unprepossessing heroine. Dr Sloper would have liked his daughter to be a replica of her dead mother, intelligent and pretty, but she is neither: '… a dull plain girl she was called by rigorous critics – a quiet lady-like girl, by those of a more imaginative sort, but by neither class was she elaborately discussed.'

When the dashing, Mr Morris Townsend presents himself as her suitor, she can scarcely believe her luck; but sadly, he is not a man in love, he is a penniless scoundrel after her fortune. Dr Sloper sees through him at once and has no intention of allowing a marriage with his daughter. But Dr Sloper is a complex and thoroughly unpleasant character who rather despises his daughter. Initially he is amused by the situation and it tickles his fancy to watch how Catherine will act.

Dr Sloper pays a visit to Townsend's sister with whom he lives, and his opinion of Townsend is confirmed: Townsend is an idle sponger, 'a plausible coxcomb'. However, he allows the affair to continue as, lacking any concern for his daughter's feelings, he enjoys the business as an interesting intellectual study. He tells Catherine his opinion of Townsend, but she is by now too much in love, and simply does not believe him: she is a simple girl who has never had a suitor and trusts Townsend entirely, and her awful Aunt, Mrs Penniman eggs her on. However, she has always been a most dutiful daughter, and she is tormented by being at odds with her father.

Eventually her father takes action: he tells her that if she marries Townsend, he will not leave her a penny, and he takes her on a tour of Europe hoping that she will forget him. He is exasperated by the fact that she has no interest at all in all the famous sites he shows her, and has not forgotten Townsend, he tells his married sister, Mrs Almond: '"She has come home exactly the same; she didn't notice a stick or stone all the while we were away – not a picture, nor a view, not a statue nor a cathedral"'. And furthermore, he learns that she has no intention at all of abandoning her lover. She is, as he says, 'glued'. Poor Catherine is desperately lonely: 'She longed for some intelligent person of her own sex to tell her story to, some kind woman'.

Probably, Townsend would have abandoned her anyway, as although Catherine has ten thousand of her own, he wanted the large fortune he expected from Dr Sloper. But in their absence Mrs Pennimann cultivates and cossets Morris, telling him that if he did marry Catherine, her father would eventually come round. Townsend is torn, wondering whether or not to take the risk; however, it soon becomes clear to him that the doctor will not be moved, and he decides to desert her. He engineers a pathetic quarrel and concludes it by saying he is leaving. She simply cannot believe it.

'She sat up half the night, as if she still expected to hear Morris Townsend ring at the door. On the morrow this expectation was less unreasonable, but it was not gratified by the appearance of the young man.'

She knows the truth but is determined to hide her suffering from the world, in particular, Mrs Pennimann, and above all, her father, and she is successful. When his more kindly and perceptive sister, Mrs Almond tells him of his daughter's suffering, he replies, '"She seems much better than when that fellow was hanging round… she has had her little dance, and now she is sitting down to rest. I suspect that on the whole she enjoys it."' His sister replies that '"she enjoys it as much as people enjoy getting rid of a leg that has been crushed."' She is right; Catherine is utterly devastated, not simply because of the betrayal by her lover, but because of the behaviour of her father.

'Morris Townsend had trifled with her affections, and her father had broken its spring. Nothing could ever alter these facts; they were always there like her name, her age and her plain face. Nothing could ever undo the wrong or cure the pain that Morris had inflicted on her, and nothing could ever make her feel towards her father as she had felt in her younger years.'

But she is brave: 'There was something dead in her life, and her duty was to try and fill the void.'

'Catherine… became an admirable old maid. She formed habits, regulated her days upon a system of her own, interested herself in charitable institutions, asylums, hospitals, and aid societies; and went, generally, with an even and noiseless step, about the rigid business of her life.' In later life she has two proposals of marriage, but she declines them both. After her father dies, Townsend returns to New York, and having wasted his life, he calls on her: 'I was in hopes that we might still have been friends.' Doubtless, he hopes to finally get hold of her money, but he is turned away; she has suffered too much. The book ends:

'Catherine meanwhile in the parlour, picking up her morsel of fancy-work, had seated herself again with it – for life, as it were.'

She has become – perhaps not too unhappily – immured in her own spinsterhood. Yet another incarcerated spinster.

'The Rector's Daughter' by F. M. Mayor

"No one has ever been near falling in love with me. I think it must be that I'm meant to do without it. I can. There may be women who can't, and she has what I might have had."

Mary Jocelyn:

Mary Jocelyn, heroine of 'The Rector's Daughter', like Catherine is plain:

'Her uninteresting hair dragged severely back, displayed a forehead lined too early. Her complexion was of a dull hue, not much lighter than her hair. She had her father's beautiful eyes, but hid them with glasses. She was dowdily dressed...'

Like Catherine she lives with her widowed father. The rector, however, unlike Dr Sloper, is not a cruel man, he simply takes his daughter's plain presence for granted. Mary, like so many of our spinsters has a life bound up with the church, early on necessarily through her father's job, and later, as compensation.

Mary, again like Catherine, is above all dutiful in nature, and spends her early years looking after a disabled sister, a contributing factor in preventing her having opportunities to go out and meet eligible men. She is also careful to look after her father as he grows old and infirm. Mr Jocelyn is a trying man whose overriding interest in life lies in studying the classics which takes up more of his time than his pastoral duties. Mary's two brothers escaped the severe classical regime early by emigrating to Canada, marrying and leading dull, but basically happy existences.

When her disabled sister dies, Mary's life opens up and a Mr Herbert, a local clergyman comes to visit; he has not come to see Mary, but her father whose classical interests he shares.

Gradually, however, they are drawn together; they think alike and share a number of interests: 'a seed of love' is planted in Mr Herbert's heart and Mary, in turn, falls in love with him. They spend a lot of time together, mostly in the garden at the rectory. Everyone sees the suitability of the marriage and expects it. Mr Herbert does not exactly propose to Mary but his intention is there, one which Mary understands and patiently awaits. His mother is unenthusiastic about Mary whom she regards as dull and inelegant, but this does not deter her son, who fully intends to propose to her. But first he has to go to Buxton to take a cure for his rheumatism: 'He did not intend to propose as an invalid'– a rather weak point in the narrative.

Mary receives two rather disappointing letters from him, but after a few weeks a third arrives and Mary is ecstatic as she skims the letter. She sees the magic words 'dear friend', 'wonderful happiness', 'the first moment I set eyes on…'. Then she reads it carefully and all her hopes are dashed:

'My dear Miss Jocelyn,

We have known each other only a few months, but I feel you are an old and dear friend to whom I must confide my wonderful happiness. I am engaged to be married to Miss Kathleen Hollins…'

Mary is heartbroken, but like Catherine she is determined to suffer in silence, and repels attempts to comfort her; she is even more shocked when she meets the new bride:

'…possibly Mrs Herbert might be something more than beautiful, rough, rude, brainless, vulgar. This was Mr Herbert's permanent choice. She had been an amusement, a very small incident. But I am superior, she thought.'

She suffers agonies of jealousy. The new bride has an equally poor opinion of Mary: "'I thought she was some sort of church person, she looked it.'" There lay the nub of the problem: Kathy was beautiful, Mary was plain.

The marriage does not go well: the scholarly Mr Herbert and the jolly, brainless Kathy have nothing in common, and Kathy, thoroughly bored, goes off to the Riviera for a holiday with a friend, where she has a riotous time. Mr Herbert is desperately unhappy, and one day seeing Mary unexpectedly, he says: "'Miss Jocelyn, sometimes one makes mistakes in life, she [Kathy] made one, I have made another.'" Mary's feelings overwhelm her: '… their eyes met, and before she knew what was happening, he kissed her… a thrill of indescribable happiness passed through her.'

But this happiness is to be short-lived: while on the Riviera Kathy has a minor operation before planning to run away with a lover; the operation goes wrong, leaving her face twisted, and she has no option but to return home to her husband. When he sees her again, Herbert's heart is filled with love and pity, and once again all thoughts of Mary are forgotten. Now Mary's suffering is doubled; she had learned to live with the marriage, but the kiss had awakened passionate feelings in her which she must now learn to repress.

Kathy with her disfigurement, and now pregnant, has become quieter and seeks a kindly companion, and of course, she chooses Mary, who good and patient as she is, acquiesces, but makes a point of avoiding Mr Herbert.

A further operation repairs the damage to Kathy's face and once she has recovered her looks and survived two pregnancies, she forgets Mary and her life goes on surprisingly well. The author concedes: '… it was not the tie it would have been with Mary. They did not know what each other was going to say before the words were uttered,' but nevertheless, he tells us, 'The Herberts' was a happy marriage.' All very well for the married pair, but what of Mary?

She has taught herself not to think of Mr Herbert now, and she is hurt by Kathy's rejection, but she is able to discover two things denied to Catherine Sloper: a renewed closeness to her father and a virtual acknowledgement from him of his love for her; and she discovers a kind of spiritual consolation from nature:

'… a winter twilight is perhaps the most beautiful of all aspects of the year; it sent a thrill of inexplicable happiness through her she felt at no other season. Today her happiness was increased. She and her father had never been so near to each other, and his praise was nectar to her; her desire of many years was accomplished.'

She has found some sort of substitution for the loss of Mr Herbert. When her father dies, Mary moves to a dreary suburb to live with an aunt, but even there she prevails and becomes a popular member of their society. However, she dies prematurely and is buried in her home churchyard. After attending the funeral Mr Herbert tells his wife of his love for Mary. Kathy is astonished that 'she, young and beautiful had been ousted by a plain middle aged woman.' In the final sentence of the book we are told:

'… no photograph, no portrait could have captured what he loved so much in her – that depth and intensity that rarely showed itself in her face or even in her words… She seemed quite close to him, walking by her side again in the garden… where he had first began to love her.'

What a pity, then, that he hadn't married her! Like Achilles, who killed Penthesilea, he realised all too late that he loved her.

These two spinsters, Catherine and Mary, were both deserving women bereft of their lovers. Would they have been happier had they married them? Catherine might have known some moments of happiness with Morris Townsend before he had spent all her money, but then he would have moved on, leaving her with nothing, just as her father had said. But Mary? Spontaneously one thinks: 'Yes, yes, yes, there was a man who loved her and to whom she was ideally suited,' but the author thinks otherwise: He concedes Mary was the one person Mr Herbert had met 'who was truly akin to him', but he concludes:

'In their marriage therefore, something would have been wanting that he had now [with Kathy'] – high spirits, geniality, light-hearted courage, which neither dreads troubles before they came nor brooded over them when they were past... she was more of a mother than Mary would have been...'

So all hunky dory for Mr Herbert, but for Mary? Would her marriage have been a happy one, or would he have tired of her plain earnestness, and would she with her keen perception, have realised that it was so, and felt that it would have been better not to have married him?

Is the truth quite crude: that for them both, sex would have been something incomprehensible, even distasteful, not at all in line with their romantic ideas? Wouldn't they perhaps have been happier if lovers had not come their way, remaining content as dutiful loving daughters, perhaps even a bit in love with their fathers? Was there something, fear, perhaps, in each of them, that put up some barrier against sex? Perhaps it wasn't the disappointment over marriage that truly ate away at their lives, but lack of sexual fulfilment. Whatever really lay at the heart of their troubles, their lives were wasted ones.

Here I look back at the rejected nymph Echo who fell in love with the beautiful but cold youth Narcissus; she may not have been a born spinster, but with her love unrequited, she too, wasted away until only her plaintive voice was left. Didn't

Catherine and Mary suffer much the same fate – reduced to little more than whispering voices? Perhaps they did not suffer as cruelly as Philomena who had her tongue torn out, but their lives too, were silenced by male cruelty. On the other hand, they were fortunate in having enough money to live in comfort. It will become increasingly apparent that money is one of the chief props of spinsterhood.

CHAPTER SIX

SCARRED SPINSTERS

Scylla was a beautiful nymph and the sea god Glaucus fell in love with her, when she spurned him, he went to Circe for a love potion, but Circe fell in love with him, and being jealous she poisoned the pool in which Scylla used to bathe. When Scylla went off for her daily dip, six ferocious dogs grew in place of her lower limbs which travelled upwards and metamorphosed into twelve feet, all waving in the air and six long necks with a frightful head on each, all with three rows of teeth, packed close together and full of black death. Any sailor journeying past is snatched up by one of her heads.
Jenny March, 'Dictionary of Classical Mythology'.

Facial Disfigurement:

This rather extreme instance of facial disfigurement makes the lots of Mary and Catherine seem relatively painless, and indeed, although they were both plain women, at least they did not suffer like the following three unfortunate, very different spinsters, all of whom suffered from the effects of facial disfigurement.

'David Copperfield' by Charles Dickens

Rosa Dartle:

In 'David Copperfield' we meet Rosa Dartle, a woman, passionate in love and in hate. Apparently illegitimate, she is a poor relation who is brought up from a young age to act as a companion to the proud Mrs Steerforth. Her son, James, vicious, spoilt and proud like his mother, had, in a fit of temper, thrown a hammer at Rosa while she was still a young girl, and the blow had left her with a marked facial scar. When David meets her for the first time the scar makes an immediate impression on him:

'She had black hair and eager black eyes and was thin, and she had a scar upon her lip, it was an old scar – I would rather call it a seam for it was not discoloured and had healed years ago – which had once cut through her mouth, downwards towards the chin, but was now barely visible across the table, except above and on her upper lip, the shape of which it had altered'.

Interestingly, he adds 'I concluded in my own mind that she was about thirty years of age and that she wished to be married.'

It transpires later that Steerforth had amused himself by seducing her before leaving her to the tender mercies of his mother. From that point on she is, as Steerforth puts it, 'sharpened... she has worn herself away with constant sharpening, she is all edge'. She is, in fact, equally consumed by love and hate for him. She continues to live with Mrs Steerforth, simulating ignorance and humility, but nevertheless, she continually asserts herself by making endless insinuations with the object of causing general unease.

Some time later David revisits the house from which Steerforth has long been absent. Rosa is beside herself with suspicion and fear:

'"What is he doing?" she asked with an eagerness that seemed enough to consume her like fire... "tell me, is it anger, is it hatred, is it pride, is it restlessness, is it some wild fancy, is it love, *what is it* that is leading him?"... As she still looked fixedly at me, a twitching and throbbing from which I could not dissociate the idea of pain, came into that cruel mark; and lifted up the corner of her lip as if with scorn, or with a pity that despised its object.'

She is terrified that he has fallen in love, and the scar with its livid presence about her lips reflects a nature now as twisted as her face.

When she hears he has run off with 'Little Em'ly', a sailor's daughter and old playmate of David's, her fury knows no bounds; she is determined to track her down, and once she has found her, she sets about tormenting her, even though the girl has run away from Steerforth who had abused her. David watches her as she vents her fury on poor little Em'ly:

'"I have come to look at you. What! You are not ashamed of the face that has done so much [harm]?" The resolute and unrelenting hatred of her tone, its cold stern sharpness and its mastered rage presented her before me... I saw the flashing black eyes and the passion-wasted figure; and I saw the scar with its white track cutting through the lips quivering and throbbing as she spoke.'

Rosa is a violent woman and her facial disfigurement is more than an ugly scar; it is the outward expression of her inner trauma; the physical wound inflicted on her by Steerforth becomes externalised into a symbol of the misery and anger that stems from her obstinate love for him; in moments of intense suffering the scar seems to speak for her, as it becomes mobile and livid; it is the voice of all she has suffered, revealing her memory of Steerforth, and the hatred he has engendered in her for all those women who have not suffered as she has.

When Steerforth dies at sea and his body is brought home, she is desperate with grief, and loud in her acclamations of love for a man whom she claims is a fallen angel ruined by his mother's indulgence:

'"I could have loved him and asked no return; if I had been his wife I could have been a slave to his caprices for a word of love a year... Look here," she said, striking the scar again with relentless hand, "when he grew into a better understanding of what he had done, he saw it and repented of it. I could sing to him and talk to him and show the ardour I felt in all he did… I attracted him when he was freshest and truest, he loved me.'"

Would she have been happy if she had been married to Steerforth? No, he is a treacherous character, as seen by his treatment of Little Em'ly; he would have treated Rosa just as badly. Had Rosa not been disfigured by Steerforth and later seduced by him, would she still have ended up as a spinster? Could she have met someone else and become a happy wife? We shall never know, but it seems unlikely. As it is, she remains one of thousands of abused women.

'Precious Bane' by Mary Webb

Prue Sarn:

Written by Mary Webb in 1928, the story is set in the late eighteenth century. It is a rural imitation of Hardy, and a bit cheesy, so I was annoyed to find myself weeping at the end! Set in a superstitious and backward rural community, Prue lives with her parents and brother, Gideon on a poor farmstead; when her father dies as a result of a blow from his son, Gideon takes Prue aside and tells her of his ambitious plans:

"'I want to make money on the place – a mort of money. Then when the time's ripe, we'll sell it. Then we'll go to Lullingford and buy a house, and you shall hold up your head with the best, and be a rich lady.'"

However, as this will involve years of back-breaking work, Prue is somewhat lacking in enthusiasm, but he claims:

"'I can do all I have a mind to do. I've got such a power in me that naught but death can bend it. And with you to give me a hand...'" Then he drops the bombshell:

"'Seeing as how things are, you'll never marry, Prue."
My heart beat soft and sad… "Not wed, Gideon. Oh, ah I'll wed for sure."
"I'm afeerd nobody'll ask you, Prue."
"Not ask me? What for not?"
"Best ask Mother for why. Maybe she can tell you why the hare crossed her path.'"

Up to now – she is in her early teens and living in a small community – she has not thought much about the effects of her hare lip, but as she grows older she senses how she is to be regarded, and this is brought home to her when she goes with her brother to market in Lullington. They enter a local inn in which a number of men are sitting:

"'Here's a queer outlandish creature."
"Here be a wench that turns into a hare by night. Her's a witch, an ugly hare-shotten witch."
Maybe in the tuthree times I'd been to Lullingford in the past, they'd stared so, but I was a child then and I didna see.
"Dunna drink when she's by. It'll pison yer innards."
"Dunna look upon the baigle. Her'll put the evil eye on you. You'll dwine and dwine away.'"

Prue, who is a kindly soul herself, cannot understand the cruelty of these men, but she resigns herself to her lot in life and works endlessly on the land, she also learns to read and write because Gideon sees this accomplishment as useful to his plans.

Then Gideon falls in love with Janice, the beautiful daughter of the local 'wizard' or wise man. Prue feels envy and dislike towards the girl, but being a good person, does her best to overcome her feelings. Now Gideon is more determined than ever to make money and becomes engaged to Janice, but he will not marry until he is a rich man. However, the acknowledgement of their engagement takes place in the traditional way when the local women meet for what is tellingly termed 'a love-spinning'; and it is there that Prue sees Kester Woodeaves and falls in love with him. '"At last," she says, "I'd found him", and she fantasises about him:

'It was strange to think that as I went about my household work and outdoor work… I should be in my own soul the bride of the weaver.''

But aware that this will never be, she hides away from Kester, but unbeknownst to her he catches sight of her partially naked, and rather likes the look of what he sees. Later on when she is subject to hostility from the local townsfolk, Kester arrives on the scene: 'He stooped, he set his arms about me. He lifted me to the saddle. It was just as in the dream I had…' Surely this is too good to be true?

'"But no," I said, "you must marry a girl like a lily. See, I be hare-shotten."
But he wouldna listen. He wouldna argufy… looking into my eyes, he said: "No more sad talk. I've chosen my bit of paradise…" And when he'd said those words, he bent his comely head and kissed me full on the mouth.'

Love and kindness have healed the scar.

It makes you squirm a bit, doesn't it, not just the cheesiness of it, but its unlikeliness? So why did I cry? Well, not for the 'hare-shotten' spinster, spinster no more.

Poor Janice has allowed Gideon to anticipate her long awaited marriage by a day, but they are caught by her father who has always hated Gideon, and so off he goes and fires the ricks, the source of all the riches for which Gideon and his family have laboured so long. Filled with fury, Gideon repudiates Janice who will return a year later, destitute, with a baby in her arms. Still unrelenting, Gideon sends her away and now desperate, she drowns herself along with her child. Gideon, maddened by his losses, goes off in his boat and drowns *himself* in the tarn in order to be near his lost bride.

So it is the girl scarred by her 'hare-shotten lip' who wins the handsome husband, and the beautiful Janice who is the deserted spinster.

'Eleanor Oliphant Is Completely Fine' by Gail Honeyman

Eleanor Oliphant:

Perhaps the most remarkable example of outward scarring that reflects the trauma and loneliness of an unmarried woman, is shown by Eleanor Oliphant.

In spite of being (our first) twenty-first century woman, Eleanor is in every way one of the most spinsterly spinsters we have met:

'I do not light up a room when I walk into it. No one longs to see me or hear my voice. I do not feel sorry for myself, not in the least. These are simply statements of fact.'

Eleanor is nearly thirty, she has a degree in classics and she works in an office; she doesn't socialise with her fellow workers who giggle at her appearance and her spinsterly ways. She has a very formal, even archaic way of speaking. Her life runs on a strictly controlled routine:

'From Monday to Friday I come in at 8.30. I take an hour for lunch… I sit in the staffroom with my sandwich and then I read the newspaper from cover to cover, and then I do the crosswords… I don't talk to anyone.' Her evenings are equally unexciting:

'After I have washed up I read a book or sometimes I watch television… I go to bed about ten, read for half an hour and then put the light out.' Every Wednesday she speaks to 'Mummy' who seems to be confined in some institution. A social worker comes to visit from time to time.

Her regime is different at the weekend because '… on Fridays I buy a margherita pizza, some chianti and two big bottles of Glen's vodka… I don't need much on Friday, just a few swigs… I drink the rest of the vodka over the weekend.'

Her life changes when she develops a crush on a local singer and, like Prue, she fantasises about her future life with him in which she fully believes (they have never met), and she starts thinking about how to glamorise her appearance; this is difficult for her because we learn:

'… it doesn't bother me at all when people react to my face, to the ridged white contours of scar tissue that slither across my right cheek, starting at my temple and running all the way down to my chin. I am stared at, whispered about.'

There is another more promising change in her life when she and a fellow office worker, Raymond witness an old man's collapse in the street and become involved with his family. Raymond is very kind to Eleanor in spite of her haughty ways and exaggeratedly formal diction: '"Let us retire to an inn or public house, Raymond,"' is a typical example. Unwillingly, she begins to see more of him, even though she disapproves of his scruffy appearance. This is the first human interaction she has had since years ago, when she lived with an abusive boyfriend who beat her up before the police intervened.

Still believing in her future life with the singer, she has her hair cut and buys some smart clothes; however, finally, realising how deluded she has been, she attempts suicide, but is discovered in time by the ever-attentive Raymond, and diagnosed with depression. She is given time off work and is referred to a psychologist, and gradually the truth emerges (spoiler): her mother had been, as Eleanor puts it, 'a bad woman', having repeatedly abused her and her sister, and had finally set fire to the house in an attempt to burn her daughters to death; Eleanor, then aged ten, had tried in vain to save her sister, but had escaped the fire alone, badly burnt. Subsequently she had been brought up by a series of foster parents. Her recent weekly 'conversations with Mummy' had been as much fantasies as her belief in her future with the singer, both attempts to find something in the way of restorative love; she tells the psychologist, '"I thought any mummy was better than no mummy."'

Her facial scar is not only the physical result of damage done to her from the fire, but is also a vivid symbol of partially repressed memories of her cruel mother and her dead sister; but between the psychologist and Raymond, Eleanor becomes able to face the truth of her history. She uses make-up to disguise her scar, and as it becomes less visible, so too her horrendous past becomes less important to her.

Scars can be cured, or at least alleviated by kindness if the sufferer is willing for this to happen. As a result of the kindness of Raymond, her psychologist and finally the people in her office who welcome her back with cards and flowers, Eleanor can attempt something like a normal life:

'I walked through the fire and I lived. There are scars on my heart just as thick, as disfiguring as those on my face. I know they're there. I hope some undamaged tissue remains, a patch through which love can come in and flow out. I hope'.

She is of course reiterating Pym's: 'Some tame gazelle, something to love / Ah, something to love.' Whether her relationship with Raymond will develop into a permanent sexual one we do not know.

All three women have been abused, but Eleanor and Prue have something besides kindness that saves them being hopeless spinsters: Eleanor, once her scar is disguised, turns out to be quite pretty, and Prue has a remarkably good figure. Poor Rosa has neither looks nor figure and remains cruel and embittered.

Sadly, it seems that it is not love alone that has the ability to heal scars whether they are emotional or physical, but it needs good looks thrown into the mix. Plain Mary Jocelyn and Catherine Sloper had no such advantages, and although they are not embittered like Rosa Dartle, their internal scars remain unhealed. Like so many other spinsters they must resort to the church and good works for consolation. Is it the case, then, that abused women can only get their lives sorted out if they are attractive?

CHAPTER SEVEN

SOILED SPINSTERS

The young bloods are not so eager now
To rattle your closed shutters with volleys of pebbles
And disturb your sleep. The door that once
Moved so very easily
On its hinges, now hugs the threshold.
Less and less often do you hear the cry "I'm yours,
And dying for your love, Lydia, night after long night,
And you lie there sleeping."
Your turn will come, when you are an old rag
In some lonely alley way, weeping at the insolence of lovers
As the wind from Thrace holds wilder and wilder orgies
Between the old moon and the new.
                                            Horace, Odes 1.

Ageing spinsters who tend to be perceived as fussy, silly,
disagreeable or simply as failures, provoke little or no male
interest and are readily dismissed by them; but those who have
been attractive and carefree in their youth, *and* have enjoyed
an active sex life, become particular objects of male ridicule
and scorn when old age finds them out.

It is the old tale of male hypocrisy: men had no problem with
enjoying their favours when they were young and seductive,
but when they cease to be so, the same men can happily regard
them with contempt. I took the translation of the ode at the
start of this chapter from an 1883 edition, and I can't resist
quoting the deliciously censorious commentary on the poem
written as the preface to the Latin text:

'A coarsely expressed ode addressed to Lydia who Horace says will soon be an old woman without the charms, but retaining the passions of her youth, and destined to meet with the same haughty contempt she now employs towards her lovers. It has no merit and may be omitted with advantage.'

It seems to me that *'It has no merit and may be omitted with advantage'* sums up the Victorian attitude not just to risqué verse, but to the state of ageing spinsterhood in the 'fallen woman'. Good time girls who fail to achieve the desired goal of marriage must be first regarded with contempt and then forgotten.

Alexander Pope in the less prudish eighteenth century took a more enlightened view. In his 'Elegy to the Memory of an Unfortunate Lady' the poet stands by the unmarked grave of 'a fallen woman' and asks, 'Is it in Heaven, a crime to love too well / To bear too tender or too firm a heart?' He takes the opposite attitude to the censorious Victorian editor of Horace, and points to the hypocrisy of those who condemn her: 'Lo! These were they whose souls the Furies steeled / And cursed with hearts unknowing how to yield.' The Furies, as we have seen earlier, do not always have right on their side, nor do the men who abuse them.

'A Streetcar Named desire' by Tennessee Williams

Blanche Dubois:

> *Did I not warn you, Prodike,*
> *" Remember that we all grow old:*
> *Decay will come and love will flee*
> *Alas, too soon? This I foretold,*
> *Now come the wrinkles and grey hairs,*
> *The shrivelled flesh, the lips gone dry;*
> *No ardent lovers climb your stairs,*

But like a tomb we pass you by .

Rufinus

Elle n'avait recontré que des hommes qui prenaient leur plaisir sans la considérer comme une personne humaine.

Simenon, 'La Patience de Maigret'.

Blanche Dubois from Tennessee Williams' 'A Streetcar Named Desire', suffers a fate closely resembling that of Horace's Lydia. Technically she is not a spinster because she has once been married, but the marriage was no marriage. She describes her husband:

'There was something different about the boy, a nervousness, a softness, a tenderness which wasn't like a man's, although he wasn't the least bit effeminate looking – still – that thing was there. He came to me for help. I didn't know that. I didn't find out anything until after our marriage when we'd run away and come back, and all I knew was I'd failed him in some mysterious way and wasn't able to give the help he needed, and couldn't speak of. Then I found out in the worst possible ways. By coming suddenly into a room that I thought was empty, but had two people in it.'

The boy was gay, and in despair shoots himself. Unsurprisingly, Blanche goes to pieces, letting her inheritance, the family home, 'Belle Reve', slip through her fingers, and she starts on a downward spiral of nymphomania. Her brother in law, Stan, tells her sister, Stella, the truth:

"She moved to the Flamingo, a second class hotel which has the advantage of not interfering in the private social life of the personalities there." Later Blanche admits:

"'Yes, I had many intimacies with strangers… not far from 'Belle Reve' before we had lost Belle Reve, was a camp where they trained young soldiers, on Saturday nights they would go into town where they would go to get drunk – and on the way back they would stagger on to my lawn and call – "Blanche, Blanche"… Sometimes I slipped outside to answer their calls…"'

But now Blanche, ageing, alcoholic, penniless and fearful of losing her looks, has come to her sister's apartment, her reputation lost, but fatally adopting a superior attitude to her brother-in law, Stan, pretending all is well. In fact, she is desperate. She confesses to her sister, Stella:

'I've run for protection, Stella, from one leaky roof to another people don't see you – *men* don't unless they are making love to you… but I'm scared I don't know how long I can turn the trick. It isn't enough to be soft and attractive. And I… I am fading now."

Sadly, her fate echoes Horace's words about Lydia. She sees an escape in Stan's friend, Mitch who is attracted to her, and she believes he will marry her, and she puts on a façade of sweet innocence, but Stan, who has seen through Blanche all along, tells Mitch the truth about her. He is staggered, and in the final scene with Blanche he lays bare not only her face, but what she has become:

'Mitch: Let's turn the light on here.
Blanche: (*fearfully*) Light? Which light? What for?' *She utters a frightened gasp… He tears the paper lantern off the light bulb which Blanche has put in place to soften her ageing looks.*
Blanche: What did you do that for?
Mitch: So I can take a look at you good and plain.'

Her last chance has gone and she sinks further and further into fantasy, asserting, amongst other fabrications that there is a millionaire awaiting her on his yacht. Possibly she believes the fabrication. When Stan returns from the hospital where he has taken his wife Stella to have her baby, in a fit of drunkenness and irritation at her pathetic pretence of superiority, he rapes her. The matter is hushed up, and in the final scene we see her being taken off to spend the rest of her days in an asylum.

Poor Blanche has been abused by so many men, and finally she has been raped by her brother-in-law. The strands of suffering that we saw originating from the Ancient World are all too cruelly woven into this poor woman's life because her fate reminds us of Philomela, the sister of Procne, also raped by her brother-in-law, Tereus who tore her tongue out to ensure her silence. Blanche's silence will be ensured by her incarceration in an asylum, but unlike Philomela she will have no means of informing her sister – or of taking revenge. Philomela was turned into a swallow so she at least had freedom. Like so many spinsters we have met, Blanche's life was to be spent in incarceration.

'Memoirs of a Geisha' by Arthur Golden

Chiyo:

We become geisha because we have no choice.

We see strands from the Ancient World twisting their way into the life of the geisha Chiyo.

In many ways I found this novel extremely distasteful. I think this was because of the matter-of-fact way in which it is written, the reader is forced to witness degrading things endured uncomplainingly by the geisha, *simply as a matter of course.*

Two young peasant girls, Chiyo, only nine, and her elder sister, Satsu, were uprooted and sold by their penniless fisherman father to a man named Mr Tanaka who took them to Kyoto. The elder sister who was less good looking than Chiyo was separated from her and taken to a red light district to become a prostitute. Chiyo who was remarkably pretty with unusually striking grey eyes, was sold on to the owners of an okiyo, a place for training girls to become geisha, so that they (the owners) could then take the profits from their trade. The owners of this okiyo, known as Granny, Mother and Auntie, although they had no relationship with each other, were typically cruel and avaricious women who virtually enslaved the girls they had bought. Chiyo has a dreadful time of it, having to work long hours as a drudge and a cleaner. Her life becomes much worse when she tries to run away with her sister, but falls and breaks her arm, and is returned to the okiyo to be punished by her mistress. Her life is made worse by Hatsumomo, a successful geisha who acts like 'an empress' in the okiyo and who takes a particular dislike to Chiyo, fearing she will develop into a rival beauty.

Then one day her fortunes change. Maneha, the most successful geisha in Kyoto, pays a visit to the okiyo. She has a request to make. It is the custom for a successful geisha to 'become' the elder sister to an apprentice geisha. She will take the girl about to various tea rooms, introduce her to influential men and generally make her well-known. Maneha will make Chiyo her 'younger sister'. She will now no longer be known as Chiyo, but adopt a new name, Sayuri. Of course Mrs Nitto ('Mother') sees the advantage in this as all Chiyo's earnings will accrue to her.

Now her training starts in earnest; she must go to a school to learn how to read and write, she will be instructed in dancing, singing and playing the shamisen. She must develop graceful behaviour, be able to perform the tea ceremony, know how to kneel with suitable subjection before her clients, and talk amusingly if she is required to speak. She must perfect her elaborate make-up and endure hours of complicated hair arrangement which she must keep in place with a special pillow while asleep, she must learn to wear the kimono gracefully (not as easy as it sounds as it is an enormous garment and extremely weighty, worn with an equally heavy and trailing obi). At the same time, she must carry out arduous tasks at the okiyo and endure the increasing torments inflicted on her by the hateful Hatsumomo.

As Chiyo becomes increasingly beautiful and well-known as 'an apprentice geisha', it is time to make money out of her, and this is the part I find most shocking. Mrs Nitto and Maneha instigate a bidding war for her 'misusage'. The man who wins the bidding, and the prices become higher and higher – to as much, in fact, as a workman would earn in a lifetime – will be the one who will take her virginity. The bidding is between two loathsome men, a dissolute baron and an infamous doctor. The latter wins. There is a particularly revolting scene where he shows Chiyo his collection of specimen bottles in which he has stored the blood from the ripped hymens of his other victims, before adding Chiyo's to his collection. What shocked me most on reading the scene was Chiyo's attitude towards it. Yes, she finds it distasteful, but she regards it as a simple *rite de passage* in becoming a fully-fledged geisha.

Now she is no longer an apprentice but a fully qualified geisha, she wears a white collar instead of a red one to show her new status. She is available to wealthy clients 'if the terms are suitable'. The next stage is to procure a wealthy 'dana': this man will take her as a mistress and spend lavishly on her and further her interests in society. Again, the man will not be chosen by Chiyo. She would have preferred the badly disfigured, but honest Nobu, but she is persuaded to take on General Cotton because, with war is on its way and shortages threatening, the corrupt general will arrange that the okiyo goes short of nothing.

As a result of her success she will now become the adopted daughter of Mrs Nitto, which means that she will eventually inherit the okiyo. However, as war ensues, the age of the geishas is waning; the district is closed down and she spends five years exiled in the country working as a peasant, preparing dyes for parachute silk. Eventually she returns to Kyoto and finds Nobu still interested in her, wanting to replace the disgraced general as her dana. Now there is a problem for her; although she is very fond of Nobu who has been kind to her, for years she has been in love with a friend of his, a man she calls 'The Chairman', who took notice of her when she was barely a teenager and whom she has encountered on many occasions since. However, it is an unwritten law that no man who is a friend of the dana can ever take his mistress away from him. Chiyo has always had hopes of the Chairman, but if she 'belongs' to Nobu, she will never get the Chairman as her dana, so she decides to make sure that Nobu who is somewhat puritanical in his views, will no longer want her. Her plan is for him to catch sight of her 'in flagrante' with a particularly revolting man known as 'the Minister'. However, she is betrayed by a jealous geisha who had once had hopes of becoming the adopted daughter of Mrs Nitta, and as a revenge takes the Chairman to view the act, instead of Nobu. However, in the end, all turns out well, Nobu rejects her and the Chairman who suspects her ruse and has always longed for her, becomes her dana.

To cut a long story short, she eventually moves to New York where she sets up her own teahouse, and where she can spend time with the Chairman who has many business interests there. This is the only solution because she can never marry him as he is already married, and an illegitimate son in Kyoto would endanger the prospects of his children. She ends up living the life of a wealthy New York woman, although she is regarded somewhat scornfully by women who know she has been a geisha, but she regards herself on the same level as them, many of whom she knows are kept women themselves.

I find Chiyo's account more shocking than the history of Blanche Dubois, which isn't really shocking at all, just very, very, sad. Now I find both the story of Chiyo or Saya, as she becomes known, both sad and shocking. If she had not been sold into the okiyo she would have spent her life living in poverty in a peasant community, probably have married and had children. She would not have been 'soiled'. The choice to become a geisha was not hers. However, once she is embarked on that path she accepts it all as a matter of course: the disgusting bidding for her virginity, the taking of a dana for whom she has no liking, the endless routine of abasement before lecherous and drunken men at various parties and tea houses where she must endure insulting comments, kneeling before them, even put on their shoes and accompany them to the toilets, and be available for their enjoyment on 'suitable terms'. I find the trick she played on Nobu to secure the Chairman a symbol of how soiled she has become.

Perhaps it is because the story concerns a culture of which I have no knowledge, or because it takes place nearly a century ago, it feels particularly abhorrent to me. I am unable to regard it in context and I do not know how to view Chiyo; I am aware that she is the object of terrible male exploitation, but nevertheless, I cannot make myself easy about her own matter-of-fact attitude. I do not know how to be fair to her. And another problem, in wondering how to view her, is the fact that the novel was written by a man. Does this distort my understanding of her?

Perhaps I should leave her with her last word: 'As a young girl I believed my life would never have been a struggle if Mr Tanaka had not torn me away [from my home]. But now I know that our world is no more permanent than a wave rising on the ocean. Whatever our struggles and triumphs, however we may suffer them, all too soon they bleed into a wash, just like watery ink on paper.'

Chiyo reminds us of the nymphs we met earlier: Callisto, raped by Zeus, and Syrinx, turned into an instrument for men's pleasure. There are horribly strong threads here, twisting their way down from the Ancient World.

'Great Expectations' by Charles Dickens

Miss Havisham:

> *"I am yellow skin and bone."*

For a long time I haven't been sure where to place Miss Havisham. She has not been seduced or led a rackety life, so she is not 'soiled' like Blanche Dubois because she has never been touched. She is not facially disfigured like the women we met earlier, but in a different way she is both soiled and scarred.

To start with scarring: as Eleanor says, 'the scars on my heart are just as thick, as disfiguring as those on my face. Scars can be internal as well as external.'

We are told that Miss Havisham 'had not shown much susceptibility up to that time', but when she was presented with a new suitor things changed. Compeyson was an unscrupulous man, a friend of her dissolute half-brother and he 'pursued her closely, practised upon her affections,' and 'all the susceptibility she possessed came out then, and she passionately loved him… There is no doubt that she perfectly idolised him…' She is warned against him because already 'he got great sums of money from her'. But Miss Havisham was too proud to listen.

'The marriage was fixed, the wedding dresses were bought, the wedding tour was planned out, the wedding guests invited.' Then on the wedding morning, as Miss Havisham, in her bridal attire sits waiting for the ceremony to take place, she receives a letter from Compeyson telling her that there will be no wedding: 'He most heartlessly broke off the marriage.' In fact, he is already married. This is a blow from which she will never recover; I suppose we would say now that her mental health was destroyed.

She makes a decision to remain exactly in the state she was in that morning. When Pip first sees her many years later:

'… she was dressed in rich materials – satins and laces and silks. And she had a long white veil dependent from her hair and she had flowers in her hair… But I saw that everything within my view which ought to be white, had been white long ago and lost its lustre. I saw that bride within the bridal dress had withered like the dress.'

So although she is not soiled by physical sexual abuse like Chiyo and Blanche, she has allowed the internal scar caused by her rejection to become vividly and horribly externalised by wearing her decaying bridal attire. Like Rosa Dartle's scar it will confront the onlooker; so, unlike Blanche who hopes that her now soiled former clothes may still bring suitors, Miss Havisham clings to the remnants of her bridal wear as an exercise in masochism. She exhibits her body in 'the once white dress' of an expectant bride, and exultingly exhibits the contrast. When the sycophantic Sarah Pocket tells her how well she looks, she retorts, 'I am yellow skin and bone'. She takes this exhibition further. She immures herself inside her house for the rest of her life, and Pip tells us: '… she has never since looked on the light of day'. She lives alongside the decaying bridal items: ' the most prominent object was a long table with a table cloth spread on it… a centre piece of some kind was in the middle of the cloth; it was so heavily overhung with cobwebs that the form was quite indistinguishable, and as I looked along the yellow expanse… it seeming to grow, like a black fungus, I saw speckle-legged spiders with blotchy bodies running home to it… I heard mice too, rattling behind the panels.' Everything around her has become soiled; 'the rotten bride cake hidden among the cobwebs' and 'the mildewed air of the feast chamber'.

But she is not content with simply exhibiting her soiled life; she has adopted a daughter, a beautiful young girl called Estella whom she trains up to be cruel and callous, as a revenge not simply against her own suitor, but against men in general. '"Break their hearts!"' She cries. In particular, she watches Pip's thwarted love for Estella 'with a mind mortally hurt and diseased.'

'"Far out of your reach, prettier than ever, admired by all who see her. Do you feel that you have lost her?" There was such malignant enjoyment in her utterance of the last words that I was at a loss what to say.'

And she succeeds; the beautiful Estella does break Pip's heart; she eschews her suitors, and finally chooses the worst of them all, a degenerate man whose life she plans to make a misery.

So the soiling extends beyond this one woman to the world outside. Only at the end of her life does Miss Havisham regret her actions: '"Oh, what have I done?"' she cries. Finally the soiling and scarring are brought to a melodramatic end. Pip tells us: 'I saw her seated in the ragged chair by the hearth. In a moment I saw a great flaming light spring up. In the same moment I saw her running at me shrieking, with a whirl of fire blazing all about her.'

Earlier we met Medusa as one of the monsters of the Ancient World, but I did not tell the whole story. Medusa had once been young and beautiful, but she was raped by the god Poseidon in the Temple of Athene; the goddess, enraged at this sacrilege, took her revenge – not on Poseidon, but on Medusa, turning her into a hideous snake-encircled gorgon who turned anyone who saw her to stone. Although Miss Havisham was not the victim of rape, her life had been violated and like Medusa she turned Estella's heart to stone in order to wreak revenge on her suitors.

However, as an example of abuse, Miss Havisham does not strike me as a credible figure, nor does she arouse any feelings of pity as say, Blanche du Bois does. She is, as the unsympathetic Sarah Pocket says, 'nobody's enemy but her own'. But there is a reason for that, one I shall be returning to her later when I discuss spectral spinsters. But for now we have had enough suffering. It is time for something different.

CHAPTER EIGHT

SCHOOL MISTRESS SPINSTERS

Single women living alone like me – and there are thousands of us up and down the country – are often the subject of pity and speculation.

Miss Read, 'A Village School'

In examining schoolmistresses we can see no obvious links with the Ancient World – I suppose Athene could be seen as a sort of schoolmistress; she certainly instructed Arachne! And in 'Some Tame Gazelle' we saw the sad cluster of Sunday School teachers who, like the Eumenides at the end of Aeschylus' play, must be content 'to do good, receive good, and be honoured as the good / are honoured.' But it is not in their professional lives that they echo their Ancient sisters but in their individual idiosyncrasies. The strands will be there, just slightly twisted.

'Villette' by Charlotte Bronte

Lucy Snowe:

Certain accidents of the weather… were almost dreaded by me, because they woke the being I was always lulling, and stirred up a craving cry I could not satisfy.

Lucy Snowe certainly has a repressed life; left (presumably an orphan) she has a relatively happy girlhood at the house of her godmother, Mrs Hope, and her son Graham; living there too, is a little motherless girl, called Polly, the daughter of an old friend of her godmother. Later, when the household is disbanded through financial problems, Lucy is forced to find employment as a companion to an elderly disabled woman, and on her death, left virtually penniless, she bravely seeks her fortune abroad where she becomes first, the nursery governess, and then teacher of English at the pensionnaire of the unscrupulous Madam Beck in the town of Villette. There she endures much hardship through loneliness.

Then she again meets her godmother's son, Graham, who is now known as Dr John; he, however, is in love with a pupil at the school, the amoral and flirtatious Ginevra Fanshawe, who is the antithesis of the self-contained and puritanical Lucy. Eventually however, the scales fall from his eyes and it seems as if he is falling for Lucy; at first she dares not let herself hope, but finally after she receives 'long' and 'kind' letters from him, she comes to believe that he is in love with her. Alas, it is not to be.

He meets or rather, re-meets Polly, the little girl whom his mother looked after in his youth. Not only has she become very beautiful, but (by some quirk) become a countess and heiress, and she is very pure and good, to boot. Lucy's chances have gone. But there is an acerbic teacher at the school, called Monsieur Paul, a fierce little man, a cousin of Madame Beck who is intrigued by Lucy, and is alternatively cruel and kind to her. Eventually, he sets Lucy up in her own school and asks her to marry him, a proposal she gladly accepts, but there is – as always with poor Lucy – a fly in the ointment: he has to go abroad for three years on business before they can marry. (Oh dear, here we are reminded of Mr Herbert taking his cure at Cheltenham before proposing to Mary; why couldn't these foolish men just have got on with it?) Lucy waits patiently, striving as ever, to work hard and make a success of her school. Eventually, he is on the ship to return, almost home, but terrible storms arise at sea, and the reader never knows whether or not he will return alive, but one feels he will not.

Bronte herself did not like her heroine, deciding her name must signify her cold nature. In a chapter on 'Villette' in his book 'Sexuality, Repression and Victorian Literature', Russell M. Goldfarb argues that Lucy Snowe is a classic case of Freudian sexual frigidity. To support this theory he quotes two passages:

1)'Conceive a dell, deep hollowed in forest secrecy; it lies in dimness and mists; its turf is dank, its herbage pale and humid. A storm or axe makes a wide gap amongst the oak trees; the breeze sweeps in; the sun looks down; the sad, cold dell becomes a deep cup of lustre; high summer pours in her blue glory and her golden light out of that beauteous sky, which till now the starved hollow never saw.'

I am at a loss to understand why this vaginal imagery implies sexual frigidity. Surely it implies the opposite. There are numerous examples which Goldfarb himself refers to, that show Lucy has a very passionate nature indeed. There is the incident where Lucy spends a long time in the Art Gallery staring with disapproval at a voluptuous picture of Cleopatra. Why does she gaze at it so long? There is the incident where Lucy revels in the storm and sits outside in it, excited by its violence:

It was wet, it was wild, it was pitch-dark… I could not go in; too resistless was the delight of staying with the wild hour'.

Then there is the visit to the theatre to see the highly sexualised play 'Vashti', which completely overwhelms her. She is obviously sexually stirred.

And finally, if Lucy is so frigid, why does she spend so much time with Genevra Fanshawe whose frivolous nature she despises, frequently allowing her to physically lean on her? Surely there is sexual attraction here.

2) Golfarb cites the occasion when Lucy buries her letters from Dr John, as she realises he has no romantic interest in her: Lucy takes her letters in a sealed jar to the foot of an old pear tree:

'The timber of the tree was sound, only there was a hole, or rather a deep hollow, near his root. I knew there was such a hollow, hidden partly by ivy and creepers, growing thickly around it, and there I meditated hiding my treasure... I cleared away the ivy and found the hole; it was large enough to receive the jar and I thrust it deep in with the jar thrust deeply in the secret hole.'

Goldfarb claims: 'Lucy re-enacts her sexual experience with Dr John before she inters it for good... Lucy has at long last purged herself of repressed sexual desires, furthermore she will have no future desire for sexual intercourse.'

If she has buried all her libido why does she change from her first asserted wish to be only M. Paul's 'sister', to allowing him to kiss her and agree to become his wife? Could it be that she looks forward to the disinterring and utilisation of the 'jar'!

It seems to me that she is quite the antithesis of frigidity, but is compelled by her situation, convention, personal experience, and unprepossessing appearance, to suppress this nature under an appearance of extreme reserve. In my opinion she is one of those spinsters, and I am sure spinster she will remain, with a nature as violent and passionate as Rosa Dartle.

'The Prime of Miss Jean Brodie' by Muriel Spark

Miss Jean Brodie:

> *" There was a Miss Jean Brodie in her prime."*

'The Prime of Miss Jean Brodie', rather like 'Some Tame Gazelle', is awash with spinsters, Scottish spinsters of the 1930s. It is a virtual overview of them.

There is Miss Mackay, headmistress of Marcia Blaine School for Girls who 'has an awfully red face, with the veins all showing', a statement much relished by Miss Brodie. There is Miss Lockhart, perceived by Sandy, the main (spinster) character in the book, as a kind of priestess in her laboratory 'wearing a white overall, with her short grey hair set back in waves from a tanned and weathered golfer's face.' She is a sort of Pythia to Sandy. There are 'the sewing sisters' 'incapable of imparting any information whatsoever, so flustered were they with their fluffed-out hair, dry blue-grey skins and birds' eyes.' There is 'a Miss Gaunt from the western isles who wore a knee length skirt made from what looked like grey blanket stuff... her head was large and bony. Her chest was a slight bulge flattened by a bust bodice, and her jersey was a dark forbidding green.'

The lives of these women are dreary, being 'of an orderly type, earning their keep, living with aged parents, and taking walks on the hills and holidays at North Berwick.'

Here is a whole gamut of spinster school teachers: 'there were legions of her kind during the nineteen-thirties, women from the age of thirty and upward who crowded their war-bereaved sisterhood with voyages into art and social welfare, education and religion.' This seeking of alternatives to the marital state reminds us of Mary Jocelyn and Catherine Sloper with their good works. But there are spinsters of a different kind as well: intellectually inclined spinsters 'who could be seen leaning over the democratic counters of Edinburgh's grocers' shops, arguing with the manager on every subject from the authenticity of the scriptures to the question of what the word 'guarantee' on a jam-jar really meant... they preached the inventions of Marie Stopes; they attended meetings of the

Oxford Group and put spiritualism to their hawk-eyed test.' There is a third category, that of 'committee spinsters' who were 'less enterprising and not at all rebellious, they were sober church-goers and quiet workers.' With them we see again the familiar strand of religion used as a crutch.

And against this backdrop of conventional spinsters we see Miss Brodie who stands in splendid uniqueness in a class of her own. She fits none of the categories into which these others fall, although she belongs in part to each: she is a strict Presbyterian, she teaches at a conventional school, she is eager to explore new avenues: 'There was nothing Miss Brodie could not learn; she boasted of it'. But from there she steps out into a world of her own. Unlike the spinsters mentioned above, she has a glamorous appearance and is much admired by the male members of the staff: 'She wore newer clothes and a kind of amber necklace'. She regards her own views as being the only correct ones and brooks no disagreement, but unfortunately she is usually misguided in her beliefs, as in her admiration for Hitler and Mussolini, for example. Nevertheless, she remains undaunted and is determined to put her own stamp on her coterie of chosen girls, her 'Brodie set'. And she has a kind of magnetic power that she exercises over her protégées, Sandy and Rose, in particular, who spend hours fantasising and even writing the fictional love life of Jean Brodie.

And that is where she differs most vividly from the other spinster schoolmistresses: she has an active love life. I say 'love life' because the liaisons she enjoys on her holidays abroad and recounts to her 'set' are somewhat ambiguous, and she is also an unashamed liar. But she does have regular sex with the music master, Mr Lloyd at whose large house she is a regular visitor, cooking him large and exotic meals, while her real love is a romantic love for the married art master, Teddy Louther; and her relations with him are platonic. Rather like Miss Havisham, albeit in a more benign way, she grooms one of her beautiful protégés, Rose; she doesn't want to wreak revenge on the male sex, but to enable Rose to become her substitute, as the lover of Teddy Louther.

Miss Brodie is an outrageous, larger than life character whose life-style is in some ways as unreal as that of Miss Havisham; how could she get away so long with her unconventional teaching methods which were in effect, no more than recounting her own often amorous experiences? Would teenage girls have been that interested in her, could she really have conjured up the gargantuan meals to which she treats her lover? Yet unlike Miss Havisham, we do believe in her.

Miss Brodie exercises fascination over men, and this sets her apart from the other spinsters and spinsterly members of the staff: '"Miss Jean Brodie", said Teddy Louther, " is a magnificent woman in her prime."' She could have married her music teacher lover, she could probably have run off with the art master, but she chose not to. But as she ages, she becomes more of a spinsterly spinster. Her later years are lonely, miserable and embittered, because like Rosa Dartle and Miss Havisham, she is 'betrayed' by the person she loves, her favourite, Sandy. The headmistress Miss Mackay, she of 'the awfully red face' had been trying unsuccessfully for years to get rid of Miss Brodie, and it is Sandy, Miss Brodie's favourite, who gives her the ammunition: '"You won't be able to pin her down on sex. Have you thought of politics... she's a born Fascist? Have you thought of that?"'
It is enough; she can sack Miss Brodie at last. But why does Sandy, who has always been her favourite betray her? It is complicated; in the first place it is Sandy, not Rose whom Miss Brodie groomed to take her place, who becomes Teddy Louther's lover; but all his portraits show a resemblance to Miss Brodie. '"Why are you obsessed with that woman," Sandy asks, "can't you see she's ridiculous?"' But it's not just sexual jealousy. Sandy is resentful of the power Jean Brodie has exercised over her throughout her adolescence: '"She

thinks she's Providence... She thinks she's the God of Calvin, that she sees the beginning and the end. And Sandy thought, "the woman is an unconscious lesbian."' And perhaps most telling of all is that Sandy, the writer of romance about Miss Brodie, who has become the lover of her lover, in the end becomes a nun, Sister Helena, thus putting a kind of seal on her own and Miss Brodie's spinsterhood.

In many ways Miss Brodie is an unique spinster among spinsters; she has fascinated, imposed herself on the imaginations of those around her, *actually* in the case of Teddy Louther's portraits, and exercised her power over them – even in adulthood they remember her. A male visitor to Sandy's convent asks: "'What were the main influences of your school days, Sister Helena, were they literary, political or personal? Was it Calvinism?" Sandy says, " There was a Miss Jean Brodie in her prime."'

But it is not a benign power that she has exercised. Like the Sirens she has sung an enticing song from a safe position, but like them she has a pile of wrecked lives beside her: she wrongly influences her students' attitudes; she was unfair and unkind towards the weakest member of her set, poor Mary Macgregor whom she leaves so bereft of confidence that she later lacks the will to save herself from death in a hotel fire; and it is under her influence Joyce Emily Hammond goes to her death in Spain – fighting for the wrong side in the Civil War. She has, by her actions even deprived Sandy of a normal life. Her warped spinsterhood has made these three women into spinsters; and if she did not kill her male lovers, she made their lives unhappy. She is nobody's victim; she has suffered no abuse; she has abused others. She is a species of harpy.

'Chronicles of Fairacre' by Miss Read

Do you want to do nothing better than be schoolmistress at Fairacre School?

Miss Read:

Miss Read is a very likeable spinster. Headmistress of the village school, she has an intelligent, humorous, pragmatic, but kindly nature, and is adept at dealing not only with her schoolchildren and their parents, but with her assistants and the various characters within the village. One can do nothing but admire and like her. Although her life is not always easy, she presents herself as a player in a sort of pastoral idyll. No woman, it seems, could be more contented with her lot.

As we shall see later with the scholarly spinsters of 'Gaudy Night', the question of the relative advantages and disadvantages of spinsterhood versus marriage come under review: Miss Read has an old friend, Amy with whom she was at college. Amy has married a prosperous businessman and has all the accoutrements of middle class comfort: an expensive car, an interest in trendy arts, and a patronising attitude towards her old friend: '"What you want," she comments, "is a husband."'

'"Tell me," she asks on another occasion: "what do you do with your time when you are not at school?"'

" I have to do all the things that other women do, I suppose, I wash my clothes and iron them, and bake cakes and mend things, and fetch in coal and clean the windows…" But I could see that was not what Amy wanted to know. How did I use my leisure, and more particularly, was I happy here, living alone – a solitary woman… would I like to change my life? Wasn't I in danger of becoming a vegetable? I don't know whether Amy believed me when I answered truthfully that I was completely happy; for single women living alone like me – and there are thousands of us up and down the country – are often the subject of pity and speculation.'

Miss Read's assertion of her contentment in her spinsterhood as opposed to the attractions of married life is vindicated when Amy later implies that all is not well with her marriage; it is obvious that her husband is being unfaithful, and all the much vaunted expensive perks that she enjoys are mere sops. Miss Read deals with this revelation with her usual kindly tact, but one cannot help feeling that she enjoys a moment of schadenfreude.

Later a newcomer arrives in the village, a Mr Mawne whom the village regards as an eligible match for Miss Read, and much insinuation is put about with suggestive comments by everyone from the vicar's wife to the school cleaner, but after he has been absent for a few weeks, a different scenario transpires. The vicar's wife arrives in an agitated state:

'"We've had some very unsettling news… about Mr Mawne."
I said I was sorry. I hoped he wasn't ill. Mrs Partridge gave a heavy sigh.
"No he's not ill" – she said, and stopped.
"Perhaps he's decided not to return to Fairacre?"
"Yes, he's coming back. That's partly the trouble," said the vicar's wife stirring her tea meditatively, "Gerald had a letter from him this morning."
"I should think that's good news, I know he's an enormous help to the vicar.."
"But, my dear… I really don't know how to tell you. To be blunt he's bringing his wife back with him."
The relief which this thunder-burst brought to me cannot be described, but Mrs Partridge looked so distraught that I could hardly let out a cheer and caper round the room… I did the next best thing.

"Believe me," I said earnestly, "that's the best news I've heard since Mr Mawne came to live here. Now I hope I shall be left in peace.'"

After the embarrassed vicar's wife has left, we are told, 'I closed the door behind her and waltzed gaily back to the kitchen, cutting the caper that had been pent-up so long.'

True, Miss Read had early claimed that she found Mr Mawne a bore, but isn't all this dancing about a rather exaggerated response to what after all is a humiliating situation? Isn't this perhaps a case of 'methinks the lady doth protest too much'? But Miss Read does not dwell on what she might have missed. She dismisses too much introspection and concludes:

'I, finding myself remarkably uninteresting, am only too pleased to observe others and the natural objects around me. Thus I am spared the pangs of self-reproach, and, as my lot is cast in pleasant places, find endless cause for happiness and amusement.'
Bully for her!

Hilary Jackson:

Her name is Hilary Jackson and she's nearly twenty-one. She seemed a conscientious, rather earnest young woman, squarish in build with a shaggy haircut and horn-rimmed glasses. She was dressed in a crumpled blouse and a gathered skirt of glazed chintz, and she wore aggressively tough sandals.

At first sight Miss Read's new assistant teacher looks a typical schoolmistress spinster, but later we see another side of Miss Jackson when she starts seeing the widower, John Franklin, whom rumour has it, is a bit of a lad. Miss Read tracks her down to his house and wastes no time in berating her:

"'By consorting with John Franklin whose affairs have been watched for many years, you are giving yourself a bad name, as a teacher you should be doubly careful of the example you set, and by flaunting the conventions – which are, after all, only the commonly accepted modes of decent living, you are not only making a fool of yourself, but jeopardising your whole career. One silly slip now may mean much future unhappiness.'"

Hilary Jackson retorts roundly:

"'I don't care a row of pins what people think of me – back-biting, narrow-minded, evil-thinking country bumpkins, as stodgy as yourself. John Franklin is a fine man and I'm proud to be seen with him. I suppose a withered old spinster like you thinks love doesn't matter. Well, it does – and for me everything else must take second place.'"

Of course, what Miss Jackson is saying is: 'I'm young, I want sex and don't want to end my life like you, never having had any.' But Miss Read wins: she contacts the girl's father and gets him to take his daughter 'out of danger'.

I don't wish to be unduly critical of Miss Read who probably really thinks she is acting for the best – but how satisfying to have vindicated her own spinsterhood! Perhaps you think I'm unkind. But amongst the different types of spinsters some will tolerate, or at least, turn a blind eye to some degree of sexual freedom, but there is this other kind that can allow no such laxity; we will see it later with Harriet Herriton in 'Where Angels Fear to Tread'. Sexual freedom threatens all the carefully constructed barriers to real life that this narrow spinsterhood has so painstakingly built. I don't think Miss Read would have taken such drastic measures as the goddess

Diana who believes her virginity besmirched when she is seen naked by the hunter Acteon and turns him into a deer, but I think she might have sympathised with her.

And there is another irony: before she met John Franklin, Hilary Jackson had been under the influence of her college psychology lecturer, an unpleasant woman, another spinster called Miss Crabbe, and she has obviously entertained sexual feelings for her before John Franklin came on the scene. And now John Franklin is out of the way, what does Miss Read do, but engineer a rapprochement between Hilary and Miss Crabbe, who immediately set off for holiday together in Switzerland, with all sorts of plans for a life together?

Does the idea of lesbianism never enter Miss Read's head? Or does Miss Read regard that particular sort of spinsterhood as preferable to a heterosexual relationship? We shall never know. We will leave her in her garden: 'The peas have done well, and I sit on the lawn shelling them, and enjoying the scent of a freshly popped pod'.

Miss Clare:

Miss Clare was taking a coat-hanger out of her big canvas holdall. She is very careful of her clothes, and is grieved to see the casual way in which children sling their coats, haphazard on the pegs in the lobby. Her own coat is always smoothed methodically over its hanger and hung on the back of the classroom door. The children watch fascinated when she removes her gloves, for she blows into them several times before folding them neatly together. Her sensible felt hat has a shelf to itself inside the needlework cupboard.'

I now turn to Miss Jackson's predecessor, as typical an old maid as you will find anywhere, as the quotation above illustrates. Miss Read gives us her history:

'Miss Clare has taught here for nearly forty years, with only one break, when she nursed her mother through her last illness twelve years ago; she started here as a monitoress at the age of thirteen, and was known officially until recently as a 'supplementary uncertified teacher'... Miss Clare is of commanding appearance, tall, slim with beautiful white hair which is kept in place with an invisible hair net. Even on the wildest days... Miss Clare walks around the playground looking immaculate. She is now over sixty and her teaching methods have of late, been looked on by some visiting inspectors with a slightly pitying eye: they are, they say, too formal; the children should have more activity, and the classroom is unnaturally quiet for children of that age.'

But that is how Miss Clare likes it: anything boisterous is a threat to her carefully nurtured spinsterhood. Again, before the annual school Christmas party we are told of the tree which 'Miss Clare had insisted on dressing on her own, and had spent all the previous evening in the shadowy classroom alone with the tree and her thoughts.' Undoubtedly, she had received much spinsterly satisfaction from that, but wouldn't it have been kinder – more generous – to have left the tree-decorating to the children? Personally, I regard Miss Clare as extremely trying, and was tempted to add her to my category of silly spinsters. Take for example the following when she is entertaining three female teachers to tea:

'A cloth of incredible whiteness, bordered with a deep edging of Miss Clare's mother's crocheting, covered the table, and in the middle stood a bowl of primroses. The best tea service patterned with pansies was in use, and cut-glass dishes held damson cheese and lemon curd of Miss Clare's own making.

The bread and butter was cut so thin as to be almost transparent.

"I've a special old carving knife," explained Miss Clare earnestly, "and I always sharpen it up on the bottom step up to the lawn. It's really quite simple.'"

And so very worthy, but is it really? What is so wonderful about transparent slices of bread? Wouldn't her guests really have preferred something to get their teeth into? I know I would. Isn't the whole episode a performance designed to assert and display the rectitude of her spinsterhood? It is this insistence on the importance of minutiae that provides her raison d'être. Later we shall see the ladies of Cranford turn minutiae into moral imperatives.

Although these schoolmistresses are extremely various: Lucy Snowe, Hilary Jackson and Miss Jean Brodie, all in their different ways, are sexually frustrated, while Miss Read and Miss Clare – outwardly, at least, appear to be lacking in libido, and content themselves with simply carrying out their duties and being respected members of a community. All of them, however, whatever their inward feelings, go to great lengths to show a brave face on the world, and refuse to be objects of scorn or pity. Perhaps our virgin goddess, Diana was really doing the same – but in a decidedly more forceful way!

CHAPTER NINE

SCHOLARLY SPINSTERS

In the room the women come and go
Talking of Michelangelo.

T.S. Eliot, 'The Love Song of J. Alfred Prufrock'

Elle travaille dans une bibliotheque municipale et c'est le type
de la vielle fille.

Simenon, 'Maigret Se Trompe'

Scholarly spinsters, although involved in the business of teaching, have not been forced into academe in the way that schoolmistresses have been forced into the schoolroom. Yes, like them, they need a salaried job, but it is, or so they believe, the love of the subject itself that has brought them there, rather than a quest for a position of respectability.

I am including a lot of these academics because they are so various, and inasmuch as each is a specialist in her own field, they can be compared with the goddesses we have met, and we shall see there are other connections, strands which twizzle down in their different ways from our spinsters in the Ancient World.

To find a whole bevy of scholarly spinsters, (there should be a collective noun for such women: 'a seclusion', perhaps?), one need look no further than Dorothy L. Sayers' 'Gaudy Night'.

'Gaudy Night' by Dorothy L. Sayers

The Dons:

This is the penultimate book in the Lord Peter Wimsey series in which its heroine Harriet Vane (the alter ego of its author) is considering exchanging her fiercely guarded spinsterhood for engagement to her titled suitor. But this is only part of the story. The plot centres around Shewsbury College, a fictional Oxford establishment; the date is 1935 and the college is all-female.

All the students and dons bar one who is engaged, are spinsters, apparently living in relative amity. The trouble starts with the appearance of obscene anonymous letters and drawings, macabre practical jokes and crude scrawls on the college walls. Who can have perpetrated these attacks? A process of elimination shows it must be one of the residents. There is the usual assortment of types: the good motherly Dean, the fiercely outspoken Miss Barton, the unworldly Miss Lydgate, the man-hating Miss Hillyard, and the somewhat mysterious Miss De Vine are amongst the protagonists; and all these ladies are united in one thing: a fierce belief that the scholarly pursuit of truth must be the overriding factor in all proceedings.

The action takes place before the Second World War which would radically change women's position and give them significance as individuals in their own right, but here in the mid 1930s, there is a stark choice between a job and a husband; there is much discussion among them on the subject: of course, marriage *is* a job, but 'one is rather apt to marry into someone's job'. And that job belongs to the man. Harriet reflects what a pity it is when an excellent scholar like Catherine Freemantle ends up married to a farmer, having to look after children and do menial work. 'What damned waste… all that brilliance, all that trained intelligence, harnessed to a load that that any uneducated girl could have done.' Condescendingly she concedes: 'The thing had its compensations, she supposed.'

Women students at the college are closely guarded against male intrusion, and relationships with men are largely disapproved of because these women's true vocation must be that of the scholar. Most of the dons have never had thoughts of marriage, only Miss de Vine had the opportunity, but decided against marrying her painter lover, because she would have had to sacrifice her career for his.

The fraught situation within the college escalates, with the dons and students receiving yet more vicious obscene anonymous letters while more pornographic drawings are found on walls, and part of Miss Lydgate's thesis is destroyed; strange and horrible 'practical jokes' take place at night.

The dons have no wish to bring in the police or private detectives, as they fear scandal and ridicule brought on them in their vulnerable spinster society, but the perpetrator must be identified and the trouble stopped. They seek the help of one of their alumnae, Harriet Vane, who reluctantly enlists the aid of her titled suitor, Lord Peter Wimsey who has considerable detective experience, and indeed it is he – a man – who will solve the enigma.

Annie, one of the college scouts had been married to a professor at a minor university; they had met when he was a student and she had been his landlady's daughter. (This marriage was an unforgiveable mistake, on his part, it is implied.) He had written a convincing thesis on an obscure historian, and all would have been well if Miss de Vine had not discovered a piece of evidence in an eastern European library that discredited his thesis; she also discovered that he knew about this piece of evidence and had stolen it. She immediately informs the authorities.

Of course, he has his professorship and even his MA taken away, along with his job. His discredited background now prevented his obtaining further employment. Bitter disappointment and the problem of supporting a wife and two children led to a downward spiral, and finally to suicide. Now his wife is bent on revenge, firstly against Miss de Vine, and more generally against the college as a whole, a nest of spinsters who, as she sees it, have the power to ruin the life of a married woman and her family.

When she is finally caught, she bursts out with a violent invective against Miss de Vine and by implication, all academic spinsters:

'You killed him and you didn't care. I say you murdered him. What had he done to you? What harm had he done to anyone? He only wanted to live and be happy. You took the bread out of his mouth and flung his children and me out to starve. What did it matter to you? You had no children. You hadn't a man to care about… you had a man once and you threw him over because it was too much bother to look after him. But couldn't you leave my man alone? He told a lie about someone who was dead and dust hundreds of years ago. Nobody was the worse for that. Was a dirty bit of paper more important than our lives and happiness? You broke him and killed him – all for nothing. Do you think that's a woman's job?… What business had you with a job like that. A woman's job is to look after her husband and children. I wish I had killed you. I wish I had killed you all. I wish I could burn down this place and all places like it – where you teach women to take men's jobs and rob them first and kill them afterwards. No wonder you can't get men for yourselves… you're ignorant and stupid and helpless. I laughed to see you look at each other; you didn't even trust each other… I wanted to see you dragged into the gutter. I wanted to see you sneered at and trampled on and degraded and despised, as we were.'

And she puts in the clincher, one they can't argue with: 'Even you, you silly old hags – you had to get a man to do your work for you.' Yes, they had had to get the help of Peter Wimsey to unmask her as the culprit.

I find this a very interesting look at spinsters from a totally different angle. Annie, a married woman, is an avenging spirit of spinsters and she admits to it, but she, of course sees them in the light of harpies, creatures who take food from deserving men and women. And vengeful as she is, she has a point: did 'the dirty bit of paper matter' when set against the happiness of family life ? This is something that these women cannot be judges of since they have no experience of it. Earlier on Lord Peter puts a test case to them: '"A false statement is published and the man who could contradict it lets it go out of charitable considerations. Would anybody here do that?" "Of course one couldn't do that," said Miss Barton, "not for ten wives and fifty children."' These spinster dons are like the Erinyes: they support justice at all cost:

'We hold we are straight and just.
If a man can spread his hands and show they are clean,
No wrath of ours shall lurk for him.'

But Miss de Vine's hands were not entirely clean, as she herself admits: '"I do blame myself, not for my original action, which was unavoidable, but for the sequel… one ought to take some thought for other people."'

However, at the height of her rage, Annie who has become something of a Fury, is led away to be given an aspirin as a panacea! Then she is to be subjected to some permanent 'medical treatment.' It has turned out that Annie's avenging spirit is powerless beside that of the spinsters. In the name of justice they have destroyed her, her husband and the life of her children, nor will they be turned aside from future similar opportunities. '"You can't carry through any principle without doing harm to somebody,"' says Miss Edwards. The dons are the true Eumenides. And Harriet, for all her principles, marries Lord Peter!

At this point I pause and ask who can be categorised as a spinster? After all, every woman is born a spinster, or rather, a potential spinster. Is the dictionary definition sufficient, or can the term be an elastic one?

We have looked at the antecedents to spinsters from the Ancient World and considered them as spinsters since they remain forever unmarried; we have looked at women who are undeniably spinsters, unmarried, ageing women like Belinda Bede or Miss Clare; I have even included Blanche du Bois, justifiably, I think, because her marriage was unconsummated. Now I want to add another woman, Vinnie Miller, who has actually been married, to the category of spinster. I did hesitate, but I think I am justified in doing so because a) her marriage had been unsatisfactory and of short duration, b) she has been on her own for many years, and c) because she has the most remarkable array of spinsterly ways. This was the clinching factor because if there are spinsters, like say, Harriet Bede, who are unmarried but not spinsterly, why should those who have been married, but behave in an unredeemedly spinsterly way, not be classed as such?

'Foreign Affairs' by Alison Lurie

Vinnie Miner

The woman's name is Virginia Miner; she is fifty-four years old, small, plain and unmarried – the sort of person no one ever notices, although she is an Ivy League college professor who has published several books, and has a well-established reputation in the expanding world of children's literature. The dog that is trailing Vinnie, visible only to her imagination, is her familiar demon or demon familiar, known to her privately as Fido and representing self-pity.

We meet her first on the plane: 'Vinnie is leaving today for six months in England. There under her professional name of V.A. Miner, she will continue her study of the folk-rhymes of children.'

It takes her some time to settle herself to her own satisfaction as she fussily sorts out her belongings:

'She has arranged her worn wool-lined raincoat, her floppy beige felt hat and her amber and beige liberty print wool scarf in her locker, in such a way that only the rudest of fellow passengers will attempt to encroach on them.' She is aware of her own anti-social behaviour, but she thinks, '... why should Vinnie Miner whose comfort has been disregarded by others for most of her adult life, disregard her own comfort?'

But someone does disregard it: Chuck Mumpson, a member of 'Sun Valley Tours'. She takes an immediate dislike to him, seeing him as a typical brash American, one who has provided himself with no reading matter, just the sort of man she despises, 'categorizing him as philistine and improvident'. Pityingly, she gives him one of the children's books she has with her. Unable to concentrate on her own novel, she visits the washroom where she allows herself one of her indulgences:

'She removes the plastic containers of blue glass cologne, skin freshener and moisturiser from their rack, and places them in her handbag, as is her custom. Vinnie has a rather nice collection of guest towels, and a very large revolving supply of coasters, matches, paper napkins, coat hangers, pencils, pens, chalk, and expensive magazines of the sort found in expensive doctors' and dentists' waiting rooms... when things are not going well she begins to look round, and annexations take place.'

In her own way, Vinnie is not unlike Miss Clare in her obsessive attention to minutiae as compensation for loneliness.

Once in London, she meets up with her established intellectual English friends, but in spite of trying to avoid Chuck Mumpson (she has given him a wrong phone number), fate persists in throwing him in her way. To cheer herself up, feeling Fido following her, Vinnie visits Fortnum and Mason.

'A blaringly mid-American voice hails her.
"Wal, hey. Aren't you, uh, Professor Miner?"
Vinnie turns.
A very large man is grinning at her; he wears a semi-transparent greenish plastic raincoat of the most repellent American sort, and locks of greying, reddish-brown hair are plastered to his broad, damp red forehead.
"Metchoo on the plane last month, Chuck Mumpson."
"Oh yes," she agrees without enthusiasm.'

However, in spite of her intellectual English friends, Vinnie is lonely and she agrees to have tea with him. Chuck is lonely too, and gradually, reluctantly, Vinnie begins to see more of him, but she remains embarrassed by his appearance and his brash American behaviour, and she is careful to keep him at a distance from her intellectual English friends so she suggests he go down to Wiltshire to look up his family roots.
Unwillingly, she considers his sexual potential because she is not without experience in such matters, but she concludes he is a typical American businessman looking for an 'outlet':

'Men of this type never think of Vinnie in connection with sex; they think of some 'cute babe' or hot little number – ideally a number under thirty. What Chuck was pressing for was sympathy, companionship, an understanding listener... Vinnie has throughout her life slept mainly with men whose interest in her was casual and comradely rather than romantic, they seldom used the word 'love' to her except in moments of passionate confusion; instead they told her they were 'very fond' of her and that that she was great in bed, and a real pal.'

Then Vinnie falls ill with a nasty cold and, neglected by her intellectual friends, she takes to her bed, but Chuck returns from Wiltshire, full of concern for her and proves his worth in arriving at her flat with comfort and food. He rises in her opinion too, when he describes how, in the course of his research about his ancestor, he has become involved in an archaeological dig, and has, in fact, been very helpful with his knowledge of engineering. His companionship makes Vinnie feel better, and she warms to him. Inevitably he makes a pass at her, but at the last minute he pulls back. Vinnie, schooled as she is in rejection, says:

'"You're going to tell me you're awfully fond of me, but you want to be honest and I should realise that your marriage is very important to you, and you really love your wife."' But Vinnie is wrong: his marriage is loveless, and he is proceeds to tell her about a car accident in which he killed a boy, he wants her to know in case this means she will want nothing more to do with him, but Vinnie does:

'"Wait," Vinnie tries to say between kisses, in which somehow she has begun to join. "I'm not sure I want…" But her voice now entirely refuses to function; and her body – rebellious greedy – presses itself against Chuck's. "Now, now," it cries, "more, more." "Very well," she says to it, "if you insist. Just this once. After all, no one will ever know."'

But the affair continues, and in spite of the amusement of her English friends Vinnie takes Chuck about, tries to educate him and improve his dress sense. Yet she is embarrassed by the gulf between them: Chuck has been brought up in a rural slum, has suffered a troubled youth, and has been only saved by the army, and a subsequent successful career in engineering. Vinnie, on the other hand, has been nurtured in an ambitious and educated family and has intellectual interests and many degrees. Nevertheless, they become increasingly happy together, and when Chuck has to return to help with the archaeological dig, he wants Vinnie to go with him, but she has her misgivings:

'The truth is Vinnie isn't temperamentally suited to a shared life; the last time Chuck was in London, nice as that was... even then she sometimes felt – how to put it – crowded, invaded. Chuck is too large, too noisy, he takes up too much room in her flat, in her bed, in her life... It had been that way with her husband almost from the start... And then when you finally got used to living like that, because you had begun loving the other person, after you had learned even to like it maybe, and depend on it – they walked out on you. No thanks.'

All the same, she relents and agrees that she will join him later. But she hears nothing from Chuck.

'It has turned out just as she feared, just as it always does for her. Chuck's affections have cooled; he has realised as so many before him, notably her former husband – that he had mistaken gratitude for love. Possibly he has also met someone else, someone younger and prettier... why should he think any more of Vinnie?'

But Vinnie is wrong again. She has a visit from his daughter who has arrived from the States; Chuck has had a heart attack climbing the stairs of a museum in pursuit of the archives about his ancestor; he is dead. Her initial reaction is one of almost satisfaction: she isn't after all, an unloved spinster:

'... that's why he didn't call, Vinnie thinks. It wasn't that he was tired of me. Joy and relief flash across her mind...'. But then the realisation of his death hits her: 'a greater pain than before, like a beam of a lighthouse that on a dark night pierces the gloom and then illuminates a frightful shipwreck. Chuck wasn't tired of her; he was dead, is dead. There is nothing left of him...

What a horribly bad joke that after fifty-four years she should have been loved by someone like Chuck, who on top of everything that is wrong with him is dead and scattered on the side of the hill somewhere in Wiltshire.'

Would Vinnie have escaped her innate spinsterhood if Chuck had lived? Could she have ever put up with his cheerful ignorance, and would he, as she had wondered, have remained fond of her? It wouldn't have worked, not with Chuck, not with anyone, because she was so unredeemably spinsterly by nature. She must live with her memories, and look forward to favourable reviews of her new book, that is all she can hope for. As she says on her return to the States: 'I have lots of friends on both sides of the Atlantic; I've just spent five very interesting months in London, and finished an important book on playground rhymes.' But even to her the list seems painfully incomplete. Once again, she becomes conscious of the presence of 'Fido', her symbol of self pity:

'"Go away," says Vinnie silently, "I'm perfectly fine. I'm not a bit sorry for myself. I'm a well-known scholar."'
Earlier we met the eponymous heroine Eleanor Oliphant; she too, claimed to be 'completely fine'. It is a mantra rehearsed by the resigned and courageous spinster. Miss Read too, declared herself to be to be 'completely happy' shelling peas in her garden. There is a tremendous pride among these women. Is it pride in spinsterhood, or a barrier put up as a defence against acknowledging an inadequacy in themselves?

'Whereabouts' by Jhumpa Lahiri.

Solitude; it's become my trade.

La Signora:

The anonymous first person speaker in 'Whereabouts', (Oh, how I wish my protagonists had names! It's a problem I shall meet again in 'Rebecca'. I shall have to call her La Signora), is the most modern of all our spinsters, living (presumably) in contemporary Italy. Unlike the Oxford dons and Vinnie, her academic life means little to her; she has more or less fallen into it because that was what was expected of her:

'I read books and studied. I listened to my parents and did what they asked me to. Even though in the end I never made them happy. I didn't like myself and something told me I'd end up alone.'

Her academic success is not a source of pride to her; it is something that has contributed to her loneliness. She is unenthusiastic about the whole business: 'I answer emails, choose what book I'd like my students to read. I'm here to earn a living, my heart's not in it.' She does not try to benefit from sexual opportunities offered by academic conferences:

'I need to spend three nights out of town for a convention. The hotel is full, besieged by my colleagues… I dread this annual event; the same convention, the same crowd… There are other groups all around, mostly men, dressed in gray, herds of them, all of them laughing too loudly, too often.'

Like Vinnie, but unlike the Oxford dons, she has had lovers: 'I'm attractive enough, but not the sort to make men's heads turn.' One ex-lover rings her, but although she has thought about him during the day, she declines his invitation to dinner, saying she has a headache, and then she leaves the house ravenous, to eat alone. There is a sort of fear that holds her back.

There is a man with whom she was involved for five years, she expected him to marry her, then one day '...someone rang my buzzer. I thought it was him; instead it was another woman who knew my boyfriend just as well as I did, who saw him on the days I didn't.'

There is the husband of a friend 'for whom I represent... what exactly, A road not taken, a hypothetical affair?' She bumps into him in the supermarket and he asks if he can help her. He is very willing: '"Sure you don't need anything? Want a few of our bags, half of it's just stuff for the pantry?"' She refuses his offer, but 'the tenderness he sets aside for me is enough'.

She has become resigned to being on her own: 'Solitude; it's become my trade,' she says. She goes to buy theatre tickets: 'I make a list of performances I'd like to attend.

"Just one ticket?" the person behind the window asks.
"Just one."'
Spring is a particularly bad time for her:

'Every blow in my life took place in spring. That's why I am afflicted by the green of the trees, the first peaches in the market, the light flowing skirts that the women in my neighbourhood start to wear. These things only remind me of loss, of betrayal of disappointment.'

Of course, I don't suppose she would describe herself as a spinster, but she displays many of the traits in others we have met: she stands outside the tenor of other peoples lives; she is self-effacing, undemanding, just someone to call on when other people need something. One friend wants someone to entertain her daughter, another comes to her house to get away from the clutter of everyday married life; once she is thinking of the friend's husband (the one from the supermarket) who is obviously fond of her, and when the phone rings she wonders what sort of assignation he will suggest, but there will be no assignation: his wife's father has had a stroke, will she come and house-sit and look after the dog while they are away? Her life is full of such disappointments; she is not heartbroken; she sees her role in life as an outsider, an onlooker.

Like Eleanor Oliphant, she sees a therapist, because like her she has had an unhappy childhood: '…sometimes I'd recount my mother's fitful rages, the quarrels I've never forgotten, terrifying scenes… I'd talk about the ways my mother would berate me.' But she gets little satisfaction from these sessions: 'I've always felt in someone's shadow.'
At the heart of her loneliness there is not too much sorrow – her life jogs along pleasantly enough, and towards the end of the book we see her leaving the familiarity of her home town to take up another job.

'"I'm thinking of leaving for a while… I've received a fellowship to go to a place I've never been before."
"What would you do there?"
"I'd work on my own in the mornings. Then twice a day I'd sit at a long table and eat lunch and dinner with other scholars. I'd get to know them, have discussions, that sort of thing."'

But there is no enthusiasm, only a sort of languor, a resignation that this is how it will be: different, but not exciting. She does not see any viable escape from spinsterhood.

'Hotel du Lac' by Anita Brookner

"As my wife you will do very well. Unmarried, I'm afraid you will soon look a bit of a fool".

Edith Hope:

Strictly speaking, perhaps I should not include Edith amongst the scholarly spinsters because unlike the others, she is not employed by a university as her father was, but she is a writer, and a highly intelligent one, and I want to include her because, although she is separated by a generation, I see her in many ways like the Italian woman mentioned above, a resigned spinster; and I would like to compare the two, chart their similarities and see if there are common attributes in these relatively modern spinsters.

Edith is a spinster in her thirties, regarding herself as resembling Virginia Woolf in looks, although another woman says she reminds her of Princess Anne. Her dress is proper and spinsterly, 'dressed for dinner, in her liberty silk smock, her long narrow feet tamed into plain kid pumps.'
There is no getting away from the fact that she is decidedly frumpish. A fellow guest, the ageing and glamorous Mrs Pusey advises her: '"You should buy yourself something pretty while you're here, dear. A woman owes it to herself to have pretty things. And if she feels good, she looks good..."'
The next morning, dressed in her tweed skirt and her long cardigan, Edith reflected that she had been perhaps a little lax in presenting an appearance to the world.'
She explains to her publisher who wants her to write sexier novels for modern women that she is a romantic; her novels always have a hare-and- tortoise theme, i.e. it is the dull girl, not the glamorous one who wins the race for the desirable male, but she knows that real life is not like that.

She has a married lover called David whom she adores, and the romantic side of her hopes that the feeling is mutual, the pragmatic side knows the truth:

'I lived for you. Yet how often did I see you? Perhaps twice a month. More if we met by accident. Sometimes less, if you were too busy. And sometimes a whole month without you. I have imagined you at home with your wife and children, and those times were bad…'

When we first meet her she has just arrived at the Swiss hotel where she is apparently escaping some disgrace at home; it is not until half way through the book that we discover what she has done. Afraid of spinsterhood, she had agreed to marry a man called Geoffrey Long, 'that kind man… I am lucky, she reminded herself looking at her drawn face in the mirror.' But just as the taxi taking her to the wedding approaches the registry office, she knows she can't go through with it, and returns home unmarried, to face all the disappointed wedding guests. She clings to her spinster's existence: 'her little house, so long her private domain, a shell for writing in, for sleeping in, silent and sunny in the deserted afternoons before the children came home from school, and turned in at other gateways.'

However, a second chance comes her way while she is at the hotel. A Mr Neville proposes to her; he tells her, in effect, that he is not in the least in love with her, but thinks she would make him a ladylike and trouble-free wife. He is a cold, unemotional man, selfish and calculating; on the other hand, he is comparatively wealthy and an owner of a fine Georgian house. He points out:

'"You are a lady, Edith. They are rather out of fashion these days, as you may have noticed. As my wife you will do very well. Unmarried, I'm afraid you will soon look a bit of a fool."'

This is putting very starkly the position of spinsterhood she will face if she does not marry him; she knows too, that her friends at home will regard her coldly after her treatment of Geoffrey Long; she takes time to consider what marriage would entail:

'She was about to enter a world which she had instinctively felt belonged to others, in which she had no claim, a world of among other things, investments, roof repairs, visitors for the weekend. And shall we take your car or mine? That was one of the remarks she had overheard David make to his wife and it had come to possess an almost totemic significance.'

She considers it carefully, weighing it up and finally decides to accept him; then she writes to her lover, breaking off their relationship and telling him what she is going to do. She is resigned to her fate:

'He assures me that I will very soon, under his guidance, develop into the sort of acceptable woman whose confidence and stamina and indeed, presumption, I have always envied. Rather like your wife, in fact.'

However, leaving her room early to post her letter, she sees Mr Neville coming out of another woman's bedroom, the bedroom of the voluptuous daughter of Mrs Pusey.

'"Of course," she thought, "of course... and then she remembered. When she had leaned against him and wept, and when he had put his arm round her, she had been aware that he had felt nothing... she saw her father's patient face. "Think again, Edith. You have made a false equation"... and if I was to marry him... knowing this, knowing too that he could so easily and so quickly look elsewhere, I should turn to stone, and I should lose the only life I have ever wanted, even though it was never mine to call my own.'

She returns to her room, destroys the letter she has written to David and orders a ticket back to London. She sends a telegram to her lover, simply saying: 'Returning.' But like La Signora, she knows full well that there is nothing much for her in the future – she has not heard from her lover since she left the country, and her friends regard her as a pariah. She has seen the stark choice that must be faced by the ageing spinster: marriage to an unloving and unfaithful husband, or spinsterhood.

Like La Signora, Edith is an outsider; yes, they both have friends, but their friends have other lives which neither of these two women actively participate in; they have both unhappy childhoods which have left them timorous about committing themselves to other people. They prefer to look on from without; Edith watches the other hotel guests: Mrs Pusey with her voluptuous daughter, the enigmatic and beautiful Veronica and her dog, the elderly countess and the hotel staff. La Signora watches the other patients in the doctor's waiting room, the girl who does her nails, the family on the train. They both wonder about them, invent stories about them, but do not reveal themselves to these people. Each has made their home their shell; each has had lovers, but each knows that no future is to be enjoyed with the only one they can imagine a future with, as he is already taken by another woman; and yet, that is not the real reason for their preference for spinsterhood. It is a sort of languid resignation that pervades them, a sort of self involvement that excludes any meaningful permanent relationship – even if it were offered; and in neither case does that seem likely. Like Cassandra, they can see their future, not as tragic as hers, but without a happy resolution; unlike her they will keep their prognostications to themselves.

'Tinker, Tailor, Soldier, Spy' and 'Smiley's People' by John le Carré

Connie Sachs:

She was a big woman... a tangle of white hair framed her sprawling face. She wore a brown jacket like a blazer and trousers with elastic at the waist, and she had a low belly like an old man's... on a trolley were the tins she ate from and the bottles she drank from.

Like so many of our spinsters, Connie could fall under several different categories: she could be classed as a Sapphic Spinster, a Suffering Spinster or even a Sleuthing Spinster, but because of her academic job and her heritage, ('her brothers were dons... her father was a professor of something'), but above all, because of her formidable brain, I have placed her here.

When George Smiley is trying to track down the mole in the headquarters of the Secret Service, known to the inner circle as the Circus, he goes to Oxford to visit Connie Sachs, who after her wrongful dismissal has returned to academia. When the door opens, 'two shrewd eyes, wet like a baby's appraised him... Finally the white face broke into a charming smile, and Miss Connie Sachs, formerly queen of research at the Circus broke into spontaneous joy.'

Connie adores George Smiley with whom she had worked closely, but time and alcohol have taken the toll on her. In fact, Connie had been in the position of Cassandra, but unlike La Signora and Edith she had not kept her prophesies to herself, she had prophesised vociferously and in vain.

She had desperately tried to pursue a suspected Russian spy called Polyakov. 'She spent three weeks in Whitehall with the Moscow Gazers, combing Soviet army bulletins for disguised entries, and finally she had tracked down three suspects, chief among them Polyakov. "Connie's little hunch has come home trumps."' But she is sent for by the boss and told:

'"You're to leave Polyakov alone. You're to put him out of your silly woman's mind, do you understand?" "And what happened?" Smiley asks. "Connie was sacked", is the laconic reply.

However, her compendious brain which remembers every detail of long-forgotten cases begins to work, and she fills Smiley in on the background of the spy Polyakov, the case which the mole had managed to put a stop to. As she recounts the details she becomes wildly animated and Smiley fears it will be too much for her: 'Connie was having a hangover. She was sitting again, slumped over her glass. Her eyes had closed and her head kept falling to one side.' However she manages to give him the complete picture.

She longs to return to the past, showing Smiley old photos of the time she had been 'Queen of Circus'. This was where she had been happy, a world where she could lose herself. '"I hate the real world"', she says. As she looks back at these halcyon days 'she was breathing heavily, not perhaps from any one emotion, but from a whole mess of them, washed around in her like mixed drinks. In her despair she cries, "Give me a kiss, George, give Connie a kiss." 'He longed to be free of her, but she was clutching him more fiercely…' He does not like to leave her, but what can he do? 'As he went down the road he heard her humming again, so loud it was like a scream.'
Connie was the victim of the Circus mole, by whose deceitful machinations she was sacked from the job she loved so much. Like Cassandra's, her accurate prophesies were ignored.

Some years later, in search of capturing his old Russian adversary, Karla, Smiley decides to consult Connie again. This time the situation is even more dire. She has now left Oxford to live in a sort of dacha; he is met by a notice: MERRILEE BOARDING ALL PETS WELCOME EGGS. Presumably it is some sort of smallholding: 'It stood in its own clearing of tree trunks and trodden mud. With a ramshackle veranda and a wood-shingle roof and a tin chimney, with smoke coming out of it. And dotted round the clearing, like allotment huts, stood the asbestos sheds and wire runs which held the chickens and all the pets welcome without discrimination.'

Connie is now revealed as 'a mountainous woman propped crookedly between two thick wooden crutches… She had white hair clipped as short as a man's and watery, very shrewd eyes.' But Connie is in her final days: 'The old fool's for the shredder. It's death, that's what I'm suffering from. The systematic encroachment of the big D… Smiley knew from experience that she was telling no less than the truth, and her skin had the leprous whiteness of death.' She is only kept going by alcohol: 'Is that booze you're toting in that bag?' she asks. Smiley fills her glass, and in spite of her terrible state, Connie can tell him in minute detail everything he wants to know about the spy Oleg Kiev. But Smiley can see it is taking its toll on her: 'The drink, the memories, the revived excitement of the chase were driving her at a speed he could not control. She was rasping like an engine with the restraints dangerously removed.'

'"Go easy, Con," Smiley warned her anxiously, "Con, come down."' However, things are worsening:

'He saw the stiffening of her face, he saw her distorted hands fly out, and her eyes screw up in disgust as if she had seen a horrible accident… her skin was cold, she was shaking from terror… her tears were all over her cheeks, he could feel them, and taste their salty sting as she pushed him away from her.'

Hilary:

But Connie is not dying alone; living with her and looking after her is a young woman of great beauty called Hilary. She too, had been part of the Circus, but something had happened to her there. Smiley had been summoned to see 'the smashed machinery, the files, the card indices and telegrams flung round the room like rubbish at a football ground; he saw the filthy graffiti daubed in lipstick on the wall. And in the centre of it all he saw Hilary herself, the culprit.' But Connie loves

Hilary: "'I should tell her to bugger off... marry some chinless fool... fulfil your foul womanhood... I'll be damned if I will, George, I want her, every gorgeous bit of her.'" Apparently the feeling is mutual '... love was a positive power, she said vaguely – ask Hils.'

Smiley has learned what he wanted to know, and he is thankful to be going; he knows he will not see Connie again. As he drives away he sees Hilary in the car's headlights:

'She was cowering among the trees waiting for him to leave before she went back to Connie... she had her hands to her face again and he thought he saw blood.'

She needs Connie as much as Connie needs her.

The story illustrates the tragedy of the academic denied recognition. If there had been no mole in the Circus and Connie had been able to continue to exploit all the power in her tremendous brain there, would this have been a fulfilled spinsterhood, or does too brilliant a brain bring with it its own seeds of destruction? Alternatively, was Connie simply a frustrated lesbian who took refuge in alcohol when it was all too late? And what about Hilary, 'that mad bitch' as Connie calls her affectionately? She, too, had been a high-powered member of the Circus; had her mental breakdown been the result of an overtaxed brain? Actually, they had both lost their lives and livelihoods because of male abuse, Connie at the hands of the mole, and Hilary lacking support in a male-orientated world.

When the nymph, Daphne lost the life she had expected because of the abuse by Apollo, and was turned into a laurel tree, she put forth new leaves and branches. Connie and Hilary too, had bravely forged something out of the remnants of their wretched lives; they too were trying to put out new leaves.

Doctor Ruth Galloway Novels by Ellie Griffiths

They met and in the course of work they fell in love. And to prove it they're getting married. Bully for them, thinks Ruth, although that sounds bitter, even to her own ears.

Doctor Ruth Galloway:

The trouble with writing about spinsters and trying to organise them into categories is that so often one category overlaps into another. Later we will meet Theodora Braithwaite as a sleuthing spinster, although she could just as easily be classed as a saintly one. For a long time I wanted to put Ruth in the Sleuthing Spinsters category too because she is one of the two protagonists of the Doctor Ruth Galloway detective novels of Ellie Griffiths. But because she thinks of herself first and foremost (that is when she is not thinking about her adored daughter) as an academic, I am including her here, although all the novels concern her sleuthing activities.

I also wanted to put her amongst her academic peers because she is the only one of them who is a single parent, and so she creates a marked contrast with those whose major, or indeed, only concern, has been with their scholastic life. And again we are faced with the question: is she really a spinster – after all she has lovers and a child. But she *is* over thirty *and* unmarried, two undeniable qualifications, so, yes!

When we first meet Ruth she foresees a lonely future ahead:

'By now I have resigned myself to spinsterhood and godmotherhood and going slightly mad, knitting clothes for my cats out of my own hair.'

But she is not unduly worried; she has a first class honours degree, a doctorate and is now Head of Forensic Archaeology at the University of North Norfolk, a job she greatly enjoys. She is proud of her academic status: 'She likes it when people use her correct title. She doesn't see why strangers should call her Ruth and she despises 'Miss'.

She is happy with her lot. However, her life changes when she receives a visit from D.I. Nelson who needs her help as a forensic expert – her speciality is bones. She feels an immediate antipathy towards him; he is everything that she despises, a philistine in his views, brash and forceful, a married man with privately educated daughters. Nelson, in turn, has no time for academics, he likes people he regards as doing a proper job, he is content with his marriage to his beautiful hairdresser wife, Michelle, hankers after Blackpool where he originates from, and leads a conventional life – at least, when he is not doing his job.

In the discrepancy of their lives we are reminded of Vinnie and Chuck, and like them, Ruth and Nelson are drawn together. They have to work closely over a particularly distressing case of two child murders and an abduction, and as the case progresses they begin to appreciate each other's good qualities: Nelson admires Ruth's efficiency, her incisive brain and her no nonsense attitude; and Ruth sees an attractive man, fair, kind, and good at his job. One night, overcome by the emotional strains of the case, they make love. And that might have been the end to it if Ruth had not fallen pregnant. She is delighted at the thought of having a child, and Nelson regards it as his duty to support her – although that does not involve telling his wife.

Ruth adores her daughter, Kate, and is a conscientious mother, although motherhood and all it involves does not come easy to her. She loathes having to involve herself in all the things young mothers are supposed to delight in. At the time of her daughter's first birthday party Ruth says:

"'I still don't really feel like a mother, one of those women who can do it all, you know, have babies, bake cakes, make potato prints.'"

She is appalled by the chaos at her daughter's first birthday party: 'It seems impossible that six children can make this much noise.'

Over the following books we see Ruth trying to juggle her academic career, do her utmost for her (rather spoilt and irritating) daughter, and help with various police investigations. But the greatest problem in Ruth's life is her relationship with Nelson; the first incident which resulted in her pregnancy has not been her last – there have been other occasions when they have made love, often when threatening circumstances have brought them together. The truth of the matter is, that she is in love with Nelson, and he with her. The problem is an insoluble one because Nelson is a family man who loves his wife and daughters.

Problems multiply when Michelle discovers Nelson is the father of Ruth's daughter. One of the things she can't understand – just like Kathy Herbert in 'The Rector's Daughter' – is how her husband could fall for a woman whom she regards as plain: 'overweight, untidy Ruth', when she herself is so beautiful. She is very like Kathy, a beautiful unintellectual wife providing her husband with a successful marriage – one that is envied by their friends.

Why on earth would her husband prefer a plain spinster? But spinsters who attract men usually have something unspinsterish about them. Although Nelson admires Ruth for her professional expertise – she is a very good forensic archaeologist – he also finds her sexually attractive: we see him admiring her in what she regards as a rather frumpish swimming costume: 'He had been surprised by how good Ruth looked in her swimming costume. He had noticed before that the fewer clothes Ruth wears, the thinner she looks. In the severely cut costume she looks curvaceous rather than overweight. 'In 'Precious Bane' we saw Kester, the weaver admiring Prue partially undressed, and showing a very seductive figure, and for him, the figure takes precedence over Prue's hare lip. These are spinsters with an extra something.

Would Ruth marry Nelson if he was free? It's a question both of them think about, and it almost looks as if he will finally leave his wife for Ruth, but then Michelle falls unexpectedly pregnant, so the chance is gone. But Ruth in her heart of hearts knows that she and Nelson are too different to actually enjoy the state of marriage; and marriage isn't the be-all-and-end-all for Ruth. She has had a relationship with an attractive archaeologist, and a long relationship with the eminently eligible American academic, Frank, but when he proposes to her with a ring in his hand, she can't bring herself to accept him – she likes him, admires him, knows he would be a good stepfather for Kate, but she refuses him. Is this because she hopes, knowing rationally that marriage with Nelson isn't feasible, that somehow it will happen, or is it because at heart Ruth is happy to be a spinster? She likes living in her lonely cottage on the Norfolk coast with her daughter and her cat; she likes being HOD at the University, she likes her subject – like Vinnie she has written acclaimed books; and unlike our other academics she has her adored daughter. Perhaps she is one of the fortunate spinsters – or perhaps not.

Anyway, Ruth Galloway is unique amongst the academic spinsters we have met. She is not alone, she does not suffer from malaise like La Signora and Edith; she has no sexual hang-ups like the dons in 'Gaudy Night'. Her life is far from easy, but perhaps it is the one that suits her best; as she says to Nelson,' "I've got to do this one on my own."'
Perhaps a child is better than a husband; at least Ruth can make her daughter live *her* sort of life, something that would be impossible with Nelson.
What a strange assortment these academic spinsters are! Unlike other spinsters who used religion as a prop, these have substituted religion with scholarship. The spinsters in 'Gaudy Night' leaned with all their weight on this crutch, eschewing

any alternative, particularly marriage. Vinnie in 'Foreign Affairs' is more ambivalent, she lays great store by her scholarship, indeed it is her life, but she hankers after another life outside academia, one that included potential husbands. However, in the end reluctantly, she has to return to the comfortable safety of scholarship.

La Signora and Edith depend financially on their scholarship, but that is all it is, they look at the world outside, but are somehow unable to engage with it. Like Vinnie, they must look to the crutch of academia, not from any love of it, but because it provides them with the only sort of lifestyle they are equipped for.

Scholarship or brainwork has been Connie's sole preoccupation; only when she is deprived of it does she discover, not the outside world which she hates, but love in a world inside a seedy boarding kennels with a mentally disturbed young woman. In her last days she will exchange the power of her brain for the comfort of love. She no longer needs the crutch of scholarship.

Ruth Galloway loves the world of academe which also provides her with her lifestyle, but she is not happy to remain confined within it; she looks outwards as well; she can divide herself – not always easily – between her job, her lover and her child. Probably she is the most successful of our academic spinsters, but then she is one of the most recent. 2021 allows spinsters freedom which was denied their earlier sisters.

In some ways most of these academic women resemble the Amazons (Ruth even has a female child!); they will fight their way through life and will fight off male intervention. Only La Signora and Edith Hope are different. Perhaps they are more like Swinburne's 'Proserpine in the Underworld':

'Here, where the world is quiet

> I watch the green field growing
> For reaping folk and sowing,
> For harvest-time and mowing,
> A sleepy world of streams.'

But even Persephone (Prosperine) was allowed up into the real world for some months of the year. Perhaps there is hope that they will be able to enjoy reality – at least, some of the time.

Let's come down from academia and look at the opposite end of the spectrum.

CHAPTER TEN

SAD AND SILLY SPINSTERS

Ah, look at all the lonely people
Ah look at all the lonely people
Eleanor Rigby
Picks up the rice where a wedding has been
Lives in a dream
Waits at the window
Wearing a face which she gives in a jar by the door
Who is it for?
The Beatles, 'Eleanor Rigby'

Silliness, of course can come in a myriad of different forms. Arachne was silly to challenge Athene at weaving; in 'Some Tame Gazelle' Miss Jenner of the wool shop is 'silly' with the travellers; Blanche du Bois is silly to imagine she is still young and desirable. Martine and Philippa are silly not to appreciate Babette's wonderful cooking. Yes, they were all silly, but here I am concerned with a particular sort of spinsterly silliness. Perhaps 'silliness' is too harsh a word; maybe they are not so much silly as sad; but one thing is certain: they are pretty irritating. Should we sympathise with them or not?

'Cranford' by Mrs Gaskell

"I daresay your mother has told you, my dear, never to let more than three days elapse between receiving a call and returning it, and also, that you are never to stay longer than quarter of an hour... you must keep thinking about the time, my dear, and not allow yourself to forget it in conversation."

Miss Matty:

Cranford is packed with silly spinsters. There is Miss Jenkyns who has been brought up by her father to believe Samuel Johnson to have the monopoly of good writing. When Captain Browne praises Dickens, Miss Jenkyns replies: "'…perhaps the author is young. Let him persevere, and who knows what may become of him, if he takes the Great Doctor for his model.'" To try and convince her of Dickens' superiority the captain reads out the latest instalment of 'Pickwick Papers', but Miss Jenkyns counters that by reading out a passage from 'Rasselas' 'in a high- pitched majestic voice… "I imagine I am now justified in my preference for Doctor Johnson…"', she concludes, full of self-satisfaction, 'and thought she would give a finishing blow or two'. "'I consider it vulgar and below the dignity of literature to publish in numbers.'"

"'How was the 'Rambler' published, Ma'am?" asked Captain Browne.' But he speaks sotto voce because he can see just how ignorant Miss Jenkyns is, and he is too much of a gentleman to offend her.

Then there is Miss Pole who regards herself as adventurous and always able to be first to impart important news. A conjuror has come to town and Miss Pole has seen 'Signor Brunoni' in the Assembly Rooms without his conjuring accoutrements; she has actually spoken to him, so when she sees him on stage announcing himself, she is incredulous: "'I don't believe him," exclaimed Miss Pole, "Signor Brunoni has not got that mufti sort of thing about his chin, but looked like a close-shaved Christian gentleman.'" She refuses to recognise him.

But the most foolish of all is Miss Matty. Some readers regard her as loveable, others may find her simply irritating:

'She owned that ever since she had been a girl she had dreaded being caught by her last leg, just as she was getting into bed… and yet it was very unpleasant to think of looking under a bed, and see a man concealed, with a great fierce face staring at you.'

I wonder what Freud would make of that! Perhaps deep down she would have liked to have seen the face staring down at her from the top of the bed, because she had in her younger years, contemplated matrimony. She had once had a suitor, a cousin of Miss Pole, a farmer by the name of Thomas Holbrook. A curious friend asks:

'"Then how came Miss Matty not to marry him?"
"Oh, I don't know. She was willing enough, I think; but you know, Cousin Thomas would not have been enough of a gentleman for the Rector [her father] and Miss Jenkyns [Matty's sister]… they did not like Miss Matty to marry below her rank. You know, somehow they are related to Sir Peter Arley; Miss Jenkyns thought a deal of that."'

But even in old age when her sister is dead and the old suitor reappears, Miss Matty is not sure whether she should return his visit: "Deborah would not have liked it."' Foolish Miss Matty.

She resigns herself to spinsterhood, but the long hours must somehow be filled and a schedule of minutiae is put in place to wear away the long empty hours:

'The greatest event was that Miss Jenkyns had purchased a new carpet for the drawing room. Oh, the busy work Miss Matty and I had in chasing the sunbeams as they fell in the afternoon right down on this carpet, through the blindless window. We spread newspapers over the places, and sat down to our books and our work; and lo! In a quarter of an hour the sun had moved, and was blazing away on a fresh spot; and down again we went on our knees to alter the position of the newspapers. We were very busy too, one morning when Miss Jenkyns gave her party, following her directions, and in cutting out and stitching together pieces of newspaper to form little paths to every chair set for the expected visitors, lest their shoes might dirty or defile the purity of the carpet.'

One's initial reaction is to think how pathetic, what an utter waste of time! But do the rest of us employ our time with validity? I suppose we like to think so. But I think what saddens one is the determination to exclude the sun, and the joy and brightness it brings. The preservation of the carpet is, as it were, a paradigm of the very ground on which they literally stand; it must be protected out of fear that any outside influence 'dirty or defile the purity' of their lives. Kazuo Ishiguro (whom we shall meet later) knew the importance of the sun all too well; it was the sun that nourished Klara and allowed her to have her being. This determination to exclude the external serves as a sort of metaphor for these spinsters' lives where daily routines must be exercised specifically to exclude the terrifying outside world.

'Emma' by Jane Austen

" I shall be sure to say three dull things as soon as ever I open my mouth, shan't I?"

Miss Bates:

In Jane Austen's 'Emma' we meet the garrulous Miss Bates. At the strawberry picking party at Donwell Abbey, the home of Mr Knightly, Emma proposes a game and 'demands from each of you either one thing very clever... or two things moderately clever – or three things very dull indeed...'

"'Oh, very well," exclaimed Miss Bates, "then I need not be uneasy. Three things very dull indeed! That will just do for me. I shall be sure to say three dull things as soon as ever I open my mouth, shan't I?"

Emma could not resist.

"Ah, Madam, but there may be a difficulty. Pardon me – but you will be limited as to number – only three at once."'

Later Mr Knightley takes Emma to task:

"'How could you be so unfeeling to Miss Bates? How could you be so insolent in your wit, to a woman of her character, age and situation?"'

At first Emma tries to make light of it: "'I daresay she did not understand me."'

Mr Knightley assures Emma that she had: "'I wish you could have heard her honouring your forbearance, in being able to pay her such attentions when her society must be so irksome."'

And Emma replies, exposing the nub of the difficulty of ageing spinsterhood: "'You must allow that what is good and what is ridiculous are most unfortunately blended in her."'

But Mr Knightley in turn, points out the tragedy inherent in this category of spinsters:

"'Were she prosperous I could allow much for the occasional prevalence of the ridiculous over the good. Were she a woman of fortune I should leave every harmless absurdity to take its chance. Were she your equal in situation – but Emma, consider how far this is from being the case. She is poor; she has sunk from the comforts she was born to; and if she live to old age she must probably sink more;. Her situation should secure your compassion."'

Emma is overcome with compunction and goes to visit Miss Bates the next day, but that doesn't alter the problem: as Mr Knightley has pointed out, the ageing spinster is on a downward path, and as Emma has pointed out, good as she is, she is nevertheless literally ridiculous, i.e. a subject for mockery. Again, there is this perennial problem with respectable spinsterhood; it can only be maintained with the possession of enough money.

Miss Bates is silly, but she also demands our sympathy in a way that the spinsters of Cranford fail to do; perhaps because they are enclosed together in a capsule of their own silliness and do not have to face the outside world alone, but Miss Bates has no equals on whom to rely; she can only look to those more fortunate than herself and court their favour.

Little Dorrit by Charles Dickens

Flora Casby:

> *"I am sure I don't know what I am saying…"*

I was uncertain whether I was justified in including Flora Casby from 'Little Dorrit' because she had been married, but I made excuses for Blanche du Bois and Vinnie Miller because of the brevity of their unsatisfactory marriages, so I shall do the same for Flora since she 'had the misfortune to lose her husband when she had been married a few months', and like the other two she is unlikely to marry again.

Arthur Clennam (the novel's hero) and Flora had been childhood sweethearts but were separated when Clennam's business interests took him to China, but now he has returned to England and the two lovebirds are to be brought together again.

Unfortunately, the years have not been kind to Flora: 'Flora, always tall, had grown to be very broad too, and short of breath… Flora who had seemed enchanting in all she said and thought, was diffuse and silly.' And we are told, 'Clennam's eye no sooner fell upon the subject of his old passion than it shivered and broke into pieces.' Flora is not unaware of her changed looks, but she *is* unaware of her foolish garrulity:

'"I am sure," giggled Flora, tossing her head with a caricature of her girlish manner… "I am ashamed to see Mr Clennam, I am a mere fright, I know he will find me fearfully changed, I am actually an old woman, it's shocking to be so found out, it's really shocking."'

However, once she has discovered he is not married 'to some Chinese lady… manderinesses, if you call them so', she thinks she may still be in with a chance, but Clennam tries to make his escape as soon as possible. Flora expostulates in her usual incoherent way:

'You could never be so unkind as to think of going, Arthur – or I suppose Mr Clennam would be far more proper – but I am sure I don't know what I am saying – without a word about the dear old days gone forever, however when I come to think of it I dare say it would be much better not to speak of them and it's highly probable that you have some much more agreeable engagement and pray let me be the last person in the world to interfere with it though there was a time… though I am running into nonsense again.'

She hopes that reminding him of the past will bring back his old affection. Sadly, this is not to be. Clennam cannot believe the change in her: 'Was it possible that Flora could have been such a chatterer in the days she referred to? Could there have been anything like her present disjointed volubility in the fascinations that had captivated him?' Flora is not stupid. '"I know I am not what you expected, I know that very well." In the midst of her rapidity she had found that out with the quick perception of a cleverer woman.' However, this doesn't stop her from continuing to indulge in fruitless hopes and fancies.

Clennam is intent on improving the lot of Little Dorrit whom he suspects has in some way been wronged by his family, and he is also falling in love with her, and in the insensitive way of such men, he has the bright idea of introducing her into the Casby family as a companion to Flora. Unaware of Clennam's feeling, Flora talks at length about her childhood romance and how she hopes that it will be renewed. Not a chance! Not only is Flora fat, silly and garrulous, she also 'very fond of porter' and other such substances. But she is a kind woman, and when finally the truth comes out that Clennam is to marry little Dorrit, in her own silly way she admits defeat. She invites Dorrit to join her in a pie shop (Flora likes her food as well as her drink), and declares (Dickens purposefully omits commas):

"'…the withered chaplet, my dear is then perished the column is crumbled and the pyramid is standing upside down on its what's it name call it not giddiness, call it not weakness, call it not folly I must now retire into privacy and look upon ashes of dear departed joys no more but taking the further liberty of paying for the pasty which has formed the humble pretext for our interview will forever say Adieu.'"

Poor Flora! She is a kindly woman, shown not only in her consideration towards Dorrit, but in also looking after an impossible old aunt, but she has committed the unforgivable sin of letting herself go and now she has only her silliness left. Apparently Dickens based her character on an experience like Clennam's: disillusionment with a childhood sweetheart.

We saw earlier how unforgiving men are to ageing spinsters, and Flora, who was such a guileless one, surely deserved a little consideration.

All of these women have been good natured in their different ways, but damned by their silliness, but perhaps their silliness was the result of their spinsterhoods, not the cause of it. 'Silly' is too dismissive an adjective, perhaps 'lonely' would be more appropriately applied, as it is to Eleanor Rigby. Yet they had a kind of courage that carried them through. We must admire that – and perhaps learn from them too.

CHAPTER ELEVEN

SPITEFUL AND SCHEMING SPINSTERS

Strife [Eris] incessantly raging, sister and comrade of murderous Ares, who, at first holds her head low, but thereafter strides the earth with head rearing to heaven.

Jenny Marsh

'Cousin Bette' by Honoré de Balzac

Lisbeth Fischer:

Jealousy lay at the root of her character, which was full of eccentricities... a peasant girl from the Vosges, with everything that implies; thin, dark with glossy black hair, heavy eyebrows meeting across the nose in a tuft, long powerful arms, and broad solid feet with some warts on her long simian face; there is a quick sketch of the spinster.

Possibly the most manipulative of all spinsters is Lisbeth Fischer, known as Cousin Bette. Indeed, she could be seen as an exact replica of Eris, the Goddess of Strife.

Lisbeth has a cousin Adeline who was made much of because of her great beauty, while Lisbeth was left to work in the fields, 'and so it happened, one day, finding Adeline alone, Lisbeth had done her best to pull Adeline's nose off... Although she was beaten for this misdeed, it did not prevent her from continuing to tear her favoured cousin's dresses and crumple her collars.'

Because of her great beauty Adeline makes an extraordinarily unexpected and advantageous marriage to the Comissionary

General Hulot who is later made a baron, and given a position near the Emperor Napoleon. As a result they begin to move in court circles in Paris. In spite of the unkind treatment by her cousin, 'Adeline who was good and kind to an exceptional degree, in Paris remembered Lisbeth and brought her there about 1809, intending to rescue her from poverty and find her a husband.' However, 'the baron found it impossible to marry off this girl with the black eyes and sooty eyebrows who could neither read nor write, as quickly as Adeline would have liked. So as a first step he gave her a trade; he apprenticed Lisbeth to the court embroiderers…'

Bette is not at all grateful for the family's kindness, but broods constantly on the difference between her lot and Adeline's, and even though various potential husbands are eventually found for her, she prefers to remain a spinster and concentrate on revenging herself not just on Adeline, but the whole Hulot family. The first step is to cultivate a façade:

'After twenty-seven years of an existence largely paid for by the Hulot family and her Uncle Fischer, Cousin Bette resigned herself to being a nobody and allowed herself to be treated with scant ceremony.'

Because she appears so unassuming she manages to ingratiate herself with all comers, because 'everyone believed that the poor spinster to be so dependent that she had no alternative but to keep her mouth shut. She called herself the family confessional.' How wrong they all are! She makes it her business to learn everyone's secret weaknesses. Her native peasant cunning too, has been sharpened by the cut-throat and callous ambience of contemporary Paris. She lays her plans.

She begins by befriending a penniless Polish refugee, Count Steinbock, who is a talented artist: 'the love of power which had lain dormant in the old maid's heart developed rapidly, she was able to satisfy her pride and find an outlet for her energy; had she not a creature of her own to scold, manage and spoil?' And by various devious and dishonest ruses she brings him into the public eye; he begins to make money of which she naturally takes her cut. She does not want to be his lover, but she wants to manipulate him to her own ends: '"You belong to me,"' she told him. Her hatred of the Hulot family is intensified when Adeline's daughter, Hortense falls in love with him and becomes his wife. Bette sees her precious possession stolen from her.

Although Adeline's marriage is apparently so wonderful, she has a far from easy time with the baron, a dissolute man who squanders the family fortune on a succession of mistresses, but she is a good, almost saintly woman who never blames him, and continues to adore him. Their son Victorin who is married to Celestine, the daughter of the rich and crooked nouveau riche Monsieur Crevel, is not a successful lawyer, and he and his family are always short of money. All these things Bette observes and spider-like, starts weaving a web of malevolent intrigue around them. Central to her plans is Madame Valerie Marneffe. This woman is anxious to use her beauty to make money and provide herself with a luxurious life style, and in aiding and abetting her, Bette finds the perfect tool:

'Lisbeth who found this courtesan existence strangely exciting, advised Valerie in everything and pursued her vengeance with relentless logic… they could laugh together over the mischief they were plotting and the stupidity of men; and count up in company the accumulating interest in their respective treasure hoards.'

The first stage in her plot is to make Baron Hulot besotted with Valerie and incur huge debts by spending enormous amounts of money on her, from which Bette takes her cut, relishing the fact that he is reducing his good wife, Adeline, to a state of poverty, while she, Bette, becomes increasingly rich and powerful; then she introduces her now-successful Polish artist to the enticing Madame Marneffe and contrives ways of getting him to fall in love with her and desert his wife.

So far then, she has brought her kind cousin to a state of ruin, while also destroying her niece Hortense's marriage to *her* artist. Then she sets about enticing Victorin's father-in-law, Crevil into Valerie's charms, thus ensuring that he too, will spend his money on the courtesan, rather than in supporting his daughter and son-in-law; and there is the bonus of having ensured enmity between the two fathers-in-law.

She delights in seeing the luxury in which her friend Valerie lives, while her cousin Adeline and her daughter Hortense are reduced to living in poverty in a few small rooms, while her nephew, Victorin, too, becomes increasingly starved of funds. She has further schemes afoot. Now she holds so many secrets, she plans to complete her revenge by marrying Baron Hulot's elderly brother, a wealthy and honourable man, and thus forcing the rest of the Hulot family to live under her control, as mistress of the house now Adeline's husband overcome by debt, has been forced into dishonesty, and has gone into hiding, mourned by his still-loving wife, Adeline.

And all the while nobody has suspected Lisbeth's part in all this, and as every one of her carefully engineered disasters occur, the family members turn to their 'dear cousin' for help; and the 'help' provided by Bette is invariably another plot to bring about further ruin for them.

Unfortunately for Bette, her prospective husband dies before the marriage takes place, and her schemes go further awry when the lynch pin of all her plots, Madame Marneffe dies. Then things begin to look up for the Hulot family who manage to recover some of their former prosperity, and now the baron is able to return to his wife; Steinbock, Hortense's artist husband also returns to her, and Victorin's financial troubles come to an end, so he too, is able to enjoy life with his wife

Celestine, who now manages the household in an efficient and kindly way. Bette cannot bear to see the family's happiness and takes to her bed:

'Lisbeth already afflicted by the family's increasingly bright circumstances, was unable to endure this latest happy turn of events. Her condition deteriorated so much that Bianchon [the doctor] gave her no more than a week to live. She must die, defeated in the end of that long struggle marked by so many victories.'

However, she is not entirely beaten:

'She kept the secret of her hatred through the terrible suffering of pulmonary tuberculosis. And she had the supreme satisfaction of seeing them, Adeline, Hortense, Hulot, Victorin, Steinbock, Celestine, and their children, all in tears round her bed, mourning her as the family's angel.'

She was, as Balzac comments, compounded of 'hate and vengeance uncompromising, for those two passions [are] the reverse side of friendship and love pushed to extremes are known absolutely in countries bathed by the sun'. But why was her hatred so extreme? Her cousin Adeline had been very good to her, her brother in law had found marriages for her, and the whole family had welcomed her and confided in her. Balzac attributes much of her sadistic behaviour to the unnatural state of spinsterhood – or, as he terms it, virginity:

'Virginity, like all abnormal states, has its characteristic qualities, its fascinating greatness. Life, whose forces have been kept unspent, takes on in the celibate individual, an incalculable power of resistance and endurance. The brain has been enriched by the sum of its untapped faculties. When they make demands on their bodies, or their minds need to resort to physical action or thought, they find steel stiffening their muscles or knowledge infused into their minds, a diabolical strength, or the black magic of the Will.'

In the recent novel, 'Hurdy Gurdy' by Christopher Wilson, we meet a very similar assertion: the fourteenth century Brother Jack Fox holds that 'woman is incomplete. She stands in regular need of the seed of man. She requires it for its liquidity to wet her humours within. If it is not forthcoming… she may suffer the condition known as suffocation of the womb… so causing mischief to that woman's health by displacing her organs within. 'Well, we have moved on a bit from that, but is there something in Balzac's assertion? In all these spinsters we see something of the prudish goddess Diana – although they are less successful. Is it after all, as Balzac claims, that the libido repressed and confined can metamorphose into a diabolical malignant strength? Cousin Bette is certainly an example, and Miss Havisham's enforced spinsterhood, too, has resulted in a long term plan to wreak revenge. But Balzac was a man, and what could he really know about the sexual feelings of such women? It seems to me that Bette was more like Eris, the goddess whose nature it was to delight in spreading discord.

'Little Dorrit' by Charles Dickens

'A Self- tormenter'

Miss Wade:

Like Cousin Bette who from her earliest years had felt resentment at being treated as a poor relation, Miss Wade has even more reason. Dickens suggests that she was illegitimate: 'My childhood was passed with a grandmother; that is to say, with a lady who represented that relative to me.' She is acutely conscious of occupying an inferior position, although it seems that she was not made to feel so by her companions, but, nevertheless, she was determined to feed and to nurture this feeling of resentment, not solely because of her position, but because of some sort of innate masochism in herself: 'I tried them over and over again… they were always forgiving me in their vanity and condescension.' She prefers alienation to affection. In adolescence she becomes attached to another girl – she has, perhaps, lesbian tendencies – whom she loves and torments in equal measure. When that comes to nothing, she feels her resentment harden into a desire for revenge against the world.

However, her life chances improve when she becomes engaged to the nephew of a wealthy family and she admits, 'I did love him once', but rather than be satisfied with her lover, she rejects him, even though he loves her, and his family put no obstacles in her way. She prefers to torment him and his family, regarding their kindness and goodwill as a subtle form of torture towards her.

Then she meets the unscrupulous Mr Gowen and she feels he understands her rage against the society in which she moves: 'He was the first person whom I had ever seen in my life who had understood me.' She deserts her fiancé for him Unfortunately:

'He amused himself as long as it suited his inclinations; and then reminded me that we were both people of the world… that there was no such thing as romance, and that we were both prepared for going different ways to seek our fortunes.'

Now she looks for solace in further revenge. Her rage is directed indiscriminately, regarding everyone as her tormenters. But she is also a masochist and indulges this inclination by watching Gowan's new bride and their family. She notices that her family have a young protégée whom she regards – with some justification – as patronised by them:

'I found a girl in various circumstances of whose position there was a singular likeness to my own, and in whose character I was pleased to see the rising against swollen patronage and selfishness, calling themselves kindness, protection, benevolence, and other fine names which I have described as inherent in my nature. I have often heard it said too, that she had an unhappy temper. Well understanding what was meant by that convenient phrase and wanting a companion with a knowledge of what I knew, I thought I would try and release the girl from her bondage and sense of injustice...'

She relishes her revenge in taking the girl away from her patrons and making her suffer, but the girl deserts her, and she is left to spend the rest of her days in bitter loneliness.

Unlike Cousin Bette, her scheming is largely unsatisfactory because she has no clear picture of exactly what she is seeking revenge for; in fact, it is her own warped nature for which she can find no solace except in indulgence in masochism. But perhaps Balzac is right, it is all the result of repressed libido.

Could she, then, have been happy had she married her fiancé and thus been satisfied sexually as well as socially? Perhaps. Would she have been different if she had married Mr Gowen? Maybe she would, because one assumes he did satisfy her sexually, but unfortunately marriage was never an option, for him she was only an amusement; his only interest was in obtaining a wealthy bride.
Sadly, there was something in her, a kind of perverted passion that would always make her opt for a masochistic outcome. As she says herself: 'I had an unhappy temper'.
We might compare her to Circe who prefers to remain alone on her island and turn men into pigs.

146

'Where Angels Fear To Tread' by E. M. Forster

Harriet Herriton:

Other spinsters are not as clever as Cousin Bette nor as passionate as Miss Wade, and their scheming is largely motivated by stupidity and pig-headedness, but the outcome is no less disastrous. In this tragic novel we see such a schemer.

'It was now nearly ten years since Charles had fallen in love with Lilia Theobold because she was pretty', and despite all his mother's efforts to prevent the match, he married her, but he had died leaving her and a daughter to the tender mercies of the Herriton family, who are a singularly unpleasant bunch: Mrs Herriton is snobbish and domineering, her son Philip weak and cynical, but afraid to defy his mother, and his sister, Harriet who, as we shall see, is a particularly malevolent spinster. Between them they make life unbearable to Lilia, and she says in an outburst to Philip later:

'For twelve years you've trained me and tortured me… do you think I'm a fool? Do you think I never felt? Ah, when I came to your house a poor young bride, how you all looked me over – and discussed me as though I might just do; and your mother corrected me and your sister snubbed me, and you said funny things about me to show how clever you were. And when Charles died I was still to run in strings for the honour of your beastly family.'

Lilia is pretty and silly and when other men show an interest in her, the family are afraid she will marry one of them and they will lose control over her and her daughter, so they hatch a plan: they will pack her off to Italy; it will improve her mind and get her out of the way of two interested curates. When she is about to leave we see Harriet exclaim bitterly:

'I believe she would take anyone. Right up to the last when her boxes were packed she was 'playing' the chinless curate. Both curates are chinless, but hers had the dampest hands. I came across them in the park.'

This is an interesting vignette of Harriet's jealousy: we may be sure that she would have been only too happy to accept either of the curates – damp hands or not – but the possession of this religious crutch is to be denied her, because she is not pretty like Lilia.

Lilia is packed off to Italy without her daughter whom Mrs Herriton and Harriet will take charge of, but she will be accompanied by a suitable companion, good sensible Miss Catherine Abbott. Philip, who regards himself as something of an expert on Italy, advises her to visit the small town of Monteriano. She agrees – with unexpected results.

A telegram arrives at the Herriton house announcing her engagement to an Italian called Gino Carella. Mrs Herriton immediately dispatches Philip off to Italy to stop the marriage. He considers that the Italian can easily be bought off: he is 'probably a ruffian and certainly a cad'. But all is much worse than the family could have imagined: not only is Gino idle and unemployed, but unbelievably, Lilia has now actually become married to him. And this has not been prevented by the dependable Miss Abbott who, it seems, has romantic ideas about love and marriage. So Philip's mission ends in total failure.

The next bombshell to hit the Herritons is the news that Lilia has died giving birth to a baby boy. At first, the family decide to wash their hands of the whole affair, but Miss Abbott who has returned to England, makes it plain to Mrs Herriton that something has to be done: the baby must be brought back to England. Afraid that people will think her less worthy than Miss Abbott, Mrs Herriton decides that *her* family will get hold of the baby and *they* will bring him up: 'If I can rescue poor Lilia's baby from that horrible man, who will bring it up as a papist or infidel – who will certainly bring it up as vicious, I shall do it'. Various letters are dispatched to Italy, but Signor Carella will not be bought off. Accordingly, Mrs Herriton dispatches Philip and Harriet to Italy with orders that they must get the baby at all costs: 'Pay all we've got for it. I will have it.'

Predictably, Harriet, 'acrid, indissoluble, large; the same in Italy as in England – changing her disposition never,' dislikes everything about Italy. There follows a revealing description of her spinsterly grievances:

'Harriet's sketchbook was stolen, and the bottle of ammonia in her trunk burst over her prayer book so that purple patches appeared on all her clothes. Then as she was going through Mantua, Philip made her look out of the window because it was Virgil's birthplace, and a smut flew in her eye, and Harriet with a smut in her eye was notorious... At Bolonga they stopped twenty-four hours to rest. It was a festa and the children blew bladder whistles night and day. "What a religion!" said Harriet.'

Here we see Harriet with all the accoutrements necessary for her spinsterhood: the sketch book, the ammonia and the prayer book, this latter comforting religious 'crutch' is damaged and she is terrified by the threat of an alien religion, one which does not confine itself to silent prayer books.

When they arrive at Monteriano they are appalled to find Miss Abbott already there, and they are terrified at the thought of her claiming the baby first, so Harriet dispatches Philip to get hold of the child, reiterating her mother's orders.

'"You see him tomorrow at ten, Philip... well, don't forget the blank cheque... I can manage the baby as far as Florence... I have told the landlady we only want the rooms for one night, and we shall keep to it... and try if you can to get poor Lilia's silver bangles... and there is an inlaid box I lent her – lent not gave... it's of no real value, but this is our only chance."'

For Harriet, the bangles and the box are as important as the baby; they are all simply objects to console her in her spinsterhood.

In the event, Philip fails to find Gino at home, and it is Catherine who finds him first, also determined to get hold of the baby. However, after she has spent time with him and seen his fondness for his son, she decides that he should keep him, and bring him up there in Italy. When Harriet learns that Catherine has 'changed sides', and suspects that Philip will join her, she takes action and orders a coach for Philip and herself to leave that night, orders which Philip obeys. But Harriet is not waiting for him at the hotel as arranged; instead, he receives a garbled message and note from the village idiot, telling him she will join him in the coach outside the town gate.

'And there she was, waiting for them in the wet. "I heard you coming," she said, and got quickly in. Not till then did he see that she was carrying a bundle.' It is the baby.

At first Philip assumes that she has come to an agreement with Gino, then it strikes him that the baby seems strangely quiet; its face is covered in tears, but it makes no noise. He demands a proper look at it. She 'dandled the baby laboriously like some bony prophetess, Judith or Deborah or Jael, but Philip begins to be worried:

"His face, do you know, struck me as all wrong, all wrong... I say you haven't hurt it, or held it the wrong way? It is too uncanny – crying and no noise... For a full quarter of a minute they contemplated the face... then there was a shout and a crash... the carriage had overturned."

Harriet's screams became coherent, 'The baby, the baby – it slipped – it's gone from my arms. I stole it.'

Of course, it is dead. Harriet takes refuge in illness:
'The details of Harriet's crimes were never known. In her illness she spoke more of the inlaid box she had lent to Lilia – lent not given – than of recent troubles.'

How telling it is that she is more concerned about the loss of her 'inlaid box' than the death of the baby for which she has been responsible.

In some ways Harriet might be considered one of the worst of all the spinsters we have met. Unlike the Eumenides, she is not concerned with pursuing justice, her motives are worse: cowardly fear of disobeying her mother is but one aspect, but more significant is her fear of Italy with its joyous exuberance of life, (rather like Miss Matty, she is fearful of the effect of the sun), and its unashamed sexuality which negates everything her cosy spinster life in England has guaranteed. The baby symbolises this terrifying sexuality, the sexuality of Lilia, of Italy, and of its father Gino. She will do anything to escape it; she does not care for the baby as a human creature, but looks on it as a triumphant trophy of her escape, and in bringing it to England, it will become an ordinary child, no longer a sexual object. And what is worse still, is that she has no compunction for what she has done:

'For Harriet after a short paroxysm of illness and remorse, was quickly returning to her normal state. She had been "thoroughly upset", as she phrased it, but soon she ceased to realise that anything was wrong beyond the death of a poor little child. Already she spoke of 'this unlucky accident', and 'the mysterious frustration of one's attempts to make things better… Harriet, like her mother, considered the affair settled.'

Forster aligns her with Judith, Deborah or Jael, legendary biblical murderesses. We have met others in the Ancient World. In a sense she is an Amazon fighting off the dreaded male, and killing a male child, but she lacks their strength; nor does she have right on her side like the Eumenides or possess their power, she cannot even stand a smut in her eye. Like the harpies she is a snatcher and a polluter, but I see most closely a resemblance with the bathing Diana: Italy is her Actaeon because it has revealed her spinster nakedness; perhaps Diana did not intend to have Acteon torn to pieces by his dogs, but she took no steps to prevent it, and it was she who had set the machinery in motion. Similarly, Harriet did not intend the baby – who was for her the embodiment of Italy's Actaeon – to die, but neither had she done anything to prevent it. She knew nothing of babies, and she had set his death in motion by her theft, after which she could return to her prayer book and her churchgoing, and maintain her godly virginity, just like the goddess Diana.

Santa Deodata:

Santa Deodata, the Patron Saint of Monteriano is another of those spinsters that twist one strand with another, because she belongs equally to the category of 'Saintly Spinsters', but she is wholly Forster's creation, and I include her here because she acts as a sort of paradigm for the senseless actions undertaken by the English spinsters.

'She was the holy maiden of the dark ages, the city's patron saint and sweetness and barbarity mingle strangely in her story. So holy was she that all her life she lay on her back in the house of her mother, refusing to eat, refusing to play, refusing to work. The devil, envious of such sanctity, tempted her in various ways; he dangled grapes above her, he showed her fascinating toys, he pushed soft pillows beneath her aching head. When all proved vain, he tripped up the mother and flung her downstairs before her very eyes. But so holy was the saint that she never picked her mother up, but lay upon her back through all, and thus ensured her throne in paradise.'

The story of the saint demonstrates not only the uselessness of the 'do-good-ing' of Harriet and Caroline, but also their totally misguided and, in the case of Harriet, callous life style. Each, like the saint, immerses herself in her own form of morality: just as the saint ignores her injured mother while imagining herself pure and holy. Harriet persuades herself of her own rectitude, while entirely ignoring the damage she has done; and Caroline will do the equivalent of the Saint lying on her bed dreaming of paradise. She will devote herself to the memory of Gino and immure herself in the stifling life of Sawston. Like the saint, she could have had a useful life, not by getting off her backside and helping her poor mother, but by marrying Philip and bringing happiness to them both.

'East Lynne' by Mrs Henry Wood

Miss Corny:

"I am a religious woman, Ma'm," she added sharply, turning to Isabel, *"and I cannot countenance Sunday travelling. I was taught my catechism."*

Cousin Bette was spiteful, but her spite was used purposefully and with great cunning, but in 'East Lynne' we meet a spinster who is too stupid to develop any long term schemes, and although she is no Athene or Diana, her motives are the same: she acts out of a blind spite when she fears losing her power and supremacy. And in acting as she does, she brings, admittedly, not such destruction as the goddesses, but she still does terrible harm, and finally brings death to her victim.

'East Lynne' is a Victorian 'sensation novel' and plenty of sensation there is in it; there are many plots, counterplots, murders and elopings; it is a long book! So I'll just outline the part that concerns the role of Miss Corny, our spiteful spinster.

The unfortunate heroine, sweet and innocent Lady Isabel, is left penniless and out of desperation she marries the worthy lawyer, Archibald Carlyle, who is himself beloved – although difficult to see why, as he is boring and lacking in empathy – by a neighbour, Barbara Hare. In spite of not loving him initially, Isabel grows to love Carlyle and is a good wife, producing three children, but she is made increasingly unhappy by the unkindness of her jealous sister-in-law, and the lack of attention and empathy from her husband. Eventually, deserting her husband and children, she allows herself to be more or less kidnapped by the wicked rake, Captain Levison. When she is believed to have been killed in a railway accident, boring Archibald marries Barbara. However, Lady Isabel has not been killed, but disfigured in a railway accident, and now unrecognisable and disguised with a green eyeshade (!), she comes to work as governess to her own children. All sorts of ramifications occur and there is a death scene reminiscent of Dickens' 'Little Nell'. And finally, the shamed Lady Isabel herself is recognised by Archibald and his family. She dies begging for *their* forgiveness. Great tear-jerking stuff, but where is the spiteful spinster in all this?

Archibald Carlyle had been brought up by his half sister, Cornelia, the daughter of his father's first wife 'and when he was a child he called her Mamma Corny… she was a woman of strong sense, but, in some things, of weak judgement; and the ruling passions in her life were love of Archibald, and love of saving money.' She does have a proposal of marriage by a young clergyman, but so appalled is she by the offer, that she throws a treacle pudding at him. Her whole life will be devoted to Archibald and his business:

'She had never relaxed her rule; with an iron hand she liked to rule him now, in great things as in small, just as she had ruled in the days of his babyhood… and Archibald generally submitted, for the force of habit is strong.'

We will meet the same force exercised by Hilda Cherrington and her hold over Eustace.

It is not surprising that Archibald does not tell his sister of his intended marriage to Isabel since she declares, '"I have warned him against it since he was in leading strings."' Instead, he intends instead to win her over with a fait accompli, but when Miss Carlyle or Miss Corny, as she is usually known, discovers the deed, she is enraged: '"I will never forgive him… and I will never forgive or tolerate her."' But she has no intention of losing her grip over him. Immediately she lets out her own house, and establishes herself at her brother's new residence, 'East Lynne', and from there she sets about making Isabel's life hell. For example, there is an early 'explosion' when 'Mr Carlyle ordered the pony carriage for church, but his sister interrupted him:

" Archibald, what are you thinking of? I will not permit it."
"Permit what?" asked Mr Carlyle.
"The cattle to be taken out on a Sunday. I am a religious woman, Ma'm," she added sharply, turning to Isabel, "and I cannot countenance Sunday travelling. I was taught my catechism, Lady Isabel."

Isabel did not feel comfortable. She knew that a walk to St Jude's church and back in the present heat would knock her up for the day, but she shrank from offending Miss Carlyle's prejudices.'

And so it goes on. Archibald is at work all day and she is at the mercy of his sister's constant petty acts of unkindness. Of course, she should have told her husband, but she is timorous and puts up with it all in silence, becoming increasingly unhappy, and the stupid Archibald has no idea of what is going on. Then she overhears gossip about Barbara Hare and begins to believe, wrongly, that it is Barbara he really loves, not her. The whole business of Miss Corny and her own suspicions about Barbara make her very ill: 'Her features white and attenuated', and the doctors suggest a change of scene, proposing that she should go to 'some place on the French or Belgian coast. Sea bathing might do wonders…' Miss Carlyle did not approve: 'What did people want with change of air… she had never wanted any…' Isabel doesn't want to go, but Archibald insists, so go she must, but without her husband, because Miss Corny, of course, insists he must attend to his business. When Isabel is finally persuaded, she begins to look forward to introducing her three children to the French coast, but naturally, Miss Corny is having none of that:

"The children are not going to the seaside," she said. "They are not ordered there."
"But they must go with me," said Lady Isabel… "why should they not go?"
"Why should they not? On account of the expense, to be sure… what with one expense and another your husband will soon be on the road to ruin…". Poor Lady Isabel laid her hand upon her children, effectually silenced, and her heart breaking with pain.'

When her husband returns, he promises her that she shall take the children. However, 'Miss Carlyle flew out when she heard the decision, and frightened her brother to repentance.'

Weak Mr Carlyle lets the heartbroken Isabel go on her own, and living there alone and forced against her will into bad company, she meets the rake Captain Levison.

She returns home, but suffering under Miss Corny's tyranny, and feeling that her husband does not love her, she disappears; everyone assumes she is dead. When her disappearance is

discovered, the servant Joyce who loves Isabel berates Miss Corny on her treatment of Lady Isabel:
"…she ordered a new frock for Miss Isabel and you countermanded it. You have told her that master worked like a dog to support her extravagant ways; when you know that she was never extravagant; that none were less inclined to go beyond the proper limits than she. I have seen her, Ma'am, come away from your reproaches with tears in her eyes, and her hands meekly clasped on her bosom, as though life was too heavy to bear. A gentle-spirited high born lady, as she was, could not fail to be driven to desperation. And I know she has been."

Even Miss Corny is made to feel her guilt: 'She did not answer… her face looked grey and ghostly; and for the first time probably, in Miss Carlyle's life words failed her.'

Mr Carlyle turned to his sister and asks: '"Can this be true?"' Silly man. Why hadn't he noticed? But his concern is short-lived; with Isabel finally dead, he can marry Barbara for whom he has always had a soft spot. When Archibald tells his sister he is going to remarry, her jealous rage knows no bounds:

'"I always thought you mad when you married before, but I shall think you doubly mad now. 'Archibald's answer shows how little he understands the spinster: "Because you have preferred to remain single and solitary yourself, is it any reason why you should condemn me to do the same? You are happier alone. I should be happier with a wife."'

Tacitly he is saying: 'You can manage without sex, I can't.' But what he doesn't understand is the reason she has remained unmarried; it is not because his sister likes being a spinster, but because she has channelled all her sexual instincts into him.

She is even more upset when she discovers whom he is to marry: "'To suffer that girl who has been angling after you for so long, to catch you at last.'" Yes, even before he had married Isabel, Miss Corny had been aware of the threat of Barbara, and she had been pleased to be the first to tell her that he was marrying Isabel. Now she comes out with all her bottled up feelings about the girl: "'She's a conceited minx, as vain as she is high.'"

But worse is to come to her: "The next consideration, Cornelia," her brother tells her, "is about your residence. You will go back, I presume, to your own home."
She argues furiously, threatening to take her money away from him, but all to no avail, she is to be exiled.

If only Archibald Carlyle had got rid of his sister when he had married Isabel, none of her tragedy would have happened. But of course, it all turns out just fine for *him*. As Miss Corny said, Barbara has 'been angling after him for so long', and now she couldn't be more delighted with her new position as wife of Mr Carlyle and mistress of East Lynne, and he is now as full of love for her as he had been with Isabel. He really is a dreadful man!

At this point we see the tragedy of Miss Corny as much as that of Isabel. Isabel at least, had known the love of a husband, and had children, Miss Corny had had nothing: no husband, no children, her love for her brother twice rejected in favour of other women, and finally she had been driven out to spend her old age alone. Some spinsters never win – no matter how spiteful they are.

All these spinsters have adopted the role of Nemesis, the goddess intent on punishing those enjoying some kind an excess or have violated the natural order of things. But whereas Nemesis was an impartial judge, each of these spinsters has appointed herself as arbiter and their judgement has been warped in some way. Bette's judgement is warped by jealousy; Miss Wade's by a feeling of inferiority, Harriet's by fear and Miss Corny's by possessiveness. None of their victims has transgressed a moral law. And none deserved their fate at the hands of these self-appointed 'goddesses'.

CHAPTER TWELVE

SUPPRESSIVE SPINSTERS

I bring foot's force crashing down
To cut the legs from under even
The runner, and spill him to ruin.'
Aeschylus, 'The Libation Bearers'

These women emerge from the unravelled strands of the scheming spinsters, but they are not malign; in fact, in their various misguided ways they intend the best for their victim.

'The Eustace and Hilda Trilogy' by L.P. Hartley

Hilda Cherrington:

"Well", said Hilda, sitting down, "I have had a busy day." "I expect you have," said Barbara , "I expect you kept other people busy too."

L.P. Hartley's 'Eustace and Hilda' trilogy examines the relationship through childhood and into early middle age of domineering Hilda and her amiable, sensitive younger brother Eustace. At the beginning of the first book, 'The Shrimp and the Anemone', he gives us an elaborate analogy of their relationship: the brother and sister had been playing on the sands at Anchorstone when Eustace spots a distressing sight:

'There fastened to a sleek green boulder, half in and half out of the water, the lovely milk-pale sea anemone was devouring its prey. Only Hilda could stop its massacre, and he called her, but she did not come; she lingered beside their pond because of something he had left undone, something she would have to scold him for later. At last she came and saw the shrimp's sad plight, wedged in the anemone's cruel mouth. Hilda knew how to bring good out of evil; with Eustace holding her ankles she sprawled across the rocks and drew the shrimp out of the honey-coloured maw. But too late; the shrimp was dead and the anemone was terribly injured, oozing out of its own lips like something that had been run over.'

This analogy works on many levels: like the anemone, Hilda, even as a child, is remarkably beautiful, and like the anemone, she is unaware of her good looks, but, as with the anemone and the shrimp, she has Eustace horribly within her grasp; she is unaware of actively doing harm, she acts instinctively. And Eustace is helpless under her control. However, Hilda's beauty will be damaged by Eustace's unwitting actions, and he himself, like the shrimp, will die prematurely.

Now for the story. Eustace and his sister have been left motherless when their mother dies giving birth to a late child, Barbara, and their upbringing at the seaside town of Anchorstone is left to the care of their uninterested father and unhappy spinster aunt; so Hilda takes it on herself to look after Eustace, an activity which largely involves bullying him and making him do things he doesn't want to do, moulding him to the shape *she* thinks he should be. She is a bully but she believes – or has brought herself to believe – that she is acting for his good, and Eustace far from resenting this, looks up to Hilda with adoration, and regards her treatment of him as unquestionably right. He is sadly lacking in will of his own; as Eustace's friend, Stephen remarks in the last book of the trilogy, he is 'her creation'. He even tells Eustace that she is '"the author of your slim gilt soul"'.

The most significant thing that Hilda makes him do and on whose consequences the hinge of the book depends, is to befriend a disabled old lady in a wheelchair. Eustace explains:

"'Hilda wanted me to speak to Miss Fothergill... partly because she thought it would be a kind of discipline for me, and also on general principles, because the Bible said you should visit the sick. She's always had my moral welfare at heart, and so one morning much against my will, I did speak to Miss Fothergill and pushed her bath chair about a bit; and she was very nice about it and asked me to tea.'"

However a naughty little girl called Nancy Steptoe whom Eustace knows through local dancing classes, scares him off: "'She's old and ugly, and I suppose you know she's a witch..,. you know about her hands. Well they're not really hands at all, but steel claws and they curve inwards...'"

Not only is Miss Fothergill apparently a witch, but the description of her claw-like hands allies her appearance to that of the harpies, and the nervous Eustace is terrified, so instead of going to tea with the harmless old lady, he takes part in a local paper chase with Nancy. But Eustace has a congenitally weak heart, and during the chase he passes out, and is rescued by the scion of the local gentry, Dick Staverley who notices his beautiful sister, and asks her to go riding with him – an invitation she scornfully refuses. When Eustace recovers, Hilda forces him to visit Miss Fothergill, and against all expectation, he grows fond of her and becomes a regular visitor. This spinster is no harpy or witch but a good fairy, and when she dies, she leaves him a small fortune. As a result Hilda fears for her influence over Eustace; for Hilda's domination over Eustace is her whole existence.

In the second book of the trilogy, 'The Sixth Heaven', we see them both grown up: Eustace, having enjoyed a successful boarding school career, has won a scholarship to Oxford, while Hilda who trained as a nurse, but predictably, couldn't get on with her colleagues, is running a clinic for crippled children, which has, of course, been financed by Eustace. Severe and unbending, and without thought for others, she runs it with ruthless efficiency. She obviously enjoys the feeling of power that the enterprise gives her. But Barbara, her much younger sister, unlike Eustace sees more deeply into her sister:

'"Well," said Hilda, sitting down, "I *have* had a busy day." "I expect you have," said Barbara, "I expect you kept other people busy too."'

Hilda is a strange mixture of selfish austerity and remarkable beauty:

'She was like a night-blooming cactus surprised in the act of flowering… now it could be seen that the foliage of the flower was extremely severe. Starting from an almost masculine white collar and a black tie descended a coat and skirt of navy-blue serge, which had the intimidating effect of a uniform without actually being one.'

What we are beginning to see is an extremely repressed young woman.

At Oxford Eustace again encounters his boyhood hero, Dick Staverley who had rescued him years earlier, and Staverley who remembers the beautiful teenage Hilda, asks them both to stay for a weekend at his ancestral home, Anchorstone Hall. Eustace amiable and naïve, has no idea of Staverley's designs and is delighted with the invitation, and persuades a reluctant Hilda to join him. Why is Hilda reluctant? The reason she gives is that any time away from the serious business of work is time wasted, but we know that she too, remembers Staverley and finally she agrees to go. Eustace is excited, not so much for himself but because he wants the world to see and appreciate Hilda. However, in spite of her beauty, she does not really fit in.

'She was not exactly overdressed in her stiff blue silk which shimmered silvery white on the top where the light caught it, her appearance was so striking that she hardly could be… In his imaginings of her at Anchorstone, this was how Eustace had wanted her to look. He could see now that it was a mistake… she wasn't a lamp that could be turned down, she had to blaze, and the more uneasy she felt, the more she clashed with her surroundings, imparting her discomfort – it seemed to Eustace, to everyone else.'

However, it becomes obvious that Staverley is fascinated by her, and during the course of the weekend he takes her for a flight in his private aeroplane; they are gone a very long time and everyone is worried for their safety. However, they return at last, and the naïve Eustace is struck by something different in Hilda. Whether or not she has been seduced by Staverley, her latent sexuality has been released.

In the last book of the trilogy we find a happy Eustace staying in Venice with Dick Staverley's rich and scheming aunt, Lady Nelly. Rumours reach him of Hilda's seeing a great deal of Dick Staverley, and given as Eustace is to daydreaming, he imagines Hilda, spending her time with him at the Ritz, giving up the clinic, marrying him, and becoming mistress of Anchorstone Hall. Hilda does, in fact, imagine that too.

However, uneasy rumours in the form of letters start to reach Eustace in Venice, although there is little from Hilda herself; his friend Stephen who like other men, has been attracted to Hilda, writes to tell him of the indications of misfortune: Hilda has been unwell, she is neglecting the clinic, she has been observed behaving strangely; clearly she is having an affair with Dick, and something is going wrong. Finally Lady Nelly tells Eustace that Dick has become engaged to an old childhood friend. The scales fall from Eustace's eyes and he concludes that Lady Nelly has invited him to Venice to leave the coast clear for Dick to seduce Hilda. However, this she denies, and she tries to comfort Eustace:

"'I admired your sister. I thought she had a fine nature – but it was a dark room, wasn't it when you weren't there, and will be brighter with the daylight let in, even if the window's broken?'"

She is trying to tell Eustace that the experience will have done his sister good, and with her beauty there will be plenty of other opportunities, but she doesn't know Hilda.

Before he leaves Venice Eustace accidently meets Staverley and confronts him, calling him 'a blackguard'. But it becomes clear that it is not entirely Dick's fault; he has made it clear from the start that he will not be tied down, and that Hilda cannot mould him to her will as she has Eustace. Much later in conversation with Dick's sister, Anne, Eustace learns something of the truth:

"'He would have asked her to marry him if she could have taken him as he was. But she marked down every moment of his time; she mixed herself up with all of his thoughts. She wanted him to do this and be that, and the more he drew away, the closer she clung to him. He was odious to her often, and in front of people, but her will was stronger than his, and she makes it seem wrong not to do what she wants... he tried to make her see they couldn't go on.'"

But with sexual awakening her possessiveness had increased, she abandons the clinic, and generally behaves in a scandalous manner; she simply will not leave him alone; he sees the only route of escape is to become engaged to an old childhood friend who will give him no trouble, and to avoid further scandal he is leaving the country, and will spend some time in the East.

And Hilda's reaction? Well, she has suddenly become paralysed and Eustace is summoned home. Apparently she cannot speak or walk, but whether this is all pretence or not, we are never told, but like our earlier spinsters, she had suffered some sort of facial disfigurement with 'her slight squint, her drooping eyelid, her embryo movements that ended in a tremor'.

On his return home Eustace thinks that some sort of shock will restore Hilda to her former self so he decides to take her out in a bath chair and pretend to lose control of it. Hilda with her disfigurement has become a replica of Miss Fothergill, and now it is Eustace who must push Hilda in a bathchair.

He embarks on his plan, but although he pretends to lose control, he has reckoned without his poor physical strength, and as the chair starts to roll towards the cliff top, he collapses. However:

'Tremors passed through Hilda, violent tremors swelling into shudderings that made the bathchair creak and rattle... her foot sought the ground, but feeling the weakness flow out of her and the strength return, she looked down at him...'.

She imagines he is dead, but he has merely fainted. Suddenly their roles are reversed, or rather, returned to their former state. It is now Hilda, restored to health, who wheels Eustace home; and that very night she is again imposing her will on him:

'"We can't have you loafing about."' She insists that instead of going to bed as he longs to do, he contacts his Oxford College: '"I should write tonight, no good putting things off."'

And of course, he must write six other letters telling the world of Hilda's recovery. He obeys her orders, but it has all been too much for him, and that night he dies in his sleep.

What sort of spinster is Hilda then? Obviously she views herself as one of the Eumenides, set on forcing first Eustace and then Dick Staverley to do what (she regards) as right; like them she is utterly intractable; her actions replicate their avowed intentions:

'For we are strong and skilled;
We have authority; we hold
Memory of evil; we are stern
Nor can men's pleading bend us.'

But she is also a harpy with a voracious appetite, and like the a harpy, she befouls everything about her: she has brought scandal on Dick Staverley, forced him into an unhappy marriage, and driven him from the country; and as for Eustace, she has given him a guilt complex which lasts a lifetime, and in the end she is (unwittingly) responsible for his death.

We can trace other mythological elements in Hilda: when Barbara, her much younger sister, gets married, and is leaving for her honeymoon, we are told:

'Fists raised in menace hurled handfuls of confetti as if they had been bombs… when a figure ran forward, wild as a bacchante and launched a new attack… Eustace could scarcely believe that the wild-eyed tear-stained dishevelled woman was his sister Hilda.'

Before Dick knew Hilda's destructive powers, he compared her to a dryad, but she is no harmless beautiful wood nymph; once she loses control she becomes a bacchante.

There is yet another classical reference. Eustace's sister does not have much sympathy with Hilda in her supposed disabled state. "How's the Medusa?" she asks Eustace when he has been to see Hilda in her room. Barbara can see the deadly effect of Hilda's gaze. Strands from the Ancient World are certainly interwoven in Hilda.

What will become of Hilda now she has lost both the men in her power? Will she take refuge in another bout of paralysis? But there will be no Eustace to rescue her. Will she, as so many spinsters do, lose herself in good works by returning to her clinic? But after her scandalous behaviour, her services will probably no longer be required. Will she become a siren, luring other men, like Eustace's friend Stephen to their destruction, even managing to marry one of them? Or will she in the end, drive them way? The author does not tell us. He leaves Hilda a lonely spinster – after all, in the author's eyes her role in the story has only been as a tool to delineate Eustace, she has never been so important in the story as he, and now his story is finished, Hilda, like her sister spinsters, is left on an empty shelf.

Hilda is the chief suppressive influence in the story, but there are other spinsters too, who play their part in stifling poor Eustace, who from his earliest years has been surrounded by single women; and all of them in some way or other, play a part in mis(s)-fashioning Eustace.

Miss Fothergill:

"She's old and ugly, and I suppose you know she's a witch."

Miss Fothergill is another dangerous and suppressive spinster; she cossets and spoils Eustace, giving him a love of the luxurious and meretricious, but in spite of all this allure she is no siren. She is more like the Scylla. Unlike the hideous monster, she does not have six rows of heads and three rows of teeth, but her large legacy has Scylla's long reach that catches and devours the man Eustace might have been. Like Hilda, she too is responsible for his 'slim gilt soul'.

Aunt Sarah:

"You will remember another time, that a small slip often makes a lot of work for other people…"

Eustace's unpleasant Aunt Sarah, repressed and spiteful, does her best to make Eustace feel wrong and guilty:

'Long ago Aunt Sarah had canalised her life; it never overflowed or enriched the land round it with the untidy detritus of living. Eustace felt he was to blame; he had grown up too much in awe of her to try and get in touch with her. He had too easily taken it for granted that she disapproved of him. Of course, Hilda, though so different and planned on so much a larger scale, had been Aunt Sarah's spiritual child; they took the same things seriously.'

The same things they took seriously were bullying Eustace and giving him a life-long sense of guilt. Mean-spirited Aunt Sarah even begrudges Eustace his legacy and tries to persuade her brother to give it up, but Mr Cherrington has no intention of doing so, relishing the benefits accruing from it to himself. '"I could do with a bit of luxury,"' he comments.

Even when Eustace finally returns to home as an adult, Aunt Sarah is ready to upbraid him. While he was in Italy Lady Nelly had expressed admiration for the watch which he had inherited from Miss Fothergill, and Eustace had left it for her when he returned home, but Lady Nelly returns it to him, writing:

'… why should I keep anything of yours as long as I have you, and if he meant it as a parting gift, then all the more she felt she must repudiate it.'

Such ideas of gifts and their generous return was something impossible for Aunt Sarah to imagine; instead, she reproves

Eustace in no uncertain terms. The parcel had been left for collection at the customs office at Victoria and Aunt Sarah has gone off to collect it:

'She had not wished to seem interfering, and it had been very difficult for her to get away… they were very understanding [at the depot], and I only had to tell them that the watch was not a purchase; it belonged to you, and you had accidentally left it behind. Such an easy thing to do, but I'm afraid it must have given your late hostess a great deal of trouble and some expense. I don't count my own, and I expect she would have plenty of help; but you were always a little forgetful, and you will remember another time that a small slip often makes a lot of work for other people… Annie gave up her afternoon out so that I should be able to make the journey…'. Her remarks take Eustace back to his boyhood, 'his conception of himself as someone who was always giving trouble.'

This vignette encapsulates everything we need to know about Aunt Sarah: '*she had not wished to seem interfering*', but of course, interfering and pointlessly interfering, was exactly what she had wanted to do, and it had given her an opportunity to portray herself as a martyr: '*it had been very difficult for her to get away*', while in fact, the excursion had given her an opportunity to go to London, and in so doing she had cheerfully made the maid sacrifice *her* afternoon out; but best of all, it had allowed her to reprimand Eustace for his carelessness – carelessness that was no carelessness, but in fact thoughtfulness; and it has reduced Eustace to the little boy she had bullied in his boyhood as '*someone who was always giving trouble.*'

The passage exemplifies everything that is unpleasant in an unhappy spinster: a need to do something pointless, and demanding adulation for doing it, while actually putting the onus on someone else; there is also a lack of understanding of another's good actions, and a resultant satisfaction in showing imagined superiority, thus enabling her to humiliate someone more fortunate than herself.

Minney:

'She bustled up, a small active woman with a kind round face and soft tidy hair.'

Minney is the Cherrington family nurse, and she gives Eustace the love that the other family members deny him,; moreover, she sees the good in Eustace: '"Do you think I am messy?" asked Eustace anxiously.

"No. You're always a good boy."' Minney is the one in the family that sees his superiority to Hilda. After the family's geography game, Eustace goes to the nursery 'to do his corrections', and finds Minney there:

'"Whatever's that?"
"It's what I've done wrong," said Eustace gloomily.
"Is it? Let me look. I don't call that much. I should be proud if I'd made no more mistakes than that."
"Would you?" asked Eustace almost incredulously.
"Yes, I should. I'll be bound Hilda didn't get as many right as you did."'

Eustace is so fond of Minney that as an adult, he buys a watch to leave her in his will.

But Minney is a spinster and a childless woman who has natural mothering instincts, and she attempts to replace Eustace's mother in a kindly way, not by bullying him as Hilda does. She knows he will be upset after Miss Fothergill's funeral, and she comes to comfort him while he is having his bath, and helps to wash and dry him while they talk. But should a woman of her years really be bathing a boy of ten?

Isn't this harmful babying, not to mention the sexual undertones that will also damage to Eustace's development? Minney, kind and good though she is, fails to treat Eustace as a boy who requires firm guidance, but as the baby she never had, and indeed, Eustace never really grows up.

There is one more spinster in Eustace's life, the lava, but she will be more appropriately addressed among the Spectral Spinsters.

Interestingly, none of these spinsters are abused women, but purposefully – in Hilda's case, and inadvertently in the cases of the others – it is they who abuse their male creature. Eustace is like Hylas who was pulled under the waves by the eager water nymphs. Another strand from Antiquity.

CHAPTER THIRTEEN

SAPPHIC SPINSTERS

Hermaphroditus was brought up by nymphs in the caves of Mount Ida, but as soon as he was fifteen he set out to see the world, travelling even as far as Lycia and Caria. Here he came to a beautiful pool where lived the nymph Salamacis. As soon as she set eyes on the handsome youth, she was overcome with desire for him. She propositioned him, but he knowing nothing yet of love, brusquely repulsed her. She pretended to go away, and then watched as he stripped to swim in the pool. As soon as he was in the cold water, she plunged in with him and clung to him, passionately as he struggled against her embraces, but she prayed to the gods that they might be united for all time. Her prayer was granted and the two bodies became one flesh, half man and half woman.

Jenny March, 'Dictionary of Classical Mythology'

Because most of the spinsters we have met have belonged to some time in the past, the mention of lesbianism is never overt. In 'Some Tame Gazelle' there are rumours that Edith once had a romance with one John Akenside in the Balkans, but it seems more likely that theirs was a working relationship, and he was in fact a homosexual since it is Count Bianco who continues to be passionately devoted to him, years after his death. We may surmise that some of the dons in 'Gaudy Night' had sapphic tendencies, but it is not even hinted at. Lucy Snowe was obviously attracted to Ginevra Fanshawe, but these are mere whispers. The only overt reference is Sandy's spoken suspicion that Miss Jean Brodie is lesbian. All these references are touched on lightly, as if of no importance, but there are two very different novels that make no bones about the subject.

'The Well of Loneliness' by Radclyffe Hall

My life is bitter with thy love; thine eyes
Blind me, thy tresses burn me, thy sharp sighs
Divide my flesh and spirit with soft sound,
And my blood strengthens, and my veins abound
                    A.C. Swinburne, 'Anactoria'.

Stephen Gordon:

The novel caused a tremendous scandal and resulted in a law suit about obscenity. It is an impassioned polemic for the rights of those known at the time as 'inverts', that they should be acknowledged as respected members of society. I will start by giving a brief outline of a very long book.

Sir Philip Gordon and his wife Lady Anna are the extremely wealthy and happy owners of a beautiful country estate, 'Morton', and all that is needed to complete their idyll is the longed-for son and heir, but when the child is born, it is a girl. Nothing daunted, they name her – somewhat unwisely, in my opinion – Stephen.

As a child, she feels different from other girls and loves dressing up to emulate her male heroes, particularly Nelson; as she grows into her teens she becomes obsessed with horses and hunting, and insists on riding astride, a shocking thing in the late nineteenth century; (there is an awful lot of sentimental gush about the mutual love and, yes, mutual conversation between Stephen and her horse, Rafferty, which continues over the course of some hundreds of pages, until thankfully, he finally pegs out). As she grows up, the neighbours become increasingly suspicious of her, but their suspicions are allayed when she becomes friendly with a young man called Martin Hallam who is visiting from Canada, but when he proposes to her, she is horror-struck and sends him packing.

Her parents become increasingly worried about her; her father who has read Kraft-Ebbing, has come to realise her nature, but does not dare to tell his conventional wife, who now shows signs of disliking her daughter who is proving so unlike the other young girls of their acquaintance. However, Sir Philip is very loving and protective towards her, not knowing how she will fit into society. But all is in vain because he meets a premature death, killed by a falling tree on his estate.

New neighbours, Roger and Angela Crosby, move in, and Stephen falls violently and passionately in love with Roger's wife, Angela who, bored and disliking her husband, encourages Stephen to a certain extent, but her feelings are shallow, and when the opportunity arises she has an affair with a man Stephen dislikes. Stephen is devastated and writes her a passionate letter demanding that she come away with her, but Angela, scared of her husband finding out about her affair, shows the letter to him, claiming she is horrified by it. She insists that she has only been seeing Stephen to try to reform her, whereupon the angry husband sends the letter to Stephen's mother who is so appalled that she makes Stephen leave the family home. This is a terrible blow to Stephen who loves the estate of Morton passionately.

Personally, I don't think it's that hard a banishment since her father has left her an enormous amount of money, and off she goes to live in London with her devoted old governess, nicknamed 'Puddle'. Increasingly now, Stephen begins to dress in as masculine way as she dares, and proud of her masculine agility, takes up fencing. She throws all her repression into writing, brings out a best-seller, and is acclaimed as an up-and-coming writer.

When the war comes she goes to France, and at great personal risk, drives ambulances and sustains a disfiguring wound to her face (making her yet another scarred spinster); in acknowledgement of her courage she is awarded the Croix de Guerre.

When the war is over she befriends a pretty Welsh girl, Mary Llewlyn, with whom she has worked in the ambulance unit. She decides to live in Paris and she buys a grand house for them both there. For some time she resists having sex with the girl, but finally succumbs, and there follows some years of great happiness as Stephen's wealth can buy every luxury for them both, but it becomes apparent that they will never be accepted by 'normal' people, and back in Paris they spend time with fellow 'inverts'.

One day Stephen's old suitor, Martin, arrives in Paris and for a while the three of them have an enjoyable 'normal' existence, since the presence of a man makes them acceptable, but eventually the inevitable happens, and Martin and Mary fall in love. For some time Stephen fights to keep possession of Mary, but when she realises that the price of having Mary is to deprive the girl of what she really wants: a respectable position in society, marriage and children, she finally makes the sacrifice and lets Mary go. The book ends with an impassioned cry to God against the injustice of her lot, and that of those like her:

'Her barren womb became fruitful – it ached with its fearful and sterile burden. It ached with the fierce yet helpless children who would clamour in vain for their right to salvation. They would turn first to God, then to the world, and then to her; they would cry out accusing: we asked for bread, would you give us a stone...? "God," she gasped, we believe, we have... we have told you we believe... we have not denied. You then, rise up and defend us. Acknowledge us, oh God, before the whole world. Give us also the right to our existence.'

The 400 page book is powerfully written and is an anguished cry of the 'invert' who can find no place for herself and her lover in the society to which she belongs by class and upbringing. Reading the book I felt very touched, particularly by Stephen's early years when she herself does not understand her own sexuality, and because she is particularly vulnerable, possessing a male sense of honour inherited from her father together with a feminine nervous sensibility to insult.

However, as the story unfolds I began to have less sympathy with her, for a start she has that staple of comfortable spinsterhood: money, and she has bucket-loads of it, living in unimaginable luxury with servants and a chauffeur; she enjoys innumerable romantic holidays with her lover and she is able to constantly lavish expensive presents on her regardless of cost; and all this is at a time of dreadful poverty in England and in France where she chooses to live. Although her largesse extends to providing two poverty-stricken inverts with food – unsuitably rich food – which makes them ill, and forks out for a lavish wedding for two of her servants, there is little evidence that she has any thoughts of alleviating anyone else's poverty. Her sole concerns are keeping her lover in luxury and becoming a famous writer; however, even in that she is abominably selfish, shutting herself up to write her novels, disregarding the emotional needs of her lover who is forced into the company of unhappy inverts; she refuses to maintain a proper contact with her mother; and she becomes increasingly obsessed with the sexuality that fate has bestowed on her, 'the Mark of Cain', as she calls it.

Well, some might think, "you were damn lucky to have all that money – far more than any other spinsters we've met. If you hadn't, your lot would have been infinitely worse; after all, you lived for years in luxury and managed to have glorious years of sex with your partner, in spite of the disapproval of society. What about other women and their problems? What about women who lost their lovers or were widowed by the war, and thus doomed to a sexless life? What about the hundreds of thousands of other sad and impoverished spinsters? We do not hear of the wealthy Stephen comparing her lot with theirs. And if she wanted to find more of her kind, why didn't she go to Berlin which was famous for sexual freedom in the twenties and thirties?

So I was torn. Yes, I thought she was very selfish, but there was much to admire in her; her courage in war and her generosity in letting her lover go, for example. And above all, I felt desperately sorry for a woman who could be so cruelly treated by a callous society, even rejected by her own mother; and her final impassioned cry, 'Acknowledge us, oh God, before the whole world. Give us also the right to our existence', is unbearably heart-rending.

Thankfully, nowadays such anguish can be avoided since the rights of the LGBT community are slowly being acknowledged. Nowadays Stephen could have become Mary's husband, adopted children and lived a happy life; no longer would she be regarded as a medusa from whom society fled. We must be thankful that we have moved on from the nineteen-twenties – even if not nearly far enough.

'Mademoiselle de Maupin' by Theophile Gautier

> *This is the golden book of spirit and sense,*
> *The holy writ of beauty.*
>> *Algernon Charles Swinburne,*
>> *'Sonnet with a copy of 'Mademiselle de Maupin'.*

Mademoiselle de Maupin:

Mademoiselle de Maupin wants to find out what men are really like; she doesn't believe that the men, or rather, *gentlemen* she meets in the rarified aristocratic society in which she moves in the eighteenth century, show their real selves to the ladies of their acquaintance, so she disguises herself as a man and sets about finding out:

'I took the most careful precautions to prevent anyone suspecting that I was a woman. I learned how to handle a sword and fire a pistol; I could ride a horse with consummate skill and with a gameness that few equestrians could have equalled…'

I am sure Radclyffe Hall must have read 'Mademoiselle de Maupin' before writing 'The Well of Loneliness' because this description is so exactly like the depiction of Stephen Gordon with her love of horsemanship and skill at fencing.

The story is written in a completely different vein from 'The Well of Loneliness', and the plot becomes somewhat farcical in its complications.

Disguised as a squire, Maupin calling herself Théodore takes a fancy for a pretty country girl, Ninon, whom she disguises as a page she calls Isnabel; but our suspicions are somewhat aroused by the close concern she feels for him:

'The little page was so exhausted that he slept in his master's arms… and the valet who showed him the way offered to relieve him of the lad, but the young squire would not entrust his page to anyone else, a mother could not be more solicitous.'

Maternal feelings, eh?

In the meantime she meets the Chevalier D'Albert, the established lover of the beautiful Rosette who adopts 'Théodore' as her page. Theatricals are to take place with 'As You Like it' being the play of choice. Théodore is to take the part of Rosamund, thus exchanging her male clothes for female attire. And then, as cross-dressing is the hinge of the play, to exchange her female clothes for male attire, in accordance with the plot. D'Albert has already fallen for Théodore, thinking her, of course, to be male, and he is worried by his 'unnatural desires', but seeing her in female clothes, he realises she is a woman, and he becomes determined to make love to her.

Meanwhile, to add to the confusion, Rosette too, has fallen deeply in love with her page, but unlike her lover does not suspect she is a woman. After further ramifications in which Isnabel's true sex is revealed, Maupin becomes uncertain of her own feelings:

'O how often have I longed to be really a man, instead of masquerading as one… if I had been a young man how deeply I would have been in love with Rosette.'

She is however, still a virgin and senses the time has come to find out what sex is all about, so she spends the night with D'Albert, and there is a graphic account of it. Needless so to say, she is delighted by this sexual awakening. But things are not so simple. The author tells us:

'Instead of returning to her own room, she paid a visit to Rosette. What she said and did there I have never been able to discover… But a maid of Rosette's told me the following peculiar circumstance: that although her mistress had not slept with her lover that night, the bed was rumpled and disarranged, and it bore the imprint of two bodies. Further, she showed me two pearls, exactly like those which Théodore wore in his hair when he acted the part of Rosalind… I pass this detail on to the intelligent reader, and leave him to draw from it whatever inferences he likes.'

After this, 'Théodore' taking 'Isnabel' with her, disappears from the scene. Years later she will write to D'Albert:

'I shall often think of you, more often than if you were with me. Comfort poor Rosette the best you can, for she must be at least as grieved at my departure as you are. Cherish a love for each other in memory of me whom both of you have loved, and utter my name sometimes when you exchange kisses.'

What are we to make of this? Unlike Stephen Gordon, Maupin, is not racked by guilt or pain, she has no particular axe to grind either for herself or other bisexuals. Initially, she had simply wanted to find out what men were really like, but her intimacy with Ninon and Rosette has made her wonder about the nature of sexuality, and she puts it to the test by sleeping with a member of each sex; we don't actually know what her preference was, although in departing with Ninon I suspect it was for women; on the other hand, she tells D'Albert that although he will be a hard act to follow, she doesn't dismiss the thought of future lovers, but she doesn't specify of which sex.

Is she a spinster, I mean a proper or improper one? Certainly, we cannot imagine her with the familiar accoutrements of spinsterliness: the knitting, the churchgoing and the preoccupation with minutiae, but I don't see her as wife material either. So, yes, I think she is, but unlike poor Stephen Gordon, a very contented one. I think Maupin would have been delighted with today's enlightened views and sexual freedom, but there again, she enjoyed it anyway some two hundred years ago, although like so many of our spinsters, her lifestyle was only made possible by the possession of money. Thankfully our sexual freedom no longer depends on wealth – or does it?

With both these spinsters we may cast a look back at Athene who sprang fully armed from the forehead of Zeus, and often pictured with the severed head of Medusa on her breastplate, but she was also a goddess, not a god, and her authority extended over the concerns of women: their spinning and weaving, even overseeing childbirth. In fact she was bisexual, but being a goddess, she was in a more powerful place than Gordon or Maupin – or women today.

CHAPTER FOURTEEN

SLEUTHING SPINSTERS

Let him hide under the ground, he shall never go free… I go
to win my right upon this man and hunt him down.
Aeschylus, 'The Libation Bearers'

Although Pym covers a number of stereotypes, we do not meet many sleuthing spinsters in 'Some Tame Gazelle'. Harriet tries to discover the truth of Mr Donne's engagement and interrogates Edith and Connie about it; and both Belinda and Harriet station themselves at a bedroom window to spy upon the departure of the archdeacon's wife Agatha, as she leaves for her health cure at Baden Baden, but Pym's characters are always low key. To discover threads of serious sleuthing we have to look further back at the Ancient World.

Of all the recent sleuths – or not so very recent, but now constantly before our eyes, thanks to film and television, is that redoubtable spinster, Miss Marple, created by Agatha Christie. Indeed, here is a spinster known all over the world over many decades as so many actresses (and I think I must use that word here, not 'actors') have portrayed her: Angela Lansbury, Joan Hixon, Geraldine MacEwan, Julia McKenzie, and of course, Margaret Rutherford, to name but a few. Nor has she been restricted to English speaking nations, she has been portrayed by Kaomi Yachingusa as a Japanese lady. And all these actresses have endeavoured in their individual ways to highlight different aspects of her spinsterhood. But before we look at film and television adaptations, let's return to the original, to the woman portrayed by Agatha Christie.

Unlike other single women we have met, Miss Marple is conscious of the outsider's perception of spinsterhood; she is fully aware of its outward signs, but she is neither ashamed nor proud of her condition. Instead, she skilfully utilises it to mask a sharp and perceptive brain, often trading on others' misconceptions of her, and even exaggerating spinsterly traits to enable her to ask apparently silly questions, or lull a suspect into a false sense of security. She turns spinsterhood on its head and uses it as a deadly weapon. To explore this, and without giving away any spoilers, let's look at 'The Body in the Library'.

'The Body in the Library' by Agatha Christie

Miss Marple:

Miss Marple's telephone rang while she was dressing. The sound of it flurried her a little. It was an unusual hour for her telephone to ring. So well ordered was her prim spinster's life that unforeseen telephone calls were a source of vivid conjecture.

In this introduction to her character we are alerted to the two aspects of her life: that she has a 'prim' spinsterhood regulated by the quotidian, and that the unusual 'flurries' her; however, it flurries her 'only a little'; while what it actually does, is stimulate the other side of her nature: her sharp brain.

At the scene of the crime Colonel Melchett asks:

'"Come now, Miss Marple, haven't you got an explanation?" "Oh yes, I've got an explanation," said Miss Marple , "quite a feasible one. But of course, it's only my own idea… Tommy Bond," she continued, "… and Mrs Martin, our new schoolmistress. She went to wind up the clock and a frog jumped out."'

Unsurprisingly, the suspect whom the colonel is questioning 'looked puzzled' and asks, '"is the old lady a bit funny in the head?"' Far from it. Like all spinsters, Miss Marple takes a keen interest in the minutiae of the neighbourhood, but unlike others she stores every incident away as data to guide her to the workings of the human mind, and she will utilise these as exempla to guide her in her enquiries and get to the root of a problem. For example, she can understand and explain the elderly Mr Jefferson's obsession with the murdered girl, by comparing it with examples from her own store of knowledge: two gullible men, Mr Harbottle's fondness for his nurse and Mr Badger's soft spot for his shop assistant.

One of the things she has particular knowledge about is the psyche of young girls, not from her own childhood memories, but because like Harriet and Belinda Bede in 'Some Tame Gazelle' she is comfortably off – a requisite we have noted earlier for enjoyable spinsterhood – and she has considerable experience of young maids, her own and those of others in her middle class circle. So when it comes to interviewing some young girls, friends of the murdered girl, Miss Marple is well-placed to spot the vital witness amongst them.

'Superintendent Harper asked curiously:
"What put you on to this particular girl?"
Miss Marple said gently:

"You haven't had as much experience with girls telling lies as I have. Florence looked at you very straight, if you remember, and stood very rigid and just fiddled with her feet like the others. But you didn't watch her as she went out of the door. I knew at once that she had got something to hide. They nearly always relax too soon. My little maid Janet always did. She'd explain quite convincingly that the mice had eaten the end of the cake, and give herself away by smirking as she left the room."'

However, like many spinsters Miss Marple knows how to be modest and self-effacing: one suspect asks:

"'Do you write detective stories?" "Oh no, I'm not nearly clever enough for *that*."
"Jane Marple is a very remarkable woman," said Mrs Bantry
"She's nice too," said Addie smiling.
"People call her a scandalmonger," said Mrs Bantry, "but she's not really."
"Just a low opinion of human nature?"
"You could call it that.'"

Unlike many spinsters, Miss Marple's opinion of human nature is not soured by bitterness; she is a realist, and her judgement is the result of her close attention to its various manifestations which she has observed, because as a well-off spinster, she has few calls on her time, and her full attention can be focussed on them. Without her spinsterhood, both its actuality and its assumed trappings, Miss Marple could not operate. For her, spinsterhood is no source of shame, it is her unique and personal modus vivendi; other people wear uniforms for their jobs, Miss Marple wears spinsterhood.

Miss Marple certainly has all the accoutrements of spinsterhood. In 'At Bertrams Hotel' we are shown her early morning routine which involves a daily reading from her prayer book – one feels this missal is not a mere prop as it was with Harriet Herriton but a genuine vade mecum – and she enjoys the old fashioned service offered by the hotel such as the perfect breakfast tray, but she is not fooled; she knows that what she is seeing is a mere performance, and that the hotel is not what it seems, but may harbour all sorts of dark secrets. Perhaps it is a paradigm for Miss Marple herself, apparently a conventional spinster, while in fact, her brain is fomenting all sorts of – not exactly nefarious schemes – but schemes, nevertheless:

'Deliberately leaving her gloves on the table, she rose and crossed the floor to the cash desk, taking a route that passed close to Lady Sedgewick's table. Having paid her bill, she 'discovered' the absence of her gloves – and returned to get them, unfortunately dropping her handbag on her return route. It came open and spilled various oddments. A waitress rushed to assist her in picking them up, and Miss Marple was forced to show a great shakiness, and dropped coppers and keys a second time.

She did not get very far by these subterfuges, but they were not entirely in vain… and it was interesting that neither of the two objects of her curiosity spared as much as a glance for the dithery old lady who kept dropping things… As Miss Marple waited for the lift, she memorised such scraps as she had heard.'

And this, of course, leads to the final successful result of the case. But does she have no compunction about pursuing a course that will lead to the culprit's execution? Lord Peter Wimsey, Dorothy L. Sayers' *male* amateur detective whom we met in 'Gaudy Night', certainly does.
Miss Marple is made of sterner stuff.

At the end of the investigation in 'At Bertram's Hotel' the mother of the true murderer has untruthfully confessed to the crime before killing herself in order to protect her beautiful daughter, who is the real culprit.

'"Well," [Miss Marple asks the inspector], "are you going to let her get away with it?"', He pauses, then he 'brought down his fist with a crash on the table.
"No," he roared, "no, by god I'm not."
Miss Marple nodded her head slowly and gravely.
"May god have mercy on her soul," she said.'

Without Miss Marple's help in the investigation and this final demand of hers, the young girl would have gone free; she is a beautiful and wealthy young lady with all her world before her. Interestingly, she is even given an angelic aspect:

'She was wearing a straight shift dress of pale blue. Her fair hair fell down on each side of her face. She looked like one of the angels in an early primitive Italian painting.'

Cynically, one could wonder if the elderly spinster does not grieve too much at the thought of this beautiful 'angel's' death, and, as we have seen with other spinsters, even places herself in some way, in alliance with the divine: 'May god have mercy on her soul'. Is she only too pleased to dismiss this angel and substitute her elderly self for the agent of God? Is she like one of the Erinyes, simply a blind instrument of divine justice? But the Erinyes were also known, admittedly as a form of hopeful flattery, as 'the Eumenides', 'the kindly ones'. That is how I prefer to think of Miss Marple.

For one reason or another this spinster has exercised an enormous power over the modern imagination, and as I mentioned above, there have been numerous film and television representations of her: each actress putting her own interpretation on Marple's spinsterhood. It is not my intention to spend much time on film or television, but here I want to refer to three interpretations to show how differently a spinster can be viewed.

In 'Murder, She Said' we first meet Margaret Rutherford's interpretation. Perhaps the most striking feature of Rutherford's Marple is her robustness, both physical and mental; this spinster is no shrinking violet, but hurling china and armed with golf clubs and knitting needles resembling weapons, she is a larger than life figure for whom spinsterhood is neither here nor there; above all, she is big and jolly – almost 'a good chap'. She is not however, without her admirers: when she refuses the offer of marriage to a wealthy landowner, admittedly, because she's a good cook, she tells him that she has another man after her. "'Who would have you?'" the disappointed suitor asks. "'Well, you for one,'" is her robust reply. Nothing 'spinsterly' about this Marple. Like Athene she has her woolcraft *and* her weapons.

Geraldine McEwan's interpretation of Miss Marple in a later adaptation of the book, (the title for some odd reason changed from Christie's original title to 'The 9.15 from Paddington') couldn't be more different; she is bubbly and almost flirtatious, pretty too, and one feels that she could probably marry who, and when she wanted, but is devoid of such desires, or if she has them, contentedly conceals them. Certainly she has the accoutrements of spinsterhood; we see her at the start of the film instructing the maid *exactly* how to lay the fire and she is seldom without her knitting. There is a nice touch is when she sweetly compels the inspector to hold the skein of wool she is winding into a ball – a sort of paradigm for her skill: taking the leading part in rolling up the case. It also reflects on the etymological origin of the word 'spinster', one who spins. Miss Marple is at the centre of the web.

Joan Hickson falls between the two extremes of Galumphing jollity and alert prettiness. But she is an altogether more august figure. In the film of 'The Body in the Library', she, unlike the other two Marples, frequently evinces repression, is unwilling to reveal any of her discoveries to the uninitiated, and has distaste for Mrs Bantry's view of 'sleuthing' as fun. And the wise old retired officer of the MET speaks of her cognisance of evil. As we observe her intense concentration on her knitting, we see an introverted persona; rather like Lucy Snowe in 'Villette', she keeps in the background, observing but not observed; but like Lucy when she confronts Madame Bec, she can conquer her introversion when there is need for action, as for example, when she bursts into the police conference in an attempt to prevent another murder.

These varying interpretations can reflect the commonly held views of spinsterhood: the large, almost masculine devil-may-care image of Rutherford's Marple, perhaps glancing at a conception of the lesbian; the sweet-but-knowing image of McEwan, reminiscent of a favourite maiden aunt; and the forbidding image of Hickson, most like the goddess Nemesis as she ruthlessly seeks out justice and punishment. But nobody except Christie knows what really goes on in the mind of any of them, and that is the intriguing thing about spinsters: we don't know what lies behind the façade.

After Marple, there have emerged dozens – possibly hundreds – of spinster sleuths, writers having seen endless potential in them, but to my mind those that followed in the wake of Chrisie, the Agatha Raisins and so on, have been but pallid imitations. However, I do think the ecclesiastical novels of D. M. Greenfield produced an interesting new genre of sleuth. Like so many of our spinsters she occupies overlapping categories, and I was tempted to include her in my section on saintly spinsters, but I think she has a powerful enough presence as a sleuth, to be included here.

'The Theodora Braithwaite Ecclesiastical Novels' by D.M. Greenwood

Theodora Braithwaite:

Standing six foot one and handsome with it, Theodora comes from eight generations of Anglicans, all in holy orders, but this being the nineteen eighties, no such privilege is afforded to Theodora, so she has settled for being 'in deacon's orders'. However, even when offered the opportunity to become a priest some years later, she refuses: "'I honestly don't care too much," she said, "I'm perfectly content in deacon's orders. There's very little that I want to do and think needs doing that I can't do as a deacon.'" Theodora is not a saint or a nun or an anchoress, but she is aware of both holiness and sin; she does her best to reach out towards the former, and to detect the latter, not to punish – she is not one of the Erinyes – but she wants to reveal the truth, with compassion and understanding.

We can appreciate her modest ambition by comparing her attitude with that of one of the top cathedral clerics. Let's look first at the terrible Canon Charles Wheeler in 'Clerical Errors'. A local vicar called Gray has been found murdered, and Canon Wheeler is anxious to make out, quite wrongly, in fact, that the dead man had had 'a problem', and he is anxious to disassociate himself from the whole business:

'There was nothing Canon Wheeler liked better than issuing orders… Canon Wheeler's ambition was to have a bishopric before he was fifty.'

He has an interview with the dean and although he likes to patronise people, Wheeler refrains here because 'the man's cousin sat in the house of lords with the bishop'. It will be well to keep in with him; however, he enjoys trying to humiliate the timorous archdeacon who has arrived a little late:
'"How very kind of you to come so promptly,"' he said contemptuously turning to his bookshelves. The Archdeacon reminded himself that an archdeacon of ten years' standing was senior to a residential canon of three. Wheeler, who was junior to them both, had contrived to have the best set of rooms in the office, and who had successfully requested both men to wait on him, cleared his throat to announce that he was ready to start the discussion:

'"We are all men of the world so of course, we know, do we not, of problems of that sort; for young clergy bring with them all kinds of undesirable connections… ? I'm sure therefore, that it is there the police will be best advised to make their enquiries.'"

Theodora knows that this selfish man has not concerned himself with visiting the widow of the murdered man, so she gets on her ancient bike and cycles off to see what she can do to help. However, Theodora is more than a kindly person: she has a first class degree in Classical Mods from Oxford and wide experience of pastoral duties in Africa, as well as the UK, and she combines her ability to observe quietly with a faculty for seeing to the heart of a thing.

When it comes to investigating the case of the murdered man, Superintendent Frost is grateful for Theodora's insight and knowledge of the workings of the hierarchy of the Church of England, and together they manage to prove that it was the pompous and self righteous Canon Wheeler himself who had committed the murder; and when the Canon himself is murdered, Theodora is again able to throw light on *his* murderer, yet in the end, although she has said earlier "'I am afraid Canon Wheeler's vision of the church is as a vehicle for his own self-advancement,'" she now thought of Wheeler as one whom she needed 'to pity and forgive.' The goddess Athene had told the Athenian jury to forgive Orestes his matricide. With her great height and commanding presence, Theodora is not unlike her.

D. M Greenfield's novels are in some ways a savage indictment on the priorities of the top Anglican clergy; in each subsequent book we see ambition and vanity getting in the way of true Christian values, but always Theodora by skill and humility manages, not only in her role as a sleuth, but as a just person, to show that virtue can win out. However, she has her faults, there are aspects of her that align her to other spinsters, holy or not. When she visits the widow of the man disregarded by Canon Wheeler, she sees toys on the lawn:

'Theodora's heart sank. If there was one thing she did not care for it was children. She had forgotten Gray had some. How many, she wondered desperately, and how young?'

It is a strange thing that spinsters seem to be sharply divided on their feelings about children; either they foolishly idolise them like Miss Matty in Cranford who in her shopkeeping days always insisted on giving children extra weight in sweets, or those like Theodora, who actively dislike them. Is this dislike a sort of repressed envy? Would Theodora actually like to be less worthy, be married, have children of her own?

There is some evidence for this: when she returned from her pastoral work in Africa, she had looked round for a suitable post as a curate. We are told she had taken an immediate liking to the Reverend Geoffrey Brighouse, vicar of the parish of St Sylvester's Betterhouse, and she accepts a curacy in his parish because 'she could learn a lot from him. 'She works closely with him: 'they laboured towards their shared ends by visiting, by being flexible in the type of formal worship offered... youth groups, wives groups, children's groups were all organized and working.' But is this all Theodora wants from him? Even when involved in a case away from the parish, she feels a need of Geoffrey, the man.

'She badly wanted to ring Geoffrey... it was, as she acknowledged, pure self-indulgence. She wanted to hear his sane voice and exchange a few words, and it did not matter what about, he would understand her, and she him.'

Is she in love with him? Does she hope to marry him, for marriage it would have to be, an affair being out of the question for the chaste Theodora and her vicar? But in the sequel, 'Holy Terrors', we see things working out rather differently. Unwisely perhaps, Theodora asks the glamorous Oenone, sister of the man wrongly accused of murder to join her and Geoffrey for a meal. Immediately she senses a mutual attraction between the two:

'Theodora was conscious of a pang of jealousy. Dammit, who helps him run his parish, Oenone or me?' She tries to make sense of her feelings:

'She coveted Geoffrey not at all, admired his professionalism, respected and shared many of his attitudes, and wanted no more of his attention than a smooth-running working relationship required. She had plans for her immediate future which certainly didn't require Geoffrey's full-time notice. Yet here she was troubled by a stab of resentment.'

Theodora is six foot one and is perhaps not very sexually attractive. For all her reasoning she is jealous. In spite of all her good works she lacks that allure which her rival possesses. And for all his good works, that is what Geoffrey wants. In a nutshell, he wants sex. And that Theodora can't comprehend; surely their mutual parish work should be enough? He marries Oenone.

In 'Mortal Spoils' Theodora reflects on the marriage as she follows the eight o'clock communion service:

'Oenone, Theodora noticed, was not present. Geoffrey, she knew, had hoped she might be drawn into the worshipping life of the church. But Oenone had kept her teaching post at a smart independent girls school in Kensington. She came to Mass on Sundays. Midweek church going was alien to her.'

Oenone, clever and attractive, is ambitious for her new husband and is determined to get him made a bishop'. Already she had revamped the whole house: 'Geoffrey's bachelor establishment in which he had camped with neat naval simplicity now looked and felt like a gentleman's residence.' All this is anathema to Theodora who believed parish life should be 'prison visiting, hospital visiting, bereavement visiting, school visiting…'.

Surely it should have been she who would have been the perfect mate for the Reverend Geoffrey Brighouse? But she notices that Geoffrey 'looked well. His thick copper-coloured hair gleamed with health. Marriage, then, agreed with him, as it did with Oenone.'

Here we have a situation akin to that of Mary Jocelyn in 'The Rector's Daughter': 'Mary was the one person Mr Herbert had met who was truly akin to him. In their marriage therefore something would have been wanting that he had now [with Kathy] – high spirits, geniality, light-hearted courage, which neither dreads troubles before they came nor brooded over them when they were past…' Neither Theodora nor Mary are sexy women, they do not attract their chosen soul mates. Sadly, each is only fitted – in male eyes – to act as indeed, Theodora does: 'Quietly, unobtrusively, efficiently she performed her welcome duties. She made no fuss and no demands, she said her Daily Office.'

Again, we are reminded of the 'privileges' given the Eumenides: 'Do good, receive good, and be honoured as the good /Are honoured. Share our country, the beloved of god.'

Like so many other spinsters we have met, saintly or unsaintly, Theodora must look to the church as a crutch, to rely on it as a sort of surrogate husband; there will always be the Daily Mass and her Daily Office to recite. Perhaps her pastoral life will be enough. Anyway, that and her sleuthing will be her lot. But this does not prevent her being one of the best of the holy spinsters we have met, and indeed one of the best sleuths.

Not until quite recently do we come upon an entirely different genre of spinster sleuths, who would greatly dislike the appellation; this, of course, coincided with the rising status of women. These sleuths will not be eccentric old spinsters, but women who enjoy equal, or greater respect than that afforded to their male colleagues; no longer are they to be regarded as oddities, laughed at by police inspectors; they are police inspectors themselves.

We have seen them predominantly recently in the Scandi Noir films, although, admittedly, they are not all spinsters, and television is currently awash with commanding female police officers, who would, I'm sure, vigorously abjure the title of spinster, although they could not deny the dictionary appellation of 'unmarried woman'.

To my mind, the most notable British sleuthing spinster of recent years is Vera whose cases have become compulsive viewing – and of course, reading. With Vera we are no longer concerned with a funny old spinster, although in many ways, she is just that, but with an extraordinarily powerful detective inspector; and if there is any laughing to be done at another's expense, it is she who will do it, and it is usually men who are her victims. But although often irascible and sometimes unreasonable in her demands on her staff, she nevertheless, commands their respect and affection.

'The Vera Novels' by Ann Cleeves

Vera:

Readers and viewers alike will have become familiar with her through the books and subsequent television series, where she is so admirably portrayed by Brenda Blethyn.

We do not know the age of Vera, but we imagine her to be in her late fifties – although the actress herself is in her seventies. Vera is large and scruffy, usually bundled up in an assortment of odd clothes against the cold weather in Northumbria, which is her stamping ground. Unlike her predecessor spinster sleuths, Vera is no lady; she has been brought up in a hard school, losing her mother at eleven, and then dragged up in squalid surroundings by a disreputable widowed father, Hector.

'She thought how different her life would have been if her mother had lived. Because her mother would have loved her, wouldn't she? Unconditionally. She would have taken her into town and bought her the sort of clothes other girls wore, had tea ready on the table when she got in from school, taken an interest. All the things that Hector had never managed to do. It occurred to her that with a mother like that, she'd have grown into a different woman. Softer, weaker. Not so good at her job. All the same, she thought, maybe that would have been a price worth paying.'

Unmarried, she is just a little sensitive on the subject. An interviewee remarks, "I never married... I valued my independence. I never met a man who was worth giving that up for."

"No," Vera said, "nor me." *Though it might have been nice to be asked,* she thought. *Just once.*' However, Vera is not much given to introspection, she is too busy solving cases because that is what she has given her life to instead of marriage, and she is extremely good at it.

In 'The Darkest Evening' Vera comes across some distant posh relatives who have never taken any notice of her, but who now expect her to give them special consideration:
'"But you're family."
"But I'm not really, am I, pet, only when it suits you? And even if I were, I'll always be a cop first."'

'The Darkest Evening' shows the many sides of Vera. Battling home through the snow, ignoring advice as usual, and relying on her own judgement, she comes across a stranded car containing only a toddler. Like Theodora, Vera is uneasy around children but she gathers the child up and drives to the nearest house, 'Brockhurst', a place she remembers well since it was owned by her father's brother, who unlike Hector, was rich and successful.

Vera deposits the child on a woman called Juliet who has inherited the estate from her father. Then Vera makes herself comfortable eating a meal in the kitchen, she will not bother mingling with the rich middle class guests. When the body of the child's mother, a young girl called Lorna, is discovered by a local farmer, Vera swings into action. And she is soon identifying the suspects: members of the Stanhope family, relations of her own, the surprisingly posh housekeeper, two farming families, the uncommunicative Falstones, parents of the dead girl and the homely Heslop family.

Then another corpse is discovered, a middle aged woman, a friend of the dead woman, called Connie, and we see Vera's compassionate side: '"She didn't deserve to die like that."' But Holly, one of her team, suggests Vera's concern might have more personal roots: 'Was it because Connie was a spinster of a certain age, and she felt some affinity for the woman?' But Vera is more complex than Holly gives her credit for. She is psychologically acute, something that her second in command, Joe Ashworth, knows and appreciates. When Vera calls him in the middle of the night she barks: '"We've got a body. We need you here."' She purposely shifts the onus on herself by couching the request as an order because she knows that Joe's wife, Sal, resents these disruptions into her family life with Joe, and she would 'give him a hard time' if Vera had asked him if he minded giving up his time off. Now she will be angry with Vera instead.

Gradually Vera begins to piece things together, getting the feel of the atmospheres of the different places around the crime. She is intrigued by the cold feel of the Felstone household, and entertained by the jollity of the Heslops; she sees the tension in the Stanhope household between Juliet and her husband,

Mark, and is intrigued by the well-spoken housekeeper. Of course, there are many ramifications and red herrings, but I don't want to give the plot away, and am only concerned to show the different sides of Vera.

Towards the end she is trapped alone in the woods on a freezing winter night with the murderer wielding a gun, but she is immensely brave in spite of her fear:

'She didn't want her career, her life to end in this place… the barrel of the shotgun was icy against her skin. She could feel the imprint of it burning like a brand. But it shifted a little and that gave her confidence.' She tries talking him through it, and seems to have quietened him down, but so great is her indignation against this man who has robbed a young girl of her life, 'that she lost all sense of caution'. She cannot resist crying out against him. But she has gone too far: '…the man put his hands round her throat and started to squeeze… As Vera began to lose consciousness, she thought this was her fault… it was her pride again, making her think she was indestructible.'

However, at the last minute she is saved by Holly, who, although she feels some animus towards Vera whom she feels never praises her enough, wants 'to keep an eye on her'. She knows that for all her skill and ability Vera is a vulnerable ageing spinster. And what does Vera say to Holly now? "Thank you?" No. "Eh lass," she said, "I didn't train you so badly, after all."' Vera had never enjoyed feeling obliged to anyone.' But she has felt affinity with the two dead women, and it is that which has driven her on; she also feels compassion for the parents of the dead girl and their toddler grandson whom she had rescued from the car on that cold winter night:

'She might be able to help out from time to time. Not babysitting. She wouldn't go that far… but when he was older, she might be there for him. Money if he needed something the couple couldn't run to. Driving lessons. Advice... then she thought the last thing they'd need was Vera butting in.'

There is great kindness in Vera, and sensitivity towards others, although she is shy of showing it.

Vera may sometimes appear like a 'bag lady' as one of her suspects describes her, even appear 'like a gaga old woman', as she describes herself when preoccupied with a case, but she is sharp, intelligent and supremely good at her job.

Was she happy with her state of spinsterhood? She didn't care for children, being 'so cack-handed she couldn't contemplate changing a nappy'. And as a wife? She was probably too independent to marry, although '*it might have been nice to be asked,* she thought. *Just once.*'

But she is a modern woman; she will not have to endure the opprobrium suffered by her forerunners; compared to them she is very lucky. Things have moved forward.

These sleuthing spinsters are strong women, a species of Erinyes in their search of justice, Amazons even, in their willingness to fight for a rewarding life that has no need of men, but they are also like the re-named harpies, the Eumenides, they are the true 'kindly ones'.

CHAPTER FIFTEEN

SINISTER AND SPECTRAL SPINSTERS

The weird sisters, hand in hand,
Posters of sea and land,
Thus do go about, about;
Thrice to thine, and thrice to mine
And thrice again to make up nine…

William Shakespeare, 'Macbeth'

Witches always seem to be spinsters; is this a patriarchal society's way of dealing with gynophobia, a fear of women who do not fit its mould? Women fall into categories: marriageable maidens and wives are okay, but those who are neither, i.e. do not fall under male control must be castigated and regarded as bad and ugly, and dismissed as something unnatural. In 'Macbeth' Macduff expresses this sentiment: 'The earth hath bubbles as the water has, /And these are of them.'

I mentioned Hecate only briefly among the goddesses of the Greek World. Here I want to describe her more fully.

Hecate is an Underworld goddess associated with sorcery and black magic. However, she was not always so. Hesiod, writing in the eighth century BCE tells us that Zeus honoured her above the other deities, and praised her as a goddess with wide powers who could bring blessings, wealth and success to both men and women. She even helped Demeter find her daughter Persephone, and became her attendant – the dreaded job of subservient companion that we shall meet later, perhaps? There is no mention of anything sinister. However, as with other ageing Classical spinsters, her good nature undergoes a sea-change. By the fifth century BC she has become menacing, associated with magic, witchcraft and creatures of the night, where she appeared accompanied by a pack of barking hell-hounds. Euripides has her invoked by Medea to aid her in her witchcraft, and she has a long-lived spinsterhood: in Macbeth she appears to the three witches: 'I, the mistress of your charms, / The close contriver of all harms', and aids them in bringing Macbeth to destruction.

We can number her too, amongst our facially disfigured spinsters. She is sculpted on the altar of Zeus at Pergamum, where she and her dog are attacking a snake-tailed giant, she has a single body, with three pairs of arms and three heads. Longevity does the spinster no favours.

The Larva:

We will move forward in time and visit Eustace Cherrington again, this time in Venice, and meet a relatively modern spectral spinster. As he returns to Lady Nelly's palazzo through the garden, he catches sight of a woman; at first he is puzzled as to who she can be:

'Stooping down, perhaps in search of something she had dropped, a woman whose dark clothes and self-effacing aspect made him think at once of Lady Nelly's maid, Elvira. This then, was the dryad of the garden, this prosaic middle-aged woman... He coughed so as not to startle her, and evidently she heard him, for though she did not turn round, she stood up, raising her hands in a wide gesture that might have been a blessing or a curse.'

He loses sight of her:

'... yet when he went out into the gallery, closing the door behind him, she was there after all, standing motionless with her back to him. "Can you tell me..?" he began, but she did not turn round, she merely moved away from him, like a taciturn guide who will not or cannot answer questions.'

But when he opens the gallery door he sees the maid Elvira on her hands and knees. 'How quickly she has got to work,' he thought...' Then realising that she can't be the woman he saw, he asks her about her identity:

'"I saw a lady in black and she brought me up here"... Elvira's whole being seemed to contract in terror, "*Allora, signore, ha visto la larva*", she gasped... And with two piercing screams she rushed from the room.'

Eustace tries to puzzle out the meaning of the word 'larva'. It is, he finally remembers, the Italian word for 'ghost'.

What is the significance of this sinister spinster – because one feels instinctively that she is a spinster? Eustace first thought the larva was a dryad, but she was something more sinister. He had made the same mistake as Dick Staverley who had initially thought Hilda a dryad, only to discover that she was one of the harpies.

With her ghostly figure and 'hands raised as blessing or curse' she is like Cassandra because she has the gift of prophecy, and like her, the larva is not understood. Eustace does not realise what she is foretelling, but from Elvira's reaction we can see that she is prophesising Eustace's own death.

On the other hand, is the larva there at all? Eustace is worried about Hilda, and having always been of an imaginative turn of mind, do his fears embody themselves in this figure which he must have heard of during his stay in Venice? Other apparently spectral spinsters can, I shall argue, be seen as figments of a troubled spinsterly imagination, (and surely Eustace is a kind of male spinster?)

'Rebecca', by Daphne du Maurier

Mrs Danvers:

Mrs Danvers? Doesn't the title exclude her from spinsterhood? I think not. I have been through the book with a toothcomb and nowhere is there any mention of a marriage, furthermore, the soubriquet was often bestowed on the housekeeper as a courtesy title; and – as a clincher – we are told that she had had spent her life at Manderley and had charge of Rebecca as a child and was called Danny by her. And besides, she has no interest in men or indeed, in anyone other than her mistress. So intense is her love that she could have been included amongst my sapphic spinsters.

Most readers will have an idea of the story, so I will only refer to the plot when it references Mrs Danvers. I start by describing the sinister nature of the housekeeper when we first meet her. On arrival at 'Manderley' Maxim de Winter's new wife (who relates the narrative) sees the row of servants lined up to welcome them home, she tells us:

'Someone advanced from the sea of faces, someone tall and gaunt, dressed in deep black, whose prominent cheekbones and great hollow eyes gave her a skull's face, parchment-white, set on a skeleton's frame... when she took my hand, hers was limp and heavy, deathly cold, and it lay in mine like a lifeless thing... I was aware of a sensation of discomfort and shame.'

Although Mrs Danvers always 'kept very much to herself', the writer is aware of her presence, and finds she has a way of appearing when least expected.

I can't keep calling her 'the writer', but it is difficult to know how to refer to the anonymous first-person, I had to resort to calling 'the writer' of 'Whereabouts' La Signora, so here again

I must settle for something. The Second Mrs de Winter is a bit of a mouthful, so I'll simply call her SMDW.

She has been intrigued by the East Wing which she has never been invited to see, and she is astounded to find it had been Rebecca's room, and all her things are still laid out, as if she was about to return. She investigates it all with a horrified fascination. She is not alone for long.

'Then I heard a step behind me, and turning round I saw Mrs Danvers. I shall never forget the expression on her face. Triumphant, gloating, excited in a strange unhealthy way. I felt very frightened… I wanted to run away, but I could not, I went on watching her eyes.

"Now you are here, let me show you everything," she said, her voice ingratiating and sweet as honey, horrible, false. "I know you want to see it all, you've wanted to for a long time, and you were too shy to ask. It's a lovely room, isn't it? The loveliest room you have ever seen."'

Slowly, ever so slowly, she takes her mistress round the room, showing her all Rebecca's beautiful things and encouraging her to touch them:

'"You've seen her brushes, haven't you?" she said, taking me to the dressing table, "there they are, just as she used them, unwashed and untouched... I used to brush her hair for her every evening. 'Come on, Danny, hair drill,' she would say, and I'd stand behind her by the stool here and brush away for twenty minutes at a time… I keep her furs in here… feel that sable wrap… She looked beautiful in this velvet. Put it against your face. It's soft, isn't it? You can feel it, can't you? The scent is still fresh, isn't it?.. You could almost imagine she had only just taken it off… these are her underclothes in this drawer… she was wearing slacks of course and a shirt when she died. They were torn from her body in the water though."

Her fingers tightened on my arm. She bent down to me, her skull's face close, her dark eyes searching mine. "The rocks had battered her to bits, you know," she whispered, "her beautiful face unrecognisable and both arms gone."'

How wonderfully Du Maurier creates this terrifyingly oppressive atmosphere. There is emphasis on touch and feel: the soft velvet, the unwashed hairbrushes, the softness of the fur, the sable and the velvet. The words: 'I *feel* (my italics) her everywhere… show Danvers' intense sensual love of Rebecca.

Max's sister Beatrice has already remarked: '"Mrs Danvers simply adored Rebecca."' She more than adored, she lusted after her, her hair, her face, her clothes, her scent; and what makes her even more frightening, is the contrast between the beauty of the living woman and the horror of her broken corpse. And the most sinister aspect of all is the fact that she is preserving the dead woman, that she has virtually mummified her, and is now luring the second Mrs de Winter into the tomb of the first. And she almost succeeds.

Mrs Danvers has tricked her into wearing the same dress that Rebecca had worn for the annual fancy dress ball. Later she finds Mrs Danvers in Rebecca's room:

'"You've done what you wanted to, haven't you?" I said, "you meant this to happen, didn't you? Are you pleased now? Are you happy?"
"Why did you ever come here?" she said. "Nobody wanted you at Manderley."
"You made me wear that dress last night," I said. "I should never have thought of it but for you. You wanted to hurt Mr de Winter, you wanted to make him suffer…"

"What do I care about his sufferings… how do you think I've liked it, watching you sit in her place, walk in her footsteps, touch the things that were hers…? You'll never get the better of her. She's mistress here, even if she's dead. She's the real Mrs de winter, not you… why don't you go… ?" She pushed me towards the open window. I could see the terrace below me, grey and indistinct in the white wall of fog. "Look down there," she said. "It's easy, isn't it? Why don't you jump? It wouldn't hurt, not to break your neck... it's a quick kind way. It's not like drowning. Why don't you try it… go, on," whispered, Mrs Danvers, "go on, don't be afraid."'

And she would have jumped, had not the siren sounding a shipwreck intervened. And once again Mrs Danvers retreats into her role of efficient housekeeper:

'"When you see Mr de Winter, Madam, will you tell him it will be quite alright if he wants to bring the men back from the ship? There will be a hot meal ready for them at any time."'

The plot unravels: Maxim confesses to his wife that he had hated Rebecca who was a thoroughly bad lot, and when she told him that she was expecting another man's child who would inherit his beloved Manderley, he killed her, and made it look like suicide, shooting her and putting her body in her boat, drilling holes in it, so it would sink and she would be lost at sea. But when the tampered boat and a body are washed up, it seems as if his crime will be discovered; but then the fact that she was dying of cancer is discovered, so the verdict of suicide given. He is a free man; but all will not be well for either Maxim or his wife; Mrs Danvers plays her last card, setting fire to Manderley and disappearing into the night.

Mrs Danvers dressed in black and intent on her malevolent purpose is a second Hecate. Perhaps when she was a young woman bringing up Rebecca, she was like the goddess, a well-meaning being, but the double influence of Rebecca's evil nature and her subsequent terrible death have turned this woman into a sorceress, a creature of the night, a dealer in death. Surely she is the most sinister of sinister spinsters.

207

It is such a thundering good story; it has all the components of a first class plot: a Cinderella heroine, an evil housekeeper, a glamorous husband, a beautiful dead wife, murder, deception and revenge. It has the lot, but only now that I have come to write about spinsters, do I see it is possible to give it an altogether different reading.

Suppose that Mrs Danvers was just an ordinary efficient housekeeper, loyal to the de Winter family, and that all her sinister behaviour is a figment of the writer's imagination? After all, Maxim sees nothing sinister in his housekeeper. When his wife breaks a precious ornament and hides the pieces and confesses that she has done so from fear of Mrs Danvers, Maxim says to his wife: "'She's not God Almighty, is she. I can't understand you. What do you mean by saying you are afraid of her?'" She stammers:

"'I did not mean afraid exactly. I don't see much of her... it's not that. I can't really explain.'"

Maxim replies that she should have simply said, "'Here, Mrs Danvers, get this mended. She'd understand that.'" She must treat Mrs Danvers, as she expects to be treated: mistress to servant.

SMDW is young, gauche and easily suggestible; she has been lifted out of her sphere and is totally overwhelmed by marriage, the splendour of her husband's house, and the legendary beauty and power exercised by her husband's first wife; she feels lonely and totally ineptitude; and from the moment of Mrs Danvers' discovery of the smashed ornament, her fears begin to assume enormous proportions and she sees the housekeeper representing a constant reproof of her own inepititude, and a reminder of her predecessor's resounding success. Then she starts to imagine Rebecca wielding an overpowering presence, exhibiting her superlative success in running Manderley, exerting the power of her beauty over

Maxim, and indeed, over everyone she met. As her own self-confidence seeps away she begins to torment herself by using the figure of Mrs Danvers to evoke the spectre of Rebecca in order to confirm her own inadequacy. An act of masochism, in fact.

Did those sessions in Rebecca's bedroom actually happen? Didn't SMDW simply come across her predecessor's bedroom, and look on it in bewilderment and envy. Perhaps there was no Mrs Danvers' gloating enumeration of Rebecca's possessions, only her own fancied image of her. And when she tells us of the second 'interview' in the bedroom, and reports Mrs Danver's urging her to death, isn't that just an expression of her own despairing thoughts? Did Rebecca's luxurious apartments stocked with all those accoutrements actually exist? After all, SMDW tells us that only Mrs Danvers comes there and preserves the objects. Surely they would have been disposed of on Rebecca's death? Furthermore, the two scenes have no witnesses, we only know what SMDW tells us.

Yes, there is the fateful copying by SMDW of the dress worn by Rebecca for the annual fancy dress ball, but does Mrs Danvers urge her mistress to adopt it to spite Maxim, or did she simply want to show the inferior figure her new mistress would cut in it ? Did she, in fact, suggest it at all, or was it simply SMDW's own unlucky idea? Again, there are no witnesses to the conversation.

Finally, was it actually Mrs Danvers who set fire to Manderley? Nowhere does the author tells us that she did; and after all, she was seen leaving the house before the fire; and if she had, why do we not hear of her being convicted of arson? Could the house simply have caught fire because the efficient housekeeper was no longer there to keep an eye on things while Maxim and his wife were away?

Yes, Mrs Danvers had adored Rebecca, and naturally she looked coldly on her replacement, contrasting her unfavourably with her old mistress, but nobody else apart from SMDW seems to find her sinister. And when SMDW finds that Maxim does love and need her, she regains her self-confidence and she views Mrs Danvers, the link with Rebecca, as a diminished creature; she doesn't need her any more; she can dismiss this personification of her ineptitude. She summons her through the footman. Mrs Danvers remonstrates: "'If Mrs de Winter wanted anything changed, she would ring me personally on the house telephone.'" But SMDW has grown in confidence and she can treat her as her husband had instructed, simply as a servant, dismissing this embodiment of her fear of Rebecca:

"'I'm afraid it doesn't concern me much what Mrs de Winter used to do... I am Mrs de Winter now, you know." She can't frighten me, any more, I thought.'

I think Rebecca is the story of two spinsters: a sad elderly housekeeper bereft of the woman she had loved, and SMDW herself. What? But she's married, continues living long subsequent years with her husband. But was the marriage ever consummated? Certainly there are no children? And didn't Maxim marry her for her purity and virginity, wanting to negate everything that Rebecca's rampant sexuality had represented to him? Could he have preferred to leave her in a state of virginity? Possibly SMDW herself was so unsophisticated that she did not know enough about sex to expect it from her husband; she would expect him to be the judge of such things.

So I think it is possible to see 'Rebecca' as the story of a gauche young woman who in her early married life is suffering from an inferiority complex – perhaps because of the lack of sexual fulfilment, but also because she does not have the personality or experience to deal with an older husband, a large estate, and its many servants; so instead, she embodies her fears and sense of insecurity into the figure of the housekeeper whose black attire and cold manner regularly suggest itself to her, and out of Mrs Danvers she allows to emerge the spectre of Rebecca, the embodiment of all she is not.

And to return to the burning of Manderley, did she herself somehow arrange it, wanting to put an end to all the failure it had represented to her, and take her husband to a new ambience where she could perhaps discard her spinsterhood, not realising that Maxim was too deeply rooted in the past, and she herself too spinsterly?

All this is a bit fanciful maybe, but if we compare SMDW with the governess in Henry James' 'The Turn of the Screw' we can see that lonely spinsters can conjure up spectres out of fear and feelings of inadequacy.

'The Turn of the Screw' by Henry James

The Young Governess:

Here the young protagonist – again, we do not know her name, an indication perhaps, in both cases of their self-effacing natures – is given complete charge of two young children, Miles and Flora; she is alone with them in a large remote country house with only a servant or two and a gullible and ignorant housekeeper, Mrs Grose, for company. She has been appointed by a handsome and wealthy young man who is the children's guardian, but insists on having nothing further to do with them. The young girl had been scared by the prospect, and taken time in deciding to accept the job, but has been finally persuaded by the handsome appearance of the children's guardian. Initially it is an apparent success. She adores the two children who are unbelievably angelic in looks and behaviour and she has a happy time with them:

'… the attraction of my small charges was a constant joy… it was all the romance of the nursery and poetry of the schoolroom'.

But she is alone – we will meet the lonely figure of the governess again later – she has no friends, and her only outings are attending church on Sundays with the children. She has no experience of the male sex apart from her interview with her employer.

One day, she sees a figure of a man staring at her, whom Mrs Grose (who does not see the figure) suggests from her description, bears a resemblance to her master's old valet, Peter Quint; she sees him more and more often, and becomes increasingly scared, making Mrs Grose a sharer in her fears; apparently the boy Miles had been very close to this man.

Then she begins to see the figure of a woman whom Mrs Grose, as in the case of Quint, does not actually see, but suggests is Flora's previous governess, Miss Jessel. However, both Peter Quint and Miss Jessel are dead. The figures can only be ghostly apparitions.

Apparently the two had enjoyed some sort of unspecified unhealthy relationship with each other; furthermore, Miles had spent a lot of time alone with Quint, as had Flora with Miss Jessel; and as time goes on, the governess begins to sense that Quint is appearing to the boy, Miles, and Miss Jessel to the girl, Flora, with, she believes, the intention of gaining some sort of terrible evil possession over them. She determines to wrest the children away from this evil pair who seem already to have some indefinable power over them. She constantly watches the children, secretly follows them, endlessly questions them, and increasingly puts pressure on them to tell her what is happening. All in vain. The pressure reduces Flora to a fatal illness and Miles, after prolonged interrogation, dies in the governess' arms.

In the introduction to the novel Kenneth B. Murdoch refers to the essay by the American critic, Edmund Wilson: 'The Ambiguity of Henry James', who 'argued that there are no ghosts in 'The Turn of the Screw', and that the horrifying apparitions seen by the governess and by her alone, are hallucinations in the tormented mind of a sexually repressed woman. She, not the supposed spirits of Miss Jessel and Peter Quint, is the real source of the children's haunted state, and little Miles' fear of her brings about the catastrophe.' He adds: 'The story can be read with this interpretation, and a few of James' own comments seem to support it.'

If we accept this reading, we can see the lonely and sexually repressed governess as a figure akin to the heroine of 'Rebecca'; each woman alone in a large remote country house with no friends to whom to confide her fears, begins to create ghostly figures who embody her own anxieties; both women fear their ghostly predecessors. SMDW uses the mediating spectral figure of Mrs Danvers to conjure up the spectre of Rebecca, while the governess in 'The Turn of the Screw' tries to use *her* housekeeper, Mrs Grose, as a mediating figure for identifying *her* fears as symbolised by Peter Quint and Miss Jessel.

Henry James' writing is always ambiguous, and there is no apparent reason why the governess should have sexual hang-ups; we only know she was attracted to her distant male employer, and that she is young and inexperienced, so perhaps the intimidating figure of Quint *could* represent a frightened attraction to male sexuality, while Miss Jessel's relationship with him could represent a fearful desire for sexual intercourse, something which in her lonely state, the governess may well have dwelt on.

However, more telling, I think, is that like SMDW, the governess suffers from a consciousness of her own inadequacy. Each woman feels crushed beneath the baneful influence of their predecessors whom they imagine to have been successful in a way they cannot emulate. Just as the former imagined Manderley unspeakably beautiful and perfect under the sway of Rebecca, the governess sees Miles and Flora's angelic appearance and behaviour emanating from the influence of Jessel and Quint. And each knows, or thinks she knows, that she cannot compete, and so each tormented herself with the creation of spectral figures.

Whether we accept this reading or not, each novel critiques the horrible plight of the lonely spinster whose only refuge lies in masochistic delusion or even madness. It is as if each has been visited by Ate, the goddess of delusion. Unlike the Bacchae who have expressed their sexual desire in their wild ecstatic dancing, these ladies must remain in a state of tight self-control. However, like the Bacchae they too suffered from the consequences of delusion. In Euripides' play Agape believes she has killed a young animal and proudly exhibits his head, only to be later faced with the horrible truth: she has killed her own son. Horrors occur when the power of Dionysus is ignored.

'Great Expectations' by Charles Dickens

Miss Havisham:

If we return to 'Great Expectations' we can view Miss Havisham as another spectral presence, although of a different sort.

Unlike the previous spectres she is a living person, but we cannot really believe in a woman spending her life sitting in a decaying wedding dress amidst a wedding feast covered in cobwebs. How could she have managed her business affairs, run a household, entertained visitors, given them meals? How did she wash, did she never have clean underwear, how did she manage a small child?

Although purportedly a creature of flesh and blood, Dickens invites us to view her as a sepulchral figure, one who lives in 'a darkened unhealthy house in which her life was hidden from the sun'. Another Hecate. And the hero, Pip describes her in spectral terms: 'an awful figure with its *ghostly* reflection thrown by the fire on the ceiling'. Later he sees her making her way along a passageway 'in a *ghostly* manner, making a low cry. She carried a bare candle in her hand and was *a most unearthly object* by its light.' Even when she is dying she is spectral:

'... though every vestige of her dress was burnt... she still had something of her old ghastly bridal appearance; for they had covered her to the throat with white cotton wool, and as she lay with a white sheet loosely overlying that, *the phantom air* of something she had been and was changed, was still upon her (my italics).'

As Angus Calder comments in the introduction to the 1965 Penguin edition: '... the lurid decay of her surroundings so described, is a mirror of Miss Havisham's diseased mind'. She has created a spectre of herself to represent the bitterness of her state of spinsterhood. She is a form of Hecate.

But Pip is not the only one to see her in ghostly form. The convict Magwitch tells Pip's friend, Herbert more details of the failed wedding; apparently Miss Havisham's ne'er do well half-brother, Arthur had colluded with Compeyson, the expected bridegroom, to cheat her of money and marriage, but time has brought its revenge: finally, he lies dying in a state of delirium tremens. Magwitch tells Herbert of his demise:

'He came a-tearing downstairs into Compeyson's parlour late at night, in only a flannel gown, with his hair all in a sweat...

"She really is upstairs alonger me now, and I can't get rid of her. She's all in white wi' flowers in her hair, and she's awful mad, and she's got a shroud hanging over her arm, and she says she'll put it on me at five in the morning... Why look at her... She's a-shaking the shroud at me... here she is. She's got the shroud again. She's unfolding it... she's lifting me up..." Then he lifted himself up hard and was dead.'"

So she is seen as a spectral form both by Pip and by Arthur. We too, are invited to see her not as a woman of flesh and blood, but as a spectre of jilted spinsterhood in its darkest form.

Ate was the daughter of Eris and personified Delusion, able to confuse and cloud men's minds. Zeus banished her from Olympus and sent her to live among mortals. He also sent his daughters The Litanies in her wake to make amends. Unfortunately they seem to have got lost when they followed Miss Havisham to her death.

CHAPTER SIXTEEN

SUPERIOR SPINSTERS

In this strand I am looking at spinsters in the context of three powerful dynasties. One might compare them to the spinster Greek goddesses who belonged to the powerful dynasty of the Olympians.

In each case wealth and status are – initially at least – taken for granted. Their misfortunes are bound up with the failing of the dynasties to which they belong, and they all suffer. Ultimately, however, each in her different way, achieves if not a triumphant spinstership in old age, one that she can sustain in comfort.

'The Leopard' by Giuseppe Tomasi di Lampedusa

Concetta, Carolina and Caterina:

It is Sicily in 1860, the time of the Unification of Italy and the last glory days of the dissolute aristocracy are fading away. We first meet the princesses Concetta, Carolina and Caterina as they attend the daily Recital of the Rosary in one of the many drawing rooms of the palace of the Prince of Salina, 'Donnafugata':

'For half an hour the steady voice of the Prince had recalled the Sorrowful and Joyful Mysteries; for half an hour other voices had interwoven a lilting hymn from which would chime some unlikely word: love, virginity and death.'

The girls who 'have been sent home for safety's sake from their convent and regretting the canopied dormitories and collective cosiness of the Holy Redeemer', are steeped in the extreme Catholicism of nineteenth century Sicily. However, Concetta is in love with her cousin Tancredi, and has hopes of marrying him, but such hopes are summarily dismissed by her father and by Tancredi himself, and together they arrange his marriage with the beautiful, rich and plebeian Angelica. Although he knows she is in love with Tancredi, the Prince has few compunctions about disappointing her. He sees that times are changing, new men are to the fore, and money is of the essence if the aristocracy is to survive. But Concetta is heartbroken; she is a haughty girl, immensely proud of her aristocratic heritage and she looks coldly on the idea of an alternative suitor.

We see the girls from time to time, attending Masses, going to balls, and enjoying the luxuries afforded by last gasp of a dying civilisation, quite unaware that the world in which they have been brought up is disappearing. Life passes them by, and all three remain unmarried. As the narrative is mainly concerned with the Prince, we see little of the girls until the final chapter of the book.

It is 1910 and the girls, now elderly spinsters have devoted themselves to the religion that they were steeped in in their youth: 'Anyone paying a visit to the old Salina ladies would be apt to find at least one priest's hat on the hall chairs.' It is what gives meaning to their lives; in fact, it is the only thing they have, apart from clinging to the remnants of their faded grandeur:

'When they inherited the palace after the death of their father, they at once thought of setting up their own oratory, they chose an out-of-the-way drawing room... they obliterated an unsuitable mythological fresco from the ceiling; decked up an altar.'

Carolina and Caterina have become obsessed with obtaining relics which they buy from an unscrupulous woman called Donna Rosa; the relics are, of course, quite bogus. They also have a picture hanging over the altar which they believe portrays the Virgin Mary, but actually shows a provocatively nubile young girl.

They are to receive a nasty shock when, in accordance with papal instructions, the Cardinal Archbishop has begun to undertake an inspection of the private chapels of his archdiocese to reassure himself about the merits of those allowed to hold services there… and the authenticity of the relics held there:

'The three Salina sisters deeply offended by the inspection of their chapel, but childish, and above all feminine in thought of receiving into their home a Prince of the Church, at being able to show him the grandeur of the Salina which, in good faith they thought still intact.'

But the visit is to be a sad disappointment; the archbishop has not put on his regalia and takes but a cursory glance at the chapel. He leaves behind his secretary to examine the relics, but he authenticates only five from the hundreds they had amassed, and substitutes the unsuitable picture hanging above the altar with a more conventional one. Caterna now in a wheelchair, has to be given smelling salts, and Carolina comments in disgust, '"This pope must be a Turk."'

Concetta's attitude is rather different. She alone among her sisters has realised that that the family prestige and fortune had declined, but in the Church and their relations with it, they had managed to maintain something of their former pre-eminence; now that too, had gone. She thinks too, of the times throughout her life she has stared at the portrait of her father, hating him for preventing her marriage with Tancredi. She has hated Tancredi too, for preferring the plebeian Angelica to her aristocratic self. Her bedroom was 'an inferno of mummified memories, pictures of dead friends, her own unused trousseau stored in cases where the ubiquitous Palermo damp had caused the contents to grow yellow and decayed'; she has even kept the embalmed body of the family dog to remind her of her long-gone happy childhood. Finally, she realises that all is meaningless:

'She rang the bell for her maid: "Anetta", she said, "this dog has really become too moth-eaten and dusty. Take it out, throw it away."' It is flung from a window, 'its dead legs seeming to dance in the air... then all found peace in a little heap of livid dust.'

This can be read as an analogy for the end of a dynasty and for the lives of the spinsters themselves. But not entirely. They still have enough money, they have each other, and they still have the crutch of their religion, even though the crutch is not as sturdy as it once was, but still, the Catholic church provides a more gilded crutch than the Anglican.

How strongly the threads of religion we first met in the Ancient World, persist. Like so many other spinsters, these sisters could have appeared under another category, that of Sacred and Saintly. Spinsters have an amazing lability to slide from one strand to another and become entangled together.

'Buddenbrooks' by Thomas Mann

'Buddenbrooks' covers the same sort of time span as 'The Leopard', the late nineteenth century and the early years of the twentieth, and it too, concerns the end of a dynasty, and here again, most of the spinsters show an amazing resilience and ability to survive. A leitmotif of the book is the contrast between marriage and spinsterhood, and it throws a whole new light on the lot of spinsters in the late nineteenth century, but before considering the different spinsters in Buddenbrooks, I need to give a very brief sketch of the narrative.

We first meet the family at the height of their success and prosperity, one of the most enviable families in the town. The patriarch Johann is still alive, but the family business is run by his son also called Johann who has three children: Tom who will succeed to the business, honest, capable and eminently fitted to carrying on the family tradition; Christian is clever, but neurotic; while pretty Antonie, known as Toni, is acutely conscious of the family's pre-eminence. (She could be seen as the German equivalent of Concetta). Later, a second daughter, Clara, is born, pallid and pious; there is also the orphaned child of a poor relative, called Clothilde who is brought up with the siblings.

When she has achieved adulthood, Toni's father, more or less forces her into a disastrous marriage with a man whom she dislikes called Herr Brunlich, because he appears, to all intents and purposes, to be a wealthy and successful businessman.

After the death of his father Johann, Tom takes over the business with great capability, but his brother Christian lacks the will or application to carry out any undertaking, and drifts from city to city failing at one job after another. One by one the older generation die off and the focus centres on the three Buddenbrook 'children': Toni's marriage fails as her husband turns out to be a swindler who has only married her for her dowry; she divorces him and returns home, but becoming bored in the family home, she marries again, this time to a man from Munich called Herr Permaneder; this marriage is not a success either; she hates living in Munich and despises the easy-going ways of her indolent husband. She divorces for the second time, a disgrace on which she puts the best face she can.

After her father's death, her sister, the pious Clara marries an apparently equally pious person, Pastor Tibutius, while Tom surprises everyone by marrying an old school friend of Toni's, Gerda from Amsterdam, beautiful, sensitive and a brilliant violinist, a great contrast to the family who have no artistic interests.

The town sees many ups and downs, but the business continues to do reasonably well and Tom becomes a senator. It is the high point of his success, after which a decline in his business affairs sets in; his marriage too, proves cold and unsatisfactory: Gerda prefers the company of Second Lieutenant Rene Maria von Throta who is billeted in the town, and with whom she can share her love of music. She has however, given her husband a son, Hanno, but he is a sickly weakling of a child, and it is obvious he is never going to be capable of carrying on the family business.

Clara who has always been sickly dies, and the 'pious' husband scoops up her share of the Buddenbrook inheritance. By her first marriage Toni has a daughter, Erica whom she now encourages to marry an unattractive insurance broker, Herr Hugo Weinschenk; this marriage, like her own, is disastrous as the husband is accused of malpractice, and he is imprisoned. Christian returns home, enfeebled, useless and dissolute, and eventually marries a woman little better than a prostitute, who manages to get him consigned to an asylum. Tom, worn out with his business and civic duties and increasingly disillusioned with his life, finally dies of a stroke.

After this very sketchy outline of a brilliant narrative I want to consider the spinsters who punctuate it and who perform something of the role of a Greek chorus, commenting on the misfortunes of the family, financial and marital.

Friederike, Henriette and Pfiffi:

Friederike and Henriette who were too tall and thin, and Pfiffi who was eighteen, and too short and fat.

These are three ugly, malign sisters, impoverished spinster cousins of the family. All through the book we see them thriving on malice and envy. After their cousin Antonie (Toni) is divorced, they have a field day:

'"Oh, heavens," said Pfiffi the youngest who was little and plump, with a droll way of shaking herself at every word. A drop of water always came in the corner of her mouth when she spoke. "Has the decree been pronounced? Are you exactly as you were before?"
"On the contrary," said Henriette who like her elder sister, was extremely tall and withered-looking. "You are much worse off than if you had never married at all."
"Yes," Frederike chimed in, "then it is ever so much better never to have married at all."'

Over the years they continue their unpleasant visits: 'They made jokes at the expense of poor innocent Clothilde. They made fun of Clara's austerity.' They have a go at Toni's daughter whom they found 'alarmingly backward in her growth. And Pfiffi in a series of little shakes drew attention to the child's shocking resemblance to the deceiver Grunlich.'

When their father dies 'the feeling was not entirely wanting that their rich relations were somehow to blame for this misfortune too.' After the birth of Tom Buddenbrooks's son, the latest heir to the family, they are seen 'shaking their heads pessimistically'; they 'declared that the child would be halt and tongue-tied to the end of his days.' They are pretty much right as the child is always unhappy and lost.

Like harpies, these are unhappy, spiteful and envious spinsters, anxious to spoil and hurt. Would they have been nicer if they had married? But if one had married how much nastier the others would have been! And if two had married, well, the remaining one would have been unspeakably nasty! They are true descendants of the malicious figures we met in the Ancient World – albeit, less successful. Like the Medusa they seek to petrify; they cannot turn their human victims to stone, but they can endeavour to petrify their hopes and aspirations.

Fraulein Weichbrodt:

Fraulein Weichbrodt was humpbacked. So humpbacked that she was not much higher than a table. She was forty-one years old, but as she had never put her faith in outward seeming, she dressed like an old lady of sixty or seventy.

In spite of her appearance she manages to run a successful educational establishment not unlike Madame Beck's in 'Villette': 'Sesemi' [the name she calls herself by] took care to have only the daughters of irreproachably refined families in her house.' She is a formidable character:

'She had shrewd, sharp brown eyes, a slightly hooked nose, and thin lips which she could compress with extraordinary firmness. In her whole insignificant figure, therein dwelt a force which was, to be sure, somewhat comic, yet exacted respect.'

Toni is sent to board with her, and this strange humpbacked lady becomes a friend of the family. We see her presence over the years, as the lives of the family change.

After her first ugly divorce Antonie goes to visit Sesemi at her old school, which, like the Buddenbrook family itself, is now falling out of fashion. Sesemi, however, has remained a staunch friend:

'She was too good and tactful even to mention the subject… she always raised herself on tiptoe to kiss Toni on the forehead with a little exploding noise.'

Later on, Antonie sends her own daughter to board with Sesemi. And every year, in spite of her straightened means, Sesemi gives the Buddenbrook family a special Christmas party. But the years pass sadly for the Buddenbrook family as the business fails, and the male heads of the family die, one by one, but it is Sesemi who is given the last words of the book.

The remaining female relations gather to say farewell to Tom's widow, Gerda, whose teenage son, the last hope of the family, has just died. Antonie, now divorced for the second time and horribly disillusioned with life, cries:

"'Tom, Father, Grandfather and all the rest, where are they? We shall see them no more. Oh, it is so sad, so hard… life crushes so much in us, it destroys our beliefs.'"

She can now only hope for something in the afterlife '"…a reunion – if that were so…'":

'And now Sesemi Weichbrodt stood up, as tall as ever she could. She stood on tiptoe, rapped on the table; the cap shook on her old head.

"It is so," she said with her whole strength; and looked at them all with a challenge in her eyes.

She stood there, a victor in the good fight which all her life she had waged against the assaults of Reason; hump-backed tiny and quivering with the strength of her convictions, a little prophetess, admonishing and inspired.'

Sesemi Weichbrodt combines the functions of the Eumenides and the Sibyl, a fighter against the odds for justice, and a prophetess who offers hope for the future. But there the author leaves us and the family, to ponder if her words are true: whether there is an afterlife, some sort of compensation for the disappointments of life bravely born, or whether these are empty words spoken by an old humpbacked spinster.

Sesemi Weichbrodt, Friederike, Henriette and Pfiffi aren't the only spinsters in 'Buddenbrooks'; there are others who also punctuate the story: Clothilde, the orphan whom the Buddenbrook family adopted, has always been marked down as a spinster; even as a child she was 'scraggy… with a long, old-maidish face.' As she became an adult her spinsterhood becomes more apparent:

'She grew thinner and thinner, and her shapeless black frock did not conceal the fact. Her face was long and straight, and expressionless as ever, her hair as smooth and ash-coloured, her nose as straight, but full of large pores and getting thicker at the end.' She is close to Toni's younger sister, Clara and they 'went always on Sunday evenings to the house of a friend where they knitted stockings for little negro children'.

Like one of the original spinners, threadwork became the purpose of her life.

Ida Jungmann:

The faithful Prussian was now in her fifties. She had begun early to grow grey, but her hair had never become quite white, having remained a mixture of brown and grey; her erect bony figure was sturdy, and her brown eyes as bright and clear and as unwearied as twenty years ago.

Ida Jungmann is a Prussian woman who has looked after two generations of the Buddenbrook children. Toni goes to visit her when she has charge of the youngest, Hanno, the delicate son of Tom Buddenbrook, now head of the family. Toni addresses her patronisingly:

'"And how are you, you old stand-by you?... You are darning, Ida – funny, I can't imagine you doing anything else."'

Darning and knitting again, the now familiar threadwork motif of the spinster. However, she has done sterling service. 'The faithful devotion of the good Ida could not be repaid with gold.' And Ida, fully conscious of her own status, apes Toni in condescension:

'She knew her own position, and when some ordinary nurse-girl came and sat down with her charge on the same bench and tried to enter into conversation, Ida Jungmann would say: "There is a draught here, Erica," and get up and go.'

It seems to me that the book is concerned with displaying the contrast between the married woman and the spinster, and surprisingly, and unlike anything we have met hitherto, the state of spinsterhood proves preferable to that of marriage. All the marriages of the Buddenbrook children are unhappy, if not disastrous: Toni makes two wretched marriages, her daughter marries a man who is first imprisoned and then disappears into obscurity. Clara ekes out a pitiful, pious existence with her pastor husband who is only too happy to profit from her premature death. Tom and his wife Gerda live sterile lives, emotionally and mentally apart, and when Gerda loses both her husband and son, her only option is to return to a dreary life in Amsterdam, restricted to playing duets with an ageing father. Christian marries a prostitute who has him incarcerated in an asylum.

Compared to them the spinsters are triumphant survivors, even poor 'ashen Clothide' who has feared for her old age, ends up living in almost luxurious accommodation as a member of the Order of St John.

'The object of these establishments was the suitable care of portionless women from old and worthy families... Poor Clothilde was now assured of a small, but certain income which would increase with the years, and finally, when she had succeeded to the highest class, would secure her a decent home in the cloister itself.'

Ida Jungmann assumes increasing power in the household, and after the death of her latest charge returns to her homeland in Prussia, presumably with a good pension. The three sisters may not have had a very happy existence, but they have gained a sort of malign pleasure from viewing the misfortunes of the Buddenbrooks in their marriages, and they have derived a bitter satisfaction described by Henriette: 'better not to have married'. They are a unit, they have survived, virginal and unscathed.

But it is perhaps the most unlikely of these spinsters, the misshapen one, Sesemi, who emerges as the most triumphant. As the women assemble to say goodbye to Gerda, it is Sesemi who 'stood there, a victor in the good fight...'

All these six spinsters have in their different ways, attained an equanimity, simply because they have fed off other peoples' marriages without having to undergo any of their drawbacks.

Ida has spent thirty comfortable years with the children of the various marriages and has revelled in the status as a member of an eminent family; Clothide who would never have had a chance of marriage and whose main interest in life is in anticipating her next meal, has enjoyed a well-fed life courtesy of the married Buddenbrooks' generosity; the sisters have also been assured – if not exactly a welcome by their married cousins, have at least have had a place to visit and vent their spleen. And Sesemi's long-standing welcome in the family like Ida's, is due to their connection with the Buddenbrook children, something they both relished.

So ultimately, wasn't the fate of these spinsters preferable to that of those women who had married? It is not they, but the twice-married Toni who cries: 'Life crushes so much in us, it destroys our beliefs.' It is a very singular for a book describing life in the nineteenth century, to privilege the lot of the spinster over that of the married woman.

Like the goddess Hestia their chastity has given them comfortable hearthside places, but unlike hers, their hearths have belonged to others.

'War and Peace' by Leo Tolstoy

Sonya:

Sonya is the third of our continental spinsters to belong in a wealthy dynastic family. Although she is an orphan, Sonya is the niece of Count Rostov and is brought up on equal status with his own children, Nicholas, Natasha and the younger Petya. She and Natasha are close friends, and from childhood she is deeply in love with her friend's brother, Nicholas, and he with her.
We meet her first when she is fifteen. '"Sonya," he says, "what is anyone in the world to me? You alone are everything."' However, Sonya suspects that marriage will be out of the question: in the first place they lie within the forbidden ties of consanguinity, but this could be fairly easily overcome; a greater barrier is the fact that Sonya is penniless, and the Rostov's are already in severe financial difficulties, due to the count's hopeless management of his affairs coupled with his

inability to conceive of a lifestyle that does not include every possible luxury for his wife and family.

The only solution is for Nicholas to marry a wealthy wife. When he goes away to fight in the Napoleonic wars, Sonya who loves the Rostov family and is eternally grateful for their kindness to her, writes to tell him that he must not consider himself bound to her. But it is obvious that they still love each other, and Sonya tells Natasha:

"'I am in love with your brother once and for all; and whatever may happen to him or me, I shall never cease to love him as long as I live.'" And she never does.

When Nicholas returns home on leave he brings with him his friend Dolokhov, who falls in love with Sonya, 'now sixteen and very pretty', and he proposes to her. She refuses him because she can think of nobody but Nicholas. He is honest enough to tell her that 'though he loves her more than anyone else… "I am young and Mama does not wish it. In a word I make no promise. And I beg you to consider Dolokhov's offer."' Sonya replies, "'Don't say that. I want nothing. I love you as a brother, I always shall, and I want nothing more.'"

Back with his regiment, Nicholas receives letters from his mother telling him of the family's increasing financial difficulties; and this compounded with his love for Sonya makes him feel 'it was all dreadfully difficult and complicated'.

When he next returns home at Christmas, he finds his mother trying to arrange a marriage for him with a wealthy heiress, and he really doesn't know what to do: he loves Sonya, but cannot bear to upset his mother, and he is aware of the increasingly worrying debts. During the Christmas festivities some exotic-looking mummers arrive unexpectedly, and the young people decide to dress up and copy them.

'Sonya's costume was the best of all. Her moustache and eyebrows were extraordinary becoming. Everyone told her she looked very handsome… Some inner voice told her that now or never her fate would be decided.'

They set off for a nearby country house in their troikas, and it is a magical moonlit night. Nicholas is entranced by Sonya in her costume and '… he slipped his arms under the cloak that covered her head, embraced her, pressed her to him and kissed her on the lips' Sonya too, 'kissed him full on the lips.' '"Sonya… Nicholas…" was all they said.'

Soon after Christmas Nicholas tells his mother of his love for Sonya and his firm resolve to marry her; the countess who has been fearing this, 'coldly told him that neither she nor his father would give blessing to such marriage…'

A few days later the countess sent for Sonya, and with a cruelty neither of them expected, reproached her niece for trying to catch Nicholas and of ingratitude. Sonya listens in silence, she is a very good person and wants to do what is right:

'She was ready to sacrifice everything for her benefactors. Self-sacrifice was her most cherished ideal… she could not help loving the countess and the whole Rostov family, but neither could she help loving Nicholas and knowing that his happiness depended on that love.'

Nicholas pleads and threatens his family, telling of his passionate love, but the matter is unresolved, and he leaves again for the war, and the countess becomes increasingly unpleasant to poor Sonya. Later, he writes to Sonya and tells her: 'Once the war is over… I will throw up everything and fly to you and press you forever to my ardent breast.' But the war will not be over for a long time.

In the course of his duties he meets the wealthy Princess Mary who must be evacuated from the family estate because of the advancing French troops; she is an extremely pious and rather plain woman, but the strangeness of the circumstances, and her possession of a sort of spirituality makes Nicholas feel strangely drawn to her.

Meanwhile, things are going very badly in the war and Napoleon is advancing on Moscow; everyone is leaving. The countess is delighted to learn from a letter of Nicholas of his meeting with Mary, and exults triumphantly in front of Sonya:

"'I had always wanted Nicholas to marry the princess, and had a presentiment that it would happen. What a good thing it would be…'" Sonya felt this was true; the only possibility of retrieving the Rostov's affairs was by Nicholas marrying a rich woman. 'It was very bitter for her.' But Sonya is pragmatic, she does not parade her grief, instead, she alone, out of the useless family, supervises the packing up of their belongings as they prepare to flee Moscow. After they move, the count dies.

'Sonya kept house, attended on her aunt, read to her, put up with her whims and secret ill will… Nicholas felt indebted to Sonya… but tried to keep aloof from her… He seemed in his heart to reproach her for being too perfect, and because there was nothing to reproach her with… He felt the more he valued her, the less he loved her.'

Oh! What about her?

Unexpectedly, Nicholas is again thrown into the company of Princess Mary, he is further drawn to her, and sees the value in marrying for money, but he feels guilt about so doing, and he also feels guilt (and so he ought!) towards Sonya. Then, under increasing pressure from the countess Sonya writes to Nicholas:

'The last unfortunate events – the loss of the almost whole of the Rostov's property and the countess' repeatedly expressed wish that he should marry Princess Mary, together with his silence and coldness of late, had all combined to make her release him from his promise, and set him completely free. It would be too painful to me to think I might be the cause of discord to the family that has been so good to me.'

How good she is – and what a contrast to her erstwhile lover!

'He had taken her at her word when she wrote giving him his freedom, and now behaved as if all that had passed between them had long been forgotten and could never in any case, be renewed.' Poor, poor Sonya and selfish, inconstant Nicholas!

'In the winter of 1813 Nicholas married Princess Mary and moved to Bald Hills [her ancestral home] with his wife, his mother and Sonya. Nicholas had told his wife all that had passed between him and Sonya, blaming himself and commending her. He had asked Princess Mary to be gentle and kind to his cousin.' How thoughtful of him! 'She could not find fault with Sonya in any way, and tried to be fond of her, but often felt ill-will towards her which she could not overcome.' When she discusses this with her sister-in-law Natasha (who is now comfortably married to the wealthy Pierre), Natasha quotes from the Bible:

'… to him that hath shall be given, to him that hath not shall be taken away. She [Sonya] is one that hath not; why I don't know, perhaps she lacks egotism… She is like a *sterile flower*, you know – like some strawberry blossoms. Sometimes I feel sorry for her, and sometimes I think she doesn't feel it, as you or I would.'

This seems a particularly callous conversation between two women who have both achieved everything they have ever wanted, good husbands and children. However, Tolstoy thinks differently:

'It really seemed that Sonya did not find her position trying, and had grown quite reconciled to her lot as a *sterile flower*. She seemed to be fond, not so much of individuals as of the family as a whole. Like a cat she had attached herself not to the people, but to the home. She waited on the old countess, petted and spoiled the children, was always ready to render the small services for which she had a gift, and all this was unconsciously accepted from her with insufficient gratitude.'

But of course Tolstoy writes as a man. As a woman, I wonder if she really was so content. We remember she had said of Nicholas all those years ago, "I shall never cease to love him as long as I live"'. I find it hard to believe that she could have enjoyed an existence living with the man she loved, *his* wife and *their* children. I think back to poor Lady Isabel in 'East Dene', forced to live with the man who was once her husband and his new wife, and look after his children (even though they were actually hers, too). Can Sonya's existence really have been such a pleasant one, particularly as nobody appreciated her and regarded all her kindness with 'insufficient gratitude'?

Ariadne had saved Theseus from the minotaur and when he sailed away with her she expected marriage, but like Nicholas, he dumped his prospective bride. Later she was given a golden crown that was set among the stars, becoming the Corona Borealis. That was her reward for her service to Theseus. Did he look up at the sky and think what a satisfactory conclusion to his adventure this had been? The Rostovs obviously felt that about Sonya.

However, like the Sicilian sisters and the Buddenbrooks spinsters, she belongs to a dynasty, no longer so wealthy and highly regarded, but nevertheless, one where they were all still able to continue to live an opulent life. Sonya would never need to worry about money or being without a family. I was going to add 'or being lonely', but I think sometimes loneliness can be most greatly experienced in the company of others who do not really care about you. But, like them, she survived – in material comfort. Money and status can be a sort of panacea.

CHAPTER SEVENTEEN

SUBORDINATE SPINSTERS

Full many a flower is born to blush unseen,
And waste its sweetness on the desert air.

Thomas Gray, 'Elegy in a Country Churchyard'

In 'The Leopard', in 'Buddenbrooks' and in 'War and Peace' we saw spinsters who in spite of loss and disappointment, managed to sustain a reasonable lifestyle, but, as we have noted so often, money was there as a prop; without that they would not have survived as they did. But what of those who do not have that necessary back-up, those with no well-to-do family to support them, no comfortably-off married relations to settle on? For them there will be a much grimmer fate. There will be a desperate need of financial support, and another need, perhaps as important, a need to have some sort of status, above all, to attain and keep the holy grail of Respectability.

'Cranford' by Mrs Gaskell

Miss Matty:

In 'Cranford' the foolish and worthy Miss Matty faces this dilemma when the bank in which all her money is invested, crashes. At first, she fails to see the danger, and is worried for the 'poor directors who must be so upset', but she is eventually brought to face the facts, the question of how to meet her financial commitments, and maintain respectability, becomes horribly pressing. Various idea are mooted:

'Teaching was, of course, the first thing that suggested itself. This, at least, would be an almost respectable occupation.' Various branches of education are considered:

'If Miss Matty could teach children, it would throw her among the little elves in whom her soul delighted.' But there are problems: she used to be able to play the piano, but 'that faint shadow of musical acquirement had faded long ago'. As a girl she was able to draw, but now her abilities are limited to inaccurate copying; there is 'fancy work and the use of globes, but as for the former, Miss Matty's eyesight was failing, and as for the latter: 'globes, equators and tropics were imaginary lines to her.' What about 'the arts'? Her artistic abilities are also somewhat limited: 'She 'excelled at making candle lighters of coloured paper, cut out to resemble feathers, and knitting garters in a variety of dainty stitches; but would anyone pay to have their children taught these arts? It seemed unlikely.'

So teaching is not an option. What then can be done, to bring in some money, and preserve her respectability? A new idea comes to her friend:

'Why should not Miss Matty sell tea – be an agent to the East India Tea company… the advantages were many – always supposing that Miss Matty could get over the degradation of condescending to anything like trade.' And this of course, is a great problem, another member of their society had been shamed by merely mentioning she had a relative in the wool trade.

However, after careful consideration her friend thinks the problem might be overcome: 'Tea was not sticky or greasy', and above all: 'No shop window would be required. A *small genteel notification* of her being licensed to sell tea, would, it is true, be necessary, but I hoped that it could be placed *where no one could see it.* (my italics).… The only thing against the plan was the buying and selling involved.' Of course, the objections of the ladies of Cranford must be overcome: 'Would Miss Matty forfeit her right to privileges of society in Cranford?' But after an anxious three days, their sanction is given, and Miss Matty's own fears are overcome:

'… men were not purchasers of tea; and it was of men she was particularly afraid. They had such sharp loud ways with them.'

However, we can see that this tea-selling isn't really a suitable occupation for Miss Matty, who is *a rector's daughter*. And fortunately, a long-lost brother returns from India to relieve her of this degradation.

Very often the spinster who looks to be rescued by a more financially secure relative must attach herself to a married relation. She will be an adjunct as it were, of another, she will be regarded like a family dog, although she will be less petted and made conscious of her position.

She will be expected to carry out duties that her more fortunate sister eschews. It is not ideal, but it is something. She is to be fed and watered and will derive respectability from being part of a marriage, as was the case with poor Sonya. Knowing that she is unlikely to wed she will perhaps connive at furthering the marriage of a relation, usually a sister whom she looks to for her survival. She is not always very skilful at this. In fact it may be the very lack of this ability that has placed her in this position in the first place.

Miss Steele:

In Austen's 'Sense and Sensibility', Eleanor and Marianne Dashwood meet the Misses Steele: 'the eldest who was nearly thirty, with a very plain and not very sensible face; but in the other, who was not more than two or three and twenty, they acknowledged considerable beauty; her features were pretty, and she had a sharp, quick eye, and a smartness of air, which though it did not give actual elegance or grace, gave distinction to her person.'

Lucy Steele is carefully manoeuvring her way to bringing about a successful conclusion to her secret engagement to Edward Ferrars; however, everyone imagines, as is in fact the case, that the gentleman in question is really in love with Eleanor. Their hostess Mrs Jennings openly praises him: '… he is one of the modestest, prettiest behaved young gentleman that I ever saw.' So Lucy is not pleased when her sister threatens to let the cat out of the bag:

'"Oh," cried Miss Steele, looking significantly round at them, "I daresay Lucy's beau is quite as modest and pretty behaved as Miss Dashwood's." 'Lucy, we are told, 'bit her lip and looked angrily at her sister. A mutual silence took place for some time.'

However, Lucy marries Edward's brother, but whether Miss Steele will be given that essential financial support by them is doubtful, as both are worthless characters.

In ' Superior Spinsters' we saw that while the situation was not ideal for the women who were reliant on the family, at least, they had no financial worries. But if the spinster has no prosperous fortunate relation to provide for her, she must look for other alternatives. One option is to become the paid companion of a well- placed woman. We can think of Hecate who was 'allowed to be Proserpine's attendant'.
If she is fortunate enough to accompany a wealthy woman, she may enjoy the benefits of foreign travel, and even manage to catch the eye of an eligible male holidaying abroad. Such a one is the nameless heroine of 'Rebecca', who accompanies the wealthy and snobbish American Mrs Van Hopper on her

vacation in Monte Carlo – although in her case, marriage to Max de Winter proves something of a mixed blessing.

Even without any prospect of marriage the spinster may, at least, enjoy some share of the privileges of wealth, and perhaps hope for a substantial legacy if she outlives her patroness, but this is by no means certain; in 'The Shrimp and the Anemone', Miss Fothergill's faithful companion, Helen Grimshaw loses out to Eustace. His father and aunt discuss the situation after the funeral.' "Miss Grimshaw certainly looked pretty sour," said Mr Cherrington chuckling reflectively.' But Aunt Sarah who is herself, only too aware of the tribulations of the unmarried woman, has every sympathy for her:

'"You could hardly expect her not to, could you after all those years? And I daresay Miss Fothergill was a bit difficult sometimes… Miss Grimshaw may still have felt and justly, that a lifetime's devotion deserved rewarding, much more than the occasional visits of a little boy who couldn't do anything to help Miss Fothergill, and must often have been in the way."'

Like Miss Grimshaw's, the lot of the companion is too often a wretched one, she is a mere dogsbody; we saw this in 'Some Tame Gazelle' where poor Connie Aspinall is forced to trail along behind the unsympathetic Edith, while hankering after her days when she was companion to Lady Grudge in the prestigious Belgrave Square. The autonomous Miss Mackenzie (whom we shall meet later) makes an impassioned cry against the lot of such women:

'"I would sooner take a broom in my hand and sweep a crossing in London than lead such a life as that. What? Make myself the slave of some old woman who would think that she had bought the power of tyrannising over me, by allowing me to sit in the same room as her? No indeed."'

'Vanity Fair' by William Makepeace Thackeray

Miss Briggs:

The perfect example of the awful lot of the companion is poor Miss Briggs in 'Vanity Fair'. To understand the position of Miss Briggs we must first learn a little of her employer, a rich and cheerful spinster:

'Old Miss Crawley was certainly one of the reprobate. She had a snug little house in Park Lane and she ate and drank a great deal too much during the season in London. She was the most hospitable and jovial of old vessels and had been a beauty in her day, she said.'

When Miss Crawley falls ill, Miss Briggs' position is usurped by the unscrupulous Becky Sharp, intent on securing Miss Crawley's money: She was denied admission to Miss Crawley's apartment and no longer allowed to administer her medicines. Briggs is a foolish and tender-hearted woman: 'She buried her crushed affections and her poor old red nose in her pocket handkerchief.' But the heartless Becky simply takes the opportunity of further ingratiating herself with the rich old woman, by imitating Miss Briggs' distress to Miss Crawley:

'Briggs' weeping snuffle and her manner of using the handkerchief were so completely rendered that Miss Crawley became quite cheerful, to the admiration of the doctors when they visited her' Becky takes her cruelty further: 'Miss Crawley liked to have Miss Briggs in a great deal... Becky used to imitate her to her face with the most admirable gravity, thereby rendering the imitation doubly piquant to her worthy patroness... Miss Briggs was not formally dismissed, but her place as companion was a sinecure and a derision; and her company was the fat spaniel in the drawing room.'

Poor foolish Miss Briggs. (She is another of those spinsters whose twisted threads could have placed her among our Sad and Silly Spinsters). You would think she might have been delighted when Miss Crawley discovers the scheming Becky's secret marriage to her nephew, Rawdon, and furiously disowns the pair of them. But the poor creature pleads for Rawdon (and by implication his wife) who is fighting at Waterloo:

'"Will my dear Miss Crawley not cast an eye of compassion on upon the heroic soldier whose name is inscribed in the annals of his country's glory," said Miss Briggs who was greatly excited by the Waterloo proceedings, and loved speaking romantically when there was occasion.'

But the worldly-wise Miss Crawley who will certainly not forgive her nephew for his improvident marriage, and who has no time for her companion, or her romanticism, replies with cruelty – and truth, pinpointing the difference between the successful married Becky and Briggs the spinster:

"Briggs, you are a fool… marry a *dame de compagne* for that is what she was, for she was no better, Briggs; no, she was just what you are, only a great deal prettier and cleverer."

Thackeray puts the lot of such spinsters in a nutshell: 'Briggs bore the attacks with meekness, with cowardice and with a resignation that was half generous, half hypocritical – with the slavish submission in a world that women of her disposition and station are compelled to show. Who has not seen how women bully women?'

Cleverness and good looks may bring the end of spinsterhood, but poor Briggs, like so many of her ilk has neither; she must put up with her employer 'with slavish submission'.

But Miss Crawley does eventually die, and Miss Briggs inherits a small annuity. You might think her problems solved, but as with the case of Miss Mackenzie whom we will meet later, a spinster with some money is at the mercy of the world. Miss Briggs' brother takes part of her capital to prop up his business, and her sister tries to make Miss Briggs pay for her son's education: '… between them, the two families got a great portion of her private savings out of her… and she fled to London, determined to seek for servitude, as less onerous than liberty.' This indeed reveals the plight of the unloved spinster; the Victorian world had no place for the lonely spinster, even one like Briggs who had a little money left.

Now, the path of the unfortunate Briggs is again to cross that of Becky who is at the height of her precarious success in fashionable London; as Becky's activities are always liable to excite suspicion, she sees the advantage of hiring Briggs as a companion and symbol of her own respectability; and when she found Briggs 'had a snug legacy from Miss Crawley… Becky instantly formed some benevolent little domestic plans concerning her.'

Not only does the foolish and gullible Briggs become a useful unpaid factotum in the house, but a ready source of cash. Between them Becky and Rawdon relieve her of the rest of her money under the pretence of investing it for her. Briggs is quite taken in: 'Mr and Mrs Crawley had kindly busied themselves on her behalf… the Colonel was so kind…'. When it becomes apparent that the money is lost, Becky tells Briggs as recompense for her losses, she is to become housekeeper at Lord Steyne's country house, Gauntly Hall:
'… she was grieved beyond measure to part with Briggs, but her means required she should practice every retrenchment, and her sorrow was mitigated by the idea that her dear Briggs would be far better provided for by her generous patron, than in her humble home… Of course the place was not to be hers yet, but she might go down on a visit.' Thackeray indulges in bitter irony: 'What words can paint the ecstatic gratitude of Briggs?'

When Becky is found by her husband with Lord Steyne, (probably) in flagrante, disgrace falls, and Rawdon leaves her, so Briggs' job – if it had ever been there – would never transpire. There is a paltry consolation: Rawdon, who unlike his wife, had some sort of conscience, entrusts his brother with £600 to return to Briggs because 'I've always felt ashamed at having taken the poor old woman's money.'

We do not hear any more of Briggs, but we can only imagine her being conned out of her remaining means, and living out her days in poverty, or suffering 'the slavish submission in a world that women of her disposition and station are compelled to show.'

The Nanny

The post of nanny will be less arduous than that of the paid companion, and it will provide pay, board and lodging. Furthermore, as a nanny the woman can claim vicariously some sense of belonging to a respectable, even wealthy household, and for the spinster who has longed for children of her own, she has access to substitutes. She can regard the children of the marriage of her employer as being effectively hers; and there is no greater triumph than bringing the bathed and freshly attired children down to greet their parents briefly before the adult dinner. The approbation of the parents and the good behaviour of the children are all due to *her*, and the parental role, she may reflect, is as nothing compared to her own. The lack of husbandly love is substituted by a love for and from the children, who, often, she knows, are closer to her than they are to their own parents. In 'Buddenbrooks' we see Fraulein Jungermann's obsessive love of Gerda's son, Hanno; in 'The Shrimp and the Anemone' we saw Minna's almost incestuous love of Eustace, as she gently bathes and dries him; even Lucy Snowe in 'Villette' is fond of Madame Beck's youngest child.

The nanny can associate herself with respectable, and sometimes wealthy or even famous families and she can enjoy or suffer the burdens of motherhood, without the ultimate responsibility. It is a compensation of sorts. And she is paid.

The Governess

Like so many of our spinsters, this one could be equally well-placed under another category, that of 'Schoolmistress Spinsters' because she has a teaching role, but unlike the classroom teacher, the position lacks authority. She does not belong to an institution which, even if it does not wholly approve of her, as in the case of Miss Jean Brodie, is in some degree, obliged to provide support. The governess is a woman alone.

The governess enjoys none of the privileges – albeit dubious one – of the companion, nor can she enjoy the quasi-maternal position of the nanny who is only responsible for the outward appearance of the children under her care; she must be responsible for their education and their behaviour.; Hers is the task of performing the unwelcome side of parenting that has been abrogated to her by those unwilling to undertake the responsibility for themselves: stern discipline may be required, but not by *them*; they must preserve the illusion that their children are perfect; *she* is the one expected to produce a silk purse out of a sow's ear. It is she who must battle with unpromising material, and if the child fails to measure up, it is *she* who will be blamed because the parents wish to hold on to their illusions about their children. And even if there are no parents present, as we saw in the case of the governess in 'Turn of the Screw' she is alone, horribly alone. A governess cannot giggle in the servants hall about the foibles of her employers because, like Miss Prior in 'Some tame Gazelle', she will be eating alone, since her position must be above the servants –

who resent her for it – and below that of her employers. Both sets of people despise her.

'Martin Chuzzlewit' by Charles Dickens

Miss Pinch:

We can see the unhappy plight of the governess in 'Martin Chuzzlewit' when Tom Pinch goes to visit his badly-treated sister 'in a house so big and fierce that its mere outside, like the outside of a giant's castle struck terror into vulgar minds and made bold persons quail....'

Tom, accosted by a footman, and surprised by the man's insolent behaviour, asks: "Pray, is Miss Pinch at home?"

"She's in," replied the footman. As much as to say to Tom, "but if you think she has anything to do with the proprietorship of this place, you had better abandon the idea."

Finally, he is shown in, and finds his sister in a very unhappy state: '"I am afraid I cannot stay here," she weeps.' The footman brings a summons from the master of the house and they are shown into an adjoining room.

'There they found a middle aged gentleman with a pompous voice and manner, and a middle aged lady with what may be termed, an excisable face, or one in which starch and vinegar were decidedly employed. There was likewise present the eldest pupil who was now weeping and sobbing spitefully.

"My brother, Sir," said Ruth Pinch timidly presenting Tom. "Oh," cried the gentleman... "you really are her brother? I don't observe any resemblance."
"Miss Pinch has a brother, I know," observed the lady.

Miss Pinch is always talking about her brother when she ought to be engaged upon my education," sobbed the pupil…

"We are very much dissatisfied with her, observed the lady.'"

Tom who is becoming increasingly angry, asks, "Will you allow me to inquire what the ground of dissatisfaction is?'"

"Yes, I will. Your sister has not the slightest innate power of commanding respect… what are my feelings as a father, when after my desire repeatedly expressed to Miss Pinch… that my daughter should be choice in her expressions, genteel in her deportment, as becomes her station in life, and politely distant to her inferiors in society, I find her only this morning, addressing Miss Pinch herself, as a beggar."

"A beggarly thing," observed the lady in correction.'

Tom then summarises the plight of his sister, and of every spinster governess:

"'No man can expect his children to respect what he degrades… your governess cannot win the respect of your children, forsooth! Let her begin by winning yours, and see what happens then.'" The gentleman expostulates violently but Tom continues:

"'When you tell me my sister is not deserving of respect of your children; I tell you it is not so… She is as well-bred, as well-taught, as well qualified by nature as to command respect as any hirer of a governess you know, but when you place her at a disadvantage in reference to every servant in your house, how can you suppose that she is not in a tenfold worse position in reference to your daughter… how can you, as an honest gentleman, profess displeasure or surprise at your daughter telling my sister she is something beggarly and humble, when you are forever telling her the same thing yourself in fifty plain out-speaking ways, though not in words, when your very porter and footman make the same delicate announcement to all comers.'"

Like Miss Matty, Tom's sister is fortunate in that he can whisk her away, and being pretty – a vital quality for shedding spinsterhood – she finally finds a suitable husband. But pity those who must stay and endure!

'Agnes Grey' by Anne Bronte

Agnes Grey:

The whole of 'Agnes Grey' is a polemic endorsing the views expressed by Tom Pinch. Agnes' first job with the Bloomfield family is a nightmare: the boy likes torturing birds, the elder girl refuses to learn, preferring to roll about on the ground, the younger girl is sly and deceitful. Agnes is horrified:

'The name of governess as applied to me was a mere mockery, my pupils had no more notion of obedience than a wild unbroken colt; the habitual fear of their father's peevish temper and the dread of the punishments he was wont to inflict when irritated, kept them generally within bounds in his immediate presence. The girls too had some fear of their mother's anger, and the boy might be occasionally bribed to do as she bid him by hope of a reward, but I had no rewards to offer, and as for punishments, I was given to understand the parents kept that privilege for themselves, and yet they expected me to keep them in order.'

We watch her as month by month, she struggles to do the impossible and she prides herself on having made *some* progress, but there is still very much left to be desired in the way of improvement.

Finally, the parents decide to attribute their children's bad behaviour to their unfortunate governess. She is summoned into the presence of Mrs Bloomfield who informs her that, 'though superior to most children of their years in their abilities, they were decidedly behind them in attainments, their manners were uncultivated, and their tempers unruly. And this she attributed to a want of sufficient firmness and diligent, persevering care on my part.' This is indeed a bitter pill:

'Unshaken firmness, devoted diligence, unwearied perseverance, unceasing care were the very qualifications on which I had secretly prided myself, and by which I had hoped in time to overcome all difficulties, and achieve success at last.'

However, she is dismissed. One feels every sympathy for poor Agnes – I will modify that – I would have felt more sympathy, if she hadn't been so dreadfully worthy and pious:

'I would carefully refrain from all useless irritability and indulgence of my own ill temper; when they behaved tolerably I would be as kind and obliging as it was in my power to be, in order to make the widest possible distinction between good and bad conduct; I would reason with them too, in the simplest and most effective manner. When I reproved them or refused to gratify their wishes, after a glaring fault, it would be more in sorrow than in anger; their little hymns and prayers I would make plain and clear to their understanding; when they said their prayers at night and asked pardon for their offenses, I would remind them of the sins of the past day, solemnly but in perfect kindness... penitential hymns should be said by the naughty, cheerful ones by the comparatively good...'

One can hardly be surprised that her charges were so difficult. All that endless preaching! What about a little fun, a little humour, a little less worthiness? But fun and humour did not constitute part of Agnes Grey's nature.

Her next job is somewhat easier as she has the care of two teenage girls, but they too, fail to live up to Miss Grey's expectations:

'Miss Matilda was a veritable hoyden… as a moral agent she was reckless, headstrong, violent and unamenable to reason. One proof of her deplorable state of mind was that, from her father's example she had learned to swear like a trooper.'

The girl's mother, not unreasonably, expects her salaried governess to improve her daughter's behaviour, and in this, too, Agnes fails. Of course, it was difficult, but a little less disapproval and a little more fun might have helped, but as I've said, that was not in her nature. One feels much empathy with Matilda who says after yet another reproof:
'"Oh Miss Grey, I've shocked you. I'm so glad."'

But the real problem for Miss Grey is the elder daughter. 'At eighteen Miss Murray was to emerge from the quiet obscurity of the schoolroom into the full blaze of the fashionable world.' She is a very pretty girl and determined to use her looks to her advantage:

'"If I could always be young I should like to be single. I should like to enjoy myself thoroughly and coquette with all the world till I am on the verge of being called an old maid; and then, to escape the infamy of that, after making ten thousand conquests, to break all their hearts, save one, by marrying some high-born, rich, indulgent husband, whom, on the other hand, fifty ladies were dying to have."'

You can imagine how well that went down with Miss Grey! But, in fact isn't that exactly what most girls secretly wanted at the time: to flirt a bit, and then move heaven and earth to escape 'the infamy of being called an old maid'? It's just that Miss Murray is disconcertingly honest about it. And I cannot help wondering if the mousey Miss Grey's moral indignation isn't fuelled by the consciousness that such powers will never belong to her.

Many young men are after the enticing Miss Murray who declares:

"'… the one I'm to have, I suppose, if I'm doomed to have any of them, is Thomas Ashby.'" The man is a notorious rake, and the shocked Miss Grey remonstrates: "'Surely not, if he's so wicked and you dislike him?'" But the heedless Miss Murray replies:

"'Oh, I don't mind his being wicked; he's all the better for that, and as for disliking him I shouldn't mind being Lady Ashby of Ashby Park.'" Another one in the eye for Agnes!

However, until she gets married, Miss Murray continues flirting with the local available men; she amuses herself by exciting and humiliating the local vicar, but then, and it is here, I think, we get to the nub of Agnes' disapproval. When Miss Murray suspects that Agnes is becoming interested in the new worthy curate, whom she has, of course, met while visiting a member of the deserving poor, she sets about luring him away from her. And now we see Agnes in a new light.

'… about this time I paid more attention to dress than ever I had done before… this is not saying much, for hitherto I'd been a little neglectful in that respect… but now also, it is not uncommon to spend as much as two minutes in the contemplation of my own image in the glass, although I could never derive any consolation from such study. I could discover no beauty in such marked features, that pale hollow cheek and ordinary dark brown hair; there might be intellect in the forehead, there might be expression in the dark grey eyes, but what of that… a low grecian brow, and large black eyes devoid of sentiment would be considered far preferable.'

She discourses humourlessly with herself, on the desirability of beauty, and concludes sententiously:

'They that have beauty, let them be thankful for it, and make good use of it, like any other talent; they that have it not, let them console themselves, and do the best they can without it.'

Oh dear, what a miserable prospect! Beautiful people must devote themselves to joining the ranks of the worthy, and unbeautiful people must suffer in silence.

However, all this worthiness is to pay off, and all this unworthiness, is punished. In spite of her plainness, Agnes finally gets her curate, while Miss Murray is left deserted in her Ashby Park, and is reduced to asking Miss Grey to come and keep her company. How Miss Grey must have relished that!

However, marriage for Agnes turns out not to be all plain sailing:

'We have had our trials, and we know we must have them again, but we bear them well together, and endeavour to fortify ourselves and each other against that final separation – that greatest of all afflictions to the survivor, but if we keep in mind that glorious heaven beyond, where we may meet again, and sin and sorrow are unknown, surely that too may be borne; and in the meantime we endeavour to live to the glory of him who has scattered so many blessings in our path.'

But however we may view her, Agnes Grey does demonstrate the plight of the spinster governess, a solitary figure, disliked, ignored and blamed by the whole household from the servants, the children and her employers. How lucky were Miss Pinch and Miss Grey to finally escape it – if indeed this was a credible fate for them. Becky Sharp did even better, but then she had the tools of escape: looks, brains and unscrupulousness.

In Victorian England there was quite another genre of governess. In an extraordinary book, partly attributed to the poet Algernon Charles Swinburne, entitled, aptly enough: 'The Whippingham Papers', we come across this fictional letter beginning:

'I hear that you are to open a birching establishment in Pimlico… your personal qualifications for *une fouetteuse* are excellent. For you cannot be above thirty, your figure, as it should, inclines to plumpness, and your arms are strong and finely rounded. With the right sleeve turned up, the movement of the biceps muscle when you are birching, must be most fetching to beholders, especially if a good view can be obtained of the round full breasts while they are heaving with the exertion.'

Whatever sort of governess you were, your lot was an unenviable one.

'Klara and the Sun' by Kazuo Ishiguro

Klara:

In Ishiguro's contemporary novel, 'Klara and the Sun', we meet a different genre of subservient spinster. Klara is hard to classify, not because she lives at some unspecified time in the future, but because her role lies somewhere between governess, nanny, and paid companion. Klara is an AF, an Artificial Friend. When the young José sees her standing in the window of an expensive American store, she is determined to own her, even though she is not the latest model. And Klara very much wants to belong to José. She is a robot with feelings. Klara is bought for José, and she comes to live with the girl and her family. José has been unwell for sometime with an unspecified illness, and Klara looks after her carefully. However, we begin to realise that the situation is odd; all this is happening in a future where some human beings are 'lifted', and some are not; this term is never fully explained but one imagines the 'lifted' ones like José, are somehow enhanced through genetic engineering, a system that has proved imperfect, and has in José's case, brought about her illness.

Klara is an ideal companion, more ideal than any other of the spinsters we have met in this section, because she needs no food or any attention, other than the 'nourishment' she receives from the sun. Like Theodora Braithwaite, 'she performed her welcome duties. She made no fuss and no demands.' Like Lucy's sister in 'Sense and Sensibility', she has no thoughts of marriage for herself – how could she? But she is anxious to further the relationship between José and her boyfriend.

Klara is almost a saintly spinster because, although she has no actual god to pray to, the sun is her god, because it is his warmth that gives her being; and she begs, or one could say, prays, to him to help José in her romance; and as José becomes more ill, she even sacrifices some of the precious fluid which keeps her mechanism going, in a mistaken attempt to try and save her.

When it seems as though the girl will die, a proposition is put to Klara, one which Jose's mother believes is possible, because Klara has become so acutely attuned to Jose and the way her brain and emotions work, what, as one might say, makes her tick as a human being. The proposition is this: if the girl does die, Klara will actually 'become' José, a substitute so like to her, that her mother will believe her to be her daughter. Klara is even willing to do that: she will cease to be herself, and become instead, a surrogate human being. A greater sacrifice, surely than has been asked of any of our previous spinsters, be they companions or holy spinsters. Perhaps she is holier than any of them.

In the event José does get better and leaves home to go off to college. Klara is no longer required. The last we see of Klara is in the scrapyard among other discarded AFs, waiting demolition – death?

We are reminded of Syrinx pursued by the god Pan, turned into a reed, and then utilised by the god to become part of a musical instrument, the pan pipes.

Like other nymphs we have met, these subservient spinsters suffer the misfortune of being powerless in the hands of those more fortunate than themselves.

CHAPTER EIGHTEEN

SANCTUARY-SEEKING SPINSTERS

Has God's supply of tolerable husbands
Fallen, in fact, so low?
                    Robert Graves, 'A Slice of Wedding Cake'.

"I don't mean to deny that men are troublesome in a house. I don't judge from my own experience, for my father was neatness itself, and wiped his shoes on coming in as carefully as any woman, but still a man has a sort of knowledge of what should be done in difficulties, that is very pleasant to have one at hand, ready to lean on."
                    Elizabeth Gaskell, 'Cranford.'.

As we have seen, the lot of the subservient spinster is a wretched one, and if she is not lucky enough to be rescued from it by marriage, her life will become even more burdensome as she grows older. For some single women, this situation is simply too ghastly to contemplate; they will expend all their energy in an attempt to discard their spinsterhood, and reach the desired sanctuary of marriage, even if a successful outcome looks unlikely. Here are three women who manage to pull it off – although, at a heavy price.

'The Expedition of Humphry Clinker by Tobias Smollett

Tabitha Bramble:

To avoid the reproachful epithet of old maid.

'Humphry Clinker' is a hilarious eighteenth century epistolary novel in which we learn of the travels through England and Scotland of Mathew Bramble, his sister, Tabitha, niece Lydia, nephew Jerry, and large entourage of servants, including the eponymous Humphry.

Matthew Bramble is a good-hearted squire who puts up with his sister out of an irritated sense of duty. His nephew has less sympathy with her:

'… Tabitha Bramble is a maiden of forty-five. In her person she is tall, raw-boned, aukward (sic), flat-chested and stooping; her complexion is sallow and freckled; her eyes are not grey, but greenish, like those of a cat and generally inflamed; her hair is of a sandy, or rather, dusty hue; her forehead low; her nose long, sharp, and towards the extremity, always red in cool weather; her lips skinny, her mouth extensive… her teeth straggling and loose, of various colours and conformation; and her long neck shrivelled into a thousand wrinkles – in her temper, she is proud, stiff, vain, imperious, prying, malicious, greedy, and uncharitable. In all likelihood her natural austerity has been soured by disappointment in love; for her long celibacy is by no means owing to her dislike of matrimony; on the contrary, she has left no stone unturned to avoid the reproachful epithet of old maid.'

From this description by a callous young man we might feel sorry for Tabitha as an archetypical spinster; she has been disappointed in love (we are later told of that she had once had a suitable lover who had died); and perhaps there is something commendable in her attempt 'to avoid the reproachful epithet of old maid.' However, during the course of the book we gain a more rounded picture of Tabitha and see that Jerry's judgement is not far off the mark. Determined to find herself a husband at the many places they visit on their journey from

London to Edinburgh. On one occasion she almost succeeds. Jerry tells us:

'This amiable maiden has actually commenced a flirting correspondence with an Irish baronet of sixty-five. He is said to be as much out at the elbows, and has received false intelligence with respect to her fortune. Be that as it may, the connection is exceedingly ridiculous and has begun to excite whispers.'

However, when he learns the truth, Sir Ulric beats a hasty retreat. Undaunted, wherever she goes, she makes ill-judged preparations for husband-hunting. We are told that in spite of having been 'several days in consultation with milliners and mantua-makers' in order to make a dramatic entry to a ball in Edinburgh, she was declared 'the worst dressed of the whole assembly'.

The most ridiculous incident occurs when a suitor appears for the squire's pretty niece and Tabitha decides it is she (Tabitha) who is the object of his affections:

'"In a word, brother, I am so sensible of Mr Barton's affections that I have been prevailed upon to alter my resolution of living a single life and put my happiness in his hands... ..."' And just to make sure, she adds, '"... the business at present is to have the writings drawn."' Poor Mr Barton is overcome with horror and rushes off home.

However she does finally succeed with Captain Lismahago who makes his first appearance by falling off his horse and displaying:

'...a headpiece patched and plastered in various colours... he would have measured above six feet in height had he stood upright; but he stooped very much; was very narrow in the shoulders and very thick in the calves of his legs which were encased in black spatterdashes – as for his thighs, they were long and slender like those of a grasshopper; his face was at least half a yard in length, brown and shrivelled, with projecting cheekbones, little grey eyes of the greenish hue, a large hook nose, a pointed chin, a mouth from ear to ear, very ill-furnished with teeth, and a high narrow forehead, well-furnished with wrinkles.'

However, he is single – and penniless, and Tabitha settles for him. He is the male counterpart of Tabitha; like Lucy's M. Paul, he is really a sort of male spinster. They get married at the end of the book, much to Matthew Bramble's contrivance and relief, but what sort of union two such peculiar persons could enjoy seems anyone's guess.

'The Vessel of Wrath' by William Somerset Maugham

Miss Jones:

'What is this? his eyes are heavy: think not they're glazed with
wine.
Go to him: it is thy duty: kiss him, take his hand in thine.'
Alfred Tennyson, 'Locksley Hall'.

I hardly like to include any of Maugham's stories since he must now be regarded as a horrible exponent of colonialism, but as 'The Vessel of Wrath' is placed in the *Dutch* East Indies in the early years of the twentieth century, I may perhaps be forgiven.

We are in the Alas Islands: 'The population of the group is estimated at about 8,000 of whom 200 are Chinese and 400 Mohammedans. The rest are heathen.' Ruling over them from the Island of Baru is the easy going Dutch Contrôleur, Mynheer Evert Gruyter. The islands are fertile ground for missionary activity, and the Contrôleur who is happy with how things are, finds the local pastor and his sister rather irritating:

'The Rev Owen Jones was a worthy man, but impossible as a companion. His sister was worse… She was flat-chested, tall and extremely thin. She had a long sallow face. She was much affected by prickly heat. Her lank brown hair was drawn straight back from her forehead. She had small eyes, grey in colour, and because they were somewhat too close, they gave her a shrewish look. Her nose was long and thin and a trifle red… She grimly looked on the bright side of things. With the ferocity of an avenging angel she sought out the good in her fellow men.'

We can see that in appearance she bears an uncanny resemblance to Tabitha Bramble.

The man known as Ginger Ted is a wastrel, a drunkard and a womaniser. Having arrived on the island some years back, he is quite content to remain there on a small remittance sent from England. The Contrôleur has mixed feelings about him; he is someone to spend a congenial evening drinking with, but on the other hand, he is liable to get drunk and break things up, often pursued by an irate father whose daughter he has seduced. One day, he goes too far in a drunken brawl and the Contrôleur sentences him to six months hard labour on a nearby island.

Meanwhile, illness breaks out on another of the islands, and the missionary who is himself ill, allows his sister to go and help as they are both skilled in medicine. She does a splendid job and when it is completed, she catches the boat back to Baru, but is somewhat nonplussed to find the boat joined by Ginger Ted who has completed his six months sentence. Worse is to follow! The launch breaks down and they have to make for a nearby uninhabited island and wait there until a new propeller can be fitted. Miss Jones is insistent that they must get back to Baru. '"Shut up, you old cow," says Ginger Ted.

'Suddenly Miss Jones gave a gasp. The truth had dawned on her, and her anger changed to fear… she saw it all. Was the broken propeller a put up job or was it an accident? Anyhow, she knew that Ginger Ted would seize the opportunity. Ginger Ted would rape her, he was mad about women… but she must pull herself together. She must keep her wits about her. She must have courage. She was determined to sell her virtue dearly, and if he killed her – well, she would rather die than yield. And if she died, she would rest in the arms of Jesus.' She finds a secluded place to sleep.

Of course, Ginger Ted has no intention of raping the old maid, and when she wakes up in the morning she finds she has had a good night's sleep and has even been covered with some sacking from the ship. Now Miss Jones revises her opinion of this man whom she has considered a reprobate.

The propeller is mended and the ship returns. Ginger Ted goes to visit the Contrôleur to collect the money accruing to him during his absence, and he is surprised to be accosted by the missionary, Mr Jones:

'"I am afraid I misjudged you in the past; I beg your pardon… you had my sister at your mercy and you spared her… I thank you from the bottom of my heart."'

When he has left, the puzzled Ginger Ted asks the Contrôleur, '"What the blazes did he mean?"' The Contrôleur finds the situation very amusing:

'"He is thanking you for having respected the virtue of Miss Jones."'

Ginger Ted is furious: "'That old cow... I wouldn't touch her with the fag end of a barge pole. It never entered my head. The nerve. I'll wring his blasted neck. Give me my money, I'm going to get drunk." "It's an insult," he shouted at the Contrôleur. "That's what it is, it's a bloody insult."'

But it seems that the missionary and his sister – especially his sister, are determined to befriend Ginger Tom. All in vain; he becomes more dissolute and drunken than ever. Undaunted, they continually offer him invitations to dinner. Finally he is persuaded by the Contrôleur to agree, but instead, he goes out and gets drunk:

'Mr Jones shook his head.
"I'm afraid it's no good, Martha, the man's hopeless."'
For a moment Miss Jones was silent, and the Contrôleur saw two tears trickle down her long thin nose.
"No one is hopeless. Everyone has some good in him. I shall pray for him every night."'

Then cholera breaks out in a number of the islands and the Contrôleur goes to seek the help of the missionary; the trouble is that the outbreak is too widespread for the two of them to deal with by themselves, but the men do not like to expose Miss Jones to danger, as some of the islanders 'are wild and treacherous'.

'"I am not afraid," she said... "Let Mr Wilson come with me. He knows the natives better than anyone, and can speak all their dialects."
"Ginger Ted... He is just getting over an attack of DTS."
"I know," she answered.
"You know a great deal, Miss Jones."
Even though the moment was so serious, Mr Gruyter could not but smile. He gave her a sharp look.'

The Contrôleur is no fool and he remembers how irresistible Ginger Ted is to women. Miss Jones' brother has no such perception.

"'Do you think it wise to trust yourself for days at a time to a man of such infamous character?' said the missionary.' But the Contrôleur, probably motivated by his penchant for amusing situations, and a pressing need of an extra pair of hands, asks Miss Jones: "'Do you think he would be of any use… ?"

"I'm convinced of it." Then she blushed. "After all nobody knows better than I that he's capable of self control." Of course, we cannot see into Miss Jones' mind, but we have our suspicions.

They send for Ginger Ted who naturally does not want to go. "'Nothing doing, Contrôleur. I'm not a philanthropist.'"

But Miss Jones perseveres; she tells him that it was her suggestion: "'The natives are so funny I was afraid to go alone. I thought if you came, I should be safer.'" Ginger Ted is not impressed:

"'What do you suppose I care if they cut your throat?' Miss Jones looked at him and her eyes filled with tears. She began to cry. He stood and watched her stupidly. She pulled herself together. "I'm being silly. I shall be alright. I'll go alone.'"

Ginger Ted stands glaring at her and shuffling his feet; finally he says:

"'Oh hell, have it your own way. I'll come with you. When do you want to start?'"
So off they go, and they are very successful: 'Out of a population of eight thousand only six hundred had died.' The Contrôleur is thankful the whole business is over.

Then one day, Ginger Ted entered. 'He was wearing a clean suit of white ducks. He looked like another man.'

The Contrôleur offers him a drink, but to his amazement his visitor refuses:

"'I don't mind having a cup of tea."
" A cup of tea?"
"I'm on the wagon. Martha and I are going to be married."
"Ginger!" The Contrôleur's eyes popped out of his head.
"You can't marry Miss Jones," he said. "Nobody could marry Miss Jones."
"She wanted it. She fell for me that night when the propeller broke. She's not a bad old girl when you get to know her. It's her last chance.""

The Contrôleur expostulates, but Ginger Ted is adamant. It seems she has really got her claws into him. She has even got him converting the natives:

"'It's no good, Contrôleur. I know you mean well, but I'm going to marry the blasted woman, and that's that. You don't know the joy of bringing all them bleeding sinners to repentance, and Christ! That girl can make a treacle pudding.""

Perhaps, like Rutherford's Marple, Miss Jones knows that the way to a man's heart is through his stomach.

The Contrôleur says he should have raped her; that way he would only have got three years imprisonment instead of a one of a lifetime. But Ginger Ted is determined, and he warns him not to let on about the imagined rape. "'Look here, Contrôleur, don't you ever let on that the thought never entered my head. Women are touchy, you know, and she'd be as sore as hell if she knew that.""

The Contrôleur goes to see the missionary to try to get him to stop the marriage, then for the first time in his life he saw a twinkle in the missionary's eye:

"'My sister is a very determined woman, Mr Gruyter, from that night he spent on the island he never had a chance."

Before anything more could be said Miss Jones swept into the room. She was radiant. She looked ten years younger. Her cheeks were flushed and her nose was hardly red at all.

"Have you come to congratulate me, Mr Gryuter? she cried, and her manner was spritely and girlish… "You see I was right after all… you don't know how splendid Edward has been all through this terrible time. He's a hero. He is a saint."'

All the Contrôleur can say is, "'I hope you will be very happy.'" Miss Jones has no doubts:

"'Oh, I know I shall… for it is the Lord who has brought us together."'

The Contrôleur could not but think it was rather a clumsy device to bring those two together, that necessitated the death of six hundred innocent persons, but not being well versed in the ways of Omnipotence, he made no remark.

"'You'll never guess where we'll be going on our honeymoon," said Miss Jones, perhaps a trifle archly… "We're going to that island where we were marooned. It has very tender recollections for both of us… it's there I want him to have his reward."

The Contrôleur caught his breath. He left quickly, for he thought that if he did not have a bottle of beer at once he would have a fit. He was never so shocked in his life.'

Well! What are we to make of the spinsterish Miss Jones? Will she marry and live happily ever after? Somehow one rather doubts it. In spite of her new skittish ways, can such a leopardess change her spots, and won't Ginger Ted revert to his old bad ways? We shall never know, but the author leaves us to ponder on it.

As so often with our spinsters, the church has been her crutch, but in her case, it has been more than a crutch; it has been used as a tool; healing the natives and converting them has brought her a husband, or rather 'it is the Lord', using the natives dead or alive to bring this about. But perhaps I am being unfair, perhaps she really *does* believe that the Lord is rewarding her – after all, she has worked for years tirelessly healing and converting the natives. Let's hope she'll be happy, or, at least let's hope that Ginger Ted doesn't disappear before the wedding, because it doesn't seem that she is really cut out to provide him with connubial bliss, but perhaps I am wrong: maybe she is looking forward to Ginger Ted's 'reward' rather more than he is. Perhaps she has been looking forward to it *and* working towards it ever since that fateful night. Perhaps Tennyson's prognosis of marriage to a worthless man: 'As the husband is the wife is; thou art mated with a clown, / And the grossness of his nature will have weight to drag thee down…' will not apply to this union.

We can see here more clearly than in any other of the churchy spinsters –the dare I say it – cynical attitude of the spinster skilled in manipulating Christianity to her own ends. How pervasive and twisted the strand of religion emanating from the Ancient World has become. However, perhaps in both Tabitha and Miss Jones we can see another quite different strand from the Ancient World: the youth Hylas gets his comeuppance by being pulled underwater by the nymph whose advances he has rejected. These ladies are no water nymphs but they are equally determined to get control of a recalcitrant suitor.

'Miss Mackenzie' by Anthony Trollope

Then said she, 'I am very dreary,
'He will not come' she said:
She wept, 'I am aweary, aweary,
Oh God, that I were dead.'
Alfred Tennyson, 'Mariana in the Moated Grange'.

Miss Mackenzie:

In Anthony Trollope's 'Miss Mackenzie' we are vividly shown the difficulties that confront the woman determined to escape spinsterhood.

The autonomous heroine has led a miserable life; her teenage years were spent looking after her invalid father, and when he died, she spent the next fifteen years of her life looking after a sickly brother: 'Her life in London had been altogether of the [Tennysonian] moated grange kind, and long before his death it had become very wearisome to her.' However, a dull friend of her brother's, a Mr Handcock, had proposed to her, and she might have accepted him, even though he was unattractive and ten years her senior, 'but the sick brother upstairs had become peevish. Such a thing should never take place without his consent, and Harry Handcock had ceased to speak tenderly.'

As so often, it is a selfish relative, mother, father, or here, brother that stands in the way of marriage.

When her brother dies, Margaret Mackenzie finds herself – totally unexpectedly – the possessor of a small fortune. Other branches of the family are aggrieved because the details behind the legacy are somewhat confused. The titled Ball family believe the legacy should have come to them, and her other brother Tom, an unsuccessful businessman – or rather, his unpleasant wife – thinks a large share should be theirs.

Hitherto, none of these family members has paid Margaret the least attention, but now they all set about renewing their acquaintance. Mr Handcock too, renews his offer of marriage.

Margaret who has lived such a lonely life does not know what she should do with her new found wealth. One thing she does decide, however, is not to marry Mr Handcock:

'She thought, or rather hoped, that society might still open to her its portals… might it not be given to her to know clever people, nice people, bright people, people who were not heavy and fat like Mr Handcock, or sick and wearisome like her poor brother Walter… she reminded herself that she was the niece of one baronet, and first cousin once removed to another, and that she had eight hundred a year, and liberty to do with it whatsoever she pleased.'

Because she is a nice woman, she wants to do some good with the money – she toys with the idea of giving it to some worthy clergyman to use as he might think fit, but she is not totally convinced that this would be a good idea, and decides instead, to help the struggling and contentious family of her brother Tom; she will undertake to give one of his daughters a good education; she won't actually adopt her because it is 'on the cards that she herself might marry… "Of course she will marry the first fool that asks her," said Mrs Tom.' But she is not right.

Margaret decides she will start a new life in the respectable town of Littlebath, taking her niece, Suzanna with her. There she receives a letter from her brother, requesting a loan of five thousand pounds, promising all sorts of securities; the letter is followed by a visit from his young business partner, Mr Rubb who is not at all averse to making the acquaintance of the wealthy spinster: 'He was a good looking man, nearly six feet high, with great hands and feet and a great forehead also, which atoned for his hands and feet.' Nevertheless, although she is partly won over by his pleasant way of talking, and his good looks, she can't help being conscious that he is not a gentleman. However, she parts with the money.

Not really knowing how to make friends, she gets drawn into the hypocritical evangelical society of Mr Stumfold and his wife. There she meets the man who will become her next suitor, the silver tongued Mr Maguire, 'the possessor of a good figure, of a fine head of jet-black hair, of white teeth, of whiskers which were almost black and very fine – and of the most terrible squint in his right eye which disfigured a face that in all other respects was fitted for an Apollo. She cannot help but be horribly fascinated by this eye.' He too, is aware of her fortune, and endeavours to ingratiate himself with her by high flown evangelical language. Margaret Mackenzie is no fool, she anticipates that both men will probably propose to her, but she is also sadly aware that it is her money, not her person that will bring these events about. She knows that she is no longer young and not particularly attractive.

The next branch of the family to make overtures to her are the titled Ball family. They have never taken any notice of her before, but now, poor themselves, and mindful of her money, they invite Margaret to stay at their rather dilapidated mansion, 'The Cedars'. The son and heir of the baronet is the widower, John Ball, 'a bald-headed stout man somewhat past forty', who has not met with much financial success in life: 'he was always thinking of his money, excusing himself to himself by the fact of his nine children.' He is a very dull man, 'with his bald head, and the weary care-worn look about his eyes and his little intermittent talk, chiefly addressed to his mother.'

Constantly egged on by his mother, the unpleasant, scheming Lady Ball, he proposes to Margaret. In fact, he is quite honest: he admits he is poor and finds it difficult to provide for his family, and he discourses at length on the hardness of his life; he doesn't claim he loves her, he only goes as far as saying, 'I like you better than any woman since I lost Rachel [his dead wife]'. He ends by saying, 'I know I haven't much to offer.'

Margaret feels sorry for him and admires his honesty, but she also knows that she doesn't yet love him; she asks for time to consider. She would like to marry and she would like to do some good with her money, but while she is trying to decide – after all she has two other suitors to take into consideration – she is summoned to his mother's room where she is subjected to a bullying and humiliating lecture. Lady Ball is determined to secure Margaret's thousands for the family. 'It is astonishing,' says Trollope, 'the harm that an old woman may do when she believes she can prevail by the means of her own eloquence... had [Margaret] been allowed to leave the house and think over it all without any argument to her other then those he [John] had used, I think she would have accepted him. But now she was up in arms against the whole thing.' She goes back to Littlebath and writes a letter of refusal.

On her return, it becomes apparent that the five thousand she has lent to her brother through the offices of Mr Rubb has been lost; in fact, the security was never there. Mr Rubb pays her what might have been a difficult visit, to explain all this, but he manages it very well by a combination of honesty and flattery and Margaret says *after* Mr Rubb has kissed her hand: '"Let there be an end to it; I will write to Tom and tell him he is welcome to the money."'

Tom is very unwell; indeed, he is dying, and asks his sister to marry Mr Rubb, his business partner – something that he has apparently already discussed with him:

'His sister understood very well; it was desirable that she by her fortune should enable the widow and orphans of her brother to live in comfort; but it was not desirable that this dependence on her should be recognised.' She refuses Mr Rubb when he comes to ask her in person.

270

Later, she receives a letter from Mr Maguire with yet another proposal which he begins with a lot of sanctimonious drivel: 'It would be my sweet privilege to wipe your eyes and comfort you in your sorrow', and he ends by saying, in effect, that with her money he could buy himself a profitable incumbency and make himself the most important clergyman in Littlebath. She writes back a letter of refusal couched in tactful terms.

Poor Margaret! She has few illusions: she knows that it is not her personal charms that have brought about all this male interest: by marrying Mr Rubb she can support her brother's family, by marrying Mr Maguire she can buy him an incumbency, or she can rescue the Ball family from poverty by marrying Sir John. In such bald terms does Trollope show the lot of the plain Victorian spinster with money.

Then everything changes. The will that has brought her her fortune is found to be false; the money now passes to John Ball, and she is left with virtually nothing. She is a nice woman and behaves very well; she will not contest this new ruling, she will manage the best she can. Lady Ball, of course, is delighted and thankful that Margaret had refused John's offer, but worried that the family will be expected to compensate her for the loss of her wealth, and she summons Margaret to a very different lecture from the previous one, to make sure she makes no demands on them:

"'I have told John that something must be done for you... I remarked to John that you were peculiarly qualified for being a lady's companion.'
'For being what, Aunt?'
'For being a companion to some lady in the decline of life, who would want to have some nice mannered person always with her. You have the advantage of being ladylike and gentle, and I think you are patient by disposition.'"

Now Margaret who, as John Ball himself has told his mother 'has behaved admirably throughout', completely loses it:

'"Aunt," said Miss Mackenzie, and her voice as she spoke, was hardly gentle, nor indicative of much patience... "I would sooner take a broom in my hand and sweep a crossing in London than lead such a life as that. What? Make myself the slave of some old woman who would think that she had bought the power of tyrannising over me by allowing me to sit in the same room as her? No indeed."'

In no uncertain terms does Margaret Mackenzie spell out the fate of the penniless spinster. Lady Ball is indignant, she had, she claims, merely been trying to be helpful. The old hypocrite! But she has underestimated Margaret's character and calculated without her son. John has been touched by Margaret's goodness and her plight, and renews his offer of marriage:

'"Margaret," said he, "you shall be my wife and the mother of my children... I loved you when I asked you at Christmas, but I did not love you then as I love you now."'

Of course, she accepts him, but she is worried about the reaction of his mother, John is too! But he tells Margaret 'to be firm', and she says she will.

But nothing will be easy for her. Mr Maguire does not believe that Margaret's fortune is lost and still thinks he is in with a chance, and that he can wrest her and the fortune away from the Ball family; to this end he goes to 'The Cedars', declaring that he is engaged to her, and when Lady Ball hears him, she sees her way forward, and maligns Margaret to her son. John Ball is a weak man and half believes his mother, and Margaret sees no alternative but to leave 'The Cedars'. John Ball is further upset when Mr Maguire goes to the press making out that he [Ball], is taking advantage of a poor woman whom he terms 'the sacrificial lamb', and stigmatises Ball himself as a 'ravening lion'.

John Ball is no lion; in fact, he is an awful coward, and he is horrified by the adverse publicity, and actually avoids making any contact with Margaret, now living in poverty with an old family servant, who treats her with scant respect. Again, we can see the awful humiliations endured by the penniless spinster; but even though Mr Rubb reappears and proposes again, seemingly out of some residual affection, and perhaps in expectation of some sort of pecuniary assistance from the Ball family, she refuses him. She decides that the only option open to her is to undertake hospital nursing as a way of earning her keep. The old servant who has now become insufferably familiar, comments of Mr Rubb: "'He really do seem a nice man, Miss. I wonder you wouldn't liefer have him than go into one of them hospitals.'" But Margaret knows she cannot marry a man who is not a gentleman, and she still has some diminishing hopes of John Ball.

However, things eventually look up for Margaret; the publicity generated by Mr Maguire's articles in the press becomes widespread, and she becomes quite a celebrity; and as a result, a rich relative of whom she has hitherto known little, decides to befriend her, and invites her to stay in her opulent London house. She proves a good friend and is determined to secure John Ball for Margaret. First, she smartens her up, then she – more or less – inveigles John Ball into renewing his proposal, and he needs all the prompting he can get, being not only a ditherer, but scared by the adverse publicity, not to mention his terrifying mother. But when Mr Maguire's scheming is finally revealed and he is sent packing, Ball proposes. Margaret Mackenzie will be married from rich relative's London house and become Lady Ball.

The novel has presented in unambiguous terms the stark choices faced by the Victorian spinster. Poor Margaret

Mackenzie, placed between the Scylla and Charybdis of the ungentlemanly and rather dishonest Mr Rubb and the scoundrely Mr Maguire, navigates her way to the shores of 'The Cedars', and the arms of its feeble owner and his nine children.

In his introduction to the novel (World's Classics 1990), A.O.J. Cockshut succinctly sums up her position:

'She has to live in a world where money is important; and the position of a dull baronet's lady is far preferable to that of a poor spinster. It is uncomfortable and painful because it is so true.'

With these three unlikely spinsters married off, we come to the end of the first part of this study. Now it is time to move on from individual spinsters and see how the ever-repeating strands of spinsterhood, as diverse as suffering, scheming, subservience, religion and disfigurement, all inherited from the Ancient World – to name but a few – have twisted and interwoven these women together into a multi-coloured fabric. Now we need to look at this material and see how and why it has become a unique textile.

PART 2: WEAVING IT TOGETHER

Each preceding chapter showed a different skein of spinsterhood and each has drawn in a greater or lesser degree from the spinsters of the Ancient World. Sometimes different skeins have overlapped. Strands from one skein have strayed into another: Theodora, for instance could belong to the saintly or to the sleuth.

Now I will endeavour to untangle these strands and weave the threads together into a composite whole, in order give a feel of the fabric of spinsterhood.

This will involve looking at family background, the rationale of spinsterhood and its external portrayal. Finally, I will come full circle and reveal how spinsterhood can be understood by reference threadwork and to its ancient etymological root in spinning. When I have finished weaving these skeins together I hope to produce a tapestry of spinsterhood that can act as an historical backdrop to the position of vulnerable women today.

SKEIN 1: SEARCHING CHILDHOOD

They fuck you up, your mum and dad,
They may not mean to, but they do.
They fill you with the faults they had
And add some extra, just for you.
Philip Larkin, 'Collected Poems'.

The first skein to be woven into the tapestry involves reaching back to the troubled childhoods of our spinsters. Although these women had very different upbringings, they are united in being blighted in a way that has left them unwilling to undertake marriage, or even form meaningful relationships. To unravel this skein we need to look into their family backgrounds.

At the beginning of this book I mentioned the vengeful Erinyes, but I didn't describe their family background.

Gaia (Earth) copulated with Ouranos (Heaven) and produced a hideous lot of children: the Titans, the Cyclopes and three hundred giants with a hundred heads and hands apiece, Briaros and Gyges, to name but two. Unsurprisingly, Ouranos did not like the look of these children, but less unsurprisingly, he stuffed them all back into Gaia's womb. Being in some discomfort, she plotted a revenge on her 'husband' by persuading her son Cronos (who had somehow managed to escape), to castrate his father. Jenny March in her 'Encyclopaedia of Mythology' vividly describes the scene: '... with the right [hand] he took the huge sickle with its long row of sharp teeth, and quickly cut off his father's genitals and flung them behind him.'
The drops of blood fell on Gaia, and after nine months, the Erinyes were the result. To add to this somewhat unusual family history, Gaia (before the incident with the sickle,

obviously) had also produced the numerous Melia nymphs who turned into ash trees; but to cap it all, there was another sister, Aphrodite. Actually she was more of a half-sister, because, while the Erinys were conceived from blood of their father's castrated genitals, she was born from the white foam that grew about the genitals when they fell into the sea. She was a much more favoured child. We are told 'Eros and Fair Desire attended her birth', and they accompanied her as she went off to Mount Olympus to join the family of gods – rather desirable foster parents. We can imagine the Erinyes thinking:

'Typical! Just because she is going to be pretty, she has the best midwives, and then goes off to live with some posh family in luxurious surroundings, while we are left with the murderous old dad, a violent mother who hates him, and a brood of delinquent brothers.' No wonder they became bitter. Gaia then incestuously copulated with her son Cronos and produced another heterogeneous set of children. Rather like Queen Victoria, Gaia seems to have enjoyed the way children were made but disliked what emerged. Cronos didn't like them either; he swallowed five of them at birth (although they were eventually disgorged).

Admittedly, none of our spinsters comes from quite such a dysfunctional family, (I think it would be hard to find one), but by considering this extreme case, we may begin to understand why some of our spinsters became warped by their unhappy childhoods and behaved as they did.

To examine these childhoods we will start with fathers because they, more than any other relation, seem to have adversely affected the lives of our spinsters.

Fathers

But my father is raging with his mind on evil – hard god that he is, a constant blight, the foiler of my plans.

Homer, 'The Iliad'.

Ecclesiastical Fathers:

There seems to be a theme of pernicious influence by the clergyman father on the daughter. This could perhaps be because of disappointment at their gender: a son could have been persuaded to follow in his father's ecclesiastical footsteps, while a daughter's sex stood in her way. Theodora Braithwaite is aware that she is tolerated, not as a person in her own right, but only as the daughter of an illustrious ecclesiastical father. Although she does not appear to have any particular emotional scars, she is made aware of being a disappointment to her family by the words of Father Tobias Angel in 'A Grave Disturbance':

"'Braithwaite. Ah, yes. A famous father. Good Catholic family. Lots of generations of priests. Pity he didn't have a son.'"

Mary Joyce's parson father was not unkind; he just unthinkingly accepted her as a familiar, inferior female presence in the house, indispensable, but not interesting, this resulted in her lack of self-confidence and a fatal dowdiness. Had she smartened herself up, made herself a bit less unsexy, she would undoubtedly have won over Mr Herbert, her erstwhile suitor who (after her death) admitted that he had loved her. It wasn't so much cruelty on the part of Reverend Joyce's part, but it was negligence, and that negligence made her the timorous spinster she was to remain.

The sisters, Martine and Philippa, are forced into spinsterhood by their father, the Dean, who will not be deprived of their hands and fills the house with an emphasis on purity, imbuing his daughters' minds with hopes of 'an ideal of heavenly love', in the place of the sexual love to which they were entitled. Instead, they were made to remain as 'precious to the community… for their dear father's sake.'

In 'Agnes Grey' the vicar father is not cruel to his daughter or his family, but he is foolish and misguided. Having lost all the family money in unwise speculation he became depressed and sickly, and unable or unwilling to care for his family. Although Agnes is not forced to become a governess, she sees that extra income is of the essence if the family is to survive, and it is her decision to become one, that embroils her in years of misery.

Although not as bad as Cronos or Ouranos these ecclesiastical fathers were not kind to their daughters.

Inadequate Fathers:

Fathers do not have to be ecclesiastical to have an adverse effect on their daughters' development, but a lack of interest and care, or simple ineptitude can be enough to blight them.

In 'Whereabouts' La Signora's father haunts her throughout her adult life because he never stepped in to intervene between her unkind mother and herself:

'"I have nothing to do with it. Why ask me?" You would repeat those two sentences, a response I found both brutal and cowardly on your part… you'd settle into an armchair in the living room in a darkness of your own making. But as a result I learned not to involve you, and never expect you to save me.'

In 'The Darkest Evening' poor Vera longs for a kindly father, a role that Hector is never going to fill, but she admits his unkindness has made her what she is, a fine and ruthless cop, although at heart she would have preferred a kindlier upbringing and at least one proposal of marriage.

Stephen Gordon's father knows about his daughter's ambiguous sexuality – he has read Kraft-Ebbing, but he can never bring himself to talk about it with her or show her he understands, nor does he dare to tell his wife who makes her daughter's life a misery by forcing her to behave in an ultra feminine fashion. Had he spoken to Stephen, perhaps in company with her mother, life would have been easier for all of them.

The god Peneius did the best he could think of at the time – but couldn't he have done better by thinking of something other than turning his daughter, Daphne, into a laurel tree?

Destructive Fathers:

There are, however, fathers whose cruelty puts them in the same class as Ouranos and his son Cronos.

The cynical and amused attitude adopted by Catherine Sloper's father produced in her a lack of self-worth, and so when the gold-digging Morris Townsend took notice of her, she was all too happy to welcome him, blind to his imperfections, and when she was subsequently dumped by him, she suffered for the rest of her life. At no point did her father offer sympathy or even understanding.

In 'Memoirs of a Geisha', Chiyo's father sells her to an unscrupulous trader in pretty girls who he knows will consign her to prostitution or to becoming a geisha. Chiyo often reflects on the contented married life she might have led, had she been allowed to remain in her home village.

Arieka in 'The Double Tongue' is similarly callously despatched, this time the father actually pays to get rid of her, by arranging for her appointment at Delphi.

Whether cruel, indifferent, or simply inadequate, these fathers have all in some degree, been responsible for their daughters unhappiness and subsequent spinsterhood.

Mothers

Grendel's mother, a woman, a she-monster brooded on her misery.

Beowulf.

Widowed Mothers:

Another source of unhappiness is the early loss of the father, altering the family dynamic, and giving unlimited power to the mother.

Eleanor Oliphant's father was unknown, and the lack of a paternal presence enabled her mother to exercise extreme cruelty on her daughters; this resulted in Eleanor turning in on herself and becoming unable to form normal relationships with anyone, let alone marriageable men. Only when she has finally managed to throw off her mother's influence does she begin to unfold and become able to socialise and develop a relationship with her friend, Raymond.

In 'Whereabouts' La Signora's father dies quite suddenly, and this results in 'my mother's fitful rages, the quarrels I've never forgotten, terrifying scenes… how severely she'd berate me… the oppressive mother… the invasive mother.' The unhappiness given her by this bad mother, coupled with the uncaring attitude of her father, resulted in her being too wary to form relationships, but doomed to always remaining an outsider.

In the 'Hotel du Lac' Edith suffers in a similar way at the hands of her Viennese mother who is filled with anger through dislike of her husband, a man who had been a kindly father to Edith, but when he died young, like La Signora's father, she was left to the untender mercy of her mother:

'She raged against her fate, deliberately, wilfully letting herself go, slatternly and scornful, mocking her pale silent daughter who slipped so modestly in and out of her aromatic bedroom, bringing cups of coffee which her mother deliberately spilled.'

Edith is left feeling insignificant, something that is to remain with her throughout her life, and although she has two proposals of marriage, the world of marriage is something she feels inadequate to face.

In 'Where Angels Fear to Tread', Harriet (and indeed, her brother) are subject to bullying by their widowed mother; it is her overriding insistence that they go to Italy, to get hold of Gino's baby that results in Harriet's crime of infanticide.

Perhaps the garrulous Miss Bates might have married if she had not been tasked with looking after *her* widowed mother.

The Goddess Gaia wasn't *exactly* widowed, but she didn't constitute the role model for motherhood!

Brothers

One husband gone, I might have found another,
Or a child from a new man in first child's place,
But with my parents hid away in death,

No brother ever could spring up for me.
Sophocles, 'Antigone'.

Antigone's words illustrate the closeness felt by the sister for the brother; it is a relationship felt to be of unique value, but brothers are a mixed lot.

There are brothers who bully their sisters into spinsterhood, and there are spinster sisters who relentlessly bully their brothers. Let's look at the first category.

Bullying Brothers:

If we cast our minds back to Margaret Mackenzie, we remember that she spent a wearisome fifteen years of her early life looking after her hypochondriac brother; she did have a proposal 'but the sick brother upstairs had become peevish. Such a thing should never take place without his consent, and Harry Handcock had ceased to speak tenderly.' In other words he condemned her to spinsterhood for his own selfish reasons.

Her other brother, Tom, bullies her in quite an opposite way, trying to persuade her to marry the unsuitable Mr Rubb in order to save his family business with her money. In effect, he resembles Chiyo's father in trying to sell her virginity.

Miss Havisham's brother (admittedly, a half-brother) colludes with Culbertson to put a stop to their wedding. This time, although money lies at the root of his actions, it is not a question of selling her virginity, but in preventing her marriage.

In 'Precious Bane' Prue is forced into spinsterhood by her brother who makes her devote her life to back-breaking work, justifying his actions by telling her that nobody will want to marry her because of her hare lip. Only after his death is she freed from her slavery and enabled to cast off her spinsterhood.

Even the much abused Miss Briggs' has a large part of her small annuity taken by her brother.

Bullied Brothers:

Not all brothers are updated versions of the hundred-handers; conversely some are subjected to bullying by their sisters, but it is this very bullying that will contribute to their spinsterhood.

Miss Corny, like Hilda Cherrington, had been tasked with bringing up a much younger brother, and like Hilda, she had allowed the brother to become all-in-all to her instead of looking outwards towards other males; but that, of course, in turn, had made both women into stern, unbending beings, cruel and scheming. And in Hilda's case, once she did feel the need for a sexual life of her own, this hard-formed intransigence cost her her marriage with Dick Staverley – his sister tells Eustace that Dick would have married her, if she had not tried to mould him, as she had her brother. Each of these two spinsters' cruelty had been allowed to flourish under the excuse of nurturing the younger brother.

In 'Where Angels Fear to Tread' Philip, like Eustace Cherrington, is lazy and malleable, a creature of both his mother and sister. When he makes his second visit to Italy with Harriet to get hold of Gino's baby, he regards the whole thing as an amusing interlude. He does not care whether they get the baby or not. However, if he kept a more careful eye on his sister, the tragedy would have been averted. He isn't exactly in awe of her, but again, like Eustace he is unwilling to thwart her plans. He should have known how selfishly determined she was to get hold of the baby and that she was never going to leave without it; instead, he was content to accept what he laughingly and so disastrously told himself was 'an honourable defeat'. The power of Harriet's will overcame his scruples, and after she had got into the carriage clutching the silent baby, he simply contented himself with saying, "'I suppose it's still breathing and all that.'" And even when his suspicions are aroused, he does nothing; she is more powerful than he, and prevails over him right up to the moment when the carriage overturns, and the baby is dead. In her own way she has bullied him as much as Hilda had bullied Eustace. Each of these women, by exercising their power over a weak brother brought about death; in Harriet's case Gino's baby; in Hilda's, the death of Eustace himself. These were strong selfish, narcissistic spinsters whose intentions had become hardened through dominating weak brothers.

In 'The Vessel of Wrath' Miss Jones had given her life to her missionary brother, and this has resulted in her becoming stern and unbending; however, these hard years have given her the strength to cow her brother to such an extent that he accepts her determination to marry. But might it not have been better if her brother had not given way, because but what sort of marriage would she have with the reprobate Ginger?

Helpful Brothers:

There are some (not many) brothers who help their sisters out of spinsterhood. Tom Pinch in 'Martin Chuzzlewit' rescues his sister from governess-ship, and he is active in promoting her subsequent marriage.

Matthew Bramble – perhaps from not altogether altruistic motives – manages to contrive a marriage between Lieutenant Lismahago and his sister Tabitha; whether or not this will be successful is uncertain, but at least he's rescued her from spinsterhood, and given her what she's been trying to achieve over the years. Without his help she would definitely have remained unmarried.

Although Miss Matty's brother does not rescue her from spinsterhood, he returns from India well-heeled and saves her from financial catastrophe.

A mixed bunch, brothers, but all have influenced their sisters, for good or ill. We are not told whether the hundred-handers, Briaros and Gyges, bullied their sisters, but I cannot think they were kindly brothers.

Sisters

Sisters, sisters
There were never such devoted sisters
All kinds of weather
We stick together
The same in the rain or sun
Two different faces
But in tight places
We think and act as one.
Irving Berlin, 'Sisters Lyrics'.

The case of sisters is different. We tend to see sisters not so much as a formative influence on the spinster's early years, but we view them in later life when they have formed a solid entity. And it is in their adult years we see them working together – or against each other – to make some sort of modus vivendi.

Spinster sisters often come in threes. We have seen the three Fates, the three Norns, there are the three Graeae, the sisters with a single eye and tooth between them; the three gorgon sisters, Medusa, Stheno and Euryale. There are the three witches in Macbeth. More recently we meet Friederike, Henriette and Pfiffi, the three spiteful sisters in 'Buddenbrooks'; there are the three Sicilian sisters, Concetta,

Carolina and Caterina, arrogantly clinging on to a decayed grandeur. Interestingly, all these threesomes seem to be fateful or unpleasant in their different ways.

More often, spinster sisters come in pairs. To begin on a light note, there are the pair of horrible sisters, described by the bardic centipede in 'James and the Giant Peach'.

'Aunt spiker was as thin as a wire,
And dry as a bone, only drier.
She was so long and thin
If you carried her in,
You could use her for poking the fire.

Aunt sponge was terrifically fat
And tremendously flabby at that.
Her tummy and waist
Were as soggy as paste.
It was worse on the place where she sat.'

More realistically, paired women have often more or less, been forced together, and while not performing the roles of husband and wife, they are 'a couple'; they are two interwoven parts of a family. In this way they achieve that desired goal: respectability. Forced into one another's company, they mould each other's adult lives. They even begin to become something of a homogenous creation. Belinda and Harriet bound together by their respective dependence on the church, become a sort of Janus-faced symbol of spinsterhood, Harriet looking outwards to the world with her cosseting of curates, colourful clothes and enjoyment of food, while Belinda looks inward, dreaming of Archdeacon Hocleve and meditating on questions of morality.

In 'Babette's Feast' Martine and Philippa become little more than an ambience of spirituality; when the pious brothers and sisters of the community visited them, they 'felt that their master's spirit was with them; here they were at home and at peace.' These sisters still haven't escaped their father.

Units are often forged at the expense of the less dominant.

In 'Cranford' Miss Matty lives with her elder sister Deborah, but it was this sister who had prevented her from marrying: Miss Matty had a suitor, a farmer by the name of Thomas Holbrook. A friend asks:

'"Then how came Miss Matty not to marry him?"

"Oh, I don't know. She was willing enough, I think; but you know, Cousin Thomas would not have been enough of a gentleman for the Rector and Miss Jenkyns... they did not like Miss Matty to marry below her rank. You know, somehow they are related to Sir Peter Arley; Miss Jenkyns thought a deal of that."'

So Miss Matty's marriage was forbidden by the sister, not to mention by yet another unkind clerical father, but even in old age, when her sister is dead and the suitor returns, Miss Matty is not sure whether she should return his visit: '"Deborah would not have liked it."' Foolish Miss Matty, always dominated by the stupid and unkind sister.

In Austen's 'Sense and Sensibility' we meet the two Miss Steeles. The younger, Lucy, is carefully manoeuvring her way to bringing about a successful conclusion to her secret engagement to Edward Ferrars and the plain elder sister tries in a maladroit way to help her, not through love – she may well resent her younger sister's good looks, but because she sees a way of the two of them being financially supported.

Whether good or bad, pleasant or unpleasant, sisters work as a unit to develop some sort of a modus vivendi – just like the Erinyes, though not as fatally.

Orphans

There are spinsters who are orphans. This would immediately condemn them to the role of subservient spinsters. Although she is not initially treated as subservient, the orphaned Sonya is continually aware of the goodness of the Rostov family in bringing her up – although they themselves do nothing as servants and governesses see to the children. But because of the indebtedness she feels, Sonya releases her beloved Nicholas from his duty to marry her, as he has always promised, and the rest of her life is spent in subservience to his family and their children.

Penniless Lucy Snowe must work first as a companion to an elderly invalid, then as a governess, and finally, as a teacher. In none of these roles is she treated with much respect.

Ruth Pinch has to endure humiliation in her work as a governess in an unkind family.

In 'Buddenbrooks' poor Clothilde, ever conscious of her inferior position, lives with the family as a poor relation.

In 'The Anchoress', when Sarah loses her mother, father and sister, she takes the decision to spend the rest of her life confined within a cell.

Admittedly, Blanche Dubois played her cards badly, but she too, had been left parentless at a young age.

And poor Klara, the Artificial Friend, is she an orphan? Well, certainly she has no definable parentage, and has to wait in the shop window until she is bought and put into a futuristic servitude.

An even greater handicap is the stigma of illegitimacy. Miss Wade is a case in point, one whose 'unhappy nature' is formed by always feeling inferior to her legitimate peers.

Of course, other women with bad fathers, mothers, and brothers, or those who are orphans, grow up, get married and live normal lives, and do not depend on relations, but sometimes, it seems, in the case of our spinsters, parents are a very real factor in the formation of their unsatisfied lives. As, Aeschylus describes the Erinyes, these spinsters too, were 'spurned, outcast from gods, driven apart to stand in light not of the sun.'

SKEIN 2: SUCCESSFUL SPINSTERHOOD?

In spite of this pernicious childhood influence or indeed other potential contributory factors, it is a mistake to see all spinsters as victims. There is a substantial number who remained spinsters by choice.

Saints, nuns and anchoresses decided to eschew marriage and keep themselves for god, (although in the case of Arieka and the Anchoress, their fate too, was the result of their family backgrounds).

Others, like Mrs Danvers and Stephen Gordon were in love with women and had no interest in men or marriage.

Like Stephen, who had her heart set on only one woman, there were women that had their heart set on only one man, and that man unfortunately already married. These were women who refused to compromise by marrying someone else, although they had other offers.

In 'War and Peace' Sonya had an offer from the eligible Denislav, but was in love with her cousin Nicholas, and so refused him.

Miss Jean Brodie could have settled for Mr Lloyd, the music master, but was in love with Teddy Lowther who was already married.

Belinda could have married Bishop Grote, but she loved her archdeacon. Ruth Galloway refused several offers because she loved Nelson, although she knew that marriage to him would be impossible, even if he was free to marry her.

In 'Hotel du Lac', Edith could have married twice, but she jilted two potential husbands because of the influence of her married lover.

Chiyo, the Geisha, settled for an unsatisfactory illicit affair, because her lover was already married.

Others chose spinsterhood for different reasons: Miss Wade jilted her eligible fiancé from a sort of innate perversity. Even Cousin Bette who eventually received offers of marriage, preferred scheming to marriage. Miss Corny scorned her single offer of marriage, preferring to remain and bully her brother.

In 'Gaudy Night' Miss de Vine gave up her lover in favour of her own life of scholarship, a decision she didn't regret.

They all made a positive decision: spinsterhood, not marriage. Why did these women not settle for second best, especially at a time when spinsterhood was despised? Romanticism? Idealism? Or did they share something different: an obstinate overwhelming desire to live life in their own ways. The goddess Hestia had offers from both Poseidon and Apollo but made an unshakeable decision to remain unmarried.

Although many of these women suffered for their decision, there were others who lived comfortable enough lives: the superior spinsters from Sicily, for example, but few positively thrived on it.

In 'Arsenic and Old Lace' there are the two old ladies who certainly enjoy life – or rather, they enjoy death, because as it transpires, they have murdered twelve old men, apparently for the best of motives – the old men were lonely! The poisonings and the burials have kept them young and active, spritely, in fact. However, 'Arsenic and Old lace' is a farce. The author intends to make us laugh at the discrepancy between what we believe about old spinsters, i.e. that they are dear old things (Martha is described as 'a sweet elderly woman with Victorian charm', and Abby is called 'a plump little darling'), while they are, in fact, murderesses. We are to assume that the whole thing is ridiculous, not just because little old spinsters would never do such things, but because they would be incapable of doing anything other than make jam and distribute broth. In fact, the play acts to reinforce the stereotype. We laugh because we know (or think we know) that spinsters are not like that. We are not expected to believe in them.

Among those we have met, I have found it difficult to track down spinsters who revel in their state. There is Margaret Rutherford's portrayal of the jolly-hockeysticks Miss Marple, but Miss Marple, as we have seen, is not always full of joie de vivre; this is another farcical portrayal. Amongst our spinsters I have found only two, and unlike the arsenic ladies, they are credible.

Harriet Bede has a robust attitude towards her spinsterhood. She likes long luxurious baths, dressing up in fashionable clothes, relishes good food, and has no time for life's losers like Miss Prior. She prefers cosseting curates to marrying either of the two men who have asked her, but then, she enjoys the confidence provided by those two invaluable assets: good looks and money.

Miss Crawley enjoys similar attributes. In 'Vanity Fair' we are told: 'Old Miss Crawley was certainly one of the reprobate. She had a snug little house in Park Lane and as she ate and drank a great deal too much during the season in London. She was the most hospitable and jovial of old vessels and had been a beauty in her day, she said.' Like Dorothy Parker's 'Little Old Lady in Lavender Silk' she might have declared:

'So I'll say, though reflection unnerves me
And pronouncements I dodge as I can,

That I think, (if my memory serves me)
There was nothing more fun than a man.'

Good looks and money would appear to form the components of an enjoyable spinsterhood, but for those who wish to escape from it there is a further vital necessity: opportunity.

Sometimes two of these three elements will be enough: Tabitha Bramble, while lacking looks, had the opportunity to meet Captain Lismahago, and there was plenty of money to clinch the deal. Miss Jones had no looks but the opportunity of meeting Ginger, and money from her missionary brother enabled her marriage. In 'Vanity Fair' Becky Sharpe had no money at all, but had the opportunity of meeting Rawdon Crawley, and the looks to win him over.

Sadly, sometimes two elements are insufficient: Mary Jocelyn possessed money and opportunity, but a dowdy appearance lost her her suitor; Catherine Sloper was plain, but she did have money, but she was given the *wrong* opportunity.

Even possessing all three elements does not guarantee success: Hilda had them all, but she still failed to win Dick Staverley.

Without any of these three elements spinsterhood is not an option but a life sentence: Miss Clare possessed neither looks, money nor opportunity and would spend her life as a 'supplementary teacher'. Fraulein Weichbrodt was hunch-backed, had no money and no opportunity, and she too had to confine herself to her scholastic duties.

There is a difference between being willing to embrace spinsterhood or having it thrust upon you. The nymphs Syrinx, Daphne and Callisto had status (an equivalent of money), looks and opportunity, but although they underwent metamorphoses, it was not from spinsterhood to marriage.

SKEIN 3: SARTORIAL DEFINITION

We have looked at the various spinsters, as it were, from the interior; we have seen their thoughts, fears and motives, but their outward appearance can be equally telling, and the personality is often defined by the clothes they chose to wear.

Most of us adopt some sort of uniform; under lockdown we tended to leave it off. Indeed, sales of men's suits plummeted and 'comfort wear' sales soared because we had no need to present an appearance to the outside world, but when lockdown ceased, and we rejoined the outside world, we once again reverted to our various uniforms, whether self-consciously casual, or purposefully formal because we felt a need to show ourselves in some particular light.

Our Greek goddesses certainly knew how to define themselves. We have met Athene as the goddess of handicraft and remember her contest with Arachne, but she was also a warlike goddess having sprung fully armed from the forehead of Zeus. She is pictured in art with helmet, aegis (a goatskin cape fringed with snakes), spear and a shield depicting the head of the gorgon, Medusa who was herself identified by her hair of snakes. Artemis (Diana) appears frequently in ancient art carrying bow and arrow and wearing animal skins.

Our spinsters are no different; a uniform or identifying dress becomes a way of defining, or conversely, hiding their state. This is often a matter of great preoccupation to them.

Clerical Garb:

Holy spinsters have an easily identifiable uniform; when St Catherine becomes a fiction rather than an actual woman – if she ever was one – she can be presented, as we have seen, in different ways, often and unrealistically, given her situation, clad in glamorous clothes, but she always has her 'prefect's badge': the wheel is always there to proclaim her chastity. Nuns, of course, have their own uniform, no matter how becomingly it is arranged, viz Audrey Hepburn in 'The Nun's Story', but the uniform is there; the black robes conceal the seductive contours of a body always alert to the whispering of the devil; the white wimple spells Chastity. No one will whip this ponderous uniform off and reveal what lies within.

Theodora Braithwaite, at six foot one, is always going to be regarded as a bit of an oddity, so like Saint Catherine with her wheel, Theodora has her own 'prefect's badge': the clerical collar, and she can always fasten it round her virginal neck when she feels danger threaten. And like the nun or the anchoress, she has the clerical robes ready to hand; and what safer uniform could there be than those? The church, as we have seen, can always be a resource for the spinster, but the accoutrement of clerical dress is the icing on the cake – or should I say a golden crosier?

Religious 'uniform' is both a protection and an assertion of pride in the choice of this lifestyle.

Academic Uniform:

The cap and gown are, like clerical attire, satisfactory ways of disguising spinsterhood: the gown hides the figure within, and the cap draws attention away from the face towards a symbol of scholarship; both proclaim the importance of the wearer; they justify spinsterhood saying: "I eschew all attempts at prettiness, my life is dedicated to higher things." In 'Gaudy Night' Harriet Vane 'observed with irritation, that most of them [the alumni] wore their caps badly, and one had the folly to put on a pale lemon frock with muslin frills which looked incongruous beneath a gown'. There can be no compromise between flirtatious femininity and austere scholarship. Harriet herself wears a black frock beneath her gown: 'Its dull surface effaced itself, not outshining the dull gleam of the academic poplin.' One of the dons, Miss Lydgate complains of her students' lack of attention to their gowns: 'these young things don't care *that* for them.' She does not like to see the young female students sunbathing in the quad: 'Miss Martin must insist on bathing dresses – backless if they like, but proper bathing dresses…'.

All this stripping-off will suggest that there is another life, a sexual one beneath the scholarly attire; she wants to keep it confined there. Backless bathing dresses are a huge concession, but the breasts, those feminine attributes must be disguised. In 'Gaudy Night', gowns play a central role in academic spinsterhood, and the plot hinges on it. When the widowed scout, Annie plots her revenge on academic spinsters, she sets fire to a number of gowns, seeking to destroy the raison d'être of the academic spinster, and reveal the nakedness of her life without her camouflage. She sees the gown as the disguise academic spinsters take because 'you can't get men for yourselves and hate the women who can.' The dons themselves, of course, would violently disagree. The gown is a symbol. It is both a protection, and a defiant assertion of the superiority of scholarship to marriage. The goddess Athene had her own cap and gown in the form of her helmet and the fringed aegis, which displayed the head of the Medusa in its centre and showed that she was more than an equal for any man.

Uniform of Effacement:

There is a quite different 'uniform', one specifically chosen for its drabness, aimed not at asserting, but specifically for obscuring the spinsterly self. In 'Hotel du Lac' Mr Neville comments on Edith's attire: "'That cardigan... I do wish you would get rid of it.'" Edith knows that he is, in effect, saying, "If you marry me, you will cast off that apparel of spinsterhood."

In 'Some Tame Gazelle' Belinda is saddened by Miss Prior's comment:

"'Oh well, Miss Bede, you never wear very fitting dresses, do you... a few inches here or there doesn't make much difference?"

"No, I suppose it doesn't," said Belinda, depressed by this picture of herself in shapeless unfashionable garments.' And when Miss Prior comments "'... now, Mrs Hocleve, she *has* got some lovely things,'" Belinda sees the difference between herself and the married Agatha Hocleve: she is defined as a spinster by her dreary clothes, while the wife of the man she loves is smartly dressed. Both Edith and Belinda are resigned to an existence, as unexciting as their clothes. Mary Jocelyn, too, presents a dowdy figure. "'I thought she was some sort of church worker'", says Kathy Herbert scornfully. Like Belinda and Edith her clothes reflect her unexciting nature.

Scheming spinsters deliberately choose to make themselves unobtrusive. Interestingly, authors tell us very little about their apparel. We know Mrs Danvers wore black, but we learn little about Harriet' Herriton's clothes in 'Where Angels Fear to Tread', or about Miss Corny's clothes in 'East Lynne'. These are women who purposefully do not draw attention to themselves because of what they are plotting. Like Ate they are not easily definable.

Two sleuthing spinsters (we have already discussed Theodora) choose to wear unobtrusive clothes, not out of any feeling of inferiority, but because they consider them appropriate to their task. Miss Marple aims for neat unobtrusiveness because she wishes to observe rather than be observed. Vera, described by one suspect as 'looking like a bag lady', has no truck with expressing her personality in clothes, but is only interested in being comfortable so she can carry out her job as easily as possible. These are spinsters for whom clothes are unimportant as symbols of spinsterhood. They prefer to subsume any complexes they might have in the pursuit of justice, after all the Erinyes were not bothered about clothes.

Suitability for the job is also the deciding factor in the chosen apparel of other spinsters. Miss Clare seeks out appropriate clothing for the classroom: '… a blue cardigan, something between a royal and a navy to wear with my grey worsted skirt in the winter', while the most extravagant item of clothing purchased by Miss Read is 'a dashing pair of brown brogues'. Again, like the sleuths, their clothing is chosen to show that their identity is synonymous with their job.

There are exceptions. Miss Jean Brodie with her string of amber beads and fashionable, striking clothes seeks to show that her personality lies outside the job. Miss Jackson in 'Village School' wears ill-chosen, unsightly, eye-catching clothes in an unsuccessful attempt to look arty and unschoolmistressy.

Hiding the libido:

In 'The Sixth Heaven' the second book of the 'Eustace and Hilda' trilogy, we are told of Hilda's choice of dress:

'Starting from an almost masculine white collar and a black tie descended a coat and skirt of navy-blue serge, which had the intimidating effect of a uniform without actually being one.' Hilda wants to assert her disregard of frivolous femininity. All very well, but when the spinster is forced to discard her uniform in favour of fashion, the effect can be disastrous, as we can see when Hilda joins the other guests, at Anchorstone Hall:

'She was not exactly overdressed in her stiff blue silk which shimmered silvery white on the top where the light caught it, her appearance was so striking that she hardly could be, and the dress which Eustace had helped her choose, only looked a little more expensive than a dress ought to look. But Hilda had not come to terms with it; it covered her up to a point, but did not clothe her. Anne and Monica seemed to have grown into their simpler dresses. They had damped down their personalities to a discreet glow, whereas Hilda wore hers like a headlight... in his imaginings of her at Anchorstone, this was how Eustace had wanted her to look. He could see now that it was a mistake... she wasn't a lamp that could be turned down, she had to blaze, and the more uneasy she felt, the more she clashed with her surroundings, imparting her discomfort – it seemed to Eustace, to everyone else.'

Eustace is anxious to marry Hilda to Dick Staverley, and to force her to cast off her spinsterhood along with her uniform. But the trouble is that Hilda has been at pains through all her adult life to suppress her passionate nature under a mask of severity, and now her habit of austerity is so deeply engrained in her, that when she casts off her uniform and is left without the habitual cover, the camouflage, as it were, she is, in fact, baring her sexual needs to the world, blazing them out, although she herself doesn't really understand this; only her awkwardness reveals her unease at the self she is revealing. In a muddled sort of way, Eustace realises that he is partly to blame for unleashing Hilda's libido: 'She wasn't a lamp that could be turned down.' And of course, this is the start of her disastrous affair with Dick Staverley.

We meet a similar case in 'Villette'. Lucy Snowe's 'uniform' is a succession of drab colourless dresses that will hide her passionate nature under a uniform of inconspicuousness; only when she has to act in the school play and take the part of a fop, does her clothing enable her to produce a spirited performance and release her repressions, revealing her closely-concealed libido. Again, her life changes when Mrs Bretton presents her with pink dress. Immediately Lucy feels what this implies – her exposure as a sexualised being.

'"That is not for me," I said hurriedly, feeling I would almost as soon clothe myself in the costume of a Chinese lady of rank... without any force at all, I found myself led and influenced by another's will, unconsulted, unpersuaded, quietly overruled. In short the pink dress went on, softened by some drapery of black lace.'

This subtle change of colour is an outward manifestation of the shedding of the uniform of spinsterhood because it comes at a time when she is falling in love with Dr John, perhaps even anticipating marriage when she could actually expose her inward feelings.

This change does not go unnoticed by the perceptive Monsieur Paul who perceives the dichotomy in Lucy's nature, the outward self-effacing persona along with the inner pent up passionate nature, and he is fascinated by it. He taunts her:

'What fatal influence had impelled me lately to introduce flowers under the brim of my bonnet, to wear '*des cols brodes*', and even appear on one occasion in a scarlet gown...'

'"Scarlet M. Paul. It was not scarlet. It was pink. Pale pink too; and further subdued by black lace."' He is not fooled:

'"Pink or scarlet, yellow or crimson, pea green or sky blue; it was all one; these were flaunting giddy colours…"'

Lucy refuses to acknowledge the change and continues to protest. Mr Paul replies, '… he only wished to counsel me, whenever I wore it, to do so in the same spirit as if its material were bure, but its hue 'gris de poussiere'.

He taunts her because he himself is a kind of male spinster, and he sees in Lucy his female counterpoint. He is small, unremarkable, dry and sarcastic, but Lucy notes: 'M. Emmanuel's taste in colour decidedly leaned to the brilliant.' But being a man, he can put his uniform on or off at will.

Once their disguises have been taken from them – neither Lucy nor Hilda had actually chosen to discard their disguises – Hilda had been persuaded to buy her dress by her brother, and Lucy's pink dress had been bought by her godmother, while Lucy had been made to wear a fop's clothing for the play, by Mr Paul. In both cases, it is the men who secretly, pruriently want to strip these women of their uniforms and scrutinise the rampant sexuality within them, sexuality that they had both been at such pains to repress. And interestingly, neither M. Paul nor Eustace had sex lives of their own; they were, in effect, voyeurs.

Disguising Femininity:

In 'The Well of Loneliness', when Stephen falls in love with Angela, she chooses a uniform, one which she will continue to wear throughout her life to disguise her feminine side, adopting as masculine attire as she can get away with at the time:

'She would go into Malvern that very afternoon and order a new flannel suit at her tailors. The suit should be grey with a little white pin stripe, and the jacket, she decided, must have a breast pocket. She would wear a black tie – no, better, a grey one to match the new suit with the little white pin stripe. She ordered not one new suit, but three, and she also ordered a pair of brown shoes.' Years later, when she is living in Paris with her lover we are told:

'Mary opened the wardrobe containing a long neat line of suits hanging from heavy mahogany shoulders… on the shelves were orderly piles of shirts, crêpe de chine pyjamas – quite a goodly selection, and the heavy silk masculine underwear that for several years now had been worn by Stephen.' She watches Stephen 'as she was frowning at herself in the glass for a second, as she twitched her immaculate neck tie.'

Stephen's masculine style of dress is intended to defiantly deny any traces of spinsterly femininity, but her disguise will cost her dear: the loss of acceptance by respectable society which, in turn, will ultimately lose her her lover.

Like Stephen, Mademoiselle de Maupin also adopts the disguise of masculinity: 'I learned how to handle a sword and fire a pistol; I could ride a horse with consummate skill… I made myself familiar with the proper way to wear my cloak and crack my riding whip, and in a few months I managed to transform a girl who was considered rather nice looking, into a young gentleman who was much nicer looking, and who lacked but a moustache.' But unlike Stephen, hers is not a choice taken because she is unhappy with her sexuality, but because she wants to find out what men are really like when they are not in the society of women, and although she discovers the pleasures of bisexuality, she is not worried by her sexuality; hers is a uniform she can put on and off at will. Both, like Athene, are able to obscure their femininity by male attire, but only Maupin is happy to reveal her feminine side. Athene too, was also interested in female crafts.

Proclaiming Respectability:

We are told little about the clothes that are worn by our superior spinsters; we don't need to be, because we know that their status and wealth will ensure that they will wear whatever they regard as suitable to their station. Their expensive clothes will be the outward proof of their comfortable spinsterhoods.

The ladies of 'Cranford', however, have very limited means, so perforce 'the materials of their clothes are in general good and plain.' And they have their own ways of coping with the lack of money to be expended and yet retain respectability in each others' eyes:

'Their dress is very independent of fashion; as they observe, "what does it signify how we dress here in Craford where everybody knows us?"' And if they go away from home, their reason is equally cogent: '"what does it signify how we dress here where nobody knows us?"'

But dowdy as they are, they all feel the need to splash out from time to time, and they have found the most economical way of doing so: the purchase of new 'caps':

'The expenditure in dress in Cranford was principally on that one article referred to. If the heads were buried in smart new caps, the ladies were like ostriches and cared not what became of their bodies. Old gowns, white and venerable collars, any number of brooches up and down everywhere – old brooches for a permanent adornment, and new caps to suit the fashion of the day.' The uniform of respectability is mutually agreed:

'The ladies of Cranford always dressed with chaste elegance and propriety, as once Miss Barker prettily expressed it.'

They have been complicit in adopting a uniform that, perhaps rather shamefacedly, expresses and excuses their spinsterly state. The well-worn clothes express their resignation to their lot and the caps and brooches are ways of lightening the tenor of that resignation.

Only when they are unwittingly presented with an alternative means of dressing do they become alarmed, and degenerate into objects of ridicule. When a friend living in Paris sends Miss Pole the frame for a crinoline, she has no idea what it is, and decides it must be a cage for her parrot:

'Mr Hoggins began to laugh in his boisterous vulgar way.

"For Polly! Ha! Ha! It's meant for you, Miss Pole, it's a new invention to hold your gown out. Ha! Ha!"'

Miss Pole sees his comments as an affront to the respectability of her spinsterhood:

'"Mr Hoggins, you may be a surgeon, and a very clever one, but nothing – not even your profession – gives you the right to be indecent."'

Miss Pole expresses the fear of male ridicule that is never far from the elderly spinster.

Combating ridicule is terribly important. Spinsters are so open to it. I remember as a child playing 'Happy Families'; all the cards bar one, must be gathered into sets of four happy smiling characters: mother, father, son and daughter. The object of the game was not to be left with the ridiculous figure of the bespectacled old maid. How we all laughed at the one who was stuck with her!

Clothes as a symbol of nubility:

Desperate spinsters may defiantly choose unsuitable clothes because they are determined to lose their spinsterhood and believe conspicuous clothing will aid them in this.

Tabitha Bramble wears ridiculously gaudy clothes resembling the ones she wore in her youth, in an attempt to present a youthful appearance; she will challenge any idea that she is ageing and ugly. She may have incurred scorn, but it has to be admitted that it paid off in the end.

Blanche du Bois 'has decked herself out in a somewhat soiled and crumpled white satin evening gown and a pair of scuffed silver slippers with brilliants set in their heels. Now she is placing the rhinestone tiara on her head in front of the mirror of the dressing table and murmuring excitedly to herself, as if to a group of spectral admirers'.

By adopting this 'uniform' consisting of the remnants of the clothes she once wore when she was young and nubile, she tries to persuade herself and others – particularly men – that she is the fascinating creature she once was, and to try and prove that she is not an ageing spinster, but a desirable and marriageable woman.

Like Blanche and Tabitha, Miss Havisham too, presents herself in clothes that she wore many years ago, the wedding dress that never saw the light of day, but unlike them, her 'uniform' is not donned to attract a husband, but to create the opposite effect: her tawdry wedding dress is intended to demonstrate to the world how she was once an object of desire, but has now become a hideous travesty of the nubile young girl she once was. It is, in fact, an outward show of her masochism.

Eleanor Oliphant is resigned to her scarred appearance and dresses in a dowdy fashion; only when she wants to attract her singer, does she start buying clothes that are fashionable, and adopts a conventional appearance. Prue Sarn's nubility is proclaimed unwittingly when Kester Woodeaves sees her naked; here it is lack of clothes that present her nubility.

In their disparate choice of clothes we see a reflection of the real women inside. Clothes are an important manifestation of the self, whether it be Stephen's tweeds or Miss Aspinall's diaphanous draperies. Like the goddess Iris' rainbow they are a hopeful sign.

SKEIN 4: STRATEGIES OF STITCHERY

"I do so hope you are interested in needlework, good plain needlework? The number of girls nowadays with no idea of simple stitchery."

Miss Read, 'Village School'.

Whatever its roots, whether or not spinsterhood has been chosen, and however long they took to select appropriate clothes, the days were often very long for our spinsters; somehow or other these women had to find ways of devising modi vivendi to pass away their time, making those wearisome hours tolerable. What strategies did they choose?

In practical terms, those who have been forced to seek employment, unpleasant though aspects of this may be, filling in those hours that are employed by her married sister, in tending to her husband and family, will not be a problem.

The subservient spinster will have her time dictated to by her employers; the schoolmistress will teach according to the timetable; the governess and the nanny will act according to the whims of her employers or pupils; the companion will spend the day obeying her rich employer; the academic will have her time dictated by her hours of lecturing and the demands of the particular study she is engaged in. The nun or anchoress will have her time spent in accordance with the set hours of prayer; the sleuthing spinster will devote her energies in tracking down the miscreants. Their hours may not be pleasant, but at least they are filled.

But what about those others who we might judge to be more fortunate, for whom money is not of the essence? How will they fill their time? The ladies of Cranford devote obsessive attention to minutiae which become as binding on them as those with prescribed tasks. Even the academic may be guilty of this. In 'Gaudy Night' we see Miss Lydgate obsessively revising her dissertation in illegible writing. Superior sisters spend their time ensuring their status is maintained. Cousin Bette and Miss Corny use all their time devising malicious schemes. Mary Joyce and Catherine Sloper both turn to good works as a panacea.

As we have noted, practising religion in one form or another can take up enormous amounts of time, whether it is relaying the prophesies of Apollo, becoming a saint or an anchoress, collecting curates like Harriet Bede, or simply by maintaining a close alliance with the church, as in the case of the Sicilian sisters. Again and again religion in one form or another becomes a vital crutch and a means of filling time.

These various strategies all tend to one end: survival, but the most important integral factor, the one that unites all our spinsters in their various endeavours to keep their heads above water, is their dependence on different forms of clothwork. This will be their lifeline.

Stitching for Living:

Firstly, and most commonly, it is used as a means of making a living. In 'Cousin Bette' we are told:
'When the count found it impossible to marry off this girl with the black eyes and the sooty eyebrows… he apprenticed Lisbeth to the court embroiderers. Her line of business *passementerie* – gold and silver lacework included… all the vast variety of brilliant decoration that formerly glittered on the handsome uniforms of the French army, and on civilian dress clothes.'
The spinster must alleviate her poverty by stitching ornamentation for the rich.

In 'Agnes Grey' we see a similar story. Agnes as the family's employee, was expected to do the lion's share of her pupil's tapestry work:

'Of fancy-work I knew nothing but what I gathered from my pupil and my own observations, but no sooner was I initiated, than she made me useful in twenty different ways; all the tedious parts of the work were lifted on to my shoulders... such as stretching the frames, stitching in the canvas, sorting the wools and silks, putting in the grounds, counting the stitches, rectifying the mistakes, and finishing the pieces she was tired of.'

Again, the subservient spinster has to be responsible for the glamorous outward show of others, more fortunate than herself.

In 'Buddenbrooks' Toni taunts Ida Jungmann: "'You are darning, Ida – funny I can't imagine you doing anything else.'" In Toni's eyes Ida's life is synonymous with threadwork. She cannot envisage her having a life outside it.

In 'Some Tame Gazelle' poor, touchy Miss Prior has to sew for others in order to make a respectable living. In all these instances we see spinsters involved with yarn as part of their designated subservient spinsterly status. As such, they must sew or starve.

Strands of Enticement:

Secondly, like the spider in the web, the spinster may do threadwork to entrap or entice a mate. In 'Some Tame Gazelle' Miss Jenner uses her wool shop to support herself and her old mother, but she also uses it to entice the visiting reps. Belinda describes her behaviour as 'silly', but she herself longs to show her affection for the archdeacon by knitting him a jumper in 'clerical grey'. The archdeacon's rival, the unmarried Father Plowman receives more pairs of embroidered slippers from his spinsterly congregation, than he knows what to do with.

In 'Villette' Lucy Snowe makes an embroidered double chain for M. Paul: 'All my materials – my whole stock of beads and silk – were used up before the chain assumed the length and richness I wished.' By her threadwork Lucy hopes to gain the attention of M. Paul. In all these cases the needle becomes a Cupid's dart, although sadly its aim is misjudged.

Threads of Justification:

Thirdly, any form of threadwork is simply a useful prop. It has no particular purpose except as a means of passing the time, while giving the appearance of doing something useful. It is adopted as a sort of symbol of respectable spinsterhood. As the writer says in 'Cranford':

"'I always took a quantity of plain sewing to Cranford, as we did not read much or walk much, I found it a capital time to get through my work.'"

Work. That is so often what sewing is referred to as. The spinster wishes to demonstrate that she is no idler, simply because she has no husband or family on whom to employ her time. She is doing her 'work.' Tellingly, in 'Some Tame Gazelle' when Mr Mould comes to propose to Harriet, he is found nervously clutching a copy of *Stitchcraft*, a magazine he is anxious to put aside, just as he wishes to remove Harriet from its spinsterly connotations.

Knitting Needles:

Work with thread, and particularly yarn, is often justified as constituting an act of altruism: in 'Buddenbrooks' Frau

Jungermann and Clara 'knit stockings for the children of negroes', although how welcome these items might be remains somewhat doubtful. Similarly, in 'Village Diary' Miss Clare is busily knitting a sweater for a young man. 'I shall give it to the cricket club. It will make a nice prize for their whist drive next winter.' But will it? What young man wants a green sweater knitted by an old schoolmistress? In 'Some Tame Gazelle' the archdeacon's spinsterly niece knits socks for Mr Donne, the curate; this is patently not an act of altruism, but a way of reminding him of her, in her absence. But in their own eyes, the working of yarn is a vindication of the worthiness of their spinsterhoods.

Knitting, in particular, becomes almost synonymous with spinsterhood. Miss Matty 'knits garters in a variety of dainty colours'. And in the various interpretations of Miss Marple we see different aspects of spinsterhood on display: McEwan's knitting represents her feminine approach to problem solving; she has the inspector hold the skein of wool for her, while she literally unravels the intricacies of the case; Rutherford's needles, on the other hand, serve as potential weapons, used for warding off unwelcome intruders. Hickson's intense concentration on the intricacies of her knitting shows her repressed and introspective nature. The use of wool comes to define spinsterhood.

Sexual Satisfaction:

Fourthly, and perhaps subconsciously, the touching of threads can provide a sort of sensual release. In 'The Anchoress' Sara reflects: 'My Rule said that I should sew only simple cloths for the church and the poor'. Nevertheless, she is delighted to be asked by Father Ranulf to 'embroider a panel for the altar cloth of St Christopher's Priory.' Unlike Clara and Ida grimly knitting away, she feels sensual delight in the work:

'When I began to sew, each stitch, each coloured thread made my fingers tingle, a warmth that flowed through my arms and chest, down into my belly.'

In her case, it seems that the embroidery acts as a kind of masturbation.

In 'Rebecca' Mrs Danvers indulges her lust for Rebecca in the feel of the material of her clothes:

'"She looked beautiful in this velvet. Put it against your face. It's soft, isn't it? You can feel it, can't you? The scent is still fresh, isn't it?"'

Even Belinda in her mild way, experiences something of the kind. She is delighted to be given the opportunity to darn the archdeacon's sock while it is actually still on his foot! This daring darning is a reaching out to his actual flesh. and it affords her great pleasure.

However, we do not know how many spinsters derived sexual satisfaction from threadwork. I think you would have to be pretty desperate as these women were in their different ways: the Anchoress shut up alone in her cell; Mrs Danvers devastated by the loss of Rebecca; and Belinda, not desperate exactly, but the darning of the sock does provide her with a feeble sort of sexual titillation, something that she may subconsciously long for.

Clothwork in its different forms has been integral to our spinsters lives.

SKEIN FIVE: SPINSTERS, SPINNERS AND SPIDERS

Two Paconians called Pigres and Mastyes wanted to seize power in their country; so when Darius had crossed into Asia, they went to Sardis with a sister of theirs, a tall and beautiful girl; they dressed the girl as finely as they could and sent her off with a jar on her head to catch water, making her at the same time spin flax and lead a horse by the halter round her arm. The sight of her as she passed was sufficiently remarkable to catch Darius' eye. Darius then asked if all the women in Paconia were as hard-working as this one, and the young men eagerly assented- which of course was the whole point of their proceeding – that they were.

Herodotus, 'Histories'.

Spiders are born to spin; they do not need to be taught. A spider's web is its home.

Hillyard, 'Spiders'.

Although our spinsters would no longer be defined by their distaffs, their intimate connection with clothing, cloth and threadwork leads us back to their etymological root, to the connection between *spinster* and *spinner,* and surprisingly, the act of spinning can still be an important part of their lives just as it was in Antiquity.

Like Ariadne who unreeled the ball of thread that guided Theseus out of the minotaur's maze and back to safety, the sleuthing spinster follows threads of evidence that will lead to a happy solution. She may sit quietly observing, behind a piece of knitting, like Miss Marple, or she can set about relentlessly tracking down loose threads of evidence, as Vera and

Theodora do, but she is spinning the fate of the culprit. A scholarly spinster uses her pen as her spindle to produce her own form of weaving, the making of *text* in the place of *textile*. La Signora and Stephen Gordon are both fascinated by stationary shops. They might eschew the spindle, but they cannot resist the fascination of paper as a loom for textual creation.

Before we take a further look at the ways in which the traditional motif of spinning continues to carry its threads down through the generations of spinsters – for a little light relief – let's take another look at 'James and The Giant Peach' and meet Miss Spider, a descendent of Arachne with a human voice.

Once aboard the Giant Peach, Miss Spider with the help of her friend The Silkworm (another spinner/spinster) works tirelessly to keep the giant peach afloat by producing threads that can be carried by seagulls to steer them through the air, and escape the pursuing Cloud Men. She laments the fate of her kind:

"'It's very unfair the way we spiders are treated… why only last week your own horrible Aunt Sponge flushed my poor dear father down the plug-hole in the bathtub.'"

Aunt Spider was unlucky, but her fate is not unlike that of other spinsters we have met, admittedly not actually washed down plugholes, but unceremoniously dumped, and left to a deadly fate, as Miss Havisham was, ending her days 'covered to the throat in white cotton wool.' She is like a spider caught in her own web.

Aunt Spider opens the way to provide an analogous view of spinsterhood. Miss Havisham is not the only spinster (or spinner) who shares characteristics of the descendants of poor Arachne. In his compact and useful book, 'Spiders', Paul

Hillyard describes some two hundred spiders, and his description of particular arachnids provides us with useful comparisons:

'The Black Widow is highly venomous, unmistakable, [and] can overcome large creatures by throwing gummy silk at them as they struggle in the web'.

Here we are reminded of Cousin Bette who spends her life weaving a complicated web of deceit and intrigue into which each member of the family is enticed, entangled and stored, ready to be devoured.

Like the Black Widow, Hilda Cherrington sought to take possession of Dick Staverley, and make him into the substance she desired to consume. In the end, he escaped her, but she still had Eustace whom she had stored away in her web since his childhood, and he did not escape; he owed his death to her desire to consume him.

The Black Widow in her dark carapace also reminds us of the black-clad, Mrs Danvers, seeking the death of SMDW, and in 'The Seventh Heaven' there is the Lava, a spectral spinster clad in a black carapace, presaging death for Eustace.

'Brown Recluse Spiders,' 'Hillyard tells us, 'like to hide in corners. They are light brown spiders.' How many spinsters have we seen unobtrusive in their drab clothing, hiding in corners? Miss Briggs, Miss Matty and Belinda are not venomous like the Black Widow, but choose to be drab and unobtrusive, because that is the way the feel safest.

There is the Black Hole Spider: 'By day it lies hidden in a tubular silk-lined retreat... it is a long-lived spider.' We might compare the Buddenbrook spinsters and the Sicilian sisters who enjoy long lives comfortable in their soft cocoons of wealth. There is the Bark Sack Spider, 'a robust spider with dark jaw. The spider makes a thick-walled retreat.' Here we think of the doughty nuns and the anchoresses enclosed behind the thick walls of their cells.

We must not push the analogy too far. Spinsters are more than spiders just as they are more than spinners; they are brave and fascinating women with their own identities. However, this closeness of spinsterhood with its etymological root in spinning is, I think, vital to understanding their nature.

Spinning is a dangerous business. In 'Precious Bane' Prue attends a 'Love Spinning' to celebrate the engagement of her brother to Janice, and it is there that she first sets eyes on Kester, the weaver. It turns out fortunately for her, but the Love Spinning spells disaster for the bride, Janice, since her marriage will not take place, her intended husband will desert her, and devastated by rejection, she will drown both herself and her child.

However, abandoning spinning or the loom can be equally disastrous for the spinster. We remember the chorus of 'The Bacchae' telling us 'of the Theban women leaving / Their spinning and their weaving/ Stung with the maddening trance / Of Dionysus.' As a result they lose control of their libido, running amok on the mountains and indiscriminately killing. We think of Hilda Cherrington who rushes wildly out at her sister's wedding and whom Eustace describes as a Bacchante. Tennyson tells the same story in 'The Lady of Shalott':

> 'She left the web, she left the loom,
> She made three paces round the room,
> She saw the water-lily bloom.
> She saw the helmet and the plume,
> Looked down on Camelot.
> Out flew the web and floated wide;
> The mirror cracked from side to side
> "The curse is come upon me," cried
> The lady of Shalott.'

When the spinner or spinster abandons the domestic sphere because her libido takes her outside it, she takes a terrible risk. Spinning and weaving spell safety – but not always. As we saw at the beginning, the Moirai and the Norns were spinsters who ruthlessly spun the threads of fate, aided by the Harpies and the Erinyes, while the Hopi Spider Woman held the power of life and death. We met Athene, the goddess in control of spinning and weaving, and we also met her victim, Arachne. Spinning has a dark and dangerous side.

Princess Rose was cursed by the Bad Fairy to prick her finger on a spindle and die; fortunately, the Good Fairy was able to soften the curse, substituting sleep for death, a sleep that could only be ended by the touch of a prince. Naturally, the King ordered all spindles to be destroyed. But one day the princess came across an old woman spinning in a forgotten attic, and of course, she found the unfamiliar object irresistible, and couldn't refrain from touching it. And that accounted for her becoming 'The Sleeping Beauty' for the next hundred years. Eventually of course, the prophecy came true, and she was awakened by a prince – who just happened to be passing by.

A strand in this story takes us back again to Ancient Greece: the Bad Fairy reminds us of the spinster prophetesses of old, the Sibyl and the Pythia, and most particularly, Cassandra, doomed never to be believed. In 'The Sleeping Beauty', even those who placed some credence on the bad fairy's words thought that an unpleasant prophesy could be ignored or diverted in some way. Idiots! It was no good banning the apparatus of spinning; things that are forbidden are enticing – even spindles! We remember too, how Arachne was attacked by Athene with her shuttle.

Some of the dark warp threads of spinsterhood, originally spun in the Ancient World have remained constant throughout; they have been woven and interwoven with a variety of colourful weft threads that have evolved and developed and been woven into the lives of disparate spinsters over subsequent millennia.

The tale of 'The Sleeping Beauty' holds some of these worn dark strands because it offers a horribly demeaning – yet totally wrong – view of spinsterhood. It celebrates an example of male privilege, (the prince) reinforcing the convenient idea that a spinster is doomed to powerlessness, unconscious of real life, without the liberating force of the male gaze. Only by accepting the gaze and subsequently mating with a male will her existence be acknowledged. Ugh!

Hopefully in this study I have been able to show that in spite of often being downtrodden and abused, our spinsters have managed to survive, sometimes happily, sometimes not. But they are the discoverers of their own identities and they have revealed themselves to us *without* the male gaze.

In their different ways these spinsters have been responsible for spinning the many yarns within this book and providing the woven material of its text. So, now I would like to conclude by imagining how they have eventually come together to form a tapestry against which we can position ourselves, and view the subject of spinsterhood with all its sadness – and its hopefulness. Let us start unrolling it.

SUPPOSING A TAPESTRY

Enthroned on high, are the austere and stately figures of the Fates, holding spindle, thread and scissors, and next to them, in contrast to the dark-haired Spider Woman, stand the blonde Scandinavian Norns; very high up they seem, as they gaze pitilessly through the dark sky at the figures below. However, the goddess Athene, some inches below, is not at all intimidated; she stands to the fore, equipped with sword and shield, emblazoned with the head of the Medusa. She is holding something that could be a spear, or perhaps it is a spindle or shuttle – she may be wearing her 'other hat' or rather, helmet, that of goddess of handicraft, because there is a very large spider dangling from the end of it, poor Arachne, no doubt.

To her left, partially obscured by a cloud, is the semi-naked figure of Diana, looking sour; perhaps she has just realised she's been spotted by Acteon; she has a thoughtful air, obviously wondering how she is to get her own back on him. She is, however, being nudged by something large and circular. What is this? Ah, it is St Catherine, looking quite glamorous, but determinedly clutching her wheel; but she, in turn, is being obscured by St Ursula who is surrounded by a blur of floating female figures, not all 11,000 of them, even this tapestry isn't large enough to portray all of her saintly followers.

Underneath, there is Saint Deodata, reclining on her couch, now floating somewhat precariously mid-air, but still looking smug, nothing is going to budge her; but she must be careful because, fluttering all about her are ominous black figures, the Eumenides, or perhaps they are harpies, it is difficult to tell.

Slightly below these august divinities are the blissfully smiling figures of Philippa and Martine, finally settled in their heavenly home; but who is that next to them? Ah, it is Babette wielding a saucepan because she is preparing to cook for the angels. Slightly lower, but still reaching upwards, are numerous dark-hooded figures with their psalters. Nuns, perhaps?

And amongst the saintly is a figure in dull drab robes, looking hesitantly upwards; it is the Anchoress who cannot decide whether she wants to join the holy throng or not, but the three Sicilian sisters have no doubt about their place in the heavens; they are holding aloft their remaining relics, as a guarantee of their admittance to those higher regions.

Piercing these heavens is the spire of some sort of church building, and as we lower our gaze, we can descry a large number of women led by a tall determined figure in full clerical robes, whose head almost seems to touch the sky, it must be Theodora Braithwaite, all six foot one of her. But who are all these other women, issuing from the church door? Who is this crossly thrusting a soiled purple prayer book forward as an emblem of her godliness? It is Harriet Herriton, but nobody seems to be taking much notice of her.

Others are clustering around the church, they too, are clutching prayer books, not aggressively like Harriet Herriton, but shyly, self-effacingly, a circle of really rather plain, uninteresting women, clutching notebooks and pencils, a gaggle of Sunday School teachers, who are hoping their good works have earned them a higher place.

Miss Marple holds her prayer book, but she is also looking quizzically about her; she knows that religious women may not be all they seem. There is Belinda Bede looking wistfully upwards, wondering perhaps, whether the Archdeacon has been translated to the heavens. Next to her, the only one of them to be colourfully dressed, and nor looking at all pious, is her sister, Harriet; she is peering back at the interior of the church, wondering whether there are any stray curates left inside. Mary Jocelyn walks behind her, but she doesn't look back at the church; she knows that neither Mr Herbert nor her father will be there.

There are other ladies who stand gossiping outside the church: Miss Bates is garrulously holding forth and Miss Briggs is smiling foolishly, as she listens, and stout Flora Casby has her mouth wide open and a breathless air about her, but Miss Matty looks worried, she does not know whether her sister Deborah would approve of her associating with ladies to whom she has not been properly introduced – and she cannot help but notice that Flora is holding a glass of something in her hand.

Next to the church is another building, I suppose it is a church hall, and – if we look carefully – we can make out a large number of figures engaged in some sort of sewing bee; we may need a magnifying glass to identify them, but no, there is a shaft of sunlight shining through the open windows; These must be 'the spinsters and the knitters in the sun'. Who can we identify? We can see two rather thin German ladies, Clothilde and Clara, busy knitting; there is already a pile of little stockings beside them; Miss Clare sits a little apart, intent on knitting something green. Lucy Snowe is there, sewing her present for Monsieur Paul; I recognise her because unlike the others who are drably dressed, she is wearing a new pink dress, although she doesn't look very comfortable in it. Miss Prior has her sewing machine out; she is working hard because she is going to be paid for whatever it is she is making. Miss Grey has an elaborate embroidery frame out in front of her, she regards it with displeasure; it is the work of her pupil which she has been told to finish. Catherine Sloper sits next to her; she is in no hurry to finish her 'piece of work'; she knows that she has nothing else to do for the rest of her life. We will leave them all to their work and turn our gaze again to outside.

But what is that conflagration over there? Something is ablaze, a great deal of orange and red wool has been used; what is it? Is it the hayrick belonging to Prue's brother that Janice's father has set alight? No, I think it is a house on fire. Is it Eleanor Oliphant's childhood home, or is it Miss Havisham's 'Satis House'? Perhaps it is Manderley. The blaze is so great we can't tell, we can only hope the occupants will escape unscarred.

Let us unroll the tapestry a little further and see who is next. Ah! The church must be part of some university building, and standing outside, as if posed for a group photo, is a stern row of ladies in academic dress, complete with gown and hood; in their hands are heavy-looking books, obviously the fruit of their labours; some are still holding pens as if they have not yet finished their work; slightly apart from them, but still obviously part of this academic community, are several other women, not so severely accoutred: here is Vinnie Miner, with her paisley scarf and Ruth Galloway in a black trouser suit, holding in one hand her latest book, and in the other, a spoilt-looking child, who is tugging at her hand, anxious to get away from all these learned women; then, there are two with their backs to the academics, looking out at the other women around them: one looks Italian and the other a bit like Virginia Woolf; they show no wish to be numbered among the other dons, but a languid air suggests they lack the energy to move away.

Below them, aware that they are lesser beings than the academics, stand the schoolmistresses with registers in their hands; they have been making their way to the village school, but they find it has been taken over by a lot of sewing women; they are not put out, they are used to difficulty. Miss Read is sporting some bright-looking brogues, and next to her stands the tall erect figure of Miss Clare, her hair tightly knotted in a bun. Looking somewhat truculent, is the ungainly figure of Miss Jackson in sandals and a flowery skirt; pointedly she stands apart from Miss Clare and Miss Read, and she is gazing admiringly at a thin, unpleasant woman who must be her adored old tutor, Miss Crabbe; further along, there are a number of dowdily dressed Scottish women, they are also schoolteachers, but regard themselves as superior to these primary school teachers as they teach at an academy, but they look a dull lot, and they are mainly obscured by a glamorous figure with a striking necklace of amber beads, who is determined to be the one noticed. This, of course, is Miss Jean Brodie. However, she has met her match in Hilda Cherrington who stands defiantly next to her in a beautiful red dress; she is a stunning looking girl, far more beautiful than Jean Brodie, but she looks awkward and unhappy, she would prefer to be wearing her usual austere uniform, and she is wondering where Eustace has got to, and whether he is behaving himself.

And here is another glamorous figure to be reckoned with, Chiyo the geisha is approaching them; she has all the assurance of Miss Brodie and none of the awkwardness of Hilda, and she is more noticeable even than the other two because she is elaborately dressed in her kimono and obi, her white face carefully made up, her hair towering above her head.

Another woman is trying to gain her place among these attractive spinsters, and she too is wearing glamorous clothes, but they are soiled and worn and the canvas itself seems to be damaged here. It must be poor Blanche du Bois.

Let us unroll the tapestry further; there is much more to see. We now seem to have left the inhabited areas behind, and it is clear we are in open countryside, because here are two beautifully dressed horsemen. What can these *men* be doing here among all these spinsters? Ah, I see, on closer inspection, they are not horse*men*, but horse*women*: Stephen Gordon is sitting here astride her horse, an angry scar on her face, and the very attractive Mademoiselle du Maupin is smiling happily as she parts her horse's mane; but they must take care, as they are in danger of being attacked by a big fierce bristling bear emerging from the bushes. No, all is well, it is only the nymph Callisto, she still has her womanly mind and would not hurt anyone.

What a lovely pastoral scene lies before us! Here are rolling fields with nymphs dancing about under a beautiful laurel tree. Oh! The tree has hands and fingers; it is poor Daphne escaping from Apollo, but under its branches – or hands – there seem to be some women huddled together who do not mind the tree's strange appearance; they seem to welcome it, for they are strange themselves: Miss Fothergill sits in her wheelchair with her red face and claw-like hands; Rosa Dartle looks on, the scar twitching on her face, the little humpbacked Frau Weichbrodt is supporting herself against the tree, and there are two other younger women with them, scarred, it's true, but looking much happier, they must be Prue Sarn and Eleanor Oliphant. An elderly Russian-looking woman with plaits around her head – it must be Sonya – approaches them, she is pretty still, in spite of her age, and she looks enquiringly towards them; she is perhaps wondering if she can offer any help, but she gets no response because they are already moving towards a slow-flowing river set about with reeds; is there someone concealed amongst them? It must be Syrinx, hiding from the god Pan. And who is this attractive girl gazing upwards at the sun? Oh, now I look closer I see it is not a girl at all, just a rusty old robot.

Now the countryside becomes rugged and we can see a sort of grim cavernous opening, and among the rocks we see Arieka, the Pythia, and the Cumaean Sibyl; they are closely watched by an unpleasant-looking dark haired woman whom I think must be Cousin Bette, and next to her, a tall thin one, Miss Corny perhaps; they are anxious to know how to proceed in their schemes and await advice. There is another prophetess there and she is also offering advice, but neither woman takes any notice of poor Cassandra. A large stocky figure regards them quizzically, it is Vera, weighing up whether there is anything to be learned from the prophetesses; she has dismissed the Sibyl and the Pythia because she knows all about falsehood, and regards them as unreliable witnesses, but she suspects that this Cassandra woman might know something.

There are other dark figures here too; they might be the evil Miss Jessel or cruel Mrs Danvers; there again, they might be mere shapes of fancy because they are not clearly depicted.

Now we can see the river emerging from the rocky cavern and wending its way towards the sea, there is a barge floating on it, bearing a single beautiful lifeless figure. I think it must be the Lady of Shalott. And if we unroll the tapestry further, we can see dark clouds overhead, no they are not clouds, but the black winged figures of the harpies. And look! The whole area is overcast, dark and gloomy, as the river enters a rough and tumultuous sea; there are islands in it, and horrible are the creatures on them; on one, sits Scylla with her nine heads, determined to catch any passing sailors, and there is Charybdis, a terrifying whirlpool on the other side. And on another island sit three hideous old crones; one holds a ghastly yellow fang, the other a bloodshot eye, while the third is trying vainly to make a grab for it. The occupant of the third island is not ugly, although she is surrounded by snuffling pigs; she is very beautiful, but oh, how sad she looks! It is Circe looking wistfully seaward, mourning the loss of Odysseus. And here sit three more hideous women, one has snakes about her head – not, I fear, for long, since Perseus will soon come and chop it off.

We have nearly finished unrolling the tapestry, but there are three women remaining on the end, determined to leave the tapestry altogether: Tabitha Bramble with her sallow face and strange jumble of clothes, Miss Jones with her thin red nose. Tabitha, now Mrs Lismahago tauntingly holds up her ring, and Miss Jones is only half shown because she is hurrying off to see what her new husband Ginger is up to. Miss Mackenzie too, is close behind; she has duties elsewhere: John Bull's nine children must be seen to. These women have no further part to play in the tapestry of spinsters.

Two people are walking past the tapestry; perhaps they have come to put it away, or perhaps they have come to restore it. The man looks at it briefly without interest, and remarks: "There are no men in it." But the woman looks more closely, and replies: "It is rather faded, I think there might have been men in the background once." She pauses, takes a second look, and adds, "actually, I think it is better, as it is now."

EPILOGUE

We have seen the many strands of suffering that our spinsters have endured dating back to the Ancient World, and we have watched them twisting their way down to the present. They have all been fictional, but their stories have been believable because they reflect the plight of real single women over the course of millennia. Now, although women are no longer termed as spinsters, and there is no dichotomy between those who are married or in relationships, and those who remain single, they still continue to be abused, not in exactly the same ways as our fictional spinsters, but their situations are often not dissimilar. They are still raped, victimised, subject to controlling relationships, paid insufficiently, forced to work in sweatshops, humiliated through disability, condemned for what they choose to wear, made to feel a lack of self-worth; they can suffer poor mental health or be forced to flee to the safety of women's refuges. So this spinsterhood we have been examining, has metamorphosed into a reflection of women as a whole – real women, alive today – and still suffering. But there is a more optimistic way of viewing modern womanhood. By fair means or foul, our spinsters were tremendous survivors, and it seems to me that there are things they can teach us.

In the course of this book we have seen there were various strategies our spinsters adopted in order to make life bearable, and we have become aware that some strategies worked, and some did not. Can we learn anything from this?

To start with the latter: spiteful scheming just brings unhappiness all round – look at Cousin Bette, Miss Corny and Harriet Herriton. Masochism doesn't work. Think of Miss Havisham, the governess in 'Turn of the Screw' and the heroine of 'Rebecca'. Suppressing the self and bullying others is no good as Hilda Cherrington learned to her cost. On the other hand, being timorous doesn't get you anywhere either: what miserable lives were lived by Miss Briggs and the other put-upon governesses and companions that we saw. And had Mary Jocelyn and Caroline Sloper been more assertive, their lives would have been very different. Retreating from life and looking on from the outside is unsatisfactory: think of La Signora and Edith Hope. Rushing desperately into relationships is very unwise. After all, it was hardly likely Miss Jones would find marital bliss with Ginger. Silliness and obsession with minutiae is tedious and unrewarding – think of the ladies of 'Cranford'.

Many of these things that didn't work were the result of the societies in which these women lived. But things that were impossible with our fictional spinsters *are* possible now. You don't have to marry a Ginger because the alternative is dire. And you can have sex without marriage: Miss Mackenzie might have enjoyed a fling with the handsome Mr Rubb! However, there are strategies and attitudes that our spinsters possessed that can still offer some very useful guidelines for us all.

They often looked for, and found a crutch, usually it was religion, and while this particular resource may not appeal now, it is always helpful to find some sort of comfort blanket: daily emails with friends, exercise, looking at nature, baking cakes, gardening; there is an individual crutch somewhere for everyone; it must be searched out and found. After all, Miss Read found contentment shelling peas in her garden. And whether or not one is a 'spinster', different forms of threadwork – sewing and knitting for example – can still be a panacea.

Patience: this is a virtue not much appreciated now in a society that looks for immediate gratification, but not expecting things to fall into your lap immediately, means you won't be disappointed when they don't. But goodies (not necessarily in the form of partners) may be out there, all the same, and by calmly persisting, they may be won. Prue Sarn got Kester Woodeaves!

Bravery: Our spinsters possessed a sort of stoicism: things might not be perfect, but they could be worse. Belinda and Harriet were reasonably happy.

And things *are* better now. If we compare the lot of single women now with those in the past, surely we must be heartened. Think of Stephen Gordon. How she would envy the LGBT community. Yes, money still has too much weight, but women can (with a bit of luck) find work that is not humiliating. Carers cannot be treated as poor Miss Briggs was. Jobs once forbidden to women, are now available, and *they* can be the bosses of men. Think of Vera. Women scholars need no longer to be on the defensive; they are respected as much as, often more than, men. And as for those women lucky enough to have money, they do not need to shut themselves away like the Sicilian sisters, the world is their oyster. Perhaps, what we must rate most highly is the fact that there is no slur, no shame, no ridicule, attached to being unmarried. Women no longer have, like Tabitha Bramble, to fear the 'opprobrious epithet of old maid'.

There is freedom – no, not enough of it – but far more than our spinsters had: sexual freedom, financial independence, laws to forbid and punish abuse; women can look for their own salvation without locking themselves in cells or convents. And there is sexual equality. Alright, not enough of it, but more, far more than our spinsters had. No woman now could be treated like Blanche du Bois, hustled off to an asylum.

If we compare the lot of single women now with that of the spinsters we have met in these pages, we must surely find consolation and inspiration for the future. I hope this book has given a (con)text against which modern womanhood now can be viewed, and readers – whether male or female – can come to realise that the weaving of womanhood is an unfinished piece of work into which we can all put new, strong, good threads, mend the gaping holes, unpick the wrong stitching and make a brighter, stronger tapestry, one that will have no shady corners or frayed edges, but emerge as something in which we will all be proud to have placed our own particular stitches, and can look at with admiration.

BIBLIOGRAPHY

Aeschylus, (transl. Lattimore, R). The Oresteia. Chicago: The University of Chicago Press, 1953.

Anonymous (ed. Swanton, Michael). Beowulf. Manchester: Manchester University Press, 1986.

Anonymous (trans. Simon Armitage) Pearl. London: Liveright Publishing Corporation, 2017.

Anonymous. The Whippingham Papers. London: Wordsworth Editions, 1995.

Artmitage, Simon. Pearl. New York: Liveright, 2017.

Austen, Jane. Emma. London: Penguin Books, 1995.

Austen, Jane. Sense and Sensibility. London: Penguin Books, 1995.

Balzac, Honoré de. Cousin Bette. London: Penguin Books, 1965.

Berlin, Irving. Sisters Lyrics. Universal Publishing Group, Concord Music Publishing LLC, 1954.

Brookner, Anita. Hotel du Lac. London: Triad Grafton Books, 1985.

Bronte, Anne. Agnes Grey. London: Penguin Books, 1988.

Bronte, Charlotte. Villette. London: Penguin Books, 1979.

Browning, Elizabeth Barrett. "A Musical Instrument". In The Poems of Elizabeth Barrett Browning. Michigan: Legare Street Press, 2020.

Cadwallader, Robyn. The Anchoress. London: Faber and Faber, 2015.

Christie, Agatha. At Bertram's Hotel. London: Fontana Paperbacks, 1990.

Christie, Agatha. The Body in the Library. London: Pan Books Ltd., 1989.

Cleeves, Ann. The Darkest Evening. London: Pan Books, 2020.

Dahl, Roald. James and the Giant Peach. London: Penguin, 2011.

Dickens, Charles. David Copperfield. London: Penguin Classics, 2002.

Dickens, Charles. Great Expectations. London: Penguin Books, 1985.

Dickens, Charles. Little Dorrit. London: Collins, 1923.

Dickens, Charles. Martin Chuzzlewit. Penguin Classics: 1999.

Di Lampedusa, Giuseppe Tomasi.The Leopard. London: Collins Harvill, 1988.

Dinesen, (Karen Blixen). Babette's Feast and Other Stories. London: Penguin, 2013.

Du Maurier, Daphne. Rebecca. Great Britain: Virago Press, 2003.

Eliot, T.S. (ed. Gardner, H). "The Love Song of J. Alfred Prufrock". In The New Oxford Book of English Verse. Oxford: Oxford University Press, 1972.

Euripides (trans. Vellacott, Philip). The Bacchae and other Plays. London: Penguin Books, 1954.

Forster, E.M. Where Angels Fear To Tread. London: Penguin Books, 1975.

Gaskell, Elizabeth. Cranford. London: Bloomsbury, 2007.

Gautier, Théophile (trans. Selver, Paul). Mademoiselle de Maupin. London: Hamish Hamilton, 1948.

Golden, Arthur. Memoirs of a Geisha. London: Chatto and Windus, 1997.

Goldfarb, Russell, M.Sexual Repression and Victorian Literature. Lewisburg: Bucknell University Press, 1970.

Golding, William. The Double Tongue. London: Faber& Faber, 1995.

Gray, Thomas. Elegy in an English Churchyard. In The New Oxford Book of English Verse. Oxford: Oxford University Press, 1972

Greenwood, D.M. Clerical Errors. London: Headline Book Publishing, 1991.

Greenwood, D.M. Every Deadly Sin. London, Headline Book Publishing, 1995.

Greenwood, D.M. Mortal Spoils. London, Headline Book Publishing, 1995.

Greenwood, D.M. Unholy Ghosts. London: Headline Book Publishing, 1991.

Griffiths, Elly. A Room Full of Bones. London: London: Quercus, 2112.

Griffiths, Elly. The Crossing Places. London: Quercus, 2009.

Griffiths, Elly. The Dark Angel. London: Quercus, 2018.

Grimm, Jacob & Wilhelm. Grimms Fairy Tales. London: Collins, 2017.

Groff, Lauren. Matrix. London: Heinemann, 2021.

Hadley, Peter (reverser). Epic to Epigram: An Anthology of Classical Verse. Bristol: Booksprint, 1991.

Hall, Radclyffe. The Well of Loneliness. London: Virago Press, 1982.

Hartley, L.P. Eustace and Hilda. London: Faber and Faber, 1971.

Hartley, L.P. The Sixth Heaven. London: Faber and Faber, 1971.

Hartley, L.P. The Shrimp and the Anemone. London: Faber and Faber, 1971.

Hillyard, Paul. Spiders. London: Collins, 2006.

Homer. (trans.Rieu, E.V.) The Odyssey. Penguin Books, 1946.

Honeyman, Gail. Eleanor Oliphant is Completely Fine. London: Harper Collins Publishers, 2018.

Horace. (eds. Gould, H.E. and Whiteley, J.L.) <u>Horace Odes: Book Two.</u> London: Macmillan and Co., Limited, 1954.

Ishiguro, Kazuo. <u>Klara and the Sun.</u> London: Faber & Faber, 2022.

James, Henry. <u>The Turn Of The Screw.</u> London: J. M. Dent & Sons Ltd., 1957.

James, Henry. <u>Washington Square.</u> London: Penguin Books, 1963.

Kesselring, Joseph. <u>Arsenic and Old Lace.</u> London: Random House, 2001.

Lahiri, Jhumpa. <u>Whereabouts.</u> London: Bloomsbury Publishing, 2021.

Larkin, P. Collected Verse. London: Faber and Faber, 2023.

Le Carré, John. <u>Smiley's People.</u> London: Hodder and Stoughton, 1979.

Le Carré, John. <u>Tinker, Tailor, Soldier, Spy.</u> Hodder and Stoughton, 2011.
Lennon-McCartney. <u>Eleanor Rigby.</u> London: Revolver, EMI, 1966.

Lurie, Alison. <u>Foreign Affairs.</u> London: Abacus, 1986.

Mann, Thomas, (trans. Lowe-Porter, H. T.). London: Penguin Books, 1957.

March, Jenny. <u>Dictionary of Classical Mythology.</u> London: Cassell, 1998.

Maugham, Somerset. Collected Short Stories: Volume Two. London: Pan Books Ltd.,1985.

Mayor, F.M. The Rector's Daughter. London: Penguin Books, 1985.

Mullett, G.M. Spider Woman Stories: Legends of the Hopi Indians. Arizona: University of Arizona Press, 1979.

Petronius. Cena Trimalchionis. Michigan: Legare Press, 2022.

Pope, Alexander. ". In The New Oxford Book of English Verse. Oxford: Oxford University Press, 1972.

Pym, Barbara. Some Tame Gazelle. London: Pan Books Ltd.,1983.

Rufinus. (transl. Page, D.) In The Cambridge Classical Texts and Commentaries. Cambridge: Cambridge University Press, 1978.

Saint, Dora (Miss Read). Chronicles of Fairacre. London: Orion, 1982.

Sayers, Dorothy, L. Gaudy Night. New York: Harper Collins, 2019.

Sélincourt, Aubrey de. (trans). Herodotus: The Histories. Middlesex: Penguin, 1954.

Shakespeare, William. (ed.Muir, Kenneth) Macbeth. London: Routledge, 1988.

Shakespeare, William. (eds Lothian, J.M. and Craik, T.W.) Twelfth Night. London: Routledge, 1988.

Simenon, Georges. La Patience de Maigret. Paris: Presses Pocket, 1965.

Simenon, Georges. Maigret Se Trompe. Paris: Presses Pocket, 1953.

Smollett, Tobias. Humphry Clinker. London: Penguin Classics, 1985.

Sophocles, (transl. Storr, F.) Antigone. London: Heinemann, 1912.

Sophocles (trans. Wyckoff, Elizabeth). Sophocles 1: Antigone. Chicago: University of Chicago Press, 1954.

Spark, Muriel. The Prime of Miss Jean Brodie. Penguin Books, 1962.

Swinburne, Charles Algernon. Poems and Ballads 1. London: William Heinemann, 1918.

Tennyson, Alfred. Selected Poems. London: Chatto and Windus, 1967.

Thackeray, William Makepeace. Vanity Fair. London: Penguin Books, 1968.

Tolstoy, Leo. War and Peace. Oxford: Oxford University Press, 1983.

Trollope, Anthony. Miss Mackenzie. Oxford: Oxford University Press, 1990.

Williams, Tennessee. A Streetcar Named Desire and Other Plays. London: Penguin Books, 1959.

Virgil, (transl. Jackson Knight, W.F.) The Aeneid. Middlesex: Penguin Books,1956.

Virgil. (trans. Lewis, C. Day.) The Aeneid. London: The World Classics, 1963.

Webb, Mary. Precious Bane. London: Jonathan Cape, 1944.

Wilson, Christopher. Hurdy Gurdy. Faber: London, 2021.

www.ingramcontent.com/pod-product-compliance
Ingram Content Group UK Ltd.
Pitfield, Milton Keynes, MK11 3LW, UK
UKHW020349280225
455614UK00033B/203

9 781835 633601

Preface

"The light shineth in darkness; and the darkness comprehendeth it not." *John 1:5.*

Most people are familiar with the Bible account of Pilate's condemnation of our Lord.

Pontius Pilate was the sixth Roman Procurator of Judea. And as such, he was an official of the Roman Empire, entrusted with the management of the financial affairs of the Province. He also had administrative powers as an agent of the Emperor of Rome.

It was the custom of the Procurator to reside in Jerusalem during all great feasts to preserve law and order in the Province, and at the time of our Lord's last Passover, Pilate was occupying his official residence in the palace of King Herod.

As Jesus was being tried for his life, Pilate asked him, in the Judgment Hall, **"Art thou the King of the Jews?"** *John 18:33.*

Jesus replied, **"My kingdom is not of this world. My kingdom is not from hence."**

"Thou sayest that I am a king."

"To this end was I born, and for this cause came I into the world, that I should bear *witness unto the truth*."

Pilate sayeth unto him, **"What is truth?"**

The Bible As Reform

Introduction

"Ye shall know the truth, and the truth shall make you free."
Christ Jesus, John 8:32.

Jesus statement regarding the freedom gained from knowing the Truth was made near the beginning of a major epoch (an extended period of time characterized by a memorable series of events, less than a period but greater than an age) extending from the start of his ministry to the present. An internal of time, the most part, two thousand years in length. An interval of time that is the subject of this book.

Great developments have been achieved during this epoch. Vast transformations in history have taken place and are taking place — though not without trial and tribulation.

This book is offered to cast light on certain aspects of these transformations — aspects that have not been understood by the majority of mankind, for reasons that will become clear as we proceed.

We are on the threshold of a new beginning — the new beginning of the twenty-first century and beyond. Mankind is beginning to experience judgement among the nations prompting them to **"beat their swords into plowshares and their spears into pruninghooks,"** in fulfillment of the prophesy that **"nation shall not lift up sword against nation, neither shall they learn war any more."** *Isaiah 2:4*

As scenes of the conflict of "error" with "truth" are presented in clearer light, the wiles of "mortal mind" (the mind of mortals) are becoming exposed and successfully overcome. **"Surely in vain the net is spread in the sight of any bird."** *Prov. 1:17.* **"For we wrestle not against principalities, against powers, against the rulers of the darkness of this world, against spiritual wickedness in high places."** *Eph. 6:12.*

But true victory is assured for the elect of God; **"For the weapons or our warfare are not carnal, but mighty through God to the pulling down of strong holds; Casting down imaginations, and every high thing that exalteth itself against the knowledge of God, and bringing into captivity every thought to the obedience of Christ."** *2 Cor. 10:4, 5.*

Mankind is now on the threshold of a new era — of a New Beginning. And the prophesy of Thomas More's poetic vision is becoming realized at last:

> *When from the lips of truth one mighty breath*
> *Shall, like a whirlwind, scatter to the breeze*
> *The whole dark pile of human mockeries,*
> *Then shall the reign of Mind commence on earth,*
> *And starting fresh, as from a second birth,*
> *Man in the sunshine of the world's new spring,*
> *Shall walk transparent like some holy thing.*

(Mis. 51:22-28)

CHAPTER 1
The Great Controversy

"Beloved, believe not every spirit, but try the spirits whether they are of God." *I John 4:1.*

The mounting attack of the mid-1700s upon the authenticity and veracity of the Bible — now called the "Higher Criticism" — has been the greatest, most far-reaching, and influential controversy of the modern world.

The first engagement of this controversial war — which has been fought for well over 200 years — was fought in silence by Hermann Reimarus, a professor of Oriental languages, at Hamburg Germany. Upon his death, in 1768, he left, cautiously unpublished, a 1400 page manuscript on the life of Christ. And six years later, in 1774, a friend — Gotthold Lessing — published it in part as the *Wolfenbuttel Fragments.*

Reimarus argued that Jesus can only be regarded as the final dominant figure in the mystical eschatology of the Jews — not as the Founder of Christianity. In other words, Reimarus claimed that Christ thought not to establish a new religion, but only to prepare men for what seemed at that time to be the imminent destruction of the world, and God's last judgement of all souls.

Later about 1836, David Strauss declared that the supernatural elements of the miracles of Jesus should be classified as myths, and that the actual history of Jesus must be reconstructed without using these elements in any form. His massive volumes made biblical criticism the storm center of German thought for a generation.

In 1840, Bruno Bauer began a series of passionately controversial works aiming to show that even Jesus was a myth — the personified form of a second century cult that evolved from the fusion of Jewish, Greek and Roman theology.

And in 1863, Earnest Renan's *Life of Jesus* alarmed millions with its rationalism, and charmed millions with its prose, gathering together the results of German criticism, bringing the controversial question of the Gospels before the entire educated world!

And throughout the following centuries, this "higher Criticism" has been countered by heroic attempts to save the historical foundations of the Christian Faith. For *history is the containing vehicle of the morality of man.*

The earliest written evidence for Jesus of Nazareth begins in the letters of Saint Paul, around the time he was imprisoned in Rome from circa 61-64 A.D.

No one has ever questioned the existence of Paul nor his repeated meetings with Peter, James and John. And Paul enviously admits that these men had known Jesus in the flesh. And the Apostles refer frequently to the "Last Supper" and to Jesus' crucifixion.

But matters are not so simple regarding the Gospels. The four that have survived the centuries, come from a much larger number of writings that were at one time circulating among the early Christians.

The gospels, *Matthew, Mark* and *Luke,* are "synoptic," meaning synonymous, in that they are *similar.* Whereas the gospel *John* embodies Christ more from a theological, metaphysical standpoint. It contradicts the other gospels in many details — as in its general depiction of Christ — not even pretending to be a biographical account.

Nevertheless, the fact remains that — despite the prejudices and theological differences of many evangelists — the Gospels record many incidents that mere inventors of myth would have desired to be concealed. Such as the competition of the Apostles for high places in the Kingdom; their flight after Jesus' arrest; Peter's denial of having known Jesus; his failure to work miracles in Galilee; the references of some auditors to his suspected insanity; his early uncertainty as to his mission; his confessions of doubt on the cross. None who read of these scenes can ever logically questions the reality of the powerful figure behind them.

That a few simply men in one generation should have fabricated so powerful and appealing a personality, so lofty an ethic, and so inspiring a vision of human brotherhood, would in itself be a miracle far more incredible than any of those recorded in the Gospels.

The original gospel compositions were apparently written at the close of the first century 60-120 A.D., and were therefore exposed to two centuries of possible error in their many trascriptions, and to possible alterations to suit the theology or aims of the copyist's sect or time.

Nevertheless, the profound story that they tell evidences the unique charm that they provide, even in the crude originals that were later enhanced for the English World by the lordly Version made for King James of England.

And after two centuries of "Higher Criticism" the outlines of the life, character and teachings of Jesus Christ have remained clear. Today they constitute the most fascinating *witness to the truth* in the history of man.

The Bible As Reform

CHAPTER 2

Truth versus Error

"Every spirit that confesseth that Jesus Christ is come in the flesh is of God." *I John 4:3.*

Christianity arose out of the esoteric Hebrew apocalyptic revelation regarding the coming Kingdom of God. It derived its profound impetus from the personality and vision of Jesus Christ, and it gained its strength from man's belief in his resurrection — which prefigures Jesus' promise of eternal life. Christianity received doctrinal form in the theology of Paul, and it grew and extended world-wide by absorbing the compromises of pagan ritual and faith. And it evolved into a triumphant Church by inheriting the organizing format and genius of Rome.

Belief in the messianic mission, and the bodily resurrection and earthly return of Christ, formed the basic faith of early Christianity, though this creed did not prevent the Apostles from continuing to abide by the teachings of Judaism.

They had received from the Holy Spirit, through Jesus, miraculous powers of inspiration, speech, and healing, and many of the sick came to them and were cured.

As the number of converts increased, the apostles ordained seven deacons to administer the affairs of the church. And in but a few years the small, and supposedly harmless sect of about 100, called Nazarenes, multiplied to well over 8000.

The rabbinate became alarmed, and Peter was arrested and questioned by the Sanhedrin. Later, in 34 A.D., Stephen (one of the seven ordained deacons) was summoned before the Sanhedrin on the charge that he had "used abusive language about Moses and about God,"

He defended himself with reckless vehemence. Whereupon the enraged Sanhedrin dragged him outside the city and stoned him to death. A young Pharisee named Saul aided the attack, thereafter going from house to house in Jerusalem, seizing all adherents of the "Way" and putting them in jail.

Many Christian converts fled to Samaria and Antioch where they established strong Christian communities, while most of the Apostles remained in Jerusalem, apparently spared in this persecution because they still observed the "Law" of the Jewish Faith.

Peter was again arrested in 62 A.D. but he soon escaped. Later in 66 A.D. the Jews revolted against Rome, and the Christians in Jerusalem left the city as soon as they could, establishing themselves in pagan, pro-Roman, Pella on the opposite bank of the Jordan. From that hour, Judaism and Christianity separated.

The Jews accused the Christians of cowardice and treason, and the Christians hailed the destruction of the temple at Jerusalem, by Titus, a fulfillment of one of Jesus' claims. Mutual antagonism inflamed the two faiths and thereafter wrote some of their most pious and controversial literature.

The Judaic form of Christianity waned in power and in numbers, finally yielding to the *new religion* which was to be later transformed by the Greco-Roman mind. Galilee turned a deaf ear to those who proclaimed the Nazarene to be the Son of God.

The Jews who thirsted for liberty from Roman domination were repelled by the concept of a Messiah who ignored their struggle for political independence. They were scandalized by the announcement that the Son of God had been born in a cave or stable in one of their local villages.

Meanwhile the apostles and the disciples were spreading the "Good News" chiefly among the Jews of the Dispersion, from Damascus to Rome. Philip made converts in Samaria and Caesarea, John developed a strong church in Ephesis, and Peter preached in the villages and cities of Syria.

And, says the book of Acts, a vision convinced Peter that he should accept pagan as well as Jewish converts into the faith, so he thereafter contented himself with baptizing rather than circumcising non-Jewish converts.

We do not know when, nor by what stages, Peter eventually made his way to Rome. But Jerome (circa 390) dates Peter's first arrival there as early as 42 A.D.. The traditional view that Peter played a leading role in establishing the Christian Community in that capital city, has survived all criticism. Peter free, and Paul in prison, labored there as rivals to win converts, until both of them suffered martyrdom, perhaps in the year 64.

Origen reports that Peter "was crucified head downward for he had asked that he suffer that way not being equal the Christ," and later stories name Nero's Circus on the Vatican field as the place of Peter's execution. At this site arose the Cathedral memorializing Saint Peter claiming to forever enshrine his bones.

Origen additionally reports (circa 220) that "Paul suffered martyrdom in Rome under Nero" and being a Roman citizen, had the distinction of not being grouped with the Christians who were crucified after the fires of 64 A.D. And Tertulian reports (cira 200) that Paul was beheaded at Rome at that time. Therefore tradition unites Paul with Peter in a simultaneous though separate martyrdom.

From Paul came the theological structure of Christianity, and from both Peter and Paul came the astonishing organization of the Christian Church. Paul found the dream of Jewish eschatology too confined by Judaic Law so he freed and broadened it into a faith that would move the world — weaving into it the ethics of the Jews and the metaphysics of the Greeks, transforming the Jesus of the gospels into the Christ of the theology we know today.

Paul created a new mystique — a new form of the resurrection drama, destined to be the survivor of all the rest. Paul replaced *conduct* with *creed* as the test of human virtue and in that sense began the Middle Ages.

This became a tragic change as humanity erroneously adjured that only a few saints could achieve the imitation of Christ — finding it easier to rise to faith and courage through hope in eternal life rather than through Christly conduct.

Paul was nearly forgotten almost for a century after his death. But when the early generations of Christianity had passed away — and the oral tradition of the Gospel had faded — and a hundred heresies had disordered the Christian mind — the epistles that he wrote provided the framework for a stabilizing system of belief that would unite the scattered congregations of Christianity into the powerful church Organization that was developing from Rome.

Even so, Paul, the man who had detached Christianity from Judaism, was still so essentially Jewish in intensity of character and sternness of morality that the Middle Ages — while adopting paganism into a colorful Catholicism — saw no kindred spirit in him, built few churches to his honor, seldom sculptured his figure, and seldom spoke his name.

Fifteen centuries passed before Martin Luther made Paul the apostle of the Reformation, and Calvin found in him the somber texts of the predestination creed.

Catholicism is the triumph of Peter. Protestantism is the triumph of Paul over Peter. Fundamentalism is the triumph of Paul of Christ.

The enslavement of man is his "Fall." This Fall is conquered not only by repentance and redemption from sin, but through the activity of man's creative abilities. And creative abilities are loosed through man's understanding of the Christ.

When man does that to which he is called by God, only then will he experience the new heaven and new earth. Only then will the Second Coming of Christ take place. Only then will His Kingdom of freedom come, in *witness to the Truth.*

CHAPTER 3

The Written Word

"Write the vision, and make it plain upon tables, that he may run that readeth it." *Habakkuk 2:2.*

Without a doubt, God is always talking to mankind through His holy spirit. He is always imparting to the world divine light by revelation to His chosen servants. **"Holy men of God speak as they are moved by the Holy Ghost."** *2 Peter 1:21.*

But throughout most of mankind's known human history, there had been no written revelation (of which we are aware) until the time of Moses, when preparation of the written Word began and thereafter continued (off and on) for some sixteen hundred years; from the writings of Moses — the historian of Creation and the Law — to the writings of John — the Recorder of the most sublime truths of the revealed Gospel of Jesus Christ.

The Bible itself points to divine inspiration as its author, yet it was written by the hands of men, and presents the varied styles and characteristics of its writers. Nevertheless, the revealed Truth it contains was **"given by the inspiration of God"** *2 Timothy 3:16* although expressed in the insufficient words of men; explaining the coincidence of the human with the divine.

It is as truly of the Bible as it is of Jesus Christ that **"the Word was made flesh, and dwelt among us."** *John 1:14.*

The Bible is a compilation of writings written in different ages by men of varied rank, occupation, and ability. Differing forms of expression are employed by its different writers. In many instances the same truth is presented, though by different writers under varied conditions and situations.

Although discrepancy or contradiction may seem apparent in certain cases, the thoughtful student discerns the basic harmony of the Bible's inspired Word. Truth, thereby revealed, forms a perfect whole adapted to meet mankind's needs in all the varied circumstances and experiences of life.

The treasure is entrusted to earthen vessels and yet it comes from above. The testimony is conveyed through the limited expressions of the human language, yet it is undeniably the testimony of God, and the sincere seeker of an understanding of God beholds in it the glorious revelation of a practical power, full of grace and truth.

Through His Word, God has revealed to mankind the complete knowledge necessary for his safety and salvation. **"Every scripture inspired of God is also profitable for teaching, for reproof, for correction, for instruction which is in righteousness; that the man of God may be complete, furnished completely unto every good work."** *2 Tim. 3:16, 17, revised.*

God revealed His will to mankind through His holy Word, and His Spirit is not given, nor can it ever be bestowed in contradiction to the inspired Word; for as the Scripture explicitly states, *the Word of God is the standard by which all moral life is to be taught, tested, and tried.*

The fallible, mortal mind of mankind convinces to have no need of guidance from the Word of God. It claims rightful government by "inner impressions" falsely thought to be the voice of God — although that influence might not be of the Holy Spirit.

This following of impressions while neglecting the Scripture can lead to confusion, deception, and to utter ruin. One must get to know the Truth, the Holy Spirit, God, as revealed in the Word of God.

One of the devices of the evil one, the one evil, is to cast contempt upon the work of the Holy Spirit through the errors of extremists, fanatics, the unfaithful, or the unwary, influencing mankind to overlook the Bible AS a source of guidance and of strength.

Even now in this present day and age the Holy Spirit is enlightening, and comforting all alert children of God. **"There is a spirit in man: and the inspiration of the Almighty giveth** them understanding." *Job 32:8.*

God, Spirit, is continuing His work, in harmony with His inspired Word, now as well as during ages past. The Holy Spirit communicates the light of understanding to individuals; but never contrary to the inspired word embodied in the sacred Canon.

"The Comforter, which is the Holy Ghost, whom the Father will send in my name, he shall teach you all things, and bring all things to your remembrance, whatsoever I have said unto you. When he, the spirit of Truth is come, he will guide you into all truth, and he will show you things to come." *John 14:26; 16:3.*

The apparent warfare of evil against good will continue to the close of time as we know it today. But Jesus assures his followers, **"I am with you always, even unto the end of the world."** *Matt. 28:20.*

Often the wrath of mortal mind has been manifested against the Church of Christ, and God has bestowed His grace and spirit upon His people to strengthen them, to help them overcome the supposed powers of the evil one, and as the Church approaches her final deliverance, he comes down **"having great wrath, because he knoweth that he hath but a short time,"** *Rev. 12:12,* and he works **"with all power and signs and lying wonders."** *2 Thes. 2:9.*

In this continuing conflict, mortal mind would employ the same policy, manifest the same false spirit, and work toward the same end, as in all preceding ages. **"He** (the evil one) **would lead astray, if it were possible, even the very elect."** *Mark 13:22 revised.* That which has been, will be, **"until he come** (the Christ) **whose right it is"** to **"overturn, overturn, overturn it."** *Ezek. 21:27.*

At this present time the same endowment of divine power and grace is no less necessary to the Church of Christ than in apostolic days. And likewise, the same disregard of the principles of God's Law, the same policy of deception by which error is made to appear as truth, and by which inhuman laws are substituted for the laws of God, can be seen repeated throughout the history of our past.

Mortal mind's misrepresentation of the Creator's character has caused mankind to cherish a false conception of the heavenly Father, and to therefore regard Him/Her with fear and contempt rather than with love and respect.

This misrepresentation of God's character — and its dire effects — accepted throughout all ages by mortal mind (unenlightened thought) can be traced throughout history in the harsh treatment of past patriarchs, prophets, apostles, martyrs, and reformers.

Mankind's humanity, or lack of it, always has been in direct proportion to our apprehension (or misapprehension) of the true nature of God and therefore of His/Her likeness, man. We need only to look at the past or the present world today to see that the crude ideals of speculative theology have made monsters of men.

How important, then that our theology be based on right ideas of God — on true ideas of the Father/Mother, received directly from Him/Her — not on human theories or speculations about Him/Her; but on God's ideas of Himself/Herself and His/Her creation, man. True theology is a divine revelation, a self-impartation of God, for only that which is of God can truly know Him as He is.

In tracing the history of the conflict of evil with good, and to shed the light of understanding upon this present age in which we live on the threshold of the twenty-first century, the author is impelled to share with others what has been communicated to his heart, as found in *the written Word.*

CHAPTER 4

Rejection of Truth

"O Jerusalem, Jerusalem, thou that killest the prophets, and stonest them that are sent unto thee, how often would I have gathered thy children together, even as a hen gathereth her chickens under her wings, and ye would not!" *Matthew 23:37.*

Had Israel as a nation preserved her allegiance to God, Jerusalem would have stood as a nation forever — the elect city of God. *Jer. 17:21-25.* But those favored people rebelled. They resisted heavens grace, abused their privileges, and slighted their opportunities.

Christ Jesus went to plead with the impenitent city, and though rewarded with evil for his good and with hatred for his love, Jesus steadfastly pursued his mission of mercy.

Never was anyone who sought his grace repelled. But Israel ignored the pleading of his love, spurned his counsels, and ridiculed his warnings.

The clouds of apostasy and rebellion that had been gathering throughout the ages, burst forth upon an unwatchful people. And he who was offering them a complete salvation from themselves, was slighted, abused, rejected, and crucified.

Jerusalem represented a symbol of the carnal mind, hardened in unbelief and rebellion. The great mistake of the Jews was their rejection of Christ. The great mistake of the Christian world today, is its rejection of the Christ and the law of God; the precepts of the one **"despised and rejected of men."**

The first temple was built during the most prosperous period of Israel's history. King David had exacted vast stores of treasure from the people for this purpose. And King Solomon, the wisest of Israel's reigning Monarchs, completed the work.

This temple was the most magnificent structure the world

had ever seen. And after its destruction by Nebuchadnezzar, it was rebuilt about five centuries before the birth of Christ by a people who had returned to a wasted and deserted country from a nearly life-long captivity in Babylon.

But the restored temple did not equal the first in grandeur nor in the manifestations of the cloud of glory and fire from heaven; nor in the abiding Shekina of the most holy place. And no voice from heaven sounded to make known the will of God.

The Jews endeavored for centuries to show wherein the promise of God, given by the prophet Haggai, had been fulfilled. Yet pride and unbelief blinded their hearts to the true meaning of Haggai's words concerning this second temple: **"The glory of this latter house shall be greater than the former. I will shake all nations, and the desire of all nations shall come; and I will fill this house with glory, saith the Lord of hosts."** *Hag. 2:9, 7.*

Many failed to see that the "Desire of all nations" had indeed come to this temple, when Jesus of Nazareth taught receptive minds and healed receptive hearts in and near its sacred courts. In this, and this only, did the second temple exceed the first in glory. But when Israel put the humble teacher from her midst, the glory forever passed away from the temple, and the Savior's words: **"your house is left unto you desolate"** *Matt. 24:2,* were fulfilled.

Jesus' disciples expected Christ's coming to be in temporal glory, to take the throne of a political empire, to punish impenitent Jews, and break off the yoke of Roman domination. After the Redeemer's sufferings and death, and the destruction of the Jewish city and temple, they fell back on his promise that he would come again to finish what was as yet undone.

The Master's words were not generally understood, but their meaning would gradually unfold, as his people should need the instruction given and be in such a state of mind as to properly benefit from it. His prophesy was two-fold in its meaning, foreshadowing the destruction of Jerusalem and prefiguring the events of these latter days as well.

During the reign of King Herod, Jerusalem had been made virtually impregnable. He, who would foretell of its destruction, would be thought of as crazed and an alarmist. And while claiming to observe the precepts of God's Law, the self-righteous rulers of Jerusalem were blindly continuing to transgress its righteous principles.

They hated Jesus because his purity of thought and action was a rebuke to them and revealed their iniquity. They accused him for all the troubles they were experiencing. Troubles which were the result of the errors of their ways.

Though they knew him to be without sin, they deemed his death necessary to ensure the safety of the nation. They feared that by letting him remain unchecked, the Romans would come and take away their positions of authority, and their nation. (*see John 11:48.*)

They reasoned that if but this one man were sacrificed, it would be better than the destruction of the whole nation of Israel; and they thought that they would once again become a strong and united people. Though they slew their savior because he reproved their self-righteousness, they claimed through the letter of the law to be God's people while they actually were not living in accord with its spirit.

Jerusalem's doom was delayed for forty years from the time of its pronouncement. This only confirmed the Jews impenitence, hatred, and cruelty towards Jesus' disciples.

They continued to spurn the graces of Christ which would have enabled them to subdue their evil impulses. Evil therefore overpowered them and became their conqueror through their cruelty, suspicion, envy, hatred, strife, rebellion, and murderous deeds.

Friends and family alike became betrayers of one another. Parents slew their children, and children their parents. Rulers could not even rule themselves, not to mention the people. The Jews had accepted false accusations against Jesus, and now false accusations against them were making their existence a dire uncertainty. For many years the Jews experienced a compounding of the great truth: **"With what measure ye meet, it shall me measured to you again"** *Mat. 7:2,* hence the anarchy, rebellion, and betrayal they experienced.

When eventually the Romans surrounded the city, under Cestius, the alert and watchful Christians were sheltered by God. The Romans unexpectedly abandoned the siege even though all conditions seemed favorable for a successful attack. The besieged and discouraged city was already at the point of surrender. Even so, the Roman general surprisingly withdrew his forces for no apparent reason.

The Jews followed him in his retreat, and while the Jews and the Romans were engaged in combat, the Christians left the city, unharmed. Not one Christian perished in the destruction of Jerusalem!

The Christians and the Jews had assembled at Jerusalem to keep the feast of tabernacles; therefore Christians throughout the land were able to make their escape, unmolested, to the land of Peraea beyond the Jordan, enabling them to spread the gospel message to another land.

The Roman siege against Jerusalem was later renewed, by Titus, at the time of the Passover, when millions of Jews were within its walls. Thousands in the besieged city perished from pestilence and starvation.

Those in power within the city walls inflicted inhuman tortures upon their fellow beings. The blind obstinacy of the Jewish leaders, and word of their perpetrated crimes excited the horror and indignation of the conquering Romans, who decided to take the fortress by storm, while not actually intending to destroy the magnificent temple.

But Titus found it impossible to check the animosity and rage of his soldiers against the detestable actions of the Jews, and their insatiable desire for plunder, so the temple was unintentionally set ablaze, and the noble edifice was abandoned to the flames.

After the destruction of the temple, the whole city soon fell into the Roman's hands. The Jews had filled, for themselves, the cup of vengeance. **"O Jerusalem, thou has destroyed thyself... thou hast fallen by thine iniquity."** *Hos. 13:9; 14:1.*

Sufferings are often falsely thought to be a visitation of the "Wrath of God." Thusly, the carnal mind conceals the results of its own work. By its stubborn rejection of divine mercy and love, the mind was loosed to govern by its baser instincts.

The destruction of Jerusalem can be treated as a solemn lesson to all who would take lightly the extended offerings of divine Love to express good.

But God's people shall be delivered! Jesus has declared that the Christ will come again to gather his faithful ones to himself, in *witness to the truth.*

The Bible As Reform

CHAPTER 5
Persecution of Truth

"Ye shall be hated of all men for my names sake: *Matthew 11:22.* **But for the elect's sake those days shall be shortened."** *Matthew 24:22.*

Jesus revealed many things to his disciples during his earthly career. He foretold of the coming experiences of his people, from the time he would leave them, to the time when Christ would appear in full power and glory for the final deliverance of mankind from the powers of darkness.

He foretold of the coming age of darkness and persecution. He told of the bitter cup which the rulers of the world would mete out on the Church of Christ. *Mat. 24:9, 21, 22.*

The Church of Christ was to tread the same pathway of humiliation, reproach, and suffering that the Master trod. The enmity which was to burst forth against the world's redeemer, would be manifested in some degree against all who believed in his name. The powers of earth would array themselves against the Christ manifested in the personage of his followers. Intolerant and unaccepting Paganism foresaw that, should the Gospel triumph, her temples, altars, false gods and financial benefits would be forever swept away.

The clouds of darkness therefore gathered in full force; intent on the destruction of the new birth of fledgling Christianity. Thusly the fires of persecution were kindled; beginning under the Roman Emperor Nero about the time of the martyrdom of Paul and continuing with greater or lesser intensity for many centuries thereafter.

Superstitious men falsely accused Christians of the most dreadful crimes and declared them to be the cause of great calamities; famine, pestilence, earthquakes. They were condemned as rebels against the state, heretics against all religions of the day, and pests against society.

The catacombs afforded shelter for thousands. Even the loss of every earthly blessing could not force them to renounce what they had come to believe concerning Christ.

But in vain were the evil-one's efforts to destroy the new-born Church of Christ. The great conflict did not cease even when faithful standard bearers fell at their posts of duty. Through defeat they did shine forth as conquerors. Although men were slain in God's work, it went steadily forward. The Gospel continued to spread and the numbers of its adherents continued to increase. It penetrated into regions unaccessible even to the Eagles of Rome.

Thousands fell; but thousands more sprang up to take their places. The sufferings they endured brought them closer together to one another, and likewise even closer to their Lord.

The wiles of mortal mind then concluded that a more successful warfare against this "scourge against society" could be waged by planting the banner of evil within the Christian Church under the guise of allegiance to the Church. The great adversary now endeavored to gain by artifice and delusion what had not been gained before by force. If the followers of Christ could be deceived and thereby led to abandon or dilute their respect and honor for God's precepts, their strength, fortitude and purpose of endeavor would fall away — a sure and easy prey to deception.

Persecution ceased and in its stead were substituted the dangerous allurements of temporal prosperity, worldly honors to man, and compromises to "the powers that be." Idolators made concessions in receiving parts of the Christian Faith while expecting true Christians in return to likewise make concessions to what *they* wanted, so all might join together on a united platform of compromised belief. Under the cloak of pretended Christianity the seamless garment of Christ was rent in twain, to be thereafter divided as spoil.

Some Christians stood firm, but most Christians, unknowingly if not willingly, at last consented to standards of a lessening degree. A union was thereby formed between Christianity and pagan practices and beliefs. The false leaven of idolatry was thereby brought into the church at this time. Unsound doctrines, superstitious rites and idolatrous ceremonies were incorporated into her worship and faith. The Church lost her purity and much of her healing power.

The true Christian studies the life of the Exemplar and earnestly seeks to correct defects shown forth in himself so as to conform to the pattern presented by Jesus Christ. Thought and action becomes more spiritualized as new light is received showing forth the fruits of continued improvement and growth, while the counterfeit Christian shuns the plain and practical truths which expose his errors. Even in her *best* estate, the Church was not wholly composed of the true, the pure, and the sincere.

Unrighteous thinking invites temptation which results in evil traits of character. This becomes evident to the discerning Christian, and the apostate one becomes angry when his faults are reproved. Thusly he is led to betray his more sincere compatriot.

Those who hold onto evil under the guise of Godliness "saying peace, peace, where there is no peace" often dislike those who disturb that peace through audible or silent condemnation of their sin, and when a favorable opportunity presents itself, will — like Judas — betray those who for their good have a reproachful effect on their lives.

Through the Spirit of Truth the hidden character of the pretender is eventually revealed. And through the example and prayers of the righteous, the pretence is dissolved or the pretender is removed from a position of influence.

This evidence of the discerning Spirit of Truth is sometimes an unconscious or conscious threat to the hypocrite. Not for long can he remain comfortable with those who in habit and disposition are constant representatives of Christ.

As long as trials and persecutions came upon the followers of Christ, they were more or less screened from the pretender and hypocrite because only those who are willing to forsake all for Christ are desirous of discipleship. As persecution ceased, converts were accepted into fellowship who were less than sincere and the door was opened for deceit.

Eventually compromised Christians were enticed further and further from the truth even to the point of persecuting those who steadfastly remained true to God. *No one knows so well how to oppose the true Christian faith as do those who were formerly its defenders.*

After a long and sever conflict, a faithful few protesting reformers dissolved their association with the apostate church that refused to free itself from falsehood and idolatry. They saw separation as an absolute necessity if they would obey the Word of God. If unity could be secured only by a compromise of truth and righteousness with error, then let there be continued difference.

The currents of religion today, though the Church often knows it not, are not the pure and holy currents of the early Christian faith in the days of Jesus and his apostles. It is only because of compromise that the Church is so popular with the world today. But let there be a revival of the faith and healing power of the early Christian faith as in the days of Jesus and his apostles, and the fires of persecution will revive, in ***witness to the truth.***

CHAPTER 6
Perversion of Truth

"Thou hast tried them which say they are apostles, and are not, and hast found them liars." *Revelation 2:2.*

The apostle Paul, in his second letter to the Thessalonians, foretold of a great apostasy that would result in the establishment of papal power.

He foretold that the day of Christ would not come **"except there come a falling away first, and that man of sin be revealed, the son of perdition** (mortal mind) **who opposeth and exalteth himself above all that is called God, or that is worshipped** (the Christ Mind)**; so that he as God sitteth in the temple of God, shewing himself that he is God."** And furthermore, **"the mystery of iniquity doth already work."** *2 Thes. 2:3, 4, 7.*

Almost imperceptibly the customs of the heathen were finding their way into the new Christian way of thinking. The pressures of conformity and compromise, restrained for a time by open persecution, were, as persecutions ceased, bringing about an adulteration of the humble simplicity of Christly teachings — incorporating the pride and pomp of pagan priests and rulers into the Church by the substitution of human hypothesis, theories and tradition, for the simple Word of God.

The Conversion of Roman Emperor Constantine, in the early part of the fourth century, caused great rejoicing. And worldly belief, cloaked in the form of righteousness, entered the Church. Paganism, while appearing vanquished, actually continued to take over. Her attitudes, doctrines, ceremonies and superstitions infiltrated the worship and faith of the professed followers of Christ.

The adulterative compromise of true Christianity with paganism, resulted in the evolvement of **"that man of sin"** opposing and **"exalting himself above all that is called God"** — a gigantic system of compromised religion — a monument to error's efforts to seat **"himself"** upon the throne of rulership — to control and govern mankind as **"he"** will.

At a former time the **"deceiver"** had come to Jesus in the wilderness of temptation, offering to give all temporal power into his hands if he would acknowledge the supremacy of the **"prince of darkness."** Jesus rebuked the tempter thus causing him to depart. But error often times meets with success when presenting its temptations to mankind.

To secure worldly honors, the Church was misled to seek favor and support from the politically powerful of that day, yielding allegiance to the Bishop of Rome.

One of the leading doctrines of Romanism is that the pope is the visible head of the universal Church, invested with supreme authority over all mankind in every part of the world. He is invested as **"Lord God the Pope."** He assumes infallibility and demands all men pay him homage — the same claim urged by Satan in the wilderness of temptation. But God's Word never even hinted of such an appointment as this whereby *any* man or woman is to be the Head of the Church of Christ. **"Call no man your father upon the earth: for one is your father, which is in heaven."** *Mat. 23:9.* The doctrine of papal supremacy is directly opposed to the Protestant teaching of Scripture.

Romanists persisted in charging Protestants with heresy and willful separation from what they claim to be the true Church of Christ, but in actuality these accusations apply rather to themselves, for only by the Word of the holy Scriptures can man discern the deceptions of error and withstand the effects of its seeming power. To every assault of the adversary, Christ stood in opposition under the shield of eternal, never changing Truth, declaring **"it is written . . ."**

But in order for man to maintain temporal authority and dominion over his fellow brethren, he often thinks he has to keep them ignorant of their God bestowed rights. And since the Bible exalts God and shows mankind their true position of freedom, mortal mind determined that the truths of the Scripture had to be determined, concealed, and suppressed; and for hundreds of years free circulation of the Bible was withheld.

The people were forbidden to read the Bible; while Priests and Prelates interpreted its teaching *for* the people, to sustain their pretensions as they saw fit, thereby maintaining temporal authority over the Church and even over the state.

This infusion of religious belief into political practice was considered to be, in the long run, **"for the good of the people,"** to enable those who considered themselves more capable to rule the **"unenlightened masses."**

Gradually, the adoration of images and relics was introduced into Christian worship. The decree of the Second Council of Nicea, in 787, firmly established this system of idolatry by expunging from the law of God the Second Commandment which forbids the worship of images, and dividing the Tenth in order to preserve the number.

By the sixth century, the seat of power in the Church was the papacy fixed in the imperial City of Rome, and the Bishop of Rome was declared to be the head of all the Church. The Dragon of paganism had given the place of **"his power, and his seat, and great authority"** to the papacy in Rome. Thus began the twelve-hundred and sixty (1260) years of papal oppression, foretold in the Prophesies of Daniel and in the Revelation of St. John. *Dan. 7:25; Rev. 13.5, 7.*

Christians were forced to choose between the dictates of papal worship and ceremonies, or the sufferings of dungeons, racks, fagots, and the headman's axe. Persecution once again came down upon the Faithful with great fury. The world once again became a vast religious battlefield, and for hundreds of years the true Church of Christ was forced to find refuge in obscurity, seclusion, and hiding.

"The woman fled into the wilderness, where she had a

place prepared of God, that they should feed her a thousand two hundred and three score (1260) days." *Rev. 12:6.* This accession to power of the Roman Church marked the beginning of what is now called the Dark Ages.

As the power of the Roman Church increased, so did the darkness deepen. Faith in Christ was transferred to faith in the pope and his representatives. People were directed to the pope, his prelates and his priests for forgiveness of sins and for eternal salvation; instead of to a trust in God and the Way of Life taught by Christ Jesus. They were wrongly taught that none could approach God except through the earthly mediation of those designated with authority by the pope.

Any deviation from his authoritative requirements was sufficient cause for the severest of punishments, and since this **"wickedness in high places"** was shrouded in the garb of sanctity, with the Scriptures suppressed, corruption flourished. It seemed at times that error and superstition would totally prevail, banishing true religion from the world forever.

False forms of religions were multiplied, and the people were burdened with rigorous exactions, long pilgrimages, the worship of relics, and the payment of vast sums of treasure and money to the Church. This invested the Church with ever increasing wealth and political power.

At the close of the eighth century came the claim of the **"universal supremacy of the pope"** — the claim of apostolic ascendancy through direct succession, back to an apostleship with Jesus in the earliest times of His ministry.

In the eleventh century, Pope Gregory VII proclaimed the perfection of the Roman Church, declaring that the Church had never erred; nor would it ever err. All this, so called, according to the Scriptures. He declared that no one could reverse any of his pronouncements; and yet it was his undeniable prerogative to reverse the decision of anyone else. The proud pontiff therefore claimed it his solemn power and prerogative to even depose emperors!

It is just as much a threat for religious beliefs to attempt to control politics — as it is for politics to attempt to govern religious beliefs.

The tyrannical character of this advocation of infallibility was illustrated in full force, when German Emperor Henry IV was declared by the pope to be excommunicated and dethroned.

Terrified by the threats and desertion of his own German Princes, Henry IV succumbed; and finally made peace with the pontiff — on the pontiff's terms! — so he could resume his exercise of the Insignia of Royalty and power.

The vast universal support provided by the exaction of great wealth from a worldwide following provided such power and governing control, that — even when exercised on the political basis — far superceded the less vast resources of more regional Kingdoms. Hence even Kings and Emperors bowed to the decrees of the Holy See. And the advancing centuries witnessed a continual increase of errors in the doctrines put forth by the Roman Church.

Such erroneous doctrines as:

1) the eternal torment of the impenitent,

2) the concept of purgatory, employed to terrify the superstitious multitudes, and,

3) full remission from the pains and penalties of sin, for those who would enlist in the pontiff's wars — wars to extend the pontiff's powerful empire, to punish his enemies, or to exterminate those who refused him their allegiance, or who dared to deny his spiritual supremacy — and,

4) the doctrine that declared that by the payment of great wealth to the Church, individuals might free both themselves and their deceased relatives and friends who were supposedly confined in Purgatory's tormenting fires of the damned.

By such means did the Church of Rome continually expand her overflowing coffers and sustain her luxurious opulence, and the vice of those pretended representatives of Him who had not a place of his own whereupon to lay His head.

All Christians were required, upon pain of death, to subscribe to and avow their faith in this debauchery; and multitudes who refused were given over to the flames when the thirteenth century brought with it that most terrible of all the engines of the papacy — the Inquisition.

In secret councils, the minds of men became drunken with the wine of apostate power and **"the blood of the saints"** and the destiny of those in subjection to their power were left almost with no hope under this terrible threat. The noontide of the papacy was the moral midnight of error and world wide ignorance. The Holy Scriptures were not only unknown to the beclouded multitudes, but even to unsuspecting priests who became ignorant perpetrators of that of which they knew not.

Even well-meaning papist leaders shunned the light which would have revealed to them their sins. With the standard of righteousness — the Bible — having been removed from them, they often — and perhaps ignorantly — exercised their power without limit; they were left to practice vice without restraint. Men shrank from no crimes by which they could obtain and extend their influence and power.

Eventually, in some instances, secular rulers endeavored to depose reigning pontiffs who were known to be guilty of crimes so revolting as to be deemed politically and humanly intolerable.

During these centuries, Europe made no progress in learning, in the arts, or in civilization. Such were the results of the banishment of the Word of God.

According to Hosea: **"My people are destroyed for lack of knowledge: seeing thou hast forgotten the law of thy God."** *Hos. 4: 6, 1, 2,* — in *witness to the truth.*

CHAPTER 7

Resistance for Truth

"No prophesy of the scriptures is of any private interpretation." *I Peter 1:20.*

Amid that night of gloom imposed upon an almost helpless world during the long dark-age period of papal supremacy, there were still active witnesses for God who held the Bible to be their only rule of life.

Posterity will never know how much the world still owes to these faithful men and woman. They were branded as heretics, their motives were impugned, their characters were maligned, their writings were suppressed, misrepresented and mutilated. Yet they stood firm from age to age maintaining the purity of their faith as a sacred heritage for generations yet to come.

But few remaining signs of their existence can be found, because it was the policy of Rome to obliterate all traces of dissent from her doctrines and dictates. Almost everything and everyone deemed heretical were destroyed, including almost every record of her cruelty toward dissenters.

Prior to the invention of printing, books were laboriously written by hand and were few in number, therefore, there was little to prevent the Romanists from desecrating the freedom-of-conscience of the masses.

Primitive Christianity had a very early start in Great Britain in the first few centuries, and the gospel received there at that time was relatively uncorrupted by the Roman apostasy. So when the Saxons invaded Britain, the conquerors refused to be influenced by their Christian slaves, so many Christians fled — not only to Scotland and Ireland, but also to Germany, Switzerland and even to Italy.

In the sixth century Rome's emissaries began to convert the

heathen Saxons in Britain and were well received by the proud "barbarians" (Sons of Arius). Many thousands of Saxons were converted to the Roman faith, but as the work progressed, the papal leaders and their converts eventually encountered the primitive Christians, their churches, their way of life, and their simple teachings.

The Emissary of Rome demanded that these primitive believers acknowledge the supremacy of the sovereign pontiff, and although the churches in Britain were eventually destroyed or forced to submit to the authority of the pope, many Christians refused and fled to lands beyond the jurisdiction of the pope where for many centuries groups of Christians remained virtually free from papal indoctrination.

Surrounded by heathenism during the lapse of ages, they were affected somewhat by its errors, but they continued to regard the Bible as their only rule of faith, and adhered to many of its truths.

Of those who resisted the encroachment of the papal power, the Waldensians stood foremost — living in Italy, the very land where the papacy had its fixed seat — so that even there its falsehoods and corruption were most steadfastly resisted.

When, after centuries of Waldensian independence, Rome insisted that the churches of the Piedmont submit to its authority, the leaders of these churches reluctantly acquiesced, but many of their members were unwilling to surrender allegiance to God, and withdrew from their native Piedmont to raise the banner of truth in foreign lands.

Others retreated behind the lofty bulwarks of the Alpine Mountains where they found a hiding place in which to keep their beliefs unsullied. Here for a thousand years their *witness to truth* maintained the independence of the original faith. And the eternal flame of truth burned on amid the darkness of the middle ages.

The surrounding mountains were a constant witness to God's creative power. And a never failing assurance of His protecting care. God had provided for them a sheltering "secret place" from the wrath and the cruelty of man.

Consider the contrast of the papal doctrines to the teachings of primitive Christianity. The view of Him with whom is **"no variableness, neither shadow of turning."** *Jas. 1:17.* God's law had been established for the government of His creation **"on earth as it is in heaven."** And in fidelity to Him God's servants should be as steadfast and as firm.

Copies of the Bible were rare so its precious words were often committed to memory. Small children were taught to look with gratitude to God as the giver of all good. They were taught that God intends life to be a discipline and that all human needs could and would be supplied by their forethought, labors, and care — through their faith. That all their powers and abilities were but reflections of God's power and inspiration. That their talents were to be improved and strengthened in and for His service. That the Bible represented the supreme and infallible authority for mankind, through the teachings and example of the Master, who **"came not to be ministered unto, but to minister."** *Mat. 20:28.*

The Bible is **God's lesson book** for all mankind — for childhood, youth, manhood and maturity — to be studied throughout all time to come. It is God's revelation of Himself to mankind, bringing us into a close walk and communion with our Creator.

The Spirit of Christ is a missionary spirit compelling the revived one to bring others also to the Savior and to let one's light shine forth to those in the darkness of midnight and old night. Compelling him or her to remove the bondage of materiality from the beloved Children of God.

When the light of Truth illuminates the darkness understanding hearts are made glad — and they long to shed forth its shining rays in order to benefit others.

The Waldensians could see that the multitudes were vainly endeavoring, under the false guidance of pope and priest, to obtain pardon through affliction while dwelling upon their sinful condition, wrongly imagining themselves exposed to a wrathful God who afflicts, yet finding no relief. Conscientious individuals thereby became enslaved and bound by the misleading doctrines of Rome.

By oft repeated fasts, scourging, midnight vigils, long prostrations, pilgrimages, fearful self-torture and humiliating penance, they sought in vain to obtain peace of mind and conscience.

Oppressed by the sense of sin and hounded by the fear of God's supposed avenging wrath, many suffered on until exhausted natures gave way, never finding the "Good News" of the gospel message of peace, nor the uplift and comfort of the promises of God.

The false doctrine that penance alone can atone for transgressions, and that reliance upon the human efforts of others is necessary and beneficial, contradicts the true view of God's infinite love, ever flowing to His beloved children.

The merits and abundant love of our beloved heavenly Father are the foundations of the Christian's faith. And Christ is our living and compassionate Savior, inviting us all to come to Him to exchange our burdens of sin, weariness and care, for the assurances of rest, pardon, and peace.

Fear of death can be vanquished. To the questioning heart, the answer can be read, **"Come unto me, all ye that labour and are heavy laden, and I will give you rest."** *Mat. 11:28.*

The purity of the gospel truths sustained the hearts of the Waldensians and were again invading the kingdoms of regimented mortal mind, arousing the seven thunders of evil. The papal leaders must have seen a great portent of danger to the security of their cause in the message of these humble people.

The simple dews of truth, coming amidst the foreboding clouds of error — if allowed to moisten the vast desert of human hope — dissolve, like the soft tender gentle beams of sunlight, forever away the foreboding clouds of error that threaten to enshroud and envelope God's dear people. Truth annihilates the manifestations of the carnal mind.

Therefore, any refusal to surrender Scriptural Canon became an offense to Rome it could not tolerate. Bitter hatred and persecution were thereby inflamed against the true believers, and the most terrible crusade against God's people began.

And example of such was the Bull issued by Pope Innocent VIII, in 1487, five centuries ago, condemning the Waldensians as heretics and delivering them, in effect, to slaughter.

He declared that the Waldensians "seduce the sheep of the true fold." That "this malicious and abominable sect of malignants, if they refused to abjure, be crushed like venomous snakes."

This papal Bull called for all members of the Roman Church to join in a crusade against those so-called heretics, offering as a reward absolution from all ecclesiastical penalties and pain; release from all former oaths taken; legalization of title to all illegally acquired property stolen in the past; the remission of all penalty for sin — including that for killing any declared heretic; and the annulling of all contracts made in favor of the heretics. It also ordered all domestics to abandon the heretics; forbade all persons to aid them in any way, and empowered anyone to freely take possession of their property.

The same influence that slew the apostles and crucified Christ was again operating to rid the earth of the beloved of God. But regardless of the crusades against these God-fearing people — and the persecutions visited upon them for those many long years — they endured by the grace of God and continued their mission of scattering the seeds of the Reformation that began in the time of Wyclif and grew broad in the days of Luther, in *witness to the Truth.*

The Bible As Reform

CHAPTER 8

Reform in England

"Blessed are they which do hunger and thirst after righteousness: for they shall be filled." *Matthew 5:6.*

The scriptural Word of God had for many ages been locked in languages predominantly unknown, except by the educated elite. Few copies of the Bible were even in existence prior to the Protestant Reformation. In those early times of Christianity, only scholars were able to find their way to the great fountainhead of revealed Truth; not available to the unschooled classes of that time.

Then, in the fourteenth century, there began in England, one of the first indications of the coming Reformation shown forth in the life of John Wyclif, an early herald of the reform that was yet to come not only to England, but to all of Christianity.

His protest against the Roman Church was thereafter never to be silenced. It was an outcry that was to eventually result in the emancipation of not only individuals, but of churches and nations as well.

He had felt a hungering need which neither scholastic studies nor the teaching of the Church could satisfy. But in reading the Word of God he found therein what he before had sought in vain. Here he saw the great plan of salvation, with Christ set forth for mankind as the only advocate with the Father.

In most cases reformers do not immediately foresee where their work will lead them. They don't intend deliberate opposition to the status quo, but sincerity and devotion to truth bring them sooner or later into conflict with the hidden falsehoods of error.

As Wyclif began to see that the Church of Rome had forsaken the Word of God for human hypothesis and the traditions of men, he fearlessly accused the priesthood of having banished the Scriptures into exile, and he demanded that the Bible be restored to its rightful place with the people for whom it was intended and that its authority be again recognized in and by the Church.

Many people had become dissatisfied with their former faith, as they too saw the iniquity that then prevailed in the Roman Church, and they welcomed with unconcealed joy the truths brought to view by Wyclif through his work. But the papists were enraged as they began to realize that this reformer was gaining an influence even superior to their own.

In addition to this, while acting as chaplain to the King of England, Wyclif took a bold stand against the exaction of tribute money claimed by the pope from the English Monarch. He pointed out to the king that the papal assumption of authority over secular rulers was presumptuous and contrary to both reason and Biblical revelation.

With the support of the king and his nobles, Wyclif's stand became a united denial of the pontiff's claim to secular authority over the kingdom. In this refusal to pay the tribute money an effectual blow was struck against papal supremacy as far as England was concerned.

Another blight that was eventually brought down by Wyclif's influence was that of the institution of the Orders of Mendicant Friars. The monk's life of idleness and beggary had brought useful labor into contempt and was a drain upon the resources of the land.

Homes were made desolate as parents were deprived of the help and society of their sons and daughters who were being enticed to join the Orders of the monks, blighting their own lives as well as bringing grief to their parents.

The sick and the poor were left to suffer, while gifts that should have been used to relieve their pressing needs went to the monks who with threats demanded the alms of the people for themselves.

Despite their outward professions of poverty, the wealth of the friars was constantly increasing. Their magnificent edifices and sumptuous tables contrasted greatly with the growing poverty of the Nation. The rapacity of the friars expressed a greed that seemed never to be satisfied, as they traversed the countryside vending the pope's pardons and his blessings.

The monks justified all this by the claim that they were following the Savior's example, declaring that since Jesus and his disciples had been supported in their ministry by the charities of the people, that they were only following his example. This claim, however, led many to the Bible to learn the truth for themselves — the last thing ever desired by Rome.

Men of learning had labored again and again, but in vain, to bring reform to these Monastic Orders, — but Wyclif, with clearer insight, struck his blow at the very root of the evil by declaring the whole system of be false and in need of total abolition.

Wyclif was appointed the Royal Ambassador of England. As a result he spent two years in the Netherlands in conference with the pope's Commissioners. There he was brought in touch with ecclesiastics from Italy, France, and Spain. This gave him an even greater insight into the "behind the scenes" situation. It was thereby revealed to him much that would have otherwise remained hidden, had he remained in England.

Upon his return, he was ever more prepared and zealous in his mission. He was appointed to the parish rectory of Lutterworth; became professor of theology at Oxford; and his influence was felt, not only in shaping the actions of the Court, but in the moulding of beliefs on a national level as well.

As a result, the papal thunders were hurled against him to bring him down. Three bulls were dispatched to England — to the university, to the king, and to the prelates of the Church. However, death came — not to the Reformer under attack — but to the pope who decreed the Reformer's destruction.

The death of Pope Gregory XI was followed, this time, by

the election of *two* popes — two professedly infallible but conflicting and rival powers.

This occurrence weakened the power of the papacy for some time, providing Wyclif with a welcome respite from harassment and persecution. And while all Christendom was filled with tumult, as the two popes waged their war, Wyclif, as professor of theology at Oxford, continued preaching in the university halls.

Furthermore, in his rectory at Lutterworth, unheeded by the storm, the Reformer applied himself to his work, and wrote the first English translation of the Bible; opening up the Word of God to all of England. Its appeal to men's reason awakened them from their passive submission to the papal dogma.

Wyclif now taught the distinctive doctrines of Protestantism — salvation through faith found in the teachings of Christ, and the inspired Word of God, found in the Bible.

This new/old faith was welcomed and accepted by nearly half the population of England; whereupon, laws were enacted and enforced, in rebuttal, to prohibit the possession and even the reading of this so newly translated Book.

Then, winning the favor of young King Richard II to their side, a synod of bishops obtained a royal decree consigning to prison all who would be found holding in their possession the condemned doctrines.

Wyclif presented an appeal before Parliament and the surprised papists saw themselves defeated when Parliament, roused by Wyclif's stirring appeal, repealed the persecuting edict.

As a result of this, Wyclif was summoned a third time for trial, this time before the highest ecclesiastical tribunal in the Kingdom. Here at last, so thought the papists, Rome would triumph. But Wyclif again persisted in repelling the accusations of his persecutors, and the power of the Holy Spirit was felt within the counsel room. The charge of heresy, which his hearers had brought against him, he with convicting power threw back upon themselves — and he withdrew from the assembly unmolested.

But the truth was to be proclaimed even to the very stronghold of the "kingdom of error." Wyclif was summoned for trial before a papal tribunal at Rome.

Although not blind to the danger that awaited him in Rome, he yet would have obeyed the summons had not a paralysing stroke prevented him from making the long and arduous journey.

Even so, from this rectory, the reformer wrote a letter to the pope, which although respectful in tone and in Christian spirit, was a keen rebuke to the pope and pride of the Papal See.

Thusly Wyclif presented to the pope and to his cardinals the meekness and humility of Christ; exhibiting not only to themselves but to all of Christendom, the contrast between themselves and the Master whose representatives they professed to be.

Wyclif fully expected that his life would be the price of his epistle, but God's providence still shielded this beloved servant. This man who for his whole lifetime had stood boldly in defense of truth, and in daily peril to his life, was not to fall victim to the hatred of this foes.

In his Church at Lutterworth, he fell stricken by another stroke, and in a short time passed on. His life had been protected, and his labors had been prolonged, until a never failing firm foundation had been laid for the great work of the coming Reformation.

Wyclif was typical of the greatness of all reformers. He expressed breadth of intellect, clearness of thought, firmness in the truth, and boldness to defend it, purity of life and diligence in study. He was untiring in labor, Christlike in love, and faithful to his ministry. And it was the Bible that made him what he was.

All the characteristics expressed by Wyclif are expressed by every sincere and able-minded reformer. **"The entrance of thy words** (says the Psalmist) **giveth light; it giveth understanding."** *Psalm 119:130.*

The great movement which Wyclif inaugurated was eventually to liberate the conscience and intellect of nations heretofore bound to Rome. But with its first leader removed, the storm clouds of persecution fell upon those remaining who dared to accept the Bible as their guide. For the first time in English history the stake was decreed against the disciples of the Gospel.

Though the papists had failed to work their will against Wyclif during his lifetime, they, by the decree of the Council of Constance, more than thirty years after he passed on, exhumed his bones and publicly burned them; and his ashes were thrown into a nearby stream.

"The stream (says an unknown writer) conveyed his ashes to the Avon, the Avon to the Severn, the Severn to the narrow seas, and they onward to the sea." Thusly did Wyclif's ashes become the symbol of his doctrine now dispersed throughout the world, and thusly did his enemies too late realize the effect of their malicious act.

Notwithstanding the continuing persecution, Wyclif's calm, earnest, and devoted protests of truth against the corruption of religious faith, continue to echo forth centuries later, in *witness to the truth.*

CHAPTER 9

Reform in Bohemia

"Stand fast therefore in the liberty wherewith Christ hath made us free." *Galations 5:1.*

To this day, to be seen as Bohemian is to be seen as an unconventional person, possible a writer or artist, living an unconventional life.

John Hus was a Bohemian of humble birth, orphaned in his early years. Later he was admitted to the University of Prague, as a charity scholar.

From the beginning of his studies he was a sincere adherent to the doctrines of the Roman Church, and an earnest seeker for the spiritual blessings it professed to bestow.

After college he entered the priesthood and soon became attached to the Court of the King. He eventually became a professor, and later Rector (director) of the University of Prague. In only a few years this humble charity scholar became the pride of his country, and his name became well known throughout Europe.

A few years after he became a priest, Hus began to denounce the terrible vices then prevalent among people of all ranks in Bohemia. He also denounced the people's great ignorance of the Bible.

Even before this time there were men in Bohemia who had come forth to openly condemn the corruption in the Church and the profligacy of the people. The labors of these men had excited widespread interest, and the fears of the hierarchy had been aroused. Persecution was directed against the dissidents, and they had been driven to the forests and the mountains.

After awhile it was decreed that all who departed from the Roman method of worship should be burned at the stake.

This inhuman action was based on the very unchristian miss-application of the Scripture: **"if a man abide not in me, he is cast forth as a branch, and is withered; and men gather them, and cast them into the fire, and they are burned."** *John 15:6.*

While Christians were fielding their lives to this debauchery, their compatriots were looking forward to the eventual triumph of their Cause.

The Word of God became even more obscured as the power of the pope increased. Pope Gregory VII issued a Bull forbidding that public worship be conducted in the Bohemian language. He made the declaration that **"God was please that His worship should be celebrated in an unknown tongue"** (Latin), while claiming that **"neglect of this rule had given rise to many evils and heresies."** The light of God's Word was to be thereby kept in obscurity, and the people thereby condemned to continuing darkness.

The Bible had been brought to Bohemia as early as the ninth century when many of the Waldensians arrived there after being driven from their homes in Italy. A Bohemian Princess had become the Queen of England by marriage, and had been converted to the teaching of Wyclif. Wyclif's writings thereafter became widely circulated in Bohemia, her native country.

Hus read these works with much interest. He believed Wyclif to be a sincere Christian, and he regarded Wyclif's advocated reforms with favor. Hus has now entered upon a path that would lead him far from the accepted precepts of Rome.

Tidings of his rebellious work at Prague were eventually carried to Rome, and Hus was summoned to appear before the pope. Hus knew that to obey the summons would expose him to certain death.

Officials at the University of Prague and in the Government, and members of the Nobility, including the King and Queen, united in appeal to the pontiff requesting that Hus be allowed to remain at Prague, and to answer the pope by deputy — whereupon the incited pope immediately proceeded with Hus's trial and condemnation in his absence. In addition to this, — the pope declared the city of Prague under Interdict.

A pontifical declaration of Interdict, whenever pronounced in that age, created widespread horror and alarm. It struck terror to a superstitious people who had been taught to regard the pope as the prime emissary of a corporeal God — himself holding the keys to heaven and to hell, possessing power to invoke harsh judgements, — temporal and spiritual as well.

The people had been taught to believe that — until it should please the pope to remove the ban — the gates of heaven were closed to all residents of the region, and their dead were thereby cutoff from the abodes of bliss.

As a result of this Indictment, religious services were suspended and the churches closed; marriages had to be solemnized outside in the churchyards, and the dead were denied burial in consecrated ground. They were instead interred in ditches or in fields, without the rites of sepulcher.

By measures that invoked terror to the imagination of men, Rome determined to control their conscience. This terror created tumult in the city of Prague, and a large class of people denounced Hus, demanding that he be turned over to the authorities of Rome.

To quiet the storm of public reaction, the Reformer withdrew to the security of his native village — but he did not cease his labors. He traveled about preaching to eager crowds, while all efforts of the pope to suppress the Gospel only furthered and extended its circulation.

All during this part of his career Hus was in a deep state of mental conflict. He had not renounced the authority of the Church, although She was seeking his destruction. To him the Roman Church was still the Spouse of Christ, and the pope was the Vicar and representative of God. Hus had merely been warring against abuses of authority, — not against authority itself.

He was trying to reconcile — through reason — why he felt so compelled to disobey an authority that claimed to be infallible and just — as he even believed it to be. And this was a doubt that tortured him from hour to hour.

He eventually became convinced that — according to the light of understanding — only Scriptural precepts should rule man's conscience. That God's Word — speaking through the priesthood — is the only infallible guide.

After a time the excitement in Prague subsided, and Hus returned to his chapel to continue preaching the Word of God. And though his enemies still were active against him, the Queen and many of the nobles were his friends.

The people were siding with him in increasing numbers because his life contrasted with the avarice and debauchery practiced by the Romanists. His teachings contrasted with the dogmas that they preached and taught.

To heal the schism in the Church and to root out heresy, the Emperor Sigismund pressured one of the now *three* rivaling popes — Pope John XXIII — into calling a General Council to meet at Constance. This demand for a Council was, however, far from welcome to Pope John. But he dared not oppose the will of the Emperor because of the rivaling pope factions.

John Hus and the contending popes were summoned to appear before the Council. But the popes — fearing to appear in person — sent delegates. The Convoker of the council — Pope John — came but with misgivings, rightly fearing to be brought into account for vices disgraceful to the tiara, and for crimes which had secured it.

Meanwhile, Hus traveled to Constance, well conscious of the dangers awaiting him there, notwithstanding letters of safe-conduct given to him by the King of Bohemia and the Emperor, Sigismund. And prior to leaving, he made arrangements for the supposed eventuality of his death.

During the journey, Hus beheld everywhere indications of the spread of his doctrines and the favor with which they were being received. People thronged to meet him, and the magistrates of many towns escorted him through the streets.

When Hus arrived at Constance he was granted liberty. The pope even added his assurance to the safe-conduct granted to Hus by the emperor and the king. But in violation of these repeated declarations, Hus was in a short time arrested by the very orders of the pope, and committed to the dungeon.

Pope John was thereafter proved before the Council to be guilty of murder, simony, and adultery, — and "crimes not fit to be named." He was deprived of the tiara and likewise thrown into prison. The two other popes were also deposed, and a new pontiff chosen.

The Council then proceeded to crush out the Reformer as well. For the last time Hus was brought before the Council, where he still refused to abjure his stand.

After his sentencing was pronounced, a ceremony of degradation then took place. Church bishops arrayed their prisoner in sacerdotal habit. They then removed the vestments one by one, with each bishop pronouncing a curse as he performed his part in the ceremonial proceedings. Finally a crown, or mitre — on which was painted the frightful figures of demons and the inscription "The Arch Heretic" — was placed upon Hus's head. The prelates then dedicated his soul to Satan, and he was — as was Jesus before him — delivered to the secular authorities, who led him to the place of execution — a large procession following behind.

When the Martyr had been fasted to the stake and all was ready for the flames, Hus was once more exhorted to save himself by simply renouncing "his error." He replied in part, "Most joyfully will I confirm with my blood that truth which I have preached." And as the flames were kindled about him he began to sing a hymn, and so continued, until his voice was forever silenced — as his *witness to the truth.*

The Bible As Reform

CHAPTER 10

Invincible Truth

"Fear not them which kill the body, but are not able to kill the soul." *Mat. 10:28.*

To mortal sense, Hus's body was no more, but the truths for which he stood could never be destroyed. His constancy and faith would encourage multitudes to stand firm for truth in the face of adversity, torture, and execution.

His execution — like that of Jesus' crucifixion — exhibited to the world the cruelty of Rome even in that later day. This repetition of the Sanhedrin error of Jesus' time —though Hus's enemies would know it not — furthered and ever extended the Cause which they had so vainly sought to destroy.

In almost every generation there are those who — while seeking to uplift the people of their time — are reproached and condemned as malefactors, as Jesus was, only to be later recognized as deserving credibility and honor.

The light of truth proclaimed — and of heroic example lived — can never be extinguished. As well might men turn back the shining of the sun, as to prevent the dawning of the day breaking newly upon an unsuspecting world.

Hus's execution kindled a flame of horror and indignation throughout Bohemia. All the nation concluded that Hus had fallen prey to the emperor's betrayal of him and the malice of the priests.

Hus was declared to be a teacher of the truth. And the council that decreed his death was charged with the crime of murder. And the Husite doctrines attracted even greater attention than before.

But Hus's murderers refused to stand by to witness the triumph of his Cause. The new pope and emperor united in an all-out effort to crush out this growing movement, and Sigismund's armies were hurled forth upon Bohemia. Again and again they were ignominiously repelled. The Husite followers were raised above the fear of death, so nothing could stand against them for very long.

Eventually the pope proclaimed a crusade against the Husites, and even greater forces were leashed upon Bohemia. Two great armies approached each other until only a river stood between them. Yet, instead of advancing boldly to attack the Husite people, the crusaders stood as if spellbound gazing at their prey.

Suddenly a mysterious terror fell upon the would-be attackers, and — without striking a blow — that mighty force broke rank and scattered to the breeze, dispelled by a powerful, but unseen, mental force.

"There were they in great fear, where no fear was: for God hath scattered the bones of him that encampeth against thee." *Psalm 53:5.*

The smaller Husite army followed in pursuit, slaughtering great numbers, and, instead of being impoverished by the war, an immense booty fell into their hands.

At last — despairing of conquest by force — the papal leaders resorted to subtlety and deceit. Though professing to grant freedom-of-conscience to the Bohemian people, a compromise was eventually arranged that in effect betrayed the Bohemians into final subjection to the power of Rome.

The Bohemians had stipulated three points as a condition of their peace with Rome. 1) The right to freely preach from the Bible, 2) the right to receive Communion in the communion service of the Church, and 3) guarantee of civil court jurisdiction, over that of the clergy or laity of the Church.

All points were agreed to by the authorities, but they stipulated that all rights to decide and explain the exact meaning of Scripture would still belong to the Roman Church.

A treaty was enacted on this basis whereby Rome gained by duplicity and fraud what she had failed to gain by conflict — for by placing her *own* interpretation upon the articles of dissent as well as upon the Bible itself — She retained her ability to pervert understanding to later suit her selfish purposes.

Many Bohemians refused to consent to the betraying compact, and once again division and dissention continued to distract the nation. Steadfast to the Gospel, the Bohemians endured the long night of their continuing persecution, until about 1470, persecution eventually ceased.

A majority had accepted the compromise with Rome, but many, adhering to the primitive unchristian Faith, formed themselves into a distinctly, Protestant Church.

And — although forced to find refuge in forests and in caves — they still assembled together for the reading of God's Word, and the united worship of His son, — and to **witness to the truth.**

The Bible As Reform

CHAPTER 11

Reform in Germany

"As cold water to a thirsty soul, so is good news." *Proverbs 25:25.*

Martin Luther was the son of a German peasant who was a worker in the mines. His father had hoped Martin would become a lawyer. Hardship, poverty, and discipline were Martin's early teachers — teachers that effectively prepared him for his later mission.

Luther's father was a hard-working man of character who had a strong and active mind, He regarded the monastic system with distrust, and he was highly displeased when his son entered a monastery without his consent. Two years went by before a reconciliation took place, and even then his father's opinion remained the same.

An earnest desire to be free from sin and to be at peace with God were motives which had led Luther to the monastic life. His harsh life in poverty as a child, often exposed him to violence and hunger.

The gloomy superstitions of religion, then prevalent, filled him with fear and he looked forward only to a very dark future. He was in constant terror of the false theory of God being a stern and unrelenting Judge — rather than a kind and loving, heavenly Father.

His situation later brightened when, at the age of eighteen, he was enrolled in the University of Erfurt where he diligently applied himself to his studies. One day — in examining the many books of the University library — he came upon a copy of the Latin Bible.

Prior to that time he had assumed the small portions of the

Gospel and epistles that were read to the people in public worship, to be the entire Bible. But he looked for the first time upon the Bible in its entirety. He found another complete Bible at the monastery where he lived, chained to the convent wall, and he thereafter took advantage of its availability. Here he led a most rigorous life endeavoring by fasting, vigils, and scourging, to subdue the evil impulses which he mistakenly believed to be his true nature — and from which his monastic life brought no relief. As a result of this painful self discipline, he lost strength and suffered from fainting spasms — effects from which he never fully recovered. Despite his most diligent efforts, his burdened conscience found no relief until a pious friend bade him look away from himself and cease the vain contemplation of infinite punishment because of the presumed violation of God's law, — and to look instead to the sin-pardoning grace of his beloved Savior, Jesus Christ. So after many a struggle with long cherished beliefs, he finally realized the truth, and peace came to his long troubled consciousness.

Eventually Luther was ordained a priest and called from the cloister to a professorship at the University of Wittenburg. Here he applied himself to the study of the Scriptures in their original tongues and he began to lecture on the Bible — opening to the understanding of the people its unbounded treasures.

Luther was still at this time a true son of the papal church, and he had no thought of being anything else. But through the providence of God he was eventually led to visit Rome.

Upon his first visit to a convent in Italy, he was filled with perplexity at the wealth, magnificence, and luxury of the monks who were endowed with princely revenue, attired in the riches and most costly robes, and who feasted at the most sumptuous of tables. This sumptuous excess contrasted greatly with the hardship and self denial of his life back home in Germany.

As he visited the churches of Rome he saw that iniquity existed among all classes of the clergy, and he was filled with horror at this discovery — that in places of sanctity there could be such profanation.

One day as Luther devotedly and on his knees climbed the steps of "Pilate's Staircase" — said to have been descended by our Savior upon his leaving the Roman judgement hall in Jerusalem, and to have been later conveyed by miracle to its present place in Rome — to acquire an indulgence promised by the pope's decree — an "inner voice" seemed to say to him, **"The just shall live by faith."** *Romans 1:17,* whereupon he sprang to his feet in dismay, and hurried from that place in shame and in utter shock.

That text thereafter never lost its influence over him and his eyes were forever opened to the delusions of the papacy. From that time forward his separation from the papal church grew wider, and he was later to sever his connection with it completely.

After his return home from Rome, Luther earned the degree of "Doctor of Divinity," from the University of Wittenburg, which now authorized him, in addition to being a monk, as a professor and herald of the Bible.

He then declared to those hungering and thirsting for the truth, that Christians should receive no doctrines but those which rest on the authority of the Scriptures.

These bold words struck at the very foundation of papal supremacy and contained the basic principle of the unfolding Reformation.

The glad tidings of a Savior's love, and the assurance of pardon and peace through Jesus' atonement for sin, brought rejoicing to the hearts of his listeners and inspired them with everlasting hope.

At Wittenburg a ray of light was kindled which would extend to the utter most ends of the earth, ever increasing in brightness, even to our present time, and beyond.

He saw that the Roman Church had made merchandise of the Grace of God. Under the plea of raising funds for the erection of Saint Peter's Church at Rome, Indulgences for the forgiveness of sins were publicly offered for sale, by the authorities of the pope.

By the price of crime was a temple to be built for the worship of almighty God.

But by this very means adopted for the aggrandizement of Rome was the deadliest blow to her power and greatness provoked. Thusly began a conflict which would shake the papal throne and jostle the triple-crown upon the pontiff's head.

The hidden purpose of the sale of indulgences was to keep superstitious people under the control of the papacy and to swell the wealth and power of her ambitious leaders. It was therefore essential that the Bible teachings be suppressed and withheld from the people.

By virtue of these Certificates of Pardon, even those sins which they should afterward desire to commit, would be forgiven the indulgence holder, in addition to those sins already committed. The purchase of indulgence was even offered as salvation for the dead.

Gold and silver flowed into the Church treasury, through a supposed salvation bought with money — money obtained more easily than a salvation that requires faith, repentance, and the diligent effort of reform.

Although many people had no faith in the papal pretensions — so contrary to reason and revelation — no prelate dared lift his voice against this inquisitous traffic in worldliness except Luther.

Though still a papist of the straightest sort, he refused to honor these purchased certificates of absolution, warning the indulgence mongers that unless they should repent and reform their lives, they would reap the consequences of their sins.

Many people, therefore, boldly demanded of the Church that their money be returned to them — while Luther the more boldly taught it impossible for man by his own works to lessen guilt or to evade the inevitable suffering that sin incurs when not forsaken.

The forgiving grace of Christ cannot be bought with worldly treasure, for it is a Gift — freely available to all who seek it *and conform*.

As the friars continued their traffic and impious pretensions, Luther decided upon a more effectual protest against their crying abuses.

On the day preceding the Festival of all Saints — a holy day when full remission of sins was granted to all who then visited the Church and made confession — Luther posted on its doors a Paper containing Ninety-five Theses contradicting the doctrine of Indulgences.

He furthermore declared his willingness to defend these theses — on the day following at the University — against all who should see fit to refute or otherwise attack them.

No one came forward to accept the challenge. Nevertheless, his propositions attracted widespread attention. Within a short while the stir and excitement they incurred resounded not only throughout all Germany, but throughout all Christendom as well.

Princes and magistrates secretly rejoiced in the prospect that a check was to be put on an arrogant power which denied any "right-of-appeal" to its decisions. But the sin-loving and superstitious multitudes were filled with fear, as the sophistries that had heretofore soothed their fear were swept away.

And seeing their lucrative gains endangered, crafty clerics interrupted their work of sanctioning crime, to rally the upholding of their fraudulent pretensions. The reformer had unquestionably stirred up a bitter and powerful opposition.

When accused of acting through pride and forwardness, Luther responded by declaring that "Christ and martyrs had in the past been put to death because they brought forth new revelations of truth, without their having first consulted the oracles of old opinion," adding, "If it be not of God, who shall then be able to forward it?"

Though barriers of prejudice were beginning to give way, and though Luther had been moved by Spirit, God, to take up this work, he was not to carry it forward without severe future conflicts.

Even the encouragement of many would-be supporters changed to reproach and condemnation as they began to realize that the acceptance of these newly preached ideas of reform would involve great sacrifices, change, and increased risk as well.

To enlighten and reform the people would be virtually to undermine the authority of Rome, stopping thousands of streams of funding now flowing into many church treasuries, curtailing the luxury and extravagance of her papal leaders, undermining the pontiff's throne, and eventually leading to the loss of personal position and authority as well. For these very reasons, the mightiest political powers of earth were becoming incensed against him.

Despite all this, Luther's teachings continued to attract the attention of thoughtful minds throughout all Germany. His sermons and his writings shed forth gentle beams of light which awakened and educated virtually thousands upon thousands of people. And the inevitable summons for Luther to appear at Rome, to answer the charge of heresy, arrived.

Through the intervention of friends, it was finally arranged that his examination be affected in Germany, instead of in Rome, but the pope's legate in Germany was *privately* informed by the pope that Luther had already been declared a heretic, and should be seized — along with his adherents — for delivery to the vengeance of Rome.

Furthermore, anyone who should fail to assist in the seizure — excepting of course the emperor — would be excommunicated from the Church.

Herein was displayed the true spirit of popery, having not a trace of Christian principle. In but one day — with Luther at great distance and without opportunity to defend himself or his position — his case had been investigated, he had been exhorted, accused, adjudged a heretic, and condemned. All this by a self-styled "holy Father," as the only supreme infallible authority in either church or state.

Augsburg was established as the site of the quasi trial, and tidings of Luther's arrival greatly satisfied the papal legate. The reformer had failed to obtain a safe-conduct from the emperor, so his friends undertook to procure one for him, urging him not to appear before the legate without it.

When the prelate saw that Luther's reasoning was unanswerable, he lost all self control, and in a rage cried out "recant, recant, or I will excommunicate you and all your partizans."

By this the large assembly present had a clear opportunity to judge for themselves the contrasting attitudes manifested by each contendant, as well as the strength and truthfulness of their positions.

Nevertheless, even with his document of safe-conduct still in hand, Luther's friends urged him to quietly return to Wittenburg — which he did in the dark of night.

Fredrick — the Emperor — resolved to stand fast as Luther's protector, writing to the legate that "none of the learned men in the principality considered Luther's doctrine to be in any way impious, unchristian, or heretical. We must therefore refuse to send him to Rome or expel him from our State."

Fredrick of Saxony had observed the general breakdown of moral restraint in society, and he felt a great work of reform to be needed. He furthermore saw that Luther was laboring to secure this same objective, so he was secretly pleased that a better influence was making itself felt within the Church.

Luther's professorship in the university had been very successful. People were flocking to Wittenburg — not for hypocritical confessions nor to adore relics — but as sincere students to fill her halls of learning, not only from all parts of Germany but from other lands as well.

The writings of Luther had kindled a new interest in the study of the Scriptures from everywhere. His work extended out from Germany, to Switzerland and Holland, to France and Spain, and to England, Belgium, and Italy. Thousands were awakening from a trance-like miasma to the joy and hope of a life of faith.

To the emperor and the nobility of Germany, in behalf of the Reformation of Christianity, Luther was declaring that **"Every institution wherein the Word of God is not diligently studied will eventually become corrupt."**

Sixty days were granted to the reformer and his adherents to recant, and if not, they were all to be excommunicated from the Church.

For centuries the threat of excommunication had struck terror even to might monarchs. Those so condemned were cut off from all traffic with their fellow-beings. They were shunned and treated as outlaws to be hunted to extermination.

When the papal Bull arrived, Luther was still defiantly resistant. Yet with others the papal Mandate was not without effect. There was still a general sympathy for Luther, however many felt life too dear to be sacrificed on the altar of reform.

But Luther — in the presence of a large crowd of prominence — publicly burned the papal bull, along with Canon Laws, decretals, and other writings sustaining papal power.

He stated that **"enemies have burned my books to injure the cause of truth, so I therefore burn *their* books in its defense. I began this work in God's name, and it will end, though perhaps without me, by His might. While on the side of the oppressor are great and mighty numbers, cast, mocking, and wealth, I stand serene and supposedly alone, but at my side is the power of the Word of God."**

The popes threat was thereupon fulfilled. A *new* Bull appeared declaring the heretic's final excommunication from the Church, denouncing as heretics, Luther and all who should receive his doctrines. There was therefore, now, no thought of turning back. His commitment was permanently established as his beginning *witness to the truth.*

CHAPTER 12

Reform in Switzerland

"By their fruits ye shall know them." *Matthew 7:20.*

Ulrich Zwingli was born in a herdsman's cottage among the Swiss Alps only a few weeks after Martin Luther's birth in Saxony.

Zwingli was reared amid natural scenes of mountain grandeur, beauty, and sublimity. His mind was early impressed with the greatness, power, and majesty of God's creation.

As with Luther, Zwingli listened early with eager interest to Bible accounts of the past grand deeds of Patriarch and Prophet and the Good News of the Bethlehem Babe — the man of Calvary — the spiritual Teacher bypassed and overlooked by many great men of the earth — the titled and the wealthy — the prideful and confident leaders so accustomed to homage and praise — those who could not be moulded for the sympathetic labor of His mission.

Zwingli learned about Jesus' disciples — men from humble circumstances, free from the pride of rank, and from the influences of bigotry, circumstance and pomp.

He learned that the "Call" to "follow me" was addressed to unlearned but teachable men, — the simple toiling fishermen of Galilee.

The less contact they had with the false teachings of their times, the more successfully could Jesus instruct and train them for God's service.

At the age of thirteen, Zwingli was sent from his native Alpine valley to Bern for further schooling. Determined efforts were put forth here by convent Friars to allure him into the monastic life.

At that time Dominican and Franciscan monks were in rivalry for popular favor. The Dominican monks of Bern endeavored to induce Zwingli to enter their monastic convent by flatteries and deceit.

Zwingli's father, however, was warned of the monks intentions and told him to return home without delay; since he had no intention of allowing his son to follow the idle and worthless life style of the monks.

The command was obeyed. But the youth was later sent to Basel where — as a student under an ancient-language teacher who had been led to the Scriptures — he first heard the Gospel of God's freely bestowed grace and love — a truth more ancient and more precious than all the theories taught by man. This was the first Ray of the light that came to Zwingli, preceding the coming of dawn.

After being ordained as a priest, his first field of labor was in an Alpine Parish not far from his native home. But the more he searched the Scriptures, the clearer became the contrast between their *witness to the truth,* in contrast to the heresies of Rome. He therefore submitted himself to the Bible as the Blessed Word of God — as the only sufficient and infallible rule of life.

And although the truth that Zwingli preached had not been received from Luther, it was yet likewise the doctrine of Christ — illustrating the uniformity of the Word of God, since they who had no communication, one with the other, still agreed closely in the doctrine of Jesus Christ.

In 1516 Zwingli was called to preach in the convent at Einsiedeln — among whose chief attractions was an image of the virgin Mary said to have the power of the working of miracles. Pilgrims at all seasons resorted to this shrine, and at the great annual festival of its consecration, multitudes came, not only from all parts of Switzerland, but from parts of France and Germany as well.

Greatly afflicted at the sight of this slavish behavior to tradition and superstition, Zwingli took (he said) this opportunity to proclaim the Gospel of the liberty of Christ.

"Regard not (he said) **that God is more in this temple than in any other part of His creation. Whereever God has fixed your dwelling, there He encompasses you with love and hears your prayers.**

" What profit (he preached) **can there be in pilgrimages, offerings, and prayers to the virgin Mary and the Saints to secure your favor with your God? What signifies efficacy in cowl or shaven crown — or priestly garments falling and adorned with gold. God looks upon the heart, and our hearts are far from God. Christ satisfies for all eternity and tones for the sins of all who believe and obey His commands."**

To many listeners these teaching were not welcome. They were content with the old ways to heaven marked out for them by Rome. It was far easier to trust their salvation to the pope and priests, than to seek for purity of heart.

But to others, the glad tidings of redemption through Christ were received with joy. For them observances enjoined by Rome had failed to bring them peace of mind, and they returned home to share with others the precious light that they had received from Zwingli.

As the truth was carried from hamlet to hamlet, the pilgrimages to the Virgin's shrine greatly decreased, and consequently also the offerings to the Church — Zwingli's salary as well. But this caused him only joy as he saw the power of fanaticism and superstition breaking down.

The authorities of the Church were not blind to the effects of Zwingli's work. But they forbore not to interfere, hoping to win him yet by flatteries.

After three years Zwingli was called to preach in the cathedral at Zurich; the most important town of the Swiss Confederacy.

The ecclesiastics by whose invitation he had been called to Zurich, desiring to prevent innovation — proceeded to instruct him of his duties: collecting revenues and exhorting the faithful to pay dues and tithes as an indication of their fidelity to the Church; — monetary proof of their devotion.

Other than preaching and personally ministering to the flock, Zwingli was told to administer the sacraments to only persons of distinction — not indiscriminately to people of all ranks.

This Zwingli refused to do, declaring his purpose to lecture on the whole of the gospel of Matthew — drawing alone on the fountain of Scripture — not a new method at all, but the old method earlier employed by the Church in former times — and this he proceeded to do.

He not only offered and proclaimed a free salvation, he fearlessly rebuked the evils and corruption of the times as well.

At first his labors were received with enthusiasm. But great opposition arose after a time. As men rose up in different lands to present to the people forgiveness and justification through the victories of Christ, the men of Rome proceeded with renewed energy to offer her pardons in exchange for the purse.

Every sin was given its special price, and men were granted unrestricted license for crime if only the Church treasury were kept filled.

Thusly, two opposing movements advanced. One offering *forgiveness of sin* for money; the other *forgiveness of sin* through Christ.

The reformers were *condemning* sin, and encouraging deliverance through reform, while Rome was *licensing* sin, making this the source of her coveted revenue.

The plague which swept over Switzerland in 1519 offered a strong impetus to reform as many were brought face to face with the "destroyer." Multitudes were led to see how worthless and vain were the purchased pardons, and they began to long for a sure foundation for their faith.

Zwingli was inflicted and brought so low that all hope for his recovery was eventually abandoned, and a report was circulated that he even was dead. But in that hour of trial, his hope and courage remained unshaken. Steadfastly trusting in his loving Savior, he was raised from the very gates of death, to preach the Gospel with even greater fervor than before.

Zwingli had arrived at a clearer understanding of its truths. He had experienced the renewing power of a knowledge of the all everpresent love of God, for **"As in Adam all die, even so in Christ shall all be made alive."** *I Cor. 15:22.*

He taught that whereever there is faith in God, there God lovingly abides, and wherever God and His all prevading love abides, there is renewal and awakened zeal, that tempers and constrains while urging the doing of good works. Step by step the Reformation in Zurich advanced. Only a year before had Luther uttered his **"no way!"** to the pope and emperor at Worms, and now everything pointed to a similar protest of reform there in Switzerland — at Zurich.

To silence the "teacher of heresy," the bishop at Constance dispatched three deputies to the Council of Zurich to accuse Zwingli of endangering the peace and good order of society by teaching the people to transgress the laws of the Church. He said that if the authority asserted by the Church were seat aside, worldwide anarchy would be a result.

Zwingli responded by pointed out that after four years of teaching the Gospel in Zurich, Zurich was more quiet and peaceful than any other town in the Confederacy.

"In every nation of every land, whoever believes with all his heart in the resurrected Christ, is wholeheartedly acceptable to God. Furthermore, Christianity provides the best safeguard for the security of the people of the land."

As a result of the Conference, at Zurich, its fruits were seen in the suppression of vice and the promotion of order and harmony.

These victories stirred the Romanists to still more determined efforts for the Reformation's overthrow. They decided to meet the reform through debate with Zwingli, and they sought to make their victory certain by designating the place of combat, and the judges too.

The dispute was designated to be resolved at Baden, but the Council of Zurich forbade their pastor to attend. Two delegates were chosen to represent the Reformers by proxy, and a host of learned doctors and prelates to champion the cause of Rome.

Official secretaries were assigned by Rome, and all others forbidden to take notes on pain of death. Notwithstanding this, Zwingli was kept daily informed of what was said at Baden.

Thusly Zwingli coached and maintained a successful debate with his clever antagonists; who resorted to insults and eventually to oaths.

The contrast between disputants was not without effect.

After eighteen days of debate — although the papists claimed the victory and their deputies sided with Rome and the Diet declared the Reformers vanquished and excommunicated from the Church — nevertheless the debate gave a strong impetus to the Protestant cause, for not long after the debate, Zurich, Bern, and Basil declared for the Reformation — as a consequence of Zwingli's *witness to the truth.*

CHAPTER 13

Continuing Reform

"If I have spoken evil, bear witness of the evil: but if well, why smitest thou me? *Christ Jesus.*

Martin Luther had passed the point of no return. He was committed to a cause that was to revolutionize the Church and the World.

A new emperor — Charles V — had just ascended to the German throne and although Rome hastened to enlist his power against the ensuing Reformation, Fredrick, the Elector of Saxony, persuaded Charles to take no steps against Luther until Luther had been granted a respectable hearing before "a tribunal of learned, pious and impartial judges."

A Convention of German States was soon to be convened in deliberative session, at Worms, to meet the youthful Monarch for the first time. This Convention presented the ideal occasion for such a hearing. Charles told Fredrick to bring Luther with him to the Diet, promising Luther protection, and freedom of speech.

The Bull declaring Luther's excommunication was published at this time, and the Saxon Reformer's Cause excited the interest of that astute assembly, whereupon the papal Legate to the Diet, Alexander, successfully remonstrated with Charles V against Luther's appearance at Worms — persuading Charles to command Fredrick to confine Luther to Wittenburg, unless he was to recant.

At the Diet, however, the vehemence, passion, and hatred manifested by the papal Legate against Luther plainly revealed the attitude of his heart, and a minority of the Diet were sympathetically inclined to favorably regard Luther's Cause.

Alexander urged the new emperor, Charles, to execute the

papal edict, but this could not be lawfully done unless the German Princes concurred. And becoming wearied by the Legate's urging, Charles ordered him to present his case to the Diet himself.

Alexander's emotional argument based on the wealth, superior power, and numbers of the Church — made a deep impression upon the Diet.

Luther was not present to counter Alexander's arguments, and Fredrich, the Elector of Saxony, had not as yet arrived, though his counsellors had preceded him in order to take notes on the Nuncio's address to the Diet.

Alexander hurled charge after charge against Luther as an enemy of Church and State, of the clergy and the dead.

Henceforth, the contrast between truth and error was the more clearly seen, and Rome's *apparent* surface victory was the signal act of her defeat.

Duke George, also of Saxony, although an enemy of Luther, responded to the Legate's address by firmly witnessing to the abominations (and deceptions) of popery and their dire results, regarding the greed and corruption of the papal Chair.

This gave even greater influence to Luther's cause by an even more forceful and able denunciation of papal abuses than Luther perhaps would have presented had be been there himself.

A committee was appointed by the Diet to prepare an enumeration of papal oppressions, resulting in a list of over one-hundred citations of abuse. This list was presented to the Emperor with the request that he take immediate action toward the correction of these abuses.

The committee petitioned that **"the ruin and dishonor of our nation must be averted. We therefore beseech you to sanction a general reformation to carry out the work of correction."**

The council then demanded the Reformer's appearance before them, notwithstanding Alexander's protests. And the Summons sent to Wittenbug included a letter of safe-conduct ensuring Luther's return to a place of safety. Upon Luther's arrival at Worms vast crowds flocked to the gates to welcome him. A greater multitude had not assembled even to greet the new Emperor himself.

At last, Luther stood before the Emperor in the spacious council hall. Never before had any man appeared in the presence of a more imposing assembly.

Although condemned by the pope, he was now standing before a tribunal, which by this very act, had set itself above the pope. The pope had placed Luther under interdict, cutting him off from all human society, yet Luther was respectfully standing before the most august assembly in the then known world.

Luther's defiance included these words, of Jesus, **"If I have spoken evil, bear witness of the evil: but if well, why smitest thou me?"** *John 18:23.*

"By the mercy of God, I implore your Imperial Majesty — or anyone else, to prove to me from the writings of the Prophets and Apostles that I am in error. God is wonderful in His counsels. Let us have a care, lest in our endeavor to arrest discord, we be found warring against the Holy Word.

"I might speak of Pharaohs and Kings, or of Israel who never more contributed to their own ruin, than when by measures only in appearance prudent, they sought alone to establish their authority apart from God. God 'removeth the mountains, and they know not'" *Job 9:5.*

Luther had been speaking to the assembly in German, and though exhausted by the speaking, he was now requested to repeat the words in Latin. God's providence was directing in this matter by providing this form of **"instant replay."**

By the first presentation, many had not seen the force of Luther's simple reasoning; but in the repetition, they clearly perceived the points which he presented.

Luther said, **"If I am not convinced by proof from the Holy Scriptures, unless by I can be dissuaded by the very texts that I have cited in my works, I neither can, nor will** retract. It cannot be right for any Christian to speak against his conscience. Here I take my stand. I can to no otherwise, so help me God."

The Christ had spoken through Luther a testimony of power and of grandeur that for a time inspired both friend and foe alike. Several of the Princes acknowledged the justice of Luther's cause, and many others were convinced of the truth of what he said. But with some the impressions received were not to last.

Then the determined Legate threatened the youthful Emperor with the folly and danger of forfeiting the friendship and support of the powerful Holy See of Rome, merely for the cause of this insignificant monk, and his words were not without effect.

Just one day later, Charles announced his decision to still follow his predecessors policy of retaining the favor and protection of the Roman Catholic Church.

Even so, he ordered that Luther's safe-conduct be respected, and that Luther be allowed to reach his home in safety. Only then could proceedings be instituted against him.

The Emperor had decided not to step beyond the wrath of custom, even though he would be upholding the papacy in the face of all its cruelty and corruption. Charles yielded to the dictates of worldly policy and pride, and in fear rejected the subtle light of truth.

However, popular enthusiasm in Luther's favor convinced the Emperor and the Diet that any injustice to Luther would endanger the Peace of the Empire and the Stability of the Throne; therefore earnest efforts were made to obtain Luther's consent to a compromise with Rome.

Had Luther yielded on even a singly point, in compromise, the carnal mind would have surely gained the victory. But Luther's unwavering firmness was the eventual seed of the Emancipation of the Church. This was the beginning of a new and more enlightened Age.

After Luther had left Worms, the papists again prevailed upon the Emperor; influencing him to issue an edict commanding that, after the expiration of Luther's safe-conduct, measures be taken again to stop his work.

All persons were forbidden to feed him, shelter him, or aid him in any way. He was to be seized and his writings were to be destroyed.

His adherents were to be imprisoned and their property confiscated. All who dared to act contrary to the Interdiction were to be included in its condemnation.

Fredrick, the Elector of Saxony, and the German Princes who were friendly to Luther's cause, had already departed for home, so with no opposition, the youthful Emperor's decree received the support of the remainder of the Diet.

As soon as Fredrick heard the threatening news he secretly had his trusted ones seize Luther first, and convey him to a secret place of safety. So with the cooperation of a few true friends, Luther was effectively hidden from the "wrath of man."

Thusly, in the hidden security of a friendly safe place in the isolated mountain castle of Wartburg, Luther was released from the heat of the battle. He could not however remain for long inactive.

While his enemies were flattering themselves that Luther had finally been effectively silence, his active although quiet ever busy pen was vigorously at work translating the New Testament into the German tongue — in *witness to the truth.*

The Bible As Reform

CHAPTER 14

Sedition and Strife

"Many false prophets are gone into the world." *I John 4:1.*

Luther's disappearance excited consternation, rumors, inquiries, and in some instances wrath.

The Emperors indictment fell powerless. It commanded far less attention than did Luther's unknown fate. This, in turn, filled the papal Legate with indignation and fear.

The tidings that Luther was safe, though yet a prisoner, calmed the fears of the people regarding his fate, and still further aroused their enthusiasm in his favor.

His writings were being read with even more interest, and the Reformation was gaining popularity and strength.

Luther's absence accomplished a greater work than perhaps his presence would have inspired. Other laborers now felt responsible for continuing the work that he had begun.

But just as there arose false Christs in the first century of the Christian Era, so there arose false prophets also in the 16th Century.

Though claiming to have been divinely commissioned from above, they were undoing the work which Luther had heretofore accomplished.

By rejecting the foundational principle of the Reformation, that the Word of God is an all-sufficient rule for faith and practice, the way was opened up for mortal mind to again mislead.

The ill effects of the incorrect teachings were quickly becoming apparent. The people were being misled to neglect the Bible, or to cast it completely aside. From self-possessed "friends" of the Reformation there arose its worst and most active enemies. Students, spurning all restraint were withdrawing from the University and confusion was running rampant.

Luther was more distressed by this *new* danger threatening

the cause of truth, than by the opposition he had experienced from the Emperor and pope. Wittenburg, the very center of the Reformation, was fast falling under the influence of lawless fanatics, and this was wrongly being blamed on Luther.

Without delay, Luther set out to return to Wittenburg, though still under the ban of the empire, so he entered upon his work with great caution and humility.

Luther did not believe in resorting to force or compulsion, nor violence, in dealing with superstitious or unbelieving people. He stood fast for liberty-of-conscience as the essence of the Christian faith

The people flocked to him from all directions and his church was often overflowing. He claimed his right to speak, but never the right to compel. He would preach and leave the rest to God.

What can be gained by force? Only cramped uniformity and hypocrisy — fair-seeming appearance — feigned allegiance — no sincerity, no faith and no love.

He knew that God will do more through the power of His Word than men and nations put together. God arrests the heart, and that taken, all is won.

Day after day Luther continued to preach, and the Word of God broke down the fanatical excitement and stilled the storm. It brought back the misguided people to the way of truth.

So successfully did his words expose the pretensions of the imposters that they quickly departed from Wittenburg. Fanaticism was in check for a time. But several years later it broke out once again, this time in even greater force.

Thomas Munzer was the most active of the fanatics. He was a man of considerable ability which, if rightly directed, could have done much good for the Reformation. But he had not assimilated the principles of true Christianity.

He was determined to obtain position, influence, and wealth — unwilling to be second even to Luther. He tried to separate the Scriptures from the spirit of true reform, ever claiming that the letter killeth, while the spirit giveth life.

Breaking away from all control — under the claim of divine sanction — Munzer and his followers gave free reign to their prejudice and passion. Scenes of sedition and strife followed in the field, and Germany became drenched in rebellious blood.

Luther saw the results of fanaticism again charged falsely against the fledgling Reformation, and he renewed his fearless defense of the gospel message, from attacks from every side.

With the word he warred again against the usurped authority of the pope, and the irrational philosophy of the schoolmen; standing firm against the fanaticism that sought to attach itself openly to the Reformation.

Upon his return to Wittenburg he finished his translating the New Testament — so faithfully begun in exile — and gave it in published form to the people of the State.

Now they were able to read god's Word for themselves and discuss its precepts with the priests, uncovering priestly ignorance which hereto fore had not been seen.

Seeing the favor with which the New Testament was received, Luther then began the translating the Old Testament as well, publishing it in parts as fast as possible.

The revealed Word of God traversed the Provinces of Germany through the efforts of reformed monks, who — having seen the scriptural unlawfulness of monastic obligations, desiring to exchange that life of indolence for one of activity and worth — traversed the Provinces of Germany selling the writings of the reformer and of his friends.

The resulting study of the Scriptures worked a mighty change in the hearts of men. The Word placed in the hands of the people aroused their dormant understanding; not only purifying and ennobling character, but importing strength and vigor to both body and mind alike.

This new found energy-of-spirit became a welcome impetus to increased industriousness in every day work and commerce, as people of all ranks became enthusiastic about defending the doctrines of the Reformation Cause.

Priests and Friars alike, were totally defeated as unlearned and heretical. The shamed ignorance of great men became apparent as their arguments were met by the simple teachings of the Word of God.

The people had found a new teaching that satisfied the longing of their heart, so they turned forever away from the worthless husks of human traditions and superstitious rites.

In vain did ecclesiastical and civil authorities resort to imprisonment, torture, fire, and the sword. Thousands of believers sealed their fate with their blood, yet the work of reform marched onward up the ascending pathway to victory, making more and more clear the contrast between the workings of evil and the work of God — in *witness to the truth.*

CHAPTER 15

Princely German Protest

"The heathen shall fear the name of the Lord, and all the kings of the earth thy glory." *Psalm 102:15.*

As a result of the protest of the Christian Princes of Germany at the Diet of Spires in 1529, the name of the reformed Church of Germany was thereafter called Protestant.

In the early fifteen-hundreds — as was previously pointed out —the youthful Charles V, under the influence of Rome, became bent on crushing the Reformation. But as he raised his hand to strike, he was forced to turn aside the blow.

Again and again the immediate destruction of all who dared to oppose themselves to Rome appeared inevitable. But always at the crucial moment some crisis would occur to force Charles to deflect his intended blow, when outsiders would make war upon him. And thus, amid the strife and the tumult of nations, the Reformation was for awhile left to strengthen and extend.

When at last the tumult had been stifled, the opposition once again renewed their common cause against the faithful reformers.

The previous Diet of Spires, three years earlier (1526), had given each German State full liberty in all matters of religion, until such time as a future meeting of the General Council was to convene for the purpose of crushing out the heresy. And if peaceful means were then to fail, Charles was prepared to resort to the use of the sword.

The papists were exultant. They appeared at Spires in great numbers, openly manifesting hostility to all reformers, and those in sympathy with the Reformation.

But the people of Spires — thirsting for the Word of God and fearless of the prohibition — flocked to services held by

Luther in the Chapel of the Elector of Saxony, and this hastened the crisis. An Imperial message was presented to the Diet stating that the granting of liberty-of-conscience had given rise to great disorder, so the Emperor was demanding that it be annulled.

But religious tolerance had been legally established, and the evangelical States were resolved to oppose any infringement of their rights.

It was finally proposed to the Diet — as a compromise — that in the evangelical States where there would be danger of revolt, no new reforms would be tolerated and no preaching on disputed points would be allowed.

What's more, opposition to celebrating the Mass would not be permitted, and no Roman Catholic would be allowed to embrace Lutheran teachings. And where the Reformation had not gained a foothold, the Edict of Worms would be rigorously enforced.

If this proposal were passed, Rome would be confirmed in the right to coerce conscience and to forbid free inquiry.

The reformers then in existence would enjoy religious freedom — but only as a stipulation of a compromise, not as a human right based on principle. And all others not under the sanction of the favored stipulation would be considered under the jurisdiction of Roman authority, where dictates of conscience would be out of the question, with Rome the "infallible judge" which must be strictly and immediately obeyed.

By this action the lifting compromise would be confined to Saxony, but freedom-of-conscience would be withheld from the remainder of Christendom. Any acceptance and profession of the Reformed faith outside of Saxony, would be a punishable crime.

The Emperor who was present at the Diet, King Ferdinand, finally and adamantly announced that the decree was to be published as an Imperial Edict, and that the only recourse remaining for those opposed to it, was to submit to the decision of the majority — whereupon he refused to consider further the conscientious convictions of the protesting princes and withdrew from the assembly.

Had the reformers depended upon human aid alone, they would have been as powerless as the papists supposed them to be, but although weak in numbers and at variance with Rome, they appealed to the Diet of Spires on the basis of the truth of Scripture through the Word of God.

A solemn Declaration of religious liberty was drawn up and presented to the Diet. In part it read: **"We hereby protest before God, our only Creator, Preserver, Redeemer, Savior, and eventually-to-be our Judge, that we neither consent to, nor adhere in any manner to the proposed decree, nor in any other thing that is contrary to our conscience, to God or to His Word.**

"His word is the only truth. He who builds on this sure foundation shall stand against all the powers of Hell, whilst all the vanities that are set up against it, shall fall before the face of God.

"We therefore reject this yoke that is to be wrongly imposed upon us."

This Protest made a deep impression on the Diet.

The majority were filled with both alarm and amazement at the strength of the Protest and the boldness of the protesters. Dissention, strife and blood shed seemed inevitable.

The Protest denied rulers with civil authority all rights to legislate in matters of conscience, and it declared, with Prophet and Apostle, **"We ought to obey God rather than men."**

The power of conscience was being raised above that of the State. The authority of Scripture was being set above the authority of the visible Church. Christ's Crown was being lifted above the emperor's Diadem and above the Tiara of the pope.

The Protest at Spires was a protest against religious intolerance and an assertion of the rights of all mankind to worship God according to the dictates of their conscience. The protestors were affirming their right to freely utter their convictions, as their *witness to the Truth.*

To quiet the dissention that greatly disturbed the empire, after the Protest of Spires, Charles V convened another Diet to be held at Augsburg a year later, and protestant leaders were summoned to attend.

Luther was forbidden to appear, at Augsburg, but he was present through his prayers and through his words.

The reformed princes wanted to have a written systematic statement of their views — including confirming Scriptural evidence — which they later could present to the Diet. And the task of the preparation of this document was committed to Luther and his friends. This **Confession of Faith** was accepted by the protesting princes as an exposition of their sincerest beliefs.

Though great dangers threatened the Reformation, its advocates reaffirmed their pledge to the gospel message, still trusting their cause to God.

When the appointed time came to appear before the emperor, the **Confession of Faith** was read to that august assembly. Errors of the papal Church were again pointed out, and truths of the Gospel were clearly set forth.

Just a few years had passed since Luther stood alone before the National Council at Worms, and now in his stead stood the noblest most powerful Princes of the German empire.

The Emperor himself was hearing Luther's written dissertation — read publicly exalting Christ — presented by illustrious confessors in so glorious an assembly in fulfillment of what the Scripture saith, declaring, **"I will speak of thy testimonies also before Kings, and will not be ashamed."** *Palm 119:46.*

That which the Emperor had declared unlawful to be proclaimed in his palace — what many had regarded even unfit for their servants to hear — was now being heard with wonder by the Masters and Lords of the Empire.

Kings and great men were the preacher, and the sermon the royal Word of God — confessing the love and power the Christ

— in *witness to the truth.*

Upon listening to the fervent **Augsburg Confession,** the Emperor, this time, declared in favor of the protesting **Confession of Faith** as being nothing but the truth.

Luther rejoiced that the Gospel was confessed by the leaders of the Empire — even the Emperor himself — but when they proposed to unite in a League of Defense against the opposition, Luther insisted that the Gospel be defended by God alone.

"The less men meddle in the Reformation work, the more striking is God's intervention in the works' behalf. The only weapon that should be employed in this warfare should be the Sword of the Spirit. Man can do more by his prayers than his enemies can do through their boasting."

There, in holy calmness and assurance, God's servants took their stand upon the promises of God, and God listened to their cries. He gave courage to the princes and ministers of His grace. He gave them victory over the rulers of the darkness of this world.

The written **Confession of Augsburg** was translated into many languages, and circulated, not only in Germany, but throughout all Europe too, and has been accepted by millions in succeeding generations.

The Protestant Reformers built their security on Christ, — and the gates of hell could not prevail, against their *witness to the truth.*

The Bible As Reform

CHAPTER 16

Reform in France

"Whatsoever a man soweth, that shall he also reap." *The Apostle Paul.*

Lefevre was one of the first to catch the light in France. He was a professor at the University of Paris — a man of extensive learning and a dedicated papist. Then came William Farel — one of Lefevre's students and the Bishop of Meux — uniting with LeFevre in proclaiming the gospel message. With Princess Margaret, the sister of King Frances I, they accepted the reformed faith even when trial and persecution awaits the disciples of Christ.

A time of relative peace intervened, and the Reformation made rapid progressive strides. Lefevre translated the New Testament into the French language, and it was published at Meux about the time when Luther's German translation was being printed in Wittenburg, Germany.

The peasants of Meux received the message of salvation as weary travelers perishing from thirst, and this reforming uplift of divine Grace brought healing change into their lives.

The wrath of the Roman hierarchy was for a time held in check by the King, who despised the narrow bigotry of the monks; but papist leaders eventually prevailed. The stake was setup and many Christians *witnessed to the truth* amid the flames.

Louis de Berquin — a brave and courtly Knight and a favorite of the King — was providentially guided to the Bible. He was three-times imprisoned by the papists, only to be set free by the King, who — in admiration of his genius and nobility of character — refused to sacrifice him to the malice of Rome.

As dangers threatened, Berquin's zeal waxed all the stronger. He not only stood in defense of the truth, but he boldly attacked the error. The charges of heresy made upon him, he rebounded back upon them.

From the writings of a learned doctor and monk at the University of Paris — one of his opponents and one of the highest ecclesiastical proponents in the nation — Berquin drew up twelve propositions contrary to the Bishop of Rome. He then appealed to the King to act as judge in the ensuing controversy, and he challenged all Romanists to defend their cause by virtue of the Bible.

But at this time, a public image of the Virgin Mary was — coincidentally, found mutilated, inciting mourning and public indignation. Berquin was blamed for this, apprehended, and condemned to the Stake.

The King was not in Paris at the time, and — lest he should interpose to save Berguin — the sentence was executed on the day of its pronouncement. Berquin was strangled at the stake and his body was consumed in the flames.

There — in 1529 — the highest literary and ecclesiastical authority in Paris set a precedent for the Paris Revolt to come 264 years later in 1793, by stifling at the Stake the final words of the dying reformer.

Lefevre then fled to Germany and Farel returned to his hometown in eastern France. But they spread the Word of God as they went.

John Calvin — a student at one of the local colleges in Paris — was a thoughtful quiet youth who evidenced a powerful and penetrating mind. He was devoted to religion, and his genius and dedication made him an excellent student, and he soon became the pride of his college.

He heard of the new Reformation with revulsion, never doubting that all heretics were deserving of their dues. Yet he was forced to test the efficacy of the Roman teachings in order to combat the Protestant Reform.

"There are but two classes of religion in the world (said the Protestant, Olivtan) **one class invented by men, whereby**

man saves himself by ritual and works, the other class revealed in the Bible, whereby salvation comes as the gracious Gift of God."

Many thoughts had been awakened in Calvin's heart which he could not banish err he tried. He saw the prayers to the saints and the ceremonies of the Church powerless to atone for sin. He felt only the blackness of eternal damnation and despair. Confession and penance were resorted to in vain, yet they did not reconcile his troubled conscience with this God.

While engaged in this fitful, fruitless struggle, Calvin witnessed a Heretic being burned at the Stake. Amid the dreadful tortuous exhibition here was a faith that contrasted with the despair and *lack of faith* he felt — though he was living in obedience to the Church. He knew that the heretical reformers rested their faith upon the Bible, and he determined to discover the secret of their joy.

Calvin had been a faithful member of the clergy since the age of twelve, but he concluded now that he could never be a consecrated priest.

For a time he turned to preparing for the law. But, abandoning this course of action, he decided to consecrate his life to the study of the gospel message.

Eventually, because of the earnest entreaties of his friends — he began to teach and preach the Word to humble peasants in their homes. The minds of these men were being stirred and this was the time to present them with the truth.

Lefevre and Farel had been rejected. But the king — influenced by political considerations — had not fully sided with Rome against the Reformation, so Paris received a second opportunity to accept their message.

Princess Margaret wanted a Protestant to preach in the churches of the city. And during an absence of the King — knowing full well that such an activity was forbidden by papal authorities — she nevertheless threw open a royal apartment in the palace for a Chapel.

Crowds thronged to the services, overflowing ante-chambers and the halls. Never before had the city been so moved by the Word of God. Thousands assembled there each day.

The spirit of temperance, purity, industry, and order was displacing drunkenness, licentiousness, idleness, and strife.

The King — upon his return to Paris — instead of ending the forbidden meetings, ordered them moved to two large churches of the city. The Word of God was preached in the capital of France for two years before the papists — regaining ascendancy — closed them and again set up the stake.

At last, when condemnation was fastened upon Calvin and the authorities determined to bring him to the flames, he fled southward to find refuge within Princess Margaret's official domain.

Calvin was determined to evangelize France, and he did not for long remain inactive. While the storm in Paris was abating, he engaged himself in a new field of ministry and love, near the university, in Potiers, outside the city, in the seclusion of a nearby cave. Here the Lord's Supper was first celebrated by Protestants in France.

Calvin returned to Paris once again where he found almost every door of labor closed to him due to the threat the Stake imposed. Scarcely had he left the country to visit Germany, when a storm of persecution descended upon the Protestants of France.

In one night reformists had placed placards all over France attacking the Catholic Mass, and the whole nation had become aroused. Instead of advancing the Protestant cause, this zealous but ill-advised action brought ruin to the Reformed faith throughout France.

One of the placards was attached to the door of the King's private chamber with obtruding boldness. This incensed his disgust and wrath, inciting him to throw his determined influence wholly on the side of Rome.

Measures were immediately taken to arrest every Lutheran in Paris. Not a house was spared. Not even the Colleges nor the University of Paris. A *new reign of terror* had begun, and its victims were put to death with cruel tortures and the flames. By this all Paris was shown the fortitude of the martyrs on their funeral pyres.

The Priests incited further agitation by circulating rumors of Protestant attempts to overthrow the government and assassinated the king, yet not a shadow of evidence could be produced to confirm their lies.

This suppression of Protestantism was to bring upon France the dire calamity of the French Revolution, within three hundred years. Suspicion, distrust, and terror began now to pervade all classes of French society.

Artisans, printers, scholars, authors, professors — and even member of the court — vanished from sight. Hundreds fled from Paris, self-exiled from their native land, giving in many cases the first indication of sympathy in favor of the Reformed faith.

The rage of the papists spent itself upon the multitudes who remained within its power.

On January 21, 1535, Francis I publicly declared for Rome and issued an Edict abolishing printing all over France, showing that intellectual culture is no safeguard against religious intolerance and persecution. Terrible became the darkness of the nation that rejected the light of truth.

France turned all progress aside, choosing darkness instead of light. Nearly three centuries later the Goddess of Reason was to be enthroned by a nation that denied the true and living God.

On January 21, 1793, 258 years later to the very day! another tumult, with a different purpose, would sweep through the streets of Paris. Again the day would close in execution and horror. This time it would be the *rabble* lashing out in fury against the intelligencia.

King Louis XVI would be dragged forward to the block and there held down by force until the waiting blade had fallen. And near that very spot more than 3000 Frenchmen would perish by the guillotine during the days of an ensuing **Reign of Terror** brought about by the anarchy of an arrogant, *rejection of the truth.*

The Bible As Reform

CHAPTER 17

Progressive Reformation

"Come unto me all ye, that labor and are heavy laden , and I will give you rest." *Christ Jesus.*

Switzerland

William Farel — upon arriving in Switzerland disguised as a schoolmaster — went on foot from village to village, and from city to city enduring weariness, hunger, and cold, in peril for his life, preaching in the market-place, and occasionally in churches and cathedrals. Though often repulsed and mercilessly attacked, he saw towns and cities open their gates in welcome to the truth.

If Geneva could be won it would become the center of the Reformation for Switzerland and France, and Italy too. But this first effort to evangelize the city did not meet early with success. Farel's efforts met only with rejection.

Eventually an inexperienced young schoolmaster named Fromont, began to quietly teach lessons from the Bible to children at school, who, in repeating the simple truths at home, gained the interest of their parents. Preachers who had previously fled, returned, and through the labors of many Protestants, the Reformation faith was finally established in Geneva.

John Calvin also found his way to Geneva after various wanderings and vicissitudes, and in this circumstance, William Farel saw the hand of God. He was confident that Calvin was a reformer with whom he could unite in the work, so he invited Calvin to accept the **Call** that would hold him irrevocably to the place he had otherwise soon planned to leave.

By this time the anathemas of the pope were thundering down against Geneva. And mighty nations threatened her with destruction. And the Jesuit Order — the most cruel, unscrupulous, and powerful of all other champions of Rome — was summoned on its behalf. All Protestants were to be menaced by this formidable foe.

The Jesuits endured great hardship in opposing the Protestant faith with the weapons of fanaticism and deception. Vowed to sincerity, humility and poverty, the Jesuits became deceitful, arrogant, and rich, by whatever means possible to overthrow the Protestant movement and reestablish papal supremacy. Their criminal, deadly purposes were concealed behind a blameless exterior of sanctity and having renounced their deadly work in order to minister to the sick and poor in the name of Jesus.

Their basic motivating rule was that **"the end would justify the means,"** however despicable those means might be. By this unbending code, lying, theft, perjury, and assassination became not only pardonable for a cause, but commendable actions serving the interest of the church.

Under secrecy and disguises, the Jesuits worked their way into offices of State, became counselors to kings, and shaped the policy of nations; establishing colleges and schools where children of Protestant parents were drawn to accept the Roman ceremonies and rites; destroying the liberty their fathers had toiled and suffered to obtain.

The Jesuits traversed Europe spreading their evil influence. To give them greater power, the pope issued a Bull reestablishing the horrors of the Inquisition. Thousands of the very flower of the nation were slain or forced to flee to their native lands.

Calvin and Farel labored in Geneva for thirty years. They established there a Protestant Church as a refuge for the hunted of western Europe — Puritans from England, Protestants from Holland, Huguenots from France, who returned later to their own countries nourished and refreshed. The torch of the Gospel carried from Geneva enlightened the darkness of every native land.

The Netherlands
Menno Simons was an educated Roman from a province of Holland. Although ordained to the priesthood, he was totally

unfamiliar with the teachings of the Bible. He feared to read the Bible, lest he be beguiled into the ranks of heresy — but in vain.

When in doubt about the doctrine of transubstantiation — *the conversion or the elements of the eucharistic at their consecration in the Mass, from the substance of bread and wine into the body and blood of Christ, with only the texture, taste, color, and smell of bread and wine remaining* — he was led to study the New Testament and the writings of Martin Luther, and was influenced to accept the Reformed faith. He withdrew from the Roman Catholic Church and devoted his life to teaching the truths he had received.

When the Munsterites arose, advocating absurd erroneous teachings and seditions — incompatible with the doctrine Menno Simons had accepted — he foresaw the results these movements could bring about if let alone, so he strenuously opposed this spurious influence.

For twenty-five years he live in peril of his life enduring hardship and great privation. He traversed the Netherlands exerting a widespread influence among the peasantry.

Simons was a man of humble spirit and gentle manners — unwavering in integrity. And this gained the confidence of the scattered and oppressed people who were confounded by the fanatical teaching of the Munsterites. And great numbers of people were converted by his labors.

Charles V had banned the Reformation, and back in Germany the protesting princes had been holding him in check. But here in the Netherlands, his power was unleashed, and persecuting edict followed edict in quick succession. Thousands perished under his reign and under the successive reign of Philip II against the continuing faith of the martyrs.

Year after year successive monarchs pressed the cruel work, but in vain. Under the noble leadership of William of Orange, Revolution at last brought the ability to freely worship God to Holland.

Denmark

In the mountains of the Piedmont, throughout Holland and on the plains of France, the progress of reform was marked in the blood of its disciples. But it found a peaceful welcome in the Scandinavian countries to the north.

Returning students from Wittenburg carried the Reformation, to their homes where hardy people welcomed the purity and simplicity of the Bible truths.

Tausen — later to be known as the reformer of Denmark — grew up in a peasant family who could not provide him with a formal education. So he entered the local cloister where it was decided that he be sent to the university of his choice, except Wittenburg, so he decided to go to Cologne — the stronghold of the Roman faith — where he became disillusioned by the dogma and mysticism taught by the professors there.

Exposed to Luther's writings he read them with delight. Offending his monastic superior, forfeiting all support, he secretly left Cologne and went to study at the forbidden University of Wittenburg.

When his studies at Wittenburg were completed he returned to his cloister in Denmark, not revealing his secret Lutheran affiliation. He intended to lead his companions to a purer faith and a holier life. When he began teaching and explaining the Bible's true meaning, he was at once confined to his cell and placed under the strict supervision of the prior. Nevertheless, to the prior's horror, several of the monks converted to the newly explained Protestant faith.

Had these Danish priests been aware of the unforgiving plans of the Church for dealing with such heresies, Tausen would not have been allowed to live. But he was instead expelled from the monastery into safety by a new royal edict extending the King's protection to teachers of the new Reformation doctrine.

The New Testament — recently translated into the Danish tongue — was being widely circulated throughout the Country. Once again papist efforts to overthrow the work greatly enforced and extended it. And Denmark erelong accepted the Protestant faith.

Sweden

Olaf and Laurentius Petri were young men who had also drunk from the well at Wittenburg. They were sons of a blacksmith of Orebro, and brought the Water of Life home to their country in Sweden.

Having studied under Luther and Melancthon, they were diligent to teach the truths that they had learned. Like Melancthon, Laurentius was reserved, thoughtful, and calm. And like Luther, Olaf aroused the people with his zeal. Both brothers were unflinchingly courageous in advancing the truth.

Sweden was divided into contending factions and continuing strife added to the misery of all. Olaf barely escaped harm with this life on several occasions, even though the reformers were favored here with the protection of the King.

The people were in poverty ground down by former oppressions. The King was therefore determined to have the Church and State reformed. And he welcomed these able soldiers to his cause.

Olaf and Laurentius were not illiterate controversialists. They were studious men of God who like their master teachers knew how to wield the weapons of reform. Not carnal weapons but **"mighty weapons through God to the pulling down of strong holds."** *2 Cor. 10:4.*

Olaf translated the New Testament into the Swedish tongue, and working together they translated the Old Testament, too.

As a result of their labors, the King of Sweden accepted the Protestant faith. And not long afterward a General Assembly declared the reforming of the State.

Freed from Roman oppression, Sweden became one of the major bulwarks of Protestantism, and attained a strength and greatness never before thought possible.

One hundred years later the armies of Sweden came to the

aid of Germany in the terrible struggles of the Thirty-Years War, helping Germany to turn the ebbing tide of the former papal success — winning toleration for the Lutherans and Calvinists — restoring liberty-of-conscience to those there who had *witness to the truth.*

England

William Tyndale completed the work that Wyclif had begun, by translating the Old Testament into the English language. When he tried to publish the newly translated Bible in England, he was forced to flee to Worms, where many there were friendly to the Reformation.

Here in Germany he published a first edition of three thousand English Bibles. These Bibles were smuggled back into England and circulated throughout the land. The demand was so great that another edition was completed within the year.

The papist Bishop of Durham — attempting to suppress the Bible — bought the complete stock of Tyndale's closest friends for the purpose of destroying them to greatly hinder the work, not realizing that by his very act of suppression, he was supplying the money needed for a subsequent, improved edition.

Tyndale was eventually imprisoned for many months, and finally met the fate of a martyr's death. But the Bibles that he produced for England enabled many to do battle throughout the centuries to come.

The foundation of the Protestant faith was not as firm in England as was supposed. Persecution diminished, but did not altogether end, and forms of the Roman doctrine were retained. The supremacy of the Pope of Rome was rejected, but the King of England was made the ruling Head of the Church, in his stead.

The great principle of religious toleration was not yet fully understood — even by the reformers. The right of every man to worship God according to the dictates of his conscience, was still not fully acknowledge.

Many of the people were still being forced to accept the

doctrines of one established, hierarchal Church. Dissenters still suffered persecution for many years.

From the loathsome dungeon of Bedford Prison came forth John Bunyan's wonderful allegory, The Pilgrim's Progress — of Pilgrims journeying from the land of destruction, on to the celestial City. And for more that 300 years this thrilling beacon has guided searching feet onto the pathway of life.

In the seventeenth century thousands of pastors were expelled from their pulpits and many still suffered persecution for their faith. Some were banished to other lands, and many were driven across the ocean to America where the foundation of civil and religious liberty was being laid — to protect multitudes from many lands, of their *witness to the truth.*

The Bible As Reform

CHAPTER 18

A Revolting Revolution

"This is the condemnation, that men loved darkness rather than the light." *John 3:19.*

The light had found entrance in France, but the darkness comprehended in not, and for centuries man struggled to gain mastery over his situation. At last the influence of evil triumphed, and the truth of heaven was thrust out.

The restraint of God's Word was removed from a people that despised the Gift of His loving Grace. Evil was allowed to come to maturity, and all the world saw the fruit of a willful and arrogant rejection of the light emanating from God's Word.

The terrible consequence of the suppression of Scripture, for so many centuries, culminated in the violent scenes of the **French Revolution** — presenting a most striking example of the workings of the carnal mind, when loosed from the guiding signs of the divine Mind that is Love.

The suppression of Scripture during **the long period of papal supremacy** was previously foretold by the prophets. The Revelation of St. John points to the terrible results that were to accrue, especially in France, from the forceful domination of **"That man of sin"** manifested to the world in the outward form of the papacy.

"The holy city (*the truth Church*) **shall they tread under foot forty and two months. And I will give power unto my two witnesses, and they shall prophesy a thousand two hundred and threescore days, clothed in sackcloth.**

And when they shall have finished their testimony, the beast that ascendeth out of the bottomless pit shall make war against them and kill them. And their dead bodies shall

lie in the street of the great city, which spiritually is called Sodom and Egypt, where also our Lord was crucified.

And they that dwell upon the earth shall rejoice over them, and make merry, and shall send gifts one to another; because these two prophets tormented them that dwelt on the earth. And after three days and a half the spirit of life from God entered into them, and they stood upon their feet; and great fear fell upon them which saw them." *Rev. 1:2-11.*

Most modern interpreters of the Bible agree that a "day" in prophetic symbolism represents a "year" in time to human sense, according to the Scripture, **"I have appointed thee each day for a year."** *Ezek. 4:6; Num. 14:34.*

Therefore the **"forty and two months,"** and the **"thousand two hundred and threescore days"** signify one and the same period of prophetic time — that time in which the Church of Christ endured great oppression under Roman persecution.

The 1260 years of papal supremacy began when the papacy became fully established in 538, and terminated when French army entered Rome and made the pope a prisoner in 1798; he later died in exile. (1260 + 538 = 1798).

Though a *new* pope was elected thereafter, the papal hierarchy has never, since, wielded the persecuting power it previously possessed. And through the influence of the Reformation, open persecution was brought to an end in 1798.

The Two Witnesses — in the material sense — represent the Old and New Testament teachings of the Bible. Two outspoken witnesses to the unfolding drama of salvation for all. *The Types and Prophesies* of the Old Testament point forward to a Savior yet to come, and *the Gospels and Epistles* of the New Testament tell of a Savior already come, in the manner prophetically foretold.

During the greater part of this period God's witnesses remained in a state of obscurity, hidden from the people by the papal power, "clothed in sackcloth," although having potential power and authority to declare the truth, during this whole time.

Then **"the beast that ascendeth out of the bottomless pit"** made **"war against them and** (for a time) **killed them"** (silenced their message).

During the French Revolution, beginning in 1793, the world for the first time heard an assembly of civilized men — *for the most part born and educated in the Church who were successfully governing one of the finest European nations of that time* — deny the most solemn truth which man's heart has ever received, when they renounced all belief in the Bible and in the one true God of its teachings.

France was the only nation in the world (up to that time) that as a nation lifted her hand in open rebellion against the God of Scripture. France stands alone in the history of the world as the single country who — by the decree of her legislative assembly — pronounced that **"there is no god."** The entire population of Paris, and a vast majority of people elsewhere, danced in the streets and sang with joy in acceptance of that announcement.

"The fool hath said in his heart, there is no God." *Psm. 14:1.*

That sorry state of corruption and immorality brings forward the similar state of mortal mind that brought destruction to the ancient cities of Sodom and Gomorrah.

Atheism and licentiousness was given free reign, converting the marriage covenant to an impermanent civil contract which could be cast aside at the merest whim of the two participants — calling forth the slang reference to it as "the sacrament of adultery." A so-called "adult" institution establishing fornication as a legally permitted national indulgence.

In no other land had contempt for the saving Christ been more forcefully displayed. In the persecution which France visited upon the Confessors of the Gospel, She crucified the Christ in the person of His disciples.

The land was laid waste with sword and axe and fagot,

converted into a vast a gloomy wilderness. These atrocities were being committed, *not during the Dark Ages of the past,* but in that brilliant era of the Age of Reason and Renaissance when science flourished and learned men of Court and Capital affected the graciousness of meekness and charity.

But that darkest history of crime was the most fiendish of all the dreadful prior Centuries. The world would shudder in shock and awe upon remembering the scenes of the most cruel and cowardly onslaught now known as the **Saint Bartholomew Day's Massacre** of 1572 in France, when the well-meaning king — *urged on by the priests and prelates of Rome* — unwittingly lent his sanction to the dreadful deed.

The Bell of the Palace was tolled in the dead of night as a signal for the slaughter. Protestants by the thousands, sleeping quietly in their homes, trusting their fate to the honor of the king, were dragged from the **sanctity of home** without warning, in the middle of the night, and were murdered in cold blood.

For seven days the massacre continued in Paris, the first three with inconceivable fury. And by special order of the king, the massacre was extended to all provinces of France. Neither age, sex, nor nobility were spared.

All over France the butchery continued for two long months. Seventy thousand (70,000) of the citizens of the nation were mercilessly slain.

And in 1793 the same deceiving influence of the carnal mind that urged on the Saint Bartholomew Day's Massacre led also to the scenes of the French Revolution, 220 years later.

At the beginning of the French Revolution, the Word of God was banned by the National Assembly. Bible were confiscated and publicly burned and arrogantly trampled under foot. And all religious institutions honoring the Bible were shut down.

The weekly day of worship and rest was set aside. In its place every tenth day was devoted to party time and revelry, and blasphemy. Baptism, Communion, and all other religious worship, were prohibited — replaced with the worship of **"Liberty."**

The Constitutionalized Bishop of Paris was brought before the people to confess that the theology that he had taught for many years was but a piece of priestcraft having no authentic foundation in the sacred truth.

He disowned the existence of the Diet and pledged to devote himself to the homage of liberty, equality, virtue, and morality. And several apostate priests, in their turn, followed suit in response to his example.

Infidel France had silenced the reproving voice of God's Two Witnesses. The Word of God lay dead in the streets of France, and those who hated the obligations of God's merciful, restraining laws, danced in the streets in jubilation.

After France had renounced the worship of the living God, it was only a matter of time until She descended to idolatry by worshiping the **Goddess of Reason** in the person of a profligate woman, when the National Convention of France rendered her public homage.

Upon being embraced by the President of the Convention, the **Goddess of Reason** was paraded amidst the immense crowd to the Cathedral of Notre Dame, and raised on the altar, receiving the adoration of the crowd, followed by a public burning of the Bible.

Atheism was completing the initial work that popery had begun — to *desecrate the truth.*

The Bible As Reform

CHAPTER 19

Flight from Fury

"Deliver me, O Lord, from mine enemies: I flee unto thee to hide me." *Psalm 143:9.*

The nation of France was being led to destruction and utter ruin by the social, political, and religious conditions wrought out by the policies of Rome.

The concepts of **Liberty** go hand in hand with the concepts of **the Bible**. Where-ever the Gospel is received, the thoughts of the people are awakened to cast off the shackles that hold them in bondage to ignorance, vice, and superstition. Men proceed to think and act like men, — instead of like animals.

Corrupt monarchs could see this effect, and they trembled in fear for the loss of their despotism. And Rome did not hesitate to inflame the jealous fears of the civil authorities.

Said the pope to the Regent of France in 1523: **"This mania** [referring to Protestantism] **will not only destroy religion, but all principalities, laws, orders and ranks besides."** A few years later, a papist dignitary warned the king: **"If you wish to keep the nations submitted to you in tranquility, manfully defend the Catholic faith and crush out all its enemies by your arms."**

Rome claimed that the purpose of the Sword of Persecution was to **"uphold the throne, preserve the nobility, and maintain the laws of the land."** But little did the rulers of the land foresee the results of that fateful Policy.

The teachings of the Bible would have infused in the hearts of the people the principles of justice, temperance, truth, benevolence and equity — of national prosperity and security.

"Righteousness exalteth a nation. [Thereby] **the throne is established...and the effect of righteousness quietness and**

assurance forever." *Prov. 14:34; 16:12; and Isa. 32:17.*

When man obeys the divine law he strives to obey the laws of the land. The man who respects and honors God will respect and honor the God-ordained Ruler in the exercise of his legitimate authority.

For decades men of principle, integrity, and moral strength — *who had the courage of their convictions and the faith to suffer for the truth* — toiled as slaves in the galleys, perished at the stake, or rotted in dungeon cells. Thousands upon thousands found safety in taking flight, and this exodus continued for years after the Revolution began.

Scarcely was there a generation of Frenchmen, during that long period, that did not see men fleeing from the fury of their persecutors, carrying with them the culture, the arts, the industry, and the law and order in which they generally excelled, to whatever nation they could find who would give them political asylum.

And as they enriched other countries with their Godly gifts, they exhausted their native land of the same. If everyone who had been driven away from France had been retained; if the industrial skill of the exiles had be cultivated on her native soil; if their industrial skill had been improving her manufactures; if their creative talents and analytical genius had been enriching her literature and her science; if their tempered wisdom had been guiding her councils; and if their bravery had been fighting for her peace; and their equity framing her laws; and their religion governing the conscience of the people, — what glory would have encompassed France in that day!

But her blind bigotry drove from her soil teachers of virtue, champions of order, honest defenders of the throne.

With the flight of the intelligencea, decline settled upon France. Flourishing manufacturing cities fell into idleness and decay. Fertile districts returned to native wilderness. Intellectual dullness and moral declension replaced a period of former progress. Paris became one vast alms-house; and it is estimated that 200,000 paupers claimed charity from the king.

Only the Jesuits flourished in the decaying nation. They ruled with tyranny over the churches and the schools; over the prisons and galleys.

The Gospel of the saving Christ would have brought to France solutions to their social and political problems. Problems that baffled the nations' clergy, her king and his legislators, plunging the nation into ruin and anarchy.

Under the dominance of Rome the people lost the Savior's lessons of sacrifice and unselfed love. They were led astray from the doctrine deny oneself for the sake of one's fellow man. The poor found no help and comfort for their degradation and servitude; the rich no rebuke for their oppression of the poor.

The selfishness of the powerful and rich grew more apparent and oppressive. The greed and profligacy of the nobility resulted in a grinding extortion of the working class. The rich suppressed the poor, and the poor grew to loath the rich.

Most of the large provincial estates were owned by the nobility. The laboring class were tenant farmers at the mercy of rich landlords, forced to submit to exorbitant demands.

The burden of supporting Church and State fell upon the middle class who become heavily taxed by civil authorities, and by the clergy as well.

The pleasure of the nobles was the ultimate consideration. The farmers and peasants could starve for all their oppressors cared. The people were compelled at every turn to bow to the exclusive interests of the landlord.

Laborers in the field lived lives of incessant work, and unrelieved misery. And if they dared to complain, they were treated with contempt.

The courts of "justice" were partial to the nobles above the peasant. Bribes were frequently demanded and accepted by the judges. The slightest caprice of the aristocracy had behind it the force of law by virtue of this system of corruption.

Of the taxes wrung from the commoners, by the magistrates, and the clergy, less than half ever found its way into the royal or episcopal treasuries. The cream of the wealth was squandered in profligate self-indulgence.

Furthermore, those who were impoverishing their fellow-subjects were themselves exempt from taxation, they were entitled by law, or custom, to all the appointments of the State. The privileged class numbered well over 15,000 and for their comfort and gratification millions were condemned to hopelessly degrading lives.

Suspicion eventually labeled all men of government "selfish and corrupt." For more than 50 years prior to the Revolution, the throne was occupied by Louis XV who, even in those prior days, was famous for his indolence, frivolousness, and sensuality.

With a depraved and cruel aristocracy, and an impoverished and ignorant lower class — the people exasperated and exhausted, and the State financially embarrassed — one did not need the eye of a prophet to foresee terrible, impending doom.

To warnings of explosive collapse, from his counsellors to the king, his only response was the philosophical reply: **"After me the deluge!"** Although he saw the evils, he had neither the courage, nor the power to meet them. In his helplessness, the doom of France was guaranteed.

Rome had learned that in order to enslave men effectually, the shackles of bondage must be fastened upon their thought with foresighted determination. The surest way to prevent men from escaping their bonds of servitude is to render them mentally incapable of freedom. And a thousand times more terrible than the physical suffering of oppression, was their mass descent into moral degradation.

Deprived of the Bible, abandoned to selfishness and bigotry, enshrouded in ignorance and superstition, and sunken in vice, the people became totally unfit for self-government, and justifying the need for force — further increasing their oppression. The widening whirlpool of self destruction wound down into the pit of bitter hopelessness and despair.

But this was not the result that Rome had originally intended.

Instead of simply holding the masses in submission to her dogma and treasuries, revolutionists, and infidels were formed. The masses grew to despise Romanism as an evil priest-craft — as the chief cause of their oppression.

The only god they knew had been interpreted to them through the perverted teaching of the church. Her false teaching had been their only religion. Her immoral example had been their only model. Unwittingly they regarded her cruelty and greed as legitimate fruitage of the Bible; and they would have none of it.

Rome had misrepresented God's character, and had perverted His laws. France had been misled to reject both the Bible and its Author. Voltaire and his associates cast God's Word aside, and spread, everywhere, infidelity to the mis-represented concept of the Lord.

Rome had ground down the people with her iron heel. And the brutalized, degraded masses recoiled at her tyranny and cast off all restraint.

Enraged by the glittering cheat which had for so long demanded their homage and allegiance, they rejected the open falsehood, and, unknowingly, truth as well. Mistaking *license* for *liberty,* and *insurrection* for *independence,* the slaves to vice exulted in their imagined freedom.

In the opening overtures of the Revolution the balance of power was quickly seized by the outraged population. But they were not prepared to use that power with wisdom and moderation. Eager to address the wrongs that they had suffered, they determined to undertake a **total reconstruction** of society, and to avenge themselves upon those whom they felt responsible for their plight.

Where France had first set up the Stake, under the prompting of the Church, to quell the beginnings of the Reformation, there on the very spot where the first martyrs of the Protestant Reformation were burned in the 16th century — the French Revolution set up its first guillotine, putting the aristocracy to the vengeance of the falling blade.

In suppressing the Gospel — the Gospel which would have

prevented this wasteful slaughter, and brought healing to her land — France, instead, opened the door to her total ruin.

When the restraining law of God was cast aside, the laws of man were inadequate to check the powerful tides of passion, and the nation was swept into the turbulent waters of anarchy and revolt.

His war against the misrepresented Bible inaugurated in France, her notorious **"Reign of Terror."**

CHAPTER 19

Sequence of Revolution

"The wicked shall fall by his own wickedness." *Proverb 11:5.*

The enraged people's thirst for vengeance was only whetted by the execution of the king. Even those who had decreed his death were soon to follow him to the scaffold. The general slaughter of all suspected of hostility to the Revolution swallowed up even the sympathetic who tried to quell it. No one was secure.

Each group of revolutionists opposed the other. France became one vast field of contention swayed by the passionate fury of the masses. One tumult succeeded another until the citizenry were melded into a seething cauldron of warring factions intent on nothing but mutual extermination. Then — adding to the misery of all — the nation became involved in a prolonged and devastating war with the major powers of Europe.

The Country was nearly bankrupt, and the armies were clamoring for arrears in pay. The Parisians were starving, and the provinces were being laid waste by thieves and robbers. Civilization was fast becoming extinguished by license and anarchy. The people had learned the lessons of cruelty and torture which Rome had diligently taught them all too well.

The persecutions which the clergy of France had for so many years dispensed, rebounded back upon them with a matching vigor.

The scaffolds ran red with the blood of priests. And the galleys and prisons became filled with the former persecutors.

Chained to the bench and toiling at the oar were the clergy of the Roman Catholic Church who, in turn, likewise experienced all those woes which their Church had so freely inflicted on the heretics.

Eventually no man could say his prayers or greet his neighbor without danger of committing a capital crime. Spies lurked in every corner, and wagon-loads of victims were carried daily through the streets of Paris to their doom.

The guillotine was early hard at work each day, and the gutters ran with blood ever onward to the Seine. The rising and falling of the gross and deadly blade was eventually deemed too slow, and other merciless means were added to the weapons of the slaughter.

In the short span of but 10 years, millions of human beings perished in the unbridled iniquity that defiled the workmanship of God.

Many who had been degraded and brutalized eventually achieved their freedom from domination. They then urged on the atrocities and excesses of unbridled license — with blame for this diabolical unbridled license — with blame for this diabolical work being mistakenly placed on the Bible.

The people were incited to regard religion as a cheat, and the Bible was the despised work of the devil — whereas true freedom lies within the proscriptions of the laws of God.

"O that thou hadst harkened to my commandments! then had thy peace been as a river, and thy righteousness as the waves of the sea: There is no peace, saith the Lord, unto the wicked. But whoso harkeneth unto me shall dwell safety, and shall be quiet from fear of evil." *Isaiah 48:18,22; Proverb 1:33.*

Nevertheless, atheists, infidels, and apostates opposed and denounced God's law. But the results of their influence only proved that man's well-being is bound up immutable in his obedience to the divine statutes. Those who refuse to reap their lessons from the Word of God are forced to reap them from the history of nations.

By the public prohibition of the Bible, the carnal mind achieved a long desired objective — a kingdom free from the restraints of the law of God. But the transgression of just and righteous law inevitably brings on misery and ruin.

"Though a sinner do evil an hundred times, and his days be prolonged, yet surely I know that it shall be well with them that fear [honor] **God. But it shall not be well with the wicked. Therefore shall they eat of the fruit of their own way, and be filled with their own devices."** *Eccl. 8:12-13; Prov. 1:31.*

Since that fateful time when France made war upon God's two witnesses, they have been honored as never before. The Revelator to St. John declares concerning them. **"They heard a great voice from heaven saying unto them, come up hither, and they ascended up to heaven in a cloud; and their enemies beheld them."** *Rev. 11:12.*

The British and Foreign Bible Society was organized in 1804. And the Bible was printed and circulated in over fifty tongues. And 12 years later, in 1816, the American Bible Society was founded. And since then the Bible has been translated into hundreds of languages and dialects.

Little attention was given to the work of foreign missions prior to the French Revolution, which began in 1793, but by the early 1800s a great change had taken place. Men had become dissatisfied with the results of rationalism and reason.

They had come to realize the absolute necessity of divine revelation and an experiential religion, for **"Ye shall know them by their fruits."** And millions have joined in the crusade on behalf of the Bible.

Whereas there were but a hundred or so Bibles in the land in Voltaire's time, there are not hundreds of thousands — nay millions — of Bibles throughout the world, in the present age in which we live. The Bible has become and **"anvil that has worn out many a hammer."**

"No weapon that is formed against thee shall prosper; and every tongue that shall rise against thee in judgement

thou shalt condemn. This is the heritage of the servants of the Lord, and their righteousness is of me, saith the Lord." *Isaiah 54:17.*

Whatever is based upon the unaided authority of man will eventually be overthrown; but that which is founded upon the immutable Word of God shall stand forever!

Vast improvements in the process of printing have given a great impetus to the publishing and circulation of the Bible. And ever-multiplying methods of communication between the various cultures and countries of the word, have broken down the ancient barriers of national prejudice and segregation.

The final loss of secular power by the Pope of Rome opened the way for the widespread entrance of the Word of God into every part of the inhabitable globe — in *witness to the truth.*

CHAPTER 21

New World Beginnings

"Stand fast therefore in the liberty wherewith Christ hath made us free, and be not entangled again with the yoke of bondage." *The Apostle Paul.*

The English reformers renounced the doctrines of Rome but established a replacement that was in many respects similar in nature. Many of Rome's customs and ceremonies were retained in the worship practices of the Church of England. It was claimed that these things were not a matter of conscience, hence not intrinsically evil.

In compromise, the retained customs and ceremonies were maintained in order to bridge the gulf of separation between the reformed churches and the Church of Rome. It was urged that this would promote the acceptance of the Protestant faith by the Romanists.

To a lot of the people this seemed quite logical and hence acceptable, but to others, that was not the case. They looked upon the compromises as badges of the slavery from which they had fought so hard to be delivered, and to which they had no deposition to return.

It was felt that God himself had established the regulations regarding his service, and that men are not at liberty to add to nor subtract from these things. Rome had begun her work by forbidding what we had explicitly enjoined.

Many people regarded the customs of the Church of England as tokens of idolatry, and they could not in conscience unite with her in worship.

The Church of England had merely replaced the authority of the pope with the authority of the king, in order to feel free of any requirement to send payments from the church collections and state treasury to Rome. The Church was now being supported by the civil authorities and they — as had Rome — permitted no dissent from her established form.

Attendance at her services was required by law, and unauthorized assembling for religious worship was forbidden under penalty of exile, imprisonment, or death, thereby guaranteeing state control of the masses and the finances of the Church.

At the opening of the seventeenth century the monarch determined to make the objecting Puritans — as they were now being called — "conform, or be harried out of the land, or else worse."

Hunted, persecuted, and imprisoned, they could discern but a bleak future, and many accepted the conviction that England had ceased forever to be a habitable spot, and some found refuge at last in Holland.

In their flight they left houses, goods, and their means of livelihood, finding refuge as strangers in a land that had a different language. Though often pinched with poverty, they thanked God for the blessings they experienced and they found joy in unmolested fellowship and spiritual communion. They knew that they were "pilgrims in a foreign land" and lifted up their eyes to Heaven — their real and dearest home — and thereby lifted up their spirits.

In the midst of exile and hardship their love and faith waxed strong. And when God's influence seemed to be prompting them to cross the sea to a land where they might establish for themselves a state of their own, — wherein they could leave for their children the precious heritage of religious freedom, — they went courageously forward into the bosom of the great unknown.

In the spirit of a solemn pledge "to forever walk in His ways made known," the pilgrim Puritans departed from Holland to find a home in the New World called America, earnestly believing that the Lord hath more truth and light yet to be revealed out of His holy Word.

John Robinson, their pastor before departing — who was prevented from going with them —said in his farewell address to the courageous band:

"Brethren, we are not erelong to part, and only the Lord knoweth whether I shall ever live to see your loving faces again, but whether the Lord hath appointed that, or not, I charge you before God and his blessed angels, to follow me no farther than I have followed Christ.

"The reformed churches are come to a period in religion where they will go no farther than the instruments of their reformation will allow. The Lutherans cannot be drawn to go any farther than what Luther saw, and the Calvinists do not go any farther than what Calvin saw, and — perchance — you may not be drawn any farther than what you presently see today. And this is a misery much to be lamented. For, though the founding reformers penetrated into the counsel of God, — were they living now, would they be as willing to embrace further light as that which they first received?

"Remember your promise and covenant with God and with one another, to receive whatever light and truth shall be made known to you from His written Word, but withal take heed, I beseech you, examine what you receive as truth, consider it and compare it with other Scripture of truth before you accept it — for it is not possible that the Christian world should come so quickly and lately out of such thick anti-Christian darkness that the **Perfection of Knowledge** breaks forth at once."

The desire for freedom-of-conscience was the motivation that pushed the Pilgrims to the perils of the long and arduous crossing of the sea. To endure the dangers and hardships of the wilderness, and — *with God's blessing* — to lay on the shores of America the foundation of a mighty nation. A nation that would eventually include such protestations of the Cradle of Liberty that would allow that **Perfection of Knowledge** referred to by John Robinson to break forth in humble birth.

And yet — honest and God fearing as they were — the Pilgrims did still not fully comprehend the great principle of religious toleration.

The freedom for which they sacrificed so much to secure

for themselves, they were not equally ready to grant to others of like desires. And so swings the pendulum of reaction.

Very few — even of the foremost thinkers and moralists of the seventeenth century — had a completely righteous and just concept of that grand principle — the outgrowth of the New Testament — which acknowledges God as the sold Judge of human faith and action.

Said one of the leading ministers of the colony of Massachusetts: "It was religious toleration that made the world anti-Christian, and the Church never took harm by the punishment of heretics."

And so the subtle regulation was adopted by the colonists that only church mangers should have a voice in the civil government of the State, — and once again a kind of State Church was formed — with all the people being required to support the clergy, and with magistrates authorized to the suppression of heresy. Thusly secular power was put back into the hands of the Church, and it was not long before these measures led to the inevitable result — religious persecution.

Roger Williams arrived in the new World eleven years after the planting of the first colony in the new soil. Like the early Pilgrims, he came to practice and enjoy religious freedom. But unlike them, he saw what so few in his time had yet seen, — that this freedom was the inalienable right of all — whatever their creed might by.

He was an earnest seeker for truth, holding — with Robinson — the conviction that it was not possible that all the light from God's Word had as yet been received.

Roger Williams was the first person in modern Christendom to assert in its plenitude, the doctrines of **liberty-of-conscience,** and **equality-of-opinions** before the law. He declared it to be the duty of the magistrate to restrain crime, but to never control the conscience. **"The public or the magistrate may decide what is due from men to men** (he said) **but when they attempt to** proscribe man's duty to God, they are out of place and there can be no safety, for it is clear that if the magistrate has the power, he may decree one set of opinions or beliefs today, and another tomorrow — as has been done in England by different kings and queens, and by the different popes and councils in the Roman Church — so that belief would become a heap of confusion, worse confounded."

When the rules are always being changed, nobody can know even how to play the game.

Attendance at the services of the established church was at this time required by law under penalty of monetary fine or imprisonment. Therefore, **"Williams reprobated the law — the worst statute of the English code — that enforced the attendance to the parish church upon the people."**

To so compel men to unite with those of a different creed, he regarded as an open violation of their natural rights; to drag to public worship the irreligious and the unwilling, "seemed like requiring hypocrisy by law."

"No one (he said) **should be forced to worship, or to maintain worship, against his own consent." "What** (exclaimed those antagonistic to his tenants) **is not the laborer worthy of his hire?" "Yes!** (he replied) **but from only those who hire him!"**

Roger Williams repudiation of the right of civil magistrates to authority over the Church, and his demand for religious liberty, could not be tolerated. The application of these principles, it was urged, would **"subvert the fundamental state and government of the Country."** And so he was banished from the Colonies, amid the cold and storms of winter, forced to seek refuge with an Indian tribe he had befriended while spreading the gospel truths.

Making his way at last to the shores of Narragansett Bay, he eventually laid there the foundations of the first State, of modern times, that in the full sense of the word recognized the right of religious freedom. The fundamental principle **"that according** to the **light and dictates of his conscience**" was the foundation of Roger William's colony.

This little Colonial State — Rhode Island — became an asylum for the oppressed. And it increased and prospered until its founding principles — civil and religious liberty — became the basic cornerstone of the American Republic.

In that grand document which our forefathers set forth as the **Declaration of Independence**, in 1776, they declared: **"We hold these truths to be self-evident, that all men are created equal; that they are endowed by their Creator with certain inalienable rights; that among these are life, liberty, and the pursuit of happiness."**

And the **Bill of Rights** of the American Constitution guarantees in the most explicit terms the inviolability of conscience: **"No religious tests shall ever be required as a qualification to any office of public trust under the United States. Congress shall make no law respecting and establishment of religion, or prohibiting the free exercise thereof,"** the Framers of the Constitution recognized the eternal principle that man's relation to his God is above human legislation, and his **right-of-conscience** inalienable. We are conscious of this **right-of-conscience** in our hearts — reason is not necessary to the existence of this basic truth. It is this conscientiousness which, in defiance of human laws, has sustained so many martyrs in torture and in the flames. It partook of the acknowledgment that one's duty to God is superior to human enactments; that men can exercise no authority over conscience. This is an inborn principle of truth which nothing can erase.

As the glad tidings spread throughout the countries of Europe — of a land where every man might enjoy the fruits of his own labor, and obey the conviction of his conscience — thousands flocked to the shores of the New World.

Massachusetts — by special law — offered free welcome and aid, at public expense, to Christians of any nation who might flee across the Atlantic "to escape from wars or famine, or the oppressions of their persecutors." Thusly the down-trodden and fugitive alike were — by state statute — made guests of the Commonwealth.

The new strangers in this foreign land were content even to earn a bore subsistence through a life of frugality and toil. They asked nothing from the soil but the reasonable returns of their own labor. They were content with the slow but steady progress of their social polity. They patiently endured the privations of the wilderness, watering the tree of liberty with the tears and the sweat of their brow, till it took root in this land of promise.

This demonstrated that the principles of the Bible are the surest safeguards of the national interest. The feeble and isolated colonies grew into a confederation of powerful states, and the world marked with wonder the peace and prosperity of **"a Church without a pope, and a State without a king."** And continually increasing numbers were attracted to America's shores.

The early requirement adopted by the colonists of only permitting members of the Church to vote or hold office in the civil government had originally been accepted as a means of preserving the purity of the State, but it lured corruption back into the Church.

Many members who joined the Church were motivated mainly by the attraction of worldly advantage, therefore they united with the Church without first having had a change of heart. Thus the churches came to consist — to a considerable extent — of unconverted persons.

Even in the ministry there were those who hold to errors of doctrine and who were ignorant of the renewing and vitalizing power of the Holy Spirit. The goal to increase the membership in numbers rather than in spirituality become foremost in the people's thought.

The aid of the State was again sought through appeals to the "powers that be" in support of the Gospel of Him who declared, **"My kingdom is not of this world."**

Any union of Church and State, be the degree ever so slight, while it may at first appear to bring the World nearer to the Church, does in actuality but bring the Church nearer to the World. And this is not true spiritual progress.

The great principles, that truth is progressive and that Christians must stand ready to accept all the light which may shine from God's Hole Word, was lost slight of by the religious descendents of the reformers — in America and Europe as well, — so highly favored in receiving the blessings of the Reformation. They failed to press forward on the path of reform and again slipped back into the formalism and error which would have otherwise been cast aside had the Church continued to walk in the light of God's Word. God's Word had been placed within the reach of all, but many valued it lightly, and neglected to read the Scriptures. They therefore continued to accept false interpretations of truth, and to cherish doctrines which have no foundation in the Word of God.

Pride and extravagance were again fostered in the Church, under the guise of religion, and the Protestant churches became corrupted with the errors of worldly ways. And the principles for which the reformers had done and suffered so much, were set aside and forgotten — in degradation — counteracting former reformist's **witness to the truth.**

CHAPTER 22

Reformation Rebuttal

The devout Catholic says to the Protestant:
We too resented our tithes going to monks who were getting out of hand. Nevertheless, we would never consider destroying the Church. We still feel that there should be room and institutions in the world for men dedicated solely to contemplation, study, and prayer.

We believe that every word of the Bible must be accepted on the basis of two provisions:

1) that the law of Christ abrogated the law of Moses;
2) that the Church was founded by the Son of God — having equal authority with the Bible, and therefore the final right to interpret the Bible and adjust its interpretation to the changing needs of life.

These provisions are considered necessary to avoid individual judgements and interpretations of ambiguous and apparently contradictory passages of Scripture, which would otherwise tear the Bible to pieces by a thousand opinions, shattering Christianity into a thousand different sects.

We feel that emphasis on faith, as opposed to deeds, is ruinous — leading to a religion whose coldness of heart becomes concealed behind the piety of its phrases. And for 100 years charity almost died in the centers of Reformation victory.

Though you ended the Confessional, you generated thousands of tensions in the struggle that you established between instinct and civilization. And the healing institution of Church was belatedly restored under dubious and hypocritical forms.

You weakened the Universities that the Church had established — to the verge of death — and you destroyed the schools.

Even your own leaders admit that the disruption of the faith let loose a chaos of individualism — in morals, philosophy, industry, and government.

You took the joy and beauty out of religious practice, and filled it with demonology and terror that condemns the masses of mankind to damnation as "reprobates," and consoles an insolent few with the pride of election and salvation.

You stifled the growth of art, and withered the study of the classics. You expropriated Church property, and gave it to the State and the rich — leaving the poor poorer than before, adding contempt to misery. You condone usury and capitalism, but you deprive the workers of the restful holidays a merciful Church had given them.

You rejected the papacy only to exalt the State; giving to selfish princes the right to dictate the religion of their subjects, and to use religion as a sanction for their wars.

You divided nation against nation, and many a nation and city against itself. You wrecked the international moral checks on national powers, and created a chaos of warring national states.

You denied the authority of a church founded, admittedly, by the Son of God, — but you sanctioned absolute monarchy, and exalted the divine right of kings.

You unwittingly destroyed the power of the Word — the only alternative to the power of the sword or money. You claimed the right of private judgment, but you denied it to others as soon as you could. And your refusal to tolerate dissent was less understandable than that of the Catholic Church. For the Catholic Church had never defended toleration; for no man can be completely tolerant — except he be indifferent.

Meanwhile, see what private judgement led to, when every man has become a pope, and has judged the doctrines of religion before being mature enough to comprehend the functions of religion in morals and society, and the need of the people for a religious faith.

A kind of disintergrative mania — unhindered by any

intergrative authority — threw the reformists and their followers into such absurd and violent disputes that men began to doubt all religion.

Christianity itself almost dissolved. This would have left men spiritually naked in the face of death, were it not that the Church stood firm amid all the fluctuations of human argument and opinion — amid all the fashionings of science and philosophy — holding the regathering flock together against the time when those who have come to understand, and are really c Christians, will submit their **pride-of-individuality** and **pride-of-intellect** to the religions needs of mankind, and will come back to the one fold that can preserve religion, despite the blasphemous ideologies of an unhappy age.

The devout Protestant says to the Catholic:

Let us not forget the cause of our divergence. Your Catholic Church had become corrupt in practice and personnel. Your priests were not functioning, your bishops were worldlings. Your popes were the scandal of Christendom. Do not your own historians confess it?

Honest men called upon you to reform, and meanwhile they kept their loyalty to the Church. You promised and pretended to reform, but you did not. On the contrary, you burned at the Stake men like Hus and Jerome of Prague because they cried out for reform.

A thousand efforts were made to reform the Church from within, They failed, until our Reformation forced you to act. And even after our revolt, the Pope who tried to cleanse the Church became the laughingstock of Rome.

You pride yourselves in producing the Renaissance, but everyone agrees that the Renaissance was issuing forth such immorality, violence, and treachery, as Europe had not known since Nero. Were we not right in protesting against this paganism; flaunting itself even in the Vatican in Rome?

Granted: morals declined for awhile, after our Reformation began. It took time to rebuild a moral life whose religious foundations and ministration had decayed. Ultimately the morality of Protestant lands became far superior to those of Catholic France or Italy.

We may owe our *mental awakening* to the Renaissance, but we owe our *moral recovery* to the Reformation. To the liberating of the intellect was added the strengthening of character.

Your Renaissance was primarily for the aristocracy and intellectuals. It scorned the people, and winked at their being hoodwinked by indulgence peddlers, and monkish profiteers of mythology. Was it not good that this crass financial exploitation of human hopes and fears, should be challenged?

We rejected the paintings and statues with which you had littered your churches, because you were allowing the people to worship the images themselves, as when you required them to fall on their knees before the sacred dolls carried in processions through the streets.

We dared to base our religion on a strong and active faith, rather than drug the people's minds with liturgy.

We acknowledge the secular authority as divinely appointed — as your own theologians had done before us — because social order requires a respected government. We rejected the international authority of the popes only after they had flagrantly used it not to arbitrate justice among nations but to advance their own material interests.

The inability of your self-seeking popes to unify Europe for a crusade against the Turks shows that the dishonesty of the papacy had broken the unity of Christendom long before the Reformation.

And though we supported the divine right of kings, we also — in England, Scotland, Switzerland, and America — favored the development of democracy, while your priests in France, Italy, and Spain were truckling to kings. And our rebellion against the authority of your church broke the spell of despotism, and induced Europe to question all absolutism — religious or secular.

You think we made the people poor, But that too was a

passing phase. The same capitalism that for awhile exploited poverty, learned to enrich the average man, as never before. And the standard of living is surely higher in Protestant England, Germany and America, than in Catholic Italy, Spain, and France.

If you are stronger today than yesterday, it is because of us. What but the Reformation compelled you to reform the Curia, to redeem your clergy from concubinage, to seat men of religion, instead of pagans, in the papal chair?

To whom do you owe it that your clergy today have so high a repute for integrity? To the Council of Trent. But to what did you owe the Council of Trent, if not to the Reformation? Without that check your Church might have continued its degeneration from Christianity into paganism until your popes would have been enthroned over an agnostic and epicurean world.

Even with the regeneration which we forced upon your Church, the peoples that accept your creed are more negligent of religion, and more skeptical of Christianity, than those that adopted the Reformation Faith. Compare France with England.

We have learned to reconcile our piety with freedom of the mind. And it is our Protestant lands that have seen the greatest flowering of Science and Philosophy. We hope to eventually adjust our Christianity to the progress of knowledge — but how is this possible to a Church that rejects the Science of the last four centuries?

The Humanist says to Both:

The honor and weakness of Protestantism is that it appeals to the intellect, which is always changing. And the strength of Catholicism lies in its refusal to adjust itself to the theories of science, which — in the experience of history — seldom survive the century in which they are born.

Catholicism proposes to meet the religious demands of a people who have barely heard of Copernicus and Darwin, and have never heard of Spinoza or Kant. Such people are many and intellectually fertile.

But how can a religion that speaks to the intellect, and centers around the sermon, adjust itself to an expanding universe in which the planet that claimed to have received God's Son is now thought to be a mere transitory speck in space — and the species for which He sacrificed so much is but a moment in the phantasmagoria of life?

And what happens to Protestantism when the Bible that it took as its sole and infallible basis is subjected to a "higher criticism" that transforms it from the Word of God into the literature of the Hebrews, and that changes the **Gospel of Christ** into the mystical **Theology of Paul**?

The Witness to Truth says to All:
The real problem for the modern mind is not between Catholicism and Protestantism, nor between the Reformation and the Renaissance; it is between Christianity and the Enlightenment — that hardly datable era which began in Europe with Francis Bacon, and hitched its hope to Reason, Science, and Philosophy.

Art was the keynote of the Renaissance, and Religion the soul of the Reformation. But Science and Philosophy became the Gods of the Enlightenment.

From this standpoint the Renaissance was in the direct line of European mental development, and the Reformation was a deviation from that line — a rejection of reason and a reaffirmation of medieval faith.

And yet despite its original intolerance, the Reformation rendered two services to the Enlightenment:

1) it broke the authority of dogma, generating a hundred sects that would formerly have died at the stake,

2) it demanded among them such a virile debate that reason was finally recognized as the Bar before which all sects — secular or religious — now have to plead their case, unless armed with irresistible physical force.

In that pleading debate — that attack and defence — all sects were weakened, all dogmas. And only a century after Luther's exaltation of faith, Francis Bacon made the proclamation that **"knowledge is power."**

And in that same 17th century, thinkers like DeCartes, Hobbes, Spinoza, and Locke offered philosophy as a substitute **basis** for religion. In the 18th century Helvetius, Holback, and La Mettrie proclaimed open atheism — and Voltaire was called a bigot because he believed in God.

This is the challenge coming between the Catholic and the Protestant versions of the medieval creed. **The effort of Christianity to survive Darwin and Copernicus is the basic drama of the past 300 years. What are the struggles of states and classes, next to this Armageddon of the mind?**

Let us remember: As we said above, the real problem for the modern mind is not between Catholicism and Protestantism, nor between the Renaissance and the Reformation. It is between the Enlightenment and Christianity.

The Renaissance liberated the mind, and beautified life, — while the Reformation quickened religious belief, and moral sense. Such limited truth as men could attain in these large matter was begotten by the union of opposites and will *ever* feel its double parentage.

The Reformation reputed the Renaissance and its emphasis on earthly affairs and joys. It returned to that aspect of the Middle Ages which counted human delights and achievements trivial and vain, calling life a veil of tears, summoning a sinful man to faith, repentance and prayer, restoring the Age of Faith, in that struggling adolescence of the Age of Reason.

Witness a Virtuous Verdict:

And as we look back over the narrative of this treatise, we perceive that our sympathy can go to all the combatants in this drama.

We can understand the anger of Luther at Roman dominance and corruption. And the reluctance of German Princes to see

German collections fatten the coffers of Italy; the resolve of Calvin and Knox to build model moral communities; the desire of Henry VII for an heir and for authority within his own realm.

But we can understand, too, the hopes of Erasmus for a reform that would not poison Christendom with hatred and strife. And we can feel the dismay of devout Roman Prelates like Contarini at the prospective dismemberment of a Church that for hundreds of years had been the nurse and custodian of Western Civilization — and was still then the strongest bulwark against immorality, chaos, and despair.

Nothing of all these efforts, however, was lost. The individual succumbs, to human sense, — but he does not die — for Jesus declared that life is eternal (*John 11:25-26*) — each individual leaves something to mankind.

Protestantism, in time, helped to regenerate the moral life of Europe. The Church purified herself into an organization, politically weaker, but morally stronger than before.

One major lesson emerges above the smoke of battle of the temporal realm. Religion and Politics are at their best when they must live with the competition of scrutiny. Intolerance ensues when and where they are left unchallenged and supreme.

The greatest gift of the Reformation was to provide Europe and America with that competition of religious faiths and political forms — which gauge each by its mettle — cautions both to tolerance — and gives the test and zest of freedom to our concepts — in *witness to the truth.*

"Thy word is a lamp unto my feet, and a light unto my path." *Psalm 119:105.*

The Bible As Reform

CHAPTER 23

American Footsteps

"He (the Lord) **will do nothing, but He revealeth his secret unto his servants the prophets."** *Amos 3:7.*

William Miller was an upright farmer from New England. His whole family was characterized by an independent, liberty-loving patriotism, and his father was a Captain in the Army of the American Revolution.

Miller did not have the advantages of a college education, but his intellect was active, and he had a keen thirst for knowledge. His love of study coupled with this habit of careful thought and critical analysis rendered him a man of sound judgement and comprehensive views.

He filled various civil and military offices with credit, and the avenues to wealth seemed quite open to him, if he so desired.

In 1816, at the age of 34, he "came under conviction" of a Savior dearly sought. And the Scriptures, which to him before were dark and contradictory, then become "A lamp unto (his) feet, and a light unto (his) path," endeavoring him to lay aside preconceived opinions.

Dispensing with commentaries, he decided to make certain for himself whether or not apparent contradictions of the Bible could be harmonized.

As a result of his studies of the books of Daniel and the Revelation of St. John, Miller accidentally discovered that the Second Coming of Christ is plainly taught within the Scriptures. It became his conclusion that not until the occurrence of this literal and predicted advent of the Christ, can God's people fully receive the Kingdom.

He concluded also that all the signs of the times of current world conditions corresponded to prophetic descriptions of the "latter days," Therefore, the period of time allotted for the continuance of world conditions in their existing state, was about to come to a close.

He discovered a chronological aspect whereby predicted events had generally been fulfilled within a given framework of historic time after having been predicted.

For instance: the 120 years from Adam to the flood; the seven days from the notification of the flood's occurrence to its start; the forty days duration of the flood's predicted rain (*Gen. 6:3; 7:4*); the 400 years of the sojourn of Abraham's seed (*Gen. 15:3*); the three days of the butler's and the baker's dream (*Gen. 40:28-54*); the seven years of Paroahs (*Gen. 41:28-54*); the 3-1/2 years of famine (*1 Kings 17:1*); the 70 years of Jewish captivity (*Jer. 25:11*); and Nubuchadnezzar's seven times (*Dan. 9:24-27*).

These events were at one time only a matter of prophesy. They were fulfilled in accordance with the times predicted. Miller therefore regarded them to be of the "times before appointed" which "God revealed unto His servants the prophets."

"The secret things (said Moses) **belong unto the Lord our God; but those things which are revealed belong unto us and to our children forever."** *Deut. 29:29.*

The prophesy that clearly reveals the time of the advent of the Comforter foretold by Jesus Christ, is that of Daniel 8:14, **"Unto two thousand and three hundred days; then shall the sanctuary be cleansed."**

Following his self-imposed rule to make Scripture its own interpreter, Miller discovered that a day in biblical time prophetic time represents a year in time to human sense — based on the Scripture: **"I have appointed thee each day for a year."** *Ezek. 4:6; Num. 14:34.* The "two thousand and three hundred days" of Daniel 8:14 indicates therefor a 2300 year period of time to human sense.

Miller then realized that this period of time extended far beyond the close of the Jewish dispensation which ended when Stephen was stoned to death in the year 34, — therefore this scriptural reference did not refer to a Cleansing of the Sanctuary in that Dispensation. It had refer to some other sanctuary at a later time.

Miller concluded that this Sanctuary of a later Age, foretold by Daniel (Daniel 8:14) represents the purification of the earth by fire, at the Second Coming of Christ. He realized that if the starting point of the 2300 year period could be made certain, the date of the Second Advent would be readily indicated in years.

The date would reveal when the present state of mankind will come to an end. The time when the curse will be removed from the earth. The time when the belief in death will be destroyed. The time when reward will be given to the servants of God — those who fear his name and obey his commands. The Dispensation when the tribulations of the earth will be no more.

Just one point in the Vision of Chapter Eight remained unexplained, the point in relation to time, the start of the 2300 year period. Upon resuming his explanation in Daniel Chapter Nine, the angel dwells exclusively on the subject of time.

"Seventy weeks are determined upon thy people (the Jews) **and upon thy holy city** (Jerusalem). **Know therefore and understand, that from the going forth of the commandment to restore and to build Jerusalem unto the Messiah the Prince shall be seven weeks, and threescore and two weeks. And after...shall Messiah be cut-off, but not for himself... and he shall confirm the covenant with many for one week; and in the midst of the week he shall cause the sacrifice and the oblation to cease."** *Dan. 9:24-27.*

Seventy weeks: [70 x 7 = 490] 490 years are to be cut-off as especially pertaining to the Jews. Since the 2300 year period of time in Chapter Eight must be the period of time from which the 490 years were predicted to be cutoff, both periods of time must begin together.

If the date of this commandment could be found, then the starting point for this 2300 years could be ascertained.

In Ezra 6:14, 15 the restoring of Jerusalem and the rebuilding of the temple of the Lord was "according to the commandment of Cyrus, and Darius, and Artaxerxes kings of Persia (now Iran)."

In originating, affirming, and completing this decree, these three kings brought the decree to completion in the autumn of 457 B.C. (*See Ezra. 7:11-28*).

Using 457 B.C. as the date in question, every aspect of the prophesy of the 70 weeks "determined upon the Jews" has been accurately fulfilled. (-457 + 490 +1 = 34).

"Seven-weeks and three-score and two-weeks" (69 weeks, 483 years) from 457 B.C. (when the decree of Artaxerxes went into effect) extends to the year 27 when Jesus was baptized by his cousin John when (according to Peter) **"God anointed Jesus of Nazareth with the Holy Ghost and with power."** *Acts. 10:38.*

After Jesus' baptism, **"he came into Galilee preaching the gospel of the kingdom of God, and saying, the time is fulfilled."** *Mark 1:14,15.* And began his 3-1/2 year ministry. He began to **"confirm the covenant with many of one week."**

And **"in the midst of the week"** (in 31) (3-1/2 years after his baptism in the fall of 27) Jesus was crucified on Calvary; ending the system of ceremony and animal sacrifices which for 4000 years had pointed forward to the Lamb of God.

Type had met anti-type. And all the sacrifices and oblations (of the ceremonial system) were to cease upon the threshold of the Sixth Dispensation of God to man. The week mentioned here refers to the final seven years of the period allotted especially to the Jews — the period of time from 27 to 34 A.D.

During this seven year period, Christ — the first half in

person and the second half through his prior instructions to his disciples — extended the gospel and **"confirmed the covenant with many** (Jews) **for one week"** (7 years).

He said to his disciples, **"go not into the way of the Gentiles, and into any city of the samaritans enter ye not; but go rather to the lost sheep of the house of Israel."** *Mat. 10:5,6.*

At the end of the 490 year period especially allotted to the Jews (in the year 34), the Jewish nation sealed its rejection of the Gospel when the Sanhedrin stoned Stephen in the year 34. The message of salvation, no longer restricted to the Jews, was thereafter taken to the Gentiles.

The disciples **"went everywhere preaching the Word."** *Acts 8:4.*

Philip went down to the city of Samaria, and preached Christ unto them *Acts 8:5,* Peter opened the gospel to Cornelius, the centurion of Ceasarea *Acts 10:21-48,* and Paul, having been redeemed to a faith in Christ, carried the glad tidings **"far hence unto the Gentiles."** *Acts 22:21.*

By taking 457 B.C. as the starting point of the great period of 2300 years **"from the going forth of the commandment to restore and to build Jerusalem"** it can readily be calculated that the time when the **"cleansing of the sanctuary"** is to begin was 1844 (-457 + 2300 + 1 = 1844). And this time was believed to coincide with the Second Coming of the Christ.

All the various figures, metaphors, parables, similitudes, etc., explained in their immediate context, or defined in other Scripture, are to be understood literally, for in-so-far as the prophesies have thus far been fulfilled, they have been fulfilled literally.

Miller came to this conclusion in 1818 after two-years of intense study of the Bible — 26 years prior to the predicted event. He studied and reviewed his conclusion during the next 5 years, before attempting to share his discovery in private to his friends.

It wasn't until eight years after that, in 1831, that he public gave the reasons for his faith — fifteen years after the start of his determined investigation.

As a result of his disclosure, Miller was called to leave his plow and explain to the people the revealed mystery of God, and in 1833, he received from the Baptist Church the license to preach.

Men of position and learning united with Miller in preaching and publishing his views prior to 1844.

From age to age the message which God has given to the world through the witness of His chosen messengers has repeatedly been scoffed at by "unbelief" as the incredible assertions of one against many.

To those engulfed in ignorance, in apathy or sin, the message of the Second Advent forebodes woe and desolation. But to those watchfully informed it inspirers joy and consolation, and satisfies the longing heart, through the promised coming of The Comforter of Christ.

CHAPTER 24

Great Disappointment

"Ye can discern the face of the sky; but can ye not discern the signs of the time?" *Christ Jesus.*

The apostle Paul instructed the Church not to look for the coming of Christ in his day and age. **"For that day shall not come** (he said) **except there come a falling away first, and that man of sin be revealed."** *2 Thes. 2:3.*

Not until after the great apostasy can we look for the Second Advent of our Lord.

The "man of sin," the "mystery of iniquity," the "son of perdition," and that "wicked" reflect the papacy, which maintained its supremacy for 1260 years, from 538 to 1798. The message of Christ's Second coming was to be proclaimed after 1798. And knowledge of the prophesies has increased since that time. Many have since proclaimed the message of the Judgement near.

In 1821, three years after Miller made his discovery Joseph Wolff, began to proclaim the Lord's soon coming.

He was born in Germany of Hebrew parentage (his father was a Rabbi) and had been convinced, as a child, of the Christian faith. He had an active, inquiring mind, and had eagerly listened to conversations that took place in this father's house.

Devout Jews of the area daily assembled themselves to recount the hopes and anticipations of their people, the glory of a Messiah to come, and the restoration of Israel.

When he inquired about Jesus, he was told that Jesus was a man of great talents, but a Jewish tribunal had put him to death because he pretended to be the Messiah.

"Why then is Jerusalem destroyed?" (Wolff questioned).

"Why are we Jews in captivity?"

He found his answer, when an elderly friend told him to read the fifty-third Chapter of Isaiah. Wolff then became convinced that Jesus was the son of God. He saw how accurately the Scripture had been fulfilled in the life of Jesus.

When almost twelve, Joseph Wolff left his father's house and to acquire an education, and to choose for himself his religion and occupation. He found shelter with relatives, but was soon expelled as an apostate. He then supported himself by teaching the Hebrew language to others.

Under the influence of a Catholic teacher, he accepted the Catholic faith, and decided to become a missionary to the Jews. He enrolled at the College of Propaganda, in Rome, where at first, he was treated with special favor, but after a time — due to his candid speech and independent thought — he was declared incorrigible and sent away again.

He made his way to England and united with the Church of England. After two years of religious study, he went out on his mission to the Jews, in 1821.

Wolff sought to lead his people to Jesus by pointing to his First Coming in humiliation. He also taught them of Jesus' Second Coming in triumph as a deliverer and a king — an event which he believed to be at hand.

His interpretation of the prophetic periods placed the "Great Consummation" to within a few years of the time Miller pointed out. And to those who scoffed, saying **"of that day and hour knoweth no man,"** men are to know nothing concerning the nearness of the Advent, according to the Scripture, he replied, "Did not the Lord give us signs of the times, so that we might at least know the approach of summer by the fig tree putting forth its leaves? Are we never to know that period?

Jesus exhorted us to not only to read the Scriptures, but to understand, **"Many shall run to and fro, and knowledge shall be increased"** during the latter days.

The exact hour and day shall not necessarily be known, but

that is not to say that the approach shall not be known. Jesus told his followers that enough shall be known, by the signs of the times, to encourage us to *prepare* for his coming, as Noah prepared his Ark for the flood

For twenty-four years, from 1821 to 1845, Wolff traveled extensively, in Africa, Asia, and in the United States he preached to Congress, in the Capital. He persevered in his missionary work until the message of the coming Judgment had been carried to a large part of the world — in ***witness to the truth.***

The Bible As Reform

CHAPTER 25

Uncertainty and Doubt

"Behold, I come quickly: hold that fast which thou hast, that no man take thy crown." *Rev. 3:11.*

When Christ did not visibly appear when first expected in the spring of the year 1844, — those who had looked for their beloved Savior were for awhile overwhelmed by uncertainty and doubt.

Many continued to study and search the Scriptures, examining anew the evidence of their faith. Still, unmistakable signs pointed to the time as near.

Interwoven with the prophesies that the people had regarded as applying to the time in question, was additional instructions especially adapted to their state of uncertainty — encouraging them to wait with patience.

"Write the vision and make it plain upon tables, that he may run that readeth it. For the vision is yet for an appointed time, but at the end it shall speak, and not lie: though it tarry, wait for it; because it will surely come, it will not tarry." *Hab. 2:1-4.*

"The word that I shall speak shall come to pass, it shall no more be prolonged... There shall none of my words be prolonged any more, but the word that I have spoken shall be done." *Ezek. 12:27,28.*

Had it not been for such portions of the Scripture admonishing them to wait, with patience, their faith would have failed them in that trying hour.

In Jesus' parable of the ten virgins *Mat. 25,* the **"tarrying of the bridegroom while the virgins slumbered,"** indicates a passing of time, *or a seeming delay,* before the expected event. One group of people in unconcern, abandoned their former faith **"they all slumbered and slept."** The other group waited, patiently, for clearer light to be received.

"The accuser of the brethren," Satan, error, induces men to watch for the errors of God's servants, holding them up to scorn, while their good deeds are bypassed without regard.

In the days of the Reformation, its detractors charged all the evils of fanaticism against the very ones who were laboring most sincerely for its Cause. The world is asleep, let the world be aroused, resurrected out of sleep. Begin in earnest the work of repentance and reform.

"And at midnight there was a cry made, Behold the bridegroom cometh, go ye out to meet him. Then all those virgins arose and trimmed their lamps." *Mat. 25:5-7.*

In the summer of 1844, halfway between the time when it had been first thought that the 2300 "days" would end, and the autumn of the same year (to which it was later found that they extended) the Advent Message was proclaimed in the very words of Scripture, **"Behold, the bridegroom cometh!"**

The discovery of that which led to this movement — the decree of Artaxerxes for the restoration of Jerusalem (the staring point of the 2300 "days") — went into effect in the autumn of the year 457 B.C. Therefore, it was assumed that the 2300 year period would terminate in the autumn of 1844, the time when **"the cleansing of the sanctuary"** was to take place.

Like the wave-sheaf, *the first ripened grain gathered before the harvest,* Christ is the first fruits of the harvest of the redeemed who shall be gathered into the garner of our Lord.

On the fourteenth day of the first Jewish month — the very day and month on which for fifteen centuries the Passover lamb had been slain, Christ (having eaten the Passover with his disciples) instituted the "Last Supper" commemorating things to come, — the **"first-fruits"** resurrection of **"them that slept."**

The great day of atonement — the beginning time for the cleansing of the sanctuary, regarding the time of the Second Coming of the Lord, fell in 1844 on the 22nd day of October.

This was in harmony with the proofs already presented that the 2300 "days" would terminate in the autumn of that year — and like a tidal wave a *new* movement swept across the land.

There was little ecstatic joy — but rather searching of the heart, confession of sin, and a forsaking of the world. There was persevering prayer and consecration of the Lord. The waiting people "arose and trimmed their lamps" with an intensity of interest heretofore unknown — though most of the churches closed their doors against this message.

Nevertheless, faith brought answers to prayer, and many hearts were melted. The assurance of their Saviors' Coming became more important to many than daily shelter and food. And if a cloud darkened their minds, they did not rest until it was driven away, and they felt the witness of their Saviors pardoning grace.

But in the autumn of 1844 they were bitterly disappointed once again. The time of expectation passed. And they did not see the appearance of their Lord. With unwavering faith they had looked forward to His coming, and like Mary at the empty tomb, they lamented: **"they have taken away my Lord, and I know not where they have laid him."** *John. 20:13.*

A feeling of awe that the message could have been true, had served as a restraint upon the unbelieving world up to that time. But now, in the light of bitter disappointment, the backlash was severe, for many scornfully renounced their faith.

With intense desire, they had prayed: **"Come Lord Jesus, and come quickly,"** but he supposedly had not come. And now, to take up again the burden of life's perplexities and care, and to endure the taunts and sneers of a scoffing world, was a terrible trial to their patience and to their faith.

Those who had been motivated more by fear than by faith, were among the first to ridicule the sorrow of the faithful. And many who suffered disappointment, lost their desire for the spiritual gifts of heaven, not remembering that it was not until their Lord had come forth from the grave, that they recognized the prophesies had foretold.

Had the disciples realized that Christ was going to be crucified and after three days be resurrected, they would not have been part of the fulfillment of this prophesy.

Those who quench the spirit, who stifle conviction because it interferes with inclinations, eventually lose the ability to distinguish truth from error, right from wrong. Worldly hope and ambitions fill the heart, and the love of God, and faith in His Word, grows cold.

While many abandoned their hopes and faith, a faithful remnant stood firm in the spirit of expectation, that the message was *still* from God, concluding that in **"yet a little while"** He that shall come, will come — *he will not tarry.*

CHAPTER 26

Dawns Early Light

"Let the heavens rejoice, and let the earth be glad...for he cometh to judge the earth...and the people with his truth." *Psalm 96:11,13.*

One of the most glorious truths revealed in the Bible is the prophesy of the Second Coming of Christ, to redeem God's people from **"the valley of the shadow of death."** The Second Advent — the Keynote of righteousness — has inspired the most sublime and impassioned appearances, of the Bible writers.

"He will swallow up death with victory; and the Lord God will wipe away tears from off all faces; and the rebuke of his people shall be taken away from off all the earth. This is the Lord; we have waited for him, we will be glad and rejoice in his salvation." *Isaiah 26:18; 25:8,9.*

"The Son of man shall come in his glory, and all the holy angels with him. Then shall he sit upon the throne of his glory, and before him shall be gathered all nations." *Mat. 25:31,32.*

"Behold, he cometh with clouds; and every eye shall see him." *Rev. 1:7.* And the long-continued rule of evil will be broken. **"The Lord God will cause righteousness and praise to spring forth before all nations (and he shall be) for a crown of glory, and for a diadem of beauty, unto the residue of his (waiting and watching) people."** *Isaiah 61:11; 28:5.*

The Coming of the Lord has been in all ages the hope of true believers everywhere. On the rocky isle of Patmos, the beloved disciple heard the promise, **"Surely I come quickly."** And his loving response, voiced the prayer of the Church in all ages. **"Even so, come, Lord Jesus."** *Rev, 22:20.*

Luther declared that, "The great day is drawing near in which the kingdom of abominations shall be overthrown." And Calvin declared that, "We must hunger after Christ until the dawning of that great day, when our Lord will fully manifest the glory of His Kingdom."

And Prophesy presents tokens by which men are to know when that great Day of Christ is near. Said Jesus, **"There shall be signs in the sun, and in the moon, and in the stars** *Luke 21:25,* **the sun shall be darkened, and the moon shall not give her light, and the stars of heaven shall fall."** *Mark 13:24-26.*

And the Revelator foretold the eventuality of **"a great earthquake"** and of the sun becoming **"black as sackcloth of hair, and of the moon becoming as blood."** *Rev. 6:12.*

The most terrible earthquake ever recorded in the history of man occurred on the **November 1, 1755**, in fulfillment of this prophesy. From its epicenter in Lisbon, Portugal, this earthquake extended throughout the greater part of Europe, North Africa, and even to America, pervading an extent of not less that four million square miles!

Twenty five years later, on **May 19, 1780**, came the next signal event mentioned in prophesy — the darkening of the sun and moon.

According to published Newspapers:

"A most mysterious and unaccountable darkening of the whole visible heavens and atmosphere in New England, not due to eclipse, the moon then being nearly full, and not being due to clouds, for in some localities, the sky had been previously so clear that the stars had been visibly bright.

"The early morning had been clear and pleasant, but by eight o'clock there was observed an uncommon appearance in the sun, and by high noon there was midnight darkness, and although the moon rose that night to the full, it had not the least effect to dispel the deathlike darkness, until after midnight, when the darkness had disappeared, the moon when first visible had the reddish appearance of blood."

Jesus said, **"Walk while ye have the light, lest darkness come upon you. He that followeth me shall not walk in darkness, but shall have the light of life."** *John 12:35; 8:12.*

Then the last of the signs foretold by Jesus as tokens of the Second Coming of Christ appeared.

"The stars of heaven fell upon the earth, even as a fig-tree casteth her untimely figs, when she is shaken of a mighty wind." *Rev. 6:13.* This prophesy was fulfilled in the great meteoric shower of November 13, 1833.

"The whole firmament, over all of the United States, was in fiery commotion for hours. Never did rain fall thicker than the meteors fell toward the earth. North, East, South, and West, it was the same, From two o'clock, the sky being perfectly cloudless and serene, an incessant play of dazzling brilliant luminosities continued in the whole heavens, until the light of day. No one who did not witness that magnificent display can form an adequate conception of its glory."

Christ had bidden mankind to watch for the signs of their coming King. **"When these things begin to come to pass** (he said) **then look up, and lift up your heads, for your redemption draweth nigh. When (the budding trees of spring) shoot forth, ye (shall) see and know of your own selves that summer is now nigh at land. So likewise ye, when ye see those things come to pass, know ye that the kingdom of God is nigh at hand."** *Luke 21:28,30,31.*

The Bible As Reform

CHAPTER 27

Lament and Rejoice

"They have taken away my Lord, and I know not where they have laid him." *John 20:13.*

Prior to the great disappointment of the Autumn of 1844, Adventists then believed, in common with the rest of the world, that the earth or some portion of it was represented by the Sanctuary of Daniel 8:11-14. They understood that the "Cleansing of the Sanctuary" typified the purification of the earth by fire, and hence the conclusion that Christ would return to the earth at that time.

All was clear and harmonious, except that it was not seen that any event answering to the Cleansing of the Sanctuary had taken place in 1844.

But to deny that the days ended at that time, was to involve the whole question in confusion, and to renounce positions which had been established by unmistakable fulfillments of prophesy.

The Adventists resolved this dilemma, when, in their investigations, they realized that there is no specific evidence for the popular view that the earth must be considered to be the Sanctuary in question. And they believed that the nature, location, and services of the Sanctuary should be found fully explained in the Bible.

In Hebrews 9:1-5, Paul refers to the tabernacle built by Moses, as "a worldly sanctuary," as the earthly dwelling place of the Most High, and after the Hebrews settled in Canaan, the tabernacle was replaced by the temple that King Soloman built, which — though a permanent structure of a much larger scale — observed the same proportions, and was similarly furnished with the Ark of the Covenant, the depository of the two tables of stone upon which were inscribed the Ten commandments of The Law. The Sanctuary had existed in this form, except while it lay in ruin in Daniel's time, until it was destroyed by Titus' Roman army in the year 70.

In the Book of Hebrews a *second* sanctuary is revealed. The Sanctuary of the New Covenant, implied in the words of Paul: **"We have such a high priest, who is set on the right hand of the throne of the Majesty in the heavens: a minister of the sanctuary, and of the true tabernacle, which the Lord pitched, and not of man."** *Heb. 8:1,2.*

The Sanctuary in Heaven, in which Christ ministers, is the great Original, of which the Sanctuary built by Moses was a Copy. The holy places of the Sanctuary in Heaven are represented by the two apartments in the Sanctuary on Earth.

Paul declares that the pattern of the Sanctuary made by Moses was the true Sanctuary which is in Heaven — the dwelling place of the Most High, God. The prophet Zecharia says concerning him **"whose name is the branch"** [meaning Christ]. **"He shall build the temple of the Lord, and he shall bear the glory, and shall sit and rule upon his (the Father's) throne; and the counsel of peace shall be between them both."** *Zech. 6:13.*

Christ is both the Foundation and the Builder of the City of God, **"The chief corner stone, in whom all the building fitly framed together groweth unto a holy temple in the Lord: in whom ye also** (says Paul) **are builded together, a habitation of God through the spirit,"** *Eph. 2:20-22.*

The term "sanctuary" as used in the Scriptures, refers to:

1) the Sanctuary built by Moses as a pattern of heavenly things, and

2) the **"true tabernacle which the Lord Pitched,"** to which the earthly sanctuary pointed. The first service ended at the crucifixion of Christ, and the **"true tabernacle"** in heaven is the sanctuary of the New Covenant.

The cleansing, both in the typical and in the actual service, had to be accomplished *literally in the former,* with the blood of sacrificial animals, and *figuratively in the latter,* with the sacrifices of the Christ, for **"without the shedding of blood** (*the shedding of materiality*)**, there is no remission."**

The priests who officiated on earth served **"unto the example and shadow of heavenly things"** *Heb. 8:5,* and since without a "putting off" of the old man, there can be no "putting on" of the new; there can be no reformation of the heart. Therefore the reformation of the heart (*the cleansing of the mind*) is the work to be accomplished.

Both ceremonies symbolize alike the transfer of sin (error) from the penitent. This was the work that began *circa* 1844 when the 2300 "days" ended. Our high Priest figuratively came to his most holy Sanctuary to perform the last division of his most holy work — *to cleans the Sanctuary* (*the consciousness of mankind*) — to blot out the record of sins which is maintained therein.

The Cleansing of the Sanctuary, therefore, involves a work of investigation — *a work of judgement* — to be performed prior to the coming of the Christ, — for when he comes, **"his reward is with him to give to every man according as his works shall be."** *Rev. 22:12.*

Adventists concluded that, instead of coming to the earth at the termination of the 2300 "days," in 1844, Christ then entered the most holy place in the heavenly Sanctuary, to perform the closing work of atonement, preparatory to his Second Coming in the flesh.

The subject of the sanctuary was thought to be the "key" which unlocked the mystery of the disappointment of 1844. The mistake (they reasoned) had not been in the reckoning of the prophetic periods, but in the specific event that was to take place at the end of the 2300 "days."

And while the Adventists had been lamenting the failure of their hope, they could have been rejoicing, for the very event that was foretold in the Bible message — which had to be fulfilled before every eye could see the coming of the Lord — was taking place: the beginning of the Cleansing of the Sanctuary, **"on earth as it is in heaven"** — in *witness to the truth.*

"Now we see through a glass darkly, but then face to face." *The apostle Paul.*

The Bible As Reform

CHAPTER 28

Thy Kingdom Come

"I will pray the Father, and he shall give you another Comforter, that he may abide with you for ever; Even the spirit of truth." — *Christ Jesus.*

Mary Baker Eddy's courageous search for desperately longed for health came to a climax in the autumn of 1844, when, at the age of twenty-three, the idea first came to her that the method of healing practiced by Christ Jesus might be a scientific method understandable and usable today.

Her life was thereafter restructured at its midpoint in 1866, when, at the age of forty-five, the idea that began to unfold for her in 1844, was confirmed as she discovered the verifiable Science of Christian Healing as the result of her spiritual recovery from the effects of a most serious accidental fall.

Mrs. Eddy contemplated, analyzed, and tested her discovery for three years from 1866 to 1869. She then proceeded to write the explanation of her discovery in the textbook *Science and Health with Key to the Scriptures,* which she "finished" in 1873 and presented to the world in 1875.

This book — though written by an unknown author and privately printed without the benefit of publisher's promotion or bookseller's interest — has nevertheless gone through hundreds and hundreds of editions, comprising literally millions of copies, purchased by individuals all over the world.

Mary Baker Eddy, a descendent of seven American generations of the Baker family, was born in the small New England farm village of Bow, New Hampshire, on July 16, 1821.

The latter half of the early 19th Century, in America, was to be a prevailing time of mental discovery. A great intellectual upheaval was stirring beneath the surface of everyday existence in preparation for the coming of a new order of spirituality.

New Ideas were crowding to the fore in both the pulpit and the press. Wherever thought was least fettered by materialistic dogma, a deep-sprung impetus could be felt that was propelling understanding upward into greater, perceptive freedom.

These new ideas being discussed with excitement and eagerness, were to grow in favor after mighty struggles with established beliefs. The broader horizon of mounting view was *inciting* thoughtful thinkers into a further comprehension of things unseen.

The age at hand had been thoroughly prepared for the fulfillment of the Master's promise that the **"Spirit of truth"** would come to men and guide them **"into all truth."** Primitive Christianity was to reappear in all the former strength of its first three-hundred years. The sick and the sinning were to be healed, and the Science of Christian healing was to be revealed.

The revival of "the Word made flesh" — truth made known by its healing effect among men — came not to the crimson carpet of religious orthodoxy — but to a humble woman meek in spirit. It came to Mary Baker Eddy — the Discoverer and Founder of the Science of the Christ — called Christian Science.

An early step was taken toward her discovery in 1833 when Mary was but twelve years of age. Her confidence in God's loving nature was challenged by her father, Mark Baker, at the time of her examination for church membership.

She could not accept the Calvinist doctrine her father explained to her, and deeply disturbed, she fell ill with a fever. A doctor was called, and when he could not relieve Mary, her mother intuitively told her to "turn to God in prayer and rest securely in his love." She wrote of this experience in later years:

"My mother, as she bathed my burning temples, bade me lean on God's love, which would give me rest if I went to Him in prayer as I was wont to do, seeking His

guidance. I prayed; and a soft glow of ineffable joy came over me. The fever was gone, and I rose and dressed myself, in a normal condition of health." *Ret. 13:18-23.*

This early evidence of God's presence and care was a distinct proof of the divine Love that heals all ills.

Whenever Mary was confronted with dogmatic opposition, her agile thought was quick to parry the blow, and alert to find a way to victory. She preferred to remain outside the boundaries of creedal safety unless she could be accepted without giving up her conviction of God as infinite divine Love.

Five years later, in 1838, at the age of seventeen, she was accepted into membership in the Congregational Church, where she remained a member, until *her church* was founded in 1879 — a Church destined to reinstate primitive, Christian healing throughout the world.

Mrs. Eddy was of little influence in the early beginnings of her mission, but today the importance of her discovery is patent to millions. Her great spiritual adventure culminated in discovery, after many years of trial, sacrifice, patience, and persistence.

Assurance at times sped her progress, but at other times she seemed caught up in the whirlpool of objectified events. Impelled by intuitive conviction, she explored the mental realm of the unseen, and presented a spiritual discovery to a watching and waiting world. The Revelation of Truth, which came to her receptive thought, began to sweep the globe in an ever-swelling tide.

The popular view of the spiritual reign of Christ for 1,000 years of righteousness and peace, before a personal coming of the Lord, is not sustained by the Word of God. It is contradictory to the teachings of the Master, Jesus, and his Apostles.

The "wheat" and the "tares" are to grow together side by side until **"the time of the harvest."** *Matt 13:30,38-41.*

And **"In the last days perilous times will come."** *2 Timothy 3:1.* The kingdom of darkness will continue until the Advent of the Lord, then it will then be destroyed in **"The brightness of his coming."** *2 Thess. 2:8.* At His coming the righteous dead will be raised, and the righteous living will be changed.

"We shall not all sleep, says the apostle Paul, but we shall all be changed, In a moment, in the twinkling of an eye, at the last trump : for the trumpet shall sound, and the dead shall be raised incorruptible, and we shall be changed. For this corruption must put on incorruption, and this mortal must put on immortality." *1 Cor. 15:51-53.*

"The dead in Christ shall rise first: (Christian concepts not understood will be given meaning) **Then we which are alive and remain shall be caught up together with them in the clouds, to meet the Lord in the clouds:** (Christian concepts already understood will be joined together with those newly revealed, having a rapturous spiritual effect) **and so shall we ever be with the Lord** (and the gentle presence of this effect shall be permanent forever). **Wherefore comfort one another with these words."** *1 Thess. 4:16-18.*

When the Son of man comes, dead thoughts are raised incorruptible, and living thoughts are changed. By this great change we are spiritually prepared to receive the Kingdom of God, for Paul says that **"flesh and blood cannot inherit the kingdom of God; neither doth corruption inherit incorruption."** *1 Cor. 15:50.*

Not until the Advent of Christ's *quickened understanding* can his people fully receive the Kingdom of God. *Consciousness must and will be spiritualized.*

Mrs. Eddy wrote:

"Today the healing power of Truth is widely demonstrated as an immanent, eternal Science, instead of a phenomenal exhibition. Its appearing is the coming anew of the gospel of 'on earth peace, good-will to men.' This coming, as was promised by the Master, is for its establishment as a permanent dispensation among men; but the mission of Christian Science now, as in the time of its earlier demonstration, is not primarily one of physical healing. Now, as then, signs and wonders are wrought in the metaphysical healing of physical disease; but these signs are only to demonstrate its divine origin, — to attest the reality of the higher mission of the Christ-power to take away the sins of the world.

"Truth's immortal idea is sweeping down the centuries, gathering beneath its wings the sick and the sinning. My weary hope tries to realize that happy day, when man shall recognize the Science of the Christ and love his neighbor as himself, — when he shall realize God's omnipotence and the healing power of divine Love in what it has done and is doing for mankind. The promises will be fulfilled. The time for the reappearing of the divine healing is throughout all time; and whosoever layeth his earthly all on the altar of divine Science, drinketh of Christ's cup now, and is endued with the spirit and power of Christian healing.

"In the words of St. John: He shall give you another comforter that he may abide with you forever. This comforter I understand to be Divine Science."

quoted from
Science and Health with Key to the Scriptures
Page 150, lines 4-17; page 55, lines 15-29.

The Bible As Reform

AFTERWORD

The Bible As Reform

The Finished Mystery

"In the days of the voice of the seventh angel, when he shall begin to sound, the mystery of God should be finished, as he hath declared to his servants the prophets." — *Revelation 10:7.*

In the concluding verses of the book of Daniel, in the Bible, Daniel is told by the Revelator — the Christ, — to **"Shut up the words, and seal the book** (*the Scriptures*) **even to the time of the end:** (*when*) **many shall run to and fro, and knowledge shall be increased."** *Daniel 12:4, see Revelation 22:10.*

And the man clothed in linen, when asked **"How long shall it be to the end of these wonders"** (*Daniel 12:6*), states that **"It shall be for a time, times, and a half; and when he shall have accomplished to scatter the power of the holy people, all these things** (*pertaining to the unfinished mystery of God*) **shall be finished."** *Daniel 12:7.*

It shall be for 3-1/2 times, or 1260 years after the abomination that maketh desolate was set up in the year 538. In other words; shortly after 1798 all the things pertaining to the unfinished mystery of God shall be finished.

Daniel then asks, **"O my lord, what shall be the end of these things?"** (*Daniel 12:8*). Whereupon Daniel is reminded by the man clothed in linen, regarding **"the time of the end"** to at that time not question him further.

"Go thy way, Daniel : for the words are closed up and sealed (*kept secret*) **until the time of the end."** *Daniel 12:9.* **"Many shall be purified, and made white, and tried, but the wicked shall do wickedly : and some of the wicked shall understand; but the wise shall understand."** *Daniel 12:10.*

The man clothed in linen then gives Daniel a time frame of two dates within which the "finishing" of "these things" will occur.

"And from the time that the daily sacrifice shall be taken away, and the abomination that maketh desolate set up (in 538), **there shall be a thousand two hundred and ninety days** (1290 years) **(even to the end of these things)."** *Daniel 12:11.*

In 1828, 1290 years after 538, Mary Baker Eddy began her healing ministry at the age of seven. *Ret. 8:1 to 9:27.*

"Blessed is he that waiteth, and cometh to the thousand three hundred and five and thirty days (1335 years)." *Daniel 12:12.* Blessed is he that cometh to 1335 years after 538 (to 1873) to finish those things.

In 1873, the Discoverer and Founder of Christian Science, Mary Baker Eddy, finished her full explanation of the scientific Principle of divine apostolic healing, in the first manuscript of the textbook of Christian Science — *"SCIENCE AND HEALTH WITH KEY TO THE SCRIPTURES"* — which she self-published in 1875 — thus finishing the mystery of God — in *witness to the truth.*

"And he shewed me a pure river of water of life, clear as crystal, proceeding out of the throne of God and of the Lamb. In the midst of the street of it, and on either side of the river, was there the tree of life (*Science and Health with Key to the Scriptures*). And the leaves (*pages*) of the tree were for the healing of the nations." *Revelation 22:1,2.*

The Bible As Reform

O dreamer, leave thy dreams for joyful waking
    O captive, rise and sing, for thou art free;
The Christ is here, all dreams of error braking,
    Unloosing bonds of all captivity.

He comes to bless thee on his wings of healing;
    To banish pain, and wipe all tears away;
He comes anew, to humble hearts revealing
    The mounting footsteps of the upward way.

He comes to give thee joy for desolation,
    Beauty for ashes of the vanished years;
for every tear to bring full compensation,
    To give thee confidence for all thy fears.

He comes to call the dumb to joyful singing;
    The deaf to hear; the blinded eyes to see;
The glorious tidings of salvation bringing,
    O captive, rise, thy Savior comes to thee.

The Christian Science Hymnal
— Hymn 202

The Bible As Reform

"Come unto me all ye that labor, and are heavy laden, and I will give you rest ... I am the way, the truth and the life." Christ Jesus

The Bible As Reform

The Bible As Refom

the Reformation of the Church
leading to the Coming of the Christ

The Bible As Healing

the Science of the Christ
outlined in the Revelation of St. John

The Bible As History

the History of Civilization
foretold in the Prophecies of Daniel

The Revelation of St. John
In Outline Form

www.ingramcontent.com/pod-product-compliance
Lightning Source LLC
LaVergne TN
LVHW020119210325
806437LV00002B/220